God has given Mike such powerful revelation on pr[...]
in *Growing in Prayer*. This book can expand your [...]
prayer and ignite your passion for true communion [...]

BIBLE TEACHER AND BEST-SELLING AUTHOR
JOYCE MEYER MINISTRIES
WWW.JOYCEMEYER.ORG

No one has earned the right to produce a book on prayer more than my friend Mike Bickle, and yet I was not prepared for how good and helpful this wonderful book actually is. It is the most practical book on prayer I have ever read.

—R. T. KENDALL
MINISTER, WESTMINSTER CHAPEL
LONDON, ENGLAND, 1977–2002
AUTHOR, *HOLY FIRE*

Mike Bickle has the unique ability to write about prayer in a way that gives every believer the longing to walk and talk with the Father. *Growing in Prayer*, like the books written by great men of God such as E. M. Bounds, will be read for generations to come. My heart burned in me to desire a deeper life of intercessory prayer as I read it.

—CINDY JACOBS
GENERALS INTERNATIONAL, DALLAS, TEXAS
WWW.GENERALS.ORG

I think I have read all the great classic books on prayer, but this is the best I have ever read. It is full of revelation and insight, but even more importantly, it compels you to pray. If you are intimidated by its size, don't be. Once you get into it, you will not want it to end.

—RICK JOYNER
SENIOR PASTOR, FOUNDER, EXECUTIVE DIRECTOR, MORNINGSTAR MINISTRIES AND
HERITAGE INTERNATIONAL MINISTRIES

Mike Bickle's pastoral leadership has always had "an edge"—one that cuts through the superficial, penetrates to the substance of prophetic insight, and communicates with a God-given love for people with truth that transforms hearts. I respect his character and honor his prayerful and practical ministry as a fellow steward of God's grace and goodness.

—JACK W. HAYFORD
FOUNDER, THE KING'S UNIVERSITY, DALLAS, TEXAS
FOUNDING PASTOR, THE CHURCH ON THE WAY, LOS ANGELES, CALIFORNIA

Enjoying God and partnering with Him in managing the earth is life's greatest privilege and should be our highest goal. For forty years Mike Bickle has relentlessly pursued this pleasure, rejecting the status quo lifestyle accepted by so many. If you have already begun a life of prayer, the insights in this book will elevate you to new heights and anchor you to new depths. If you're just getting started, they will save you years of trial and error. *Growing in Prayer* is an outstanding work!

—DUTCH SHEETS
DUTCH SHEETS MINISTRIES
WWW.DUTCHSHEETS.ORG

The journey of God's people in a nation is not easy. We experience many struggles, but we emerge triumphant. God's people in Indonesia realize that only through the power of prayer can Indonesia stand in righteousness and justice. Mike Bickle is an intercessor who has greatly inspired us by teaching us about the importance of 24/7 prayer, which we now see in many cities in Indonesia. This book will push you toward the fulfilment of God's call to enter a new dimension by growing in prayer and worship.

—DANIEL H. PANDJI
NATIONAL PRAYER NETWORK
MY HOME INDONESIA

Twenty years ago God moved powerfully across the earth, pouring out His new wine of refreshing. We were privileged in Sunderland, England, to be part of the global outpouring. One book became for us the theme of all we were discovering and experiencing and was foundational during this season: *Passion for Jesus* by Mike Bickle.

Since that time, our prophetic journey has intertwined with Mike's over and over again in an unusual and undeniable way. A true servant of God, Mike has pioneered the way with commitment, focus, and wisdom that both inspire and provoke. He has kept the Word of God central, shown us the keys to sustaining 24/7 prayer and worship, and refused to deviate from his divinely inspired course.

Today, as God moves powerfully upon the earth raising up a global prayer movement, Mike is leading the way once again. He has written a classic that is essential reading for all of us pursuing a lifestyle of prayer. *Growing in Prayer* is one of the most inspiring, helpful, informative, and practical books on prayer I have ever read. It is rooted in biblical truth and is theologically sound.

Mike Bickle has my admiration. He has kept a great ship on course in safe waters without altering his direction while at the same time fulfilling a great call and learning much in the process. We are privileged he has committed to print what can only become a must-read for every sincere believer.

—KEN GOTT
HOUSE OF PRAYER EUROPE
SUNDERLAND, UNITED KINGDOM

If you want to glean from a man who has taught, modeled, and lived a genuine life of prayer, then here you are. I personally know of no other leader in the earth as committed to prayer and to awakening the church to the necessity of prayer as Mike Bickle. The closer we draw to the return of Jesus, the more crucial it will become for every Christian to live out the many lessons found throughout this truly momentous work.

—JOEL RICHARDSON
NEW YORK TIMES BEST-SELLING AUTHOR, TEACHER

God has used Mike Bickle to spark the end-time prayer movement. He has been an inspiration to us in the East. He imparted the urgency of raising up a generation in an atmosphere of prayer, praise, and worship to prepare the way for the Second Coming of Jesus. We in Hong Kong, China, and Asia are so happy to see this book published. *Growing in Prayer* crystallizes the principles of planting and equipping end-time praying churches, the new wineskin for this momentous season in church history.

—EDDIE MA
INCUBATOR MINISTRIES, HONG KONG SAR, CHINA
WWW.ANHOP.ASIA

I have known Mike Bickle for almost twenty-five years. I have watched his life and ministry, related closely to IHOPKC, and am not surprised that he has written this book. It really represents Mike's life, who he is, and what he does. It is a comprehensive manual of prayer like no other. It is deep, faithful, truthful, and challenging. This manual reflects the lessons of the ministry of the International House of Prayer. To spend time at IHOPKC is to see the principles of this book in action and indeed to be changed as you watch more than one thousand young people engage in 24/7 prayer. This book provides a key to spiritual warfare without going in strange directions that cannot be proven by Scripture. It has my highest recommendation.

—Daniel Juster, ThD
Tikkun International, Jerusalem, Israel

This is a very timely book on prayer that can serve an emerging generation of catalysts whose DNA is to seek after God. Mike has provided them with a broad and deep look at the principles of prayer—a very powerful tool to help them live out their destinies. I think every young person who wants to make a significant impact on his or her generation should read this book.

—Jerome Ocampo
Senior pastor, Jesus' Flock Inc.
Founder, Jesus Revolution Now
Empowered 21 Asia
World Prayer Assembly

Mike Bickle is one of the great prayer leaders of our day. The Lord has used him and his team so significantly in the 24/7 prayer movement. I pray that this book will be a source of great insight and instruction on how we can pray more effectively. I look forward to profiting from Mike's insights in my own prayer life and ministry.

—Paul Cedar
Chairman, Mission America Coalition

This book is like Mike Bickle's giving you a key to the innermost chamber of his heart, where he has stored up his most cherished possessions. Through intimacy and intercession Mike has influenced the world. What he has garnered through years of experience and study, we can have for the taking. This book expresses Mike's desire to multiply those treasures through us.

—Asher Intrater
Revive Israel Ministries

What a gift to our generation! This is a comprehensive handbook that will travel with me. It is an essential aid for leaders involved in training others, yet it can also be consumed in small bites as a devotional reading that nourishes the soul. I found myself reading excerpts to my seventeen-year-old daughter. Like her, you may be on a quest, exploring the ways of God. This is perfect material for those hungry to know God intimately. My wife, Julie, and I enjoyed a chapter a day as inspiration and instruction for our times of prayer together. Here are the keys to both a world-changing movement and a joy-filled heart.

—John Dawson
President emeritus, Youth With A Mission International

Few leaders have impacted my life as Mike Bickle has. The hours we have spent together in prayer and vision sharing are some of my most treasured memories of being in the presence of one who wonderfully embodies a passion for Jesus. *Growing in Prayer* is the remarkable outflow of a worship-saturated prayer life that powerfully captures this passion page after page. Be prepared to be blessed!

—DICK EASTMAN
INTERNATIONAL PRESIDENT, EVERY HOME FOR CHRIST
WWW.EHC.ORG

I can't think of anyone who can write an inspiring and practical manual on prayer better than Mike Bickle, who virtually lives in the prayer room day after day, month after month, and year after year. My own heart was stirred with a fresh call to prayer while reading this book.

—DR. MICHAEL L. BROWN
PRESIDENT, FIRE SCHOOL OF MINISTRY,
HOST OF THE LINE OF FIRE RADIO BROADCAST

Mike Bickle is a friend and a man whom I admire as a leader in one of the largest prayer movements throughout the world. Because of his close walk with the Lord, the revelation he receives—as well as his interpretation and activation based on that revelation—has authenticity and relevance in our lives. When he speaks, I want to listen; when he writes, he impacts the lives of his readers. I thank God for this man and his ministry.

—LOREN CUNNINGHAM
FOUNDER, YOUTH WITH A MISSION

Mike Bickle's *Growing in Prayer* is:

+ A unique book for our times—I have looked for this all my life.

+ Instructive—a practical manual for starting and growing in prayer

+ Interesting—a fascinating history of prayer from the pen of a modern pioneer, a 24/7 praying practitioner

+ Insightful—candid input from the writer's own prayer life and an encouraging reminder that prayer has always been the key factor in revivals

+ Inspiring—an intriguing, priority *must*—especially for a leader's retreat or a church study group

—DAVID PYTCHES
BISHOP, CHURCH OF ENGLAND
FOUNDER, NEW WINE

Growing in Prayer by Mike Bickle is a real-life guide to talking with God. It describes the anticipated consequence of growing in prayer in a believer's life. You will find it to be both biblical and highly practical.

—LUIS BUSH
INTERNATIONAL FACILITATOR, TRANSFORM WORLD CONNECTIONS

GROWING
IN
PRAYER

MIKE
BICKLE

CHARISMA
HOUSE

Most CHARISMA HOUSE BOOK GROUP products are available at special quantity discounts for bulk purchase for sales promotions, premiums, fund-raising, and educational needs. For details, write Charisma House Book Group, 600 Rinehart Road, Lake Mary, Florida 32746, or telephone (407) 333-0600.

GROWING IN PRAYER by Mike Bickle
Published by Charisma House
Charisma Media/Charisma House Book Group
600 Rinehart Road
Lake Mary, Florida 32746
www.charismahouse.com

Unless otherwise noted, all Scripture quotations are from New King James Version®. Copyright © 1982 by Thomas Nelson. Used by permission. All rights reserved.

Scripture quotations marked KJV are from the King James Version of the Bible.

Scripture quotations marked NAS are from the New American Standard Bible, copyright © 1960, 1962, 1963, 1968, 1971, 1972, 1973, 1975, 1977, 1995 by The Lockman Foundation. Used by permission. (www.Lockman.org)

Scripture quotations marked NIV are taken from the Holy Bible, New International Version®, NIV®. Copyright © 1973, 1978, 1984, 2011 by Biblica, Inc.™ Used by permission of Zondervan. All rights reserved worldwide. www.zondervan.com The "NIV" and "New International Version" are trademarks registered in the United States Patent and Trademark Office by Biblica, Inc.™

All italics in Scripture quotations reflect the author's emphasis.

Cover design by Justin Evans

Visit the author's website at www.ihopkc.org.

Library of Congress Control Number: 2014908844
International Standard Book Number: 978-1-62136-046-9
E-book ISBN: 978-1-62136-047-6

14 15 16 17 18 — 9 8 7 6 5 4
Printed in the United States of America

I dedicate this book to the faithful intercessory missionaries who have been on the staff at the International House of Prayer of Kansas City over the last fifteen years.

CONTENTS

ACKNOWLEDGMENTS

I AM INDEBTED TO the team who helped me write this book for their excellent work. I especially want to thank Anne House, Kathi DeCanio, Maggie Syrett, and Barb Dycus for preparing the manuscript for Maureen Eha to pore over and turn into a book. Thank you, Maureen. Your contribution was invaluable. I am grateful for the many long hours they all invested in the project. Without their help, this book would not exist. I am also grateful to Jono Hall for his extensive research. Thank you, team.

FOREWORD

IT IS AN honor to write this commendation and a pleasure to recommend this book. Mike Bickle's latest book, *Growing in Prayer*, is the most practical book on prayer I have read. It will go down as a classic and will stand alongside the greatest books on prayer in church history.

And yet this is not surprising. No one I know has earned the right to speak on this subject more than Mike Bickle. Mike's ministry and the subject of prayer are virtually interchangeable. He is the founder of the famed International House of Prayer in Kansas City, Missouri—a place where intercessory prayer continues nonstop day and night. Mike aspires to see one million full-time intercessors praying for the great revival—the end-time harvest, the conversion of the lost, God's blessing upon Israel, His intervention in troubled spots of the world, the prevalence of social justice, excelling in worship, and everything in between.

I first met Mike Bickle in 1992 when John Wimber invited my wife, Louise, and me to spend time at the Vineyard conference in Anaheim, California. One of the first persons I met there was Mike. I enjoyed an instant rapport with him. He preached for me at Westminster Chapel. He introduced me to John Paul Jackson. He has since founded IHOPKC, and now he ministers all over the world.

What impresses me most about Mike is his transparent love for Jesus. His love for God and His Son oozes out of every sentence in this wonderful book.

You will be impressed by Mike's total commitment to prayer and his absolute persuasion of the power of *persistent* prayer. This is a book that will make you want to pray. Prayer begins as a discipline and ends up a delight. Here is a book written for the newest and youngest Christian and yet one that will thrill and inspire older veterans like me. It is clear and simple while focusing upon the honor and glory of God. It is God-centered and Bible-centered prayer that Mike is after.

Mike not only inspires us to *want* to pray but also shows us *how* to pray. He reminds us of the need for a prayer list, the importance of having a regular time to pray (he assumes this should be an hour at least), and what to include—intercession, personal petition, and devotion. He equally stresses that there be corporate prayer—the gathered people of God interceding according to the will of God. He stresses gratitude, worship, never giving up, speaking Scripture to God. That is what John Calvin emphasized, that the best way to pray is to remind God of His own Word! I loved his affirming references to the Jonathan Edwardses and the Martyn Lloyd-Joneses of this world. All Christians—reformed, charismatic, Pentecostal, and other believers—will esteem this book.

One of the greatest fringe benefits of reading *Growing in Prayer* is what it will do for you—particularly your own personal life. Caution: you cannot follow Mike's principles of prayer and remain a nominal Christian. A consistent, godly lifestyle will characterize the person who follows his suggestions. *Growing in Prayer* is an apt title. You will certainly grow from reading this book!

What an incalculable privilege is ours—to know that the great God of heaven and Earth would stoop to our weakness and be moved by our little prayers. Oh, yes. That is the wonderful thing. You will be addressing the One who has no equal—and discover He listens to you as if there were no one else in the world!

Now start reading this book. You might consider reading it on your knees, although posture is not the most important thing. Just read it. And start praying like you have never prayed in your life. You will never be the same again.

—R. T. KENDALL
MINISTER, WESTMINSTER CHAPEL
LONDON, ENGLAND (1977–2002)

INTRODUCTION

THIS BOOK COVERS many important topics related to prayer: its biblical foundations; its practical applications; its historical expressions throughout the generations; and its prophetic significance in the generation in which the Lord returns.

Why write a book about prayer? Across the nations the Lord is awakening a deep desire in many believers to grow in prayer. Multitudes have a fresh hunger to go deeper in God but are not sure where to start or what to do. They want biblical answers that are practical and proven. They want solutions on growing in prayer that will actually work in their lives.

Believers want to know what to do during their prayer times. They want to know how to overcome distractions and hindrances to prayer; what to do when they do not feel like praying; how much time they should give to prayer. They want to know if it is possible for busy people to have a deep and strong prayer life.

In this book I will address these issues and many more. My aim is threefold: first, to give practical instruction on what to do to develop a life of prayer; second, to give a biblical understanding of different types of prayer and the principles associated with them—that is, to give a hands-on biblical theology of prayer; and third, to give a big-picture perspective of what the Holy Spirit is doing in emphasizing prayer across the earth in this hour.

Perhaps you are one of those who longs to go deeper in prayer and to participate in God's plan. If so, you're in the right place.

To make certain we're all "on the same page" as we begin our discussion on prayer, I'll give you a definition of the word. You may remember it from Sunday school. Very simply, *prayer* is "talking with God."

As a young Christian I had the idea that prayer was complicated, mysterious, and difficult, but on my journey of growing in prayer, I found that it is instead simple, immensely practical, and often very enjoyable. Prayer can take many forms, but all prayer is essentially a two-way conversation with the Lord that has life-changing results.

Just think about this for a moment: We can talk to the God of the universe! And we can know that not only does He *listen* attentively and with great affection but also He *responds* in various ways—by revealing His heart, giving us direction, blessing our circumstances, transforming our emotions, touching our loved ones, reviving the church, saving the lost, releasing justice, impacting society, and so on. Prayer is a great privilege and has significant implications for our own lives and for the world around us. It is worth whatever it takes to cultivate a strong prayer life.

During the last forty years of seeking to develop a strong prayer life, I have learned many important things about prayer. I still have much to learn, but I would like to share some principles and practical tools that have helped me sustain a life of prayer and grow closer to God. This is not an in-depth look at prayer—that book will hopefully come later—but an introduction to help you on your journey of developing a vibrant and fruitful life of prayer.

Prayer is a high calling and an amazing privilege, yet many see it as a burdensome duty. Why? Prayer can be a fierce struggle. I know this struggle and have experienced it often. In my early years prayer was especially difficult.

My friend Larry Lea encouraged me by declaring that when we persist in prayer, our prayer life progresses from duty to discipline to delight. Long ago I determined that I was going to know what it meant to delight in prayer. I was not sure how it would happen, but I fiercely resolved to find out.

By the grace of God, it "worked." I have enjoyed prayer for many years and have received answers to untold numbers of prayers. I'm not saying prayer is never a struggle for me today, but I now know the way to get through the times of resistance and difficulty so enjoyable prayer that brings real results is the norm.

Isaiah prophesied that the Lord would make His servants joyful in His house of prayer (Isa. 56:7). Here Isaiah referred to a new paradigm for prayer: prayer characterized by joy. It is what I like to call "enjoyable prayer." The Lord desires that the church be surprised by joy in communicating with Him.

Enjoyable prayer is prayer that refreshes our souls and invigorates our spirits. Imagine what it is like for prayer to be enjoyable! We will want to engage in it continually. On the other hand, if it is not enjoyable, we will pray only intermittently—or not at all.

Many believers are aware that the Lord is calling them to grow in their prayer lives, but other things always seem to get in the way. The good news is that the Holy Spirit will help all of us who desire to pray more effectively (that's His job!), and we will begin to enjoy praying. For our part, we must ask Him for help, put into practice the biblical principles related to prayer, and stick with the process, even when we feel as if it isn't working.

It is not enough to desire to pray; we must resolutely stay with it. We must fight for our prayer lives because they will not develop on their own.

Thankfully God desires to strengthen us by His grace to develop consistent, meaningful prayer lives. Though we are all weak, ordinary people, His grace is sufficient to motivate us to remain faithful.

Being a person of prayer is the most important calling in one's life. It is a higher calling than being a spouse, a parent, a pastor, a preacher, or a leader in the marketplace. We will all be far better spouses, parents, and leaders as we take time to grow in prayer.

Not every believer is called to preach, but every Christian is called to pray. Prayer is essential for our spiritual well-being. It is not an optional activity.

With that in mind, are you ready to join the multitudes now being sovereignly stirred by the Lord to grow in prayer and to begin a new chapter in your spiritual life? If so, let's get started!

PART I

THE FOUNDATION
for PRAYER

The main lesson about prayer is just this: Do it! Do it! Do it![1]
—JOHN LAIDLAW

Chapter 1

CALLED *to* PRAY

As it is the business of tailors to mend clothes and cobblers to
make shoes, so it is the business of Christians to pray.[1]
—MARTIN LUTHER

WE BEGIN OUR journey of growing in prayer by acknowledging that prayer is not only for beginners but also for mature believers. Otherwise there would be no point in trying to grow in it! The Lord calls *every* believer to a life of prayer—no matter how long he has been saved or how experienced he is in this discipline. The best thing all of us can do to improve ourselves, our lives, and our relationships is to grow in prayer.

Prayer is a means of connecting with the Holy Spirit, who energizes us to love God. Our love for God then causes us to overflow in love for others. Jesus made an absolute statement about our inability to walk in the fullness of our destinies in God without growing in prayer. He said that unless we abide in Him, we can do nothing related to bearing fruit or maturing in our spiritual lives:

> He who abides in Me, and I in him, bears much fruit; for without Me you can do nothing.
>
> —JOHN 15:5

Because we are not the source of spiritual life ourselves, we cannot generate it, nor can we receive it unless we abide in Christ. Just as it is impossible for us to jump a hundred feet even if we push ourselves, it is impossible for us to generate spiritual life. It is not an issue of practice; we were not created to be able to jump a hundred feet! And neither were we created to have Spirit-life while living independently of the Spirit. We must abide in Christ and grow in prayer to make our lives work. (For more about abiding in Christ, see chapter 4.)

The Holy Spirit will move in a new and powerful way in your heart and life as you take to grow in prayer. The change may not happen overnight, but it will most certainly happen. The discipline of prayer will eventually become delight in prayer. Dryness in prayer will gradually be replaced by a vibrant dialogue with God that will change your life and result in many answered prayers.

I invite you to begin the next stage of your journey in prayer right now. There is no better time than today. Do not wait for a special spiritual experience to begin to grow in prayer. We grow in prayer by actually *praying*. Beginners in prayer mature by praying more. It is the same principle we embrace when learning to play a musical instrument—we become better the more we practice.

FROM DUTY TO DELIGHT

In my younger days I loved Jesus, but I dreaded spending time in prayer. I saw prayer as a necessary duty that I had to endure if I wanted to receive more blessing. I never dreamed that I would one day be one of the leaders of a 24/7 prayer ministry such as the International House of Prayer of Kansas City.

My desire to have a strong prayer life was kindled some forty years ago when I was about eighteen years old. My youth leaders told me that I had to develop a prayer life if I wanted to experience the deeper things of God and enter into the fullness of my calling. I wanted to live radically for God, so I listened carefully to them. However, the idea of actually taking time to pray was terrible.

I also read a few books on prayer. Especially memorable are those written by Leonard Ravenhill and E. M. Bounds, who wrote some of the classics on prayer and revival. After reading their books, I was even more convinced of my need to grow in prayer, but the thought was daunting. The books inspired me but left me feeling guilty about the lack of prayer in my life. I felt spiritually "stuck" and desperate for a breakthrough.

In the summer of 1974 one of my youth leaders exhorted me to set aside an hour every day for prayer, and I determined to try. I was a freshman at the University of Missouri, living in a student apartment with three other believers. I told them, "I will pray an hour a day, even if it kills me." My announcement brought an element of accountability, knowing that each night they would watch me to see if I actually kept my commitment. So I set my prayer time from nine to ten each night. I referred to it as the "hour of death" because it was so boring I felt as if I was going to die.

At 9:00 p.m. I began my hour of prayer by mentioning everything I could think of to God. I exhausted my entire list in about two minutes: "Thank You, Jesus, for my health, for food, for my friends. Please help me score touchdowns on the university football team, help me get a good wife, and help me make good grades...." I looked at my watch, and I still had fifty-eight minutes to go! Some of those prayers were never answered. I did make the university football team, but I never made any touchdowns, and I made only average grades. But hey, I did get the girl—and a really good one at that! Diane and I have been married for thirty-seven years. She is an amazing wife and mother and a genuine woman of God who has sought the Lord diligently and consistently throughout our years together.

I endured that dreadful hour of prayer night after night. I did not like it at all. I enjoyed activities such as going to worship services and attending Bible studies to hear teaching. I liked engaging in ministry activity and going on missions trips. But when I got alone to pray or read the Bible, I found it confusing and boring. However, I really wanted to grow in God, so I knew I had to stick with this "prayer thing" until I developed a real life in prayer. I was determined—but not very hopeful that it would work for me.

A New View of Prayer

To be successful, I needed a new perspective on prayer: I needed to know what prayer is and why the Lord insists on it. As I discovered answers to these questions, I began to see prayer as so much more than a religious duty to endure. I learned that it is a place of encounter, a way to receive blessing, an act of partnership with God, and much more.

Prayer is a place of encounter.

At first I thought of prayer as a necessary duty that was mostly results-oriented. I imagined that the Lord wanted me to "endure" talking to Him to prove my dedication. I saw it as paying the price in prayer, and if I endured it long enough, then He would surely give me the blessing I was asking for.

Thankfully the Lord never intended for prayer to be something we do merely out of duty or to get specific results. First and foremost, prayer is about encountering God and growing in relationship with Him. It is the means by which we most feel His presence and receive love from Him as we gain understanding of what He is like. It is the time when we receive fresh insight into His heart and when new desires in our hearts are formed so that we may commune deeply with Him. Prayer positions us to be energized to love—to love God and people. This is the foundational principle of prayer. Yes, it is biblical to pray to get answers and to see God's power. But prayer is first of all an opportunity to commune with God.

The call to prayer is a call to participate in the love that has forever burned in God's heart. From eternity past the Father has loved the Son with all His heart, and the Son has loved the Father with the same intensity. The primary factor in the Father's relationships, both within the Godhead and with His people, is wholehearted love. The family dynamics among the Father, Son, and Spirit are based on and flow in this wholehearted love. This love is the foundational reality of the kingdom of God. It is this very reality that we participate in as we grow in prayer, and it is what prayer is mostly about—that is, participating in the family dynamics of the Godhead. We do this by receiving God's love and responding to the Lord and people in His love.

We were created to receive and express the burning love that originates in God's heart. God created the human race to share His love. Why? Simply because "God is love" (1 John 4:16). No lack in the fellowship within the Trinity prompted God to create humans. The Father was not lonely, and He had no needs. The Father, Son, and Holy Spirit are fully satisfied in the joy of the love they have shared together from eternity past. Yet the Lord created us to share the joy of His love with us. He created us in His image, for love—to receive His love, reflect it back to Him, and share it with others. Love is at the core of our relationship with God, the essence of salvation, and the foundation for understanding prayer.

God's heart burns with love, and He calls us to experience it—to enter into what I refer to as "the fellowship of the burning heart." Salvation is an invitation to this fellowship, which we will learn more about in the next chapter.

Prayer is a way to receive blessing.

We do not pray "just to pray." Yes, we pray to commune with God, but we also pray so that things will change and God's blessings will be released in us and through us. There is a point to our prayers. In the apostle James's teaching on prayer, he wrote of the power of prayer: "The effective, fervent prayer of a righteous man avails much" (James 5:16). Effective prayer accomplishes much and leads to real results. Jesus taught His disciples, saying, "If you ask anything in My name, I will do it" (John 14:14). We are to pray in faith that our prayers will actually produce results—believing that God will answer them by releasing a greater measure of His blessing and power. In the lesson of the withered fig tree in Mark's Gospel, Jesus underlined the importance of praying with faith, or confidence:

> Jesus answered and said to them, "Have faith in God. For assuredly I say to you, whoever says to this mountain, 'Be removed and be cast into the sea,' and does not doubt in his heart, but believes that those things he says will be done, he will have whatever he says. Therefore I say to you, whatever things you ask when you pray, believe that you receive them, and you will have them."
>
> —MARK 11:22–24

Jesus often affirmed people who had faith to receive from Him. One example is His response to the Roman centurion, who did not consider himself worthy to receive Jesus under his roof but knew that if Jesus spoke just a word, his servant would be healed. The Bible tells us that when Jesus heard the centurion's reply to His offer to come and heal the servant, "He marveled, and said to those who followed, 'Assuredly, I say to you, I have not found such great faith, not even in Israel'" (Matt. 8:10). Again, it was in response to their faith that two blind men received their sight. Having asked them if they believed He was able to heal them, Jesus said to them, "According to your faith let it be to you" (Matt. 9:29).

On the other hand, Jesus rebuked those who could not receive because of their lack of faith in Him. Matthew 17:14–21 recounts the story of the man who brought his epileptic son to the disciples to be healed but was disappointed because "they could not cure him." Publicly Jesus expressed pain over the "faithless and perverse generation" and then healed the boy instantly. Later, in private, when the disciples asked why they could not drive the demon out of the boy, Jesus stated the reason simply and categorically: "'Because of your unbelief.'" He added that nothing would be impossible for those who pray with faith. Other accounts show that Jesus was unable to do mighty works where there was great unbelief (Matt. 13:58; Mark 6:5–6).

Just before He ascended into heaven, Jesus "rebuked their [the eleven disciples'] unbelief and hardness of heart, because they did not believe those who had seen Him after He had risen" (Mark 16:14). That He would issue a rebuke at this point is surprising because it was after the disciples had walked with Him through the entire three years of His ministry. But with His next breath, immediately after He rebuked them, Jesus commissioned them to go into all the world and preach the gospel, assuring them that "those who believe" would cast out demons in His name and see the sick healed when they laid their hands on them (vv. 17–18).

We are called to be channels of His blessing and healing to others. Mark's final verse reports that after Jesus sat down at the right hand of God, the eleven went out preaching, and the Lord was "working with them and confirming the word through the accompanying signs" (v. 20). The disciples learned much from Jesus: when they prayed in faith and obedience, things changed.

Some people think of prayer solely as communion with God, and others think of it only as the way to obtain more blessing in their circumstances. But we do not need to choose one over the other; we can expect results from our prayers as we grow in communion with God. Praying in faith is a God-ordained way to receive His blessing in both our internal lives and our external circumstances.

I know some believers who have a passive, indifferent attitude toward receiving God's blessings. They do not seem to care whether their prayers avail much in their own lives, and they believe their attitude is an expression of humility: they consider it selfish to want to receive answers to their prayers.

Jesus never affirmed a passive attitude of indifference about receiving from Him. It is not true humility but false humility that disregards the blessings Jesus has ordained for His people. We do not need to choose between the two views on prayer; we can have both greater intimacy with God and more blessing in our circumstances from answered prayer.

God has chosen to give some blessings only as His people pray for them with confidence. Prayer is one of the primary means of securing the full blessing God has ordained to give us. God opens doors of blessing and closes doors of oppression in direct response to our prayers. Indeed, His Word declares, "The LORD longs to be gracious to you, and therefore He waits on high to have compassion on you....He will surely be gracious to you at the sound of your cry; when He hears it, He will answer you" (Isa. 30:18–19, NAS).

The Lord longs to be gracious, to release a greater measure of His grace and blessing to us. He will surely do this at the sound of our cry—when He hears it, He will answer us. Receiving more from God is not about convincing Him to be willing to give us more. Rather, it is about God's convincing His people to pray for more with confidence.

God leads His kingdom by giving more in response to prayer because He desires a deep relationship with us. In prayer we position ourselves to receive abundant grace and blessing. Never imagine that we earn or deserve blessing because of our prayers. Rather, prayer is the place of receiving blessing in response to interacting with Him. It is through our praying and His answering that He strengthens our relationship with Him.

Some of God's promises for increased blessing are not guarantees but invitations to partner with Him in holy, believing, persevering prayer. If we fulfill the conditions—and prayer is one of the conditions—then the promises are guaranteed. Many promises include the conditional word "if"—if we call out to Him, then God promises to answer in specific ways. Here are just a few:

> You will seek the LORD your God, and you will find Him if you seek Him with all your heart and with all your soul.
>
> —DEUTERONOMY 4:29

> If My people who are called by My name will humble themselves, and pray and seek My face…then I will hear from heaven, and will forgive their sin and heal their land.
>
> —2 CHRONICLES 7:14

> How much more will your heavenly Father give the Holy Spirit to those who ask Him?
>
> —LUKE 11:13

Blessings are promised to those who come to God and ask. Therefore, if we pray, the quality of our natural and spiritual lives will improve. For example, the measure in which we receive insight from the Holy Spirit will increase, and our thirsty hearts will encounter God more deeply.

By praying, we can both release God's blessing in greater measure and cut off the work of the enemy, who seeks to devour our finances, break our bodies, ruin our relationships, oppress our hearts, and destroy our families. Through prayer we can hinder his destruction in our lives. God opens doors of blessing and closes doors of oppression in response to prayer. When we pray, doors of demonic oppression can be shut. We have authority in Jesus's name to stop demonic activity and to release angelic activity in our lives and the lives of others.

God will not do our part, and we cannot do His part. God requires that we cooperate with Him according to His supernatural grace. This is an expression of His desire for intimate partnership with us. Only through a lifestyle of prayer can we receive the fullness of what God has promised.

Prayer is partnership with God.

The Lord wants much more from His people than for them to be His workforce. He longs to have relationship with those who love Him and to partner with them in accomplishing His purposes.

God governs the earth in partnership with His people who reign with Him through prayer. We learn from the Book of Revelation that we are destined to reign with Jesus: "To him who overcomes I [Jesus] will grant to sit with Me on

My throne" (Rev. 3:21). The twenty-four elders sing of the redeemed that Jesus has "made us kings and priests to our God; and we shall reign on the earth" (Rev. 5:10). He gives us a dynamic role in determining a measure of the quality of life that we experience in this age as we respond to Him in prayer, obedience, faith, and meekness.

When my boys were little, God used a simple episode from our family life to teach me about partnering in prayer with His purposes. One day when I came home, my wife, Diane, was in the kitchen with our son Luke, who was about five years old at the time. They had just finished washing the dishes together. My son's shirt was soaked with water. My wife's hair was damp and sticking up, and there was a broken plate on the floor. Things were a little messy. I asked, "What happened?"

Luke smiled and said with great pride, "Hey, Dad, I just washed the dishes."

I said, "Well, tell me about it."

Diane said, "Well, I took a dirty plate and handed it to him. He sort of washed it and then I rewashed it. Then I handed the plate back to him so that he would put it away. He dropped one, and it broke. He also splashed water everywhere as he 'helped' me."

So Luke made a big mess, broke a dish, and got water everywhere, yet in his mind he "washed the dishes." But he was happy, and his big smile said, "Dad, look what I did—I washed the dishes."

In that moment I gained a new insight into how prayer works. Diane could have washed the dishes much faster without Luke's help, but she wanted to involve him. The Lord can easily build His kingdom without using us, but He wants to involve us because He is committed to a relationship of partnership with us. Jesus is not just a King with power; He is also a Bridegroom with a desire for relationship. He has joy in our friendship and in our partnering together in the work of the kingdom with Him.

As you will learn in chapter 3, the essence of effective prayer is that we speak in agreement with God. Therefore, one important aspect of prayer is telling God what He tells us to tell Him. The Word shows us what He promises to release to His people, and we simply pray these things back to Him. It is as if He is handing us a dish to wash, and then we hand it back to Him. He fulfills His kingdom purposes as we talk with Him.

The Importance of Asking

One foundational principle of the kingdom is that God releases more blessing if we ask for it. He could easily release all His blessings to us without our asking, but He wants us to be involved in the process. Most of us know the Bible verse that teaches us we have not because we ask not (James 4:2). God wants us to do more than simply *think* about our needs; He wants us to *ask* Him to meet them. Many complain about their lives or their circumstances and even talk to others about them, but they do not speak their needs out to the Lord.

It is easy to think about our needs without verbalizing them. Why does God insist on our asking? It is because the "asking" leads to a greater heart-connect with Him. Therefore, He "starves us out" of our prayer-less lives by withholding certain blessings until we ask—until we actually *talk* to Him about them. When the pressure caused by the lack of His blessing is greater than our busyness, then we pray more. And in the process of praying, we connect with Him relationally.

In Philippians 4:6 Paul instructs us, "In everything by prayer...let your requests be made known to God." The Lord knows our needs without our asking, yet He waits to give us many things until we ask Him for them.

Jesus called us to pray with perseverance for God's help and blessing:

> Ask, and it will be given to you; seek, and you will find; knock, and it will be opened to you. For everyone who asks receives, and he who seeks finds, and to him who knocks it will be opened.
>
> —MATTHEW 7:7–8

Jesus called us to ask and keep on asking, to seek and keep on seeking, to knock and keep on knocking. The verbs in the Greek are in the continuous present tense, indicating that we are to do this consistently and keep on doing it. Asking is important.

In addition to a deeper relationship with God and blessings in our circumstances, a greater measure of grace awaits those who will seek the Lord for more. We have established that asking God for our needs is a mark of our humility and dependence on Him. James, quoting from Proverbs, says that "God...gives grace to the humble" (James 4:6). Born-again believers are invited to come to the throne of grace to experience more of God's grace, which is already theirs in Christ. Hebrews 4:16 urges us to "come boldly to the throne of grace, that we may obtain mercy and find grace to help in time of need." God's grace is available to all who boldly and consistently come to Him. Part of the breakthrough in our experience comes as we pray for it. We receive a greater measure of God's grace, which renews our minds and emotions.

There is a difference between our *legal position* in Christ—what we freely receive in the Spirit—and our *living condition*—what we actually experience in our everyday lives. We seek to experience more grace in our everyday lives because we are confident that God's grace has been freely given to us in our legal position in Christ.

Our *legal position* is the way God views us in Christ and what has freely been made available to us in the Spirit. Our *living condition* is how much we actually experience of that which is freely available. In our legal position before God we, as believers, have received the fullness of grace as a free gift because of what Jesus did for us on the cross. It is free, full, and final.

Second Corinthians 5:21 declares that we have become "the righteousness of God" in Christ. When God looks at our born-again spirits, He sees the very righteousness of Christ in us. This is our legal position before God. We will never have more grace available than is ours on the day that we are born again. But in our living condition we want to experience more of what is freely ours. James was referring to our living condition when he taught that God "gives more grace" to believers (James 4:6).

OUR PRAYERS DON'T HAVE TO BE PERFECT

Prayer is one of God's brilliant strategies, the most brilliant way to rule the universe. Why? Because when we speak God's Word back to God, it draws us into intimacy with His heart and unifies us with others who pray the same things. And it humbles us and transforms us at the same time. In other words, the result of the Father's ruling the universe through prayer is that His people are established in intimacy, community, and humility while engaged in governmental partnership with Jesus to change the earth.

The good news is that our prayers don't have to be perfect to accomplish God's purposes. They are effective because of the authority of Jesus, which is based on His finished work on the cross. Therefore, our prayers work even when they are short, when they are weak, and when they are poorly worded.

The value of ninety-second prayers

Short prayers are effective. Even ninety-second prayers matter and can connect our hearts with God while releasing His blessing to us. Do not put off praying until you have a full hour to pray. Even while you are rushing to an appointment, waiting at a stoplight, or standing in line at a store, you can offer ninety-second prayers that will make a difference in your life and the lives of others.

The value of "weak" prayers

Some people assume that because they do not feel anything when they pray, God must not feel anything either. They conclude that their weak prayers are ineffectual and may even despise them. The truth is that we offer our prayers in human weakness, but they ascend to God in power because of the sufficiency of the blood of Jesus and because they are in agreement with God's heart. Others believe they are growing in prayer only if they feel good during their prayer times. They wrongly conclude that their prayers are meaningless when they feel dry and distracted.

What should we do when our prayers feel weak or ineffective? Instead of measuring the effectiveness of our prayers by the emotions we feel in a particular prayer time, we must measure it by what God says in His Word. Jesus declared in the Word that everyone who asks and keeps on asking will receive, and everyone who seeks and keeps on seeking will find (Matt. 7:7–8).

Our prayers—all of them—are heard, even if we do not feel anything when we offer them. Do not measure your prayers by how you feel when you pray them but by the extent to which they are in agreement with God's will and Word. Beloved, our weak prayer times may not move us, but they move the heart of

God. The apostle John emphasized that we can have confidence that our prayers are heard regardless of how we feel while we are praying.

> Now this is the confidence that we have in Him, that if we ask anything according to His will, He hears us.
> —1 JOHN 5:14

Why? Because God views our weak prayers through the blood of Jesus and the riches of His glory. The phrase "the riches of glory" is mentioned often by the apostle Paul in his epistles. Ephesians 1:18 is a good example.[2]

> ...that you may know what is the hope of His calling, what are the riches of the glory of His inheritance in the saints.

God assesses the activity in our lives very differently from the way we assess it with our natural minds. The fullness of the glory of our lives in Christ is hidden from our own eyes as well as from the eyes of others in this age. Yet it will become evident to all when Jesus appears at His Second Coming.

> For you died, and your life is hidden with Christ in God. When Christ who is our life appears, then you also will appear with Him in glory.
> —COLOSSIANS 3:3–4

The challenge is that often we do not feel or see the glory of God in our lives. Because it is indiscernible and hidden from our emotions and our five senses, we cannot measure it. We look at our lives as small, weak, and boring, and yet Jesus sees them through the lens of the riches of glory. He sees what we don't see, and that includes our prayers.

Our many small acts of obedience, including our prayers, are glorious in God's eyes. By understanding the value of our weak prayers, we are empowered to see them as relevant and powerful. Though they may seem weak according to the flesh, every prayer in God's will matters to God.

The value of poorly worded prayers

God values our prayers even when we do not say them in the "right" way. We sometimes think we must have perfect wording when we pray. But we come boldly to the "throne of grace" (Heb. 4:16) not the "throne of literary accuracy." The Lord hears the groan of the prisoner (Ps. 79:11; 102:20) as well as the eloquence of biblical scholars and powerful preachers. Remember, God knows our hearts—and He has given us His Spirit to intercede with us and for us.

ALL PRAYER MOVES GOD'S HEART

In the summer of 1988 I had a life-changing encounter at a Saturday morning prayer meeting. I had been leading this prayer meeting each Saturday for nearly four years. We had about twenty people who regularly attended.

One Saturday I arrived around fifteen minutes early. The only two cars already in the parking lot belonged to the young guys who were running the sound system.

As I approached the door to enter the building, I heard music that was incredibly loud. It sounded like something from the "Hallelujah Chorus" in Handel's *Messiah*. It was glorious and beautiful and very loud. I thought, "Oh no, the sound techs are playing with the sound system, and they will surely blow out the speakers by having the volume up so loud." I ran to open the door and ask them to turn the volume down, but when I opened the door, everything was quiet. I thought, "What is going on?"

I hurried into the sanctuary, and the only two guys there were not in the sound booth but rather at the front of the sanctuary praying together. I was perplexed and wondered, "What was that 'Hallelujah Chorus'-type thing that I just heard at such a loud volume?" Then it dawned on me, with a sense of awe, that I had literally heard angelic choirs.

I quickly assumed that the meeting was going to be the most powerful Saturday morning prayer meeting I had ever attended and that something special would happen. My anticipation was very high. Surely hearing the angelic voices was a sign that we were about to witness a dramatic breakthrough of God's presence!

The prayer meeting began, and I thought that at any moment the glory of God would manifest in an unusual way. But nothing of the sort happened. It was as run-of-the-mill as it was on many other Saturdays. Then I went up to pray on the microphone as I did each Saturday morning, thinking that something powerful might happen, but I felt very dull as I prayed. I thought, "What about the angelic choirs? Why did I hear them?" I was perplexed.

After the prayer meeting was over and everyone else had left the building, I sat quietly by myself for about twenty minutes and thought, "Hearing that angelic choir was one of the strangest things that has ever happened to me. What did it mean?" I prayed, "Lord, I am confused. Why didn't something dynamic happen today in the prayer meeting?"

I was trying to figure it out but could not come up with an answer. Then suddenly the Lord gave me a very clear word. It came as an impression. The Holy Spirit said, "This is what happens every time a few of My people gather to pray." I understood in that moment that angelic choirs rejoice every time God's people gather to pray, even in a small, seemingly uninspired or "unanointed" Saturday morning prayer meeting.

Beloved, our private times of prayer and our public prayer meetings may not move us, but they move the angels, and more importantly, they move the heart of God. Never measure your prayers by what you feel; when we pray in agreement with God's will, our "weak prayers" move the heart of God even if they do not move ours.

God's response to the Roman soldier Cornelius, as recorded in the Book of Acts, is proof that this is so. While Cornelius was praying, an angel suddenly appeared to him with a message from God, telling him his prayers would be remembered forever (Acts 10:3–4): "He [the angel] said to him, 'Your prayers and your alms have come up for a memorial before God'" (v. 4).

Perhaps, like most of us, Cornelius felt that his prayers were weak and not very effective. It must have been quite a shock to hear that God would remember his prayers as a memorial before His throne. I like to imagine Cornelius praying with his soldiers. I envision three or four soldiers gathered to pray, without worship music and without Bibles. Because they were not born again, they did not possess the indwelling Spirit. Therefore, I assume their prayer meetings were "pretty rough," and I don't think I would have enjoyed being in them. Imagine: no Bible, no indwelling Spirit, and no anointed worship music! Yet Cornelius's prayers moved God's heart so much that He sent an angel to tell him He will remember them forever as a memorial before Him.

If God will eternally remember the prayers of a man who was not yet born again, how much more will He treasure the prayers of born-again believers who speak God's Word back to their Father? Indeed, our prayers move God's heart and are remembered forever. The Lord views our short, weak, poorly worded prayers through the cross of Jesus. He sees things very differently from the way we view them through our human perspective.

Our prayers matter to God, regardless of how we feel when we pray. On our journey of growing in prayer, let us be mindful of the value of "weak" prayers. As I eventually learned on my prayer journey, the key to experiencing delight rather than a sense of duty in our prayer lives is understanding the fullness of what prayer is and discovering that it is the means by which we participate in the fellowship of the burning heart along with the three persons of the Trinity.

Chapter 2

THE FELLOWSHIP *of the* BURNING HEART

Prayer should not be regarded as a duty which must be performed, but rather as a privilege to be enjoyed, a rare delight that is always revealing some new beauty.[1]
—E. M. BOUNDS

CONTRARY TO WHAT some people think, salvation is much more than a means of escaping hell. As we read in 1 Corinthians, it is an invitation to fellowship with God: "God is faithful, by whom you were called into the fellowship of His Son, Jesus Christ our Lord" (1 Cor. 1:9). The apostle John echoed this high calling in his first letter when he wrote, "Truly our fellowship is with the Father and with His Son Jesus Christ" (1 John 1:3). The implications for this truth are vast, far beyond what we may think.

Salvation is also more than a means of gaining earthly happiness by receiving God's blessing on one's circumstances. Those who see salvation this way pray only for that which will make their lives more comfortable—financial provision, relational blessings, physical health, and anointed ministry—but this is not the ultimate purpose of salvation.

As I mentioned in the previous chapter, salvation is an invitation to enter into "the fellowship of the burning heart." It is God's work through His Son to make a way for us to enter that fellowship. God is after our hearts; He is looking for our love; He is searching for those who will freely enter into and participate in the love shared within the Trinity. This is the glorious destiny of those who say yes to His salvation.

As John pointed out in his Gospel, the essence of eternal life is to know God—to have experiential knowledge of Him.

> This is eternal life, that they may know You, the only true God, and Jesus Christ.
>
> —JOHN 17:3

It is much more than having information about God—His ways and plans. He wants us to come to know Him intimately by talking to Him and living in the experience of His love in this age and the age to come.

Jesus was after so much more than making our lives easy and comfortable when He became a man to die on the cross for us. There is something much bigger going on, and His agenda goes far beyond our temporary earthly happiness. We have been offered the great privilege of knowing God, and the call to grow in prayer is a call to participate in the fellowship of His burning heart—to participate in some of the family dynamics within the Godhead.

13

FIVE EXPRESSIONS OF GOD'S LOVE

As we grow in prayer, we experience more of the love that has burned in God's heart from eternity past. The ultimate reality of the kingdom is the burning love that has existed within the fellowship of the three persons of the Trinity from before the creation of the world.

God is love. His very being is wholehearted love (1 John 4:16). In other words, the essence of how God thinks and feels flows from His heart of unwavering, passionate, infinite, wholehearted love. There is a perpetual "volcanic explosion" of intense love among the three persons of the Trinity. From eternity past, the Father has loved the Son with all His heart, mind, and strength, and Jesus has loved the Father and the Spirit with this same intensity. Each person of the Trinity loves the other two persons with deep, powerful, eternal love. We were created to receive *and* express a measure of this all-consuming love that dwells in God's heart and is the crux of the kingdom of God.

The Father, Son, and Spirit are each fully satisfied in the fellowship of the Trinity. But the joy of love compelled the triune God to create beings who could share their love. Love demands expression; thus, it must be shared and multiplied. God wanted others to experience the joy of the Trinity's perfect love.

Love is the foundation of our relationship with God, the essence of salvation, and the key to understanding how to pray. The call to participate in the fellowship of the burning heart that exists in the relationship among the persons of the Godhead is the cornerstone of the call to prayer.

One foundational premise in Scripture is that God loves us with the same intensity with which God loves God. Impossible as it seems to us weak and sinful mortals, it's true. Jesus declared to His disciples (and by extension, to us), "As the Father loved Me, I also have loved you; abide in My love" (John 15:9). Later Jesus prayed "that the world may know that You [the Father] . . . have loved them as You have loved Me" (John 17:23). Jesus was saying that He loves us as much as He loves the Father and that the Father loves us as much as He loves Jesus.

Think about that for a minute. The Father loves Jesus and us with the same intensity! It's a difficult concept to grasp when we compare ourselves with Jesus, who was sinless. But it's one I never tire of contemplating. Sometimes I wonder: "How does Jesus feel about that? Does it bother Him that God loves me as much as He loves Him?" Of course Jesus is delighted because He loves me as much as the Father does.

As we noted in chapter 1, the love burning in God's heart has at least five expressions. First, God loves God—the Father, Son, and Spirit love each other with fiery love. Second, God loves His people with all His heart and strength. Third, our love for God springs from His love imparted to us. Fourth, God's people love themselves in God's love and for God's sake. Finally, God's people love one another in the overflow of the love that we receive from God. Together these five expressions of love constitute what I call "the fellowship of the burning heart." We are invited to enter into the relationship of burning love that is shared within the fellowship of the Trinity. What a glorious destiny! This radically changes how we view our lives and how we understand salvation.

God's love for God

The first expression of perfect love is found in the relationships within the Trinity. The Son loves the Father (John 14:31), and the Father loves the Son (John 3:35; 5:20; 15:9; 17:23). Each person of the Trinity loves the others with all their heart, mind, and strength.

I fully embrace the truth of the Trinity as commonly taught throughout church history. There is one God who forever dwells in three distinct, divine persons. They are coequal in that the Father, Son, and Spirit each fully possess all God's attributes, while they differ in function and authority in work.

The way God loves within the Trinity is the same way—the only way—He loves us. He cannot love partially; He always loves in fullness and wholeheartedly. His love neither diminishes nor grows because it is infinite in measure and eternal in duration. He never loves us with just part of His love—that would be to deny His own character.

God's love for His people

It is a cause for much rejoicing that God's love does not end with Him but is poured out on and imparted to human beings. Jesus loves the redeemed with the same intensity of love with which the Father loves Him: "As the Father loved Me, I also have loved you; abide in My love" (John 15:9). The Father loves the redeemed with this same intense love, as we see from Jesus's prayer to Him "that the world may know that You ... have loved them as You have loved Me" (John 17:23).

Our love for God

The Pharisees sought to trick Jesus with a question. One day, in response to their question about which was the greatest commandment in the law, Jesus implied that wholehearted love for God was to be the first priority in our lives: "You shall love the Lord your God with all your heart, with all your soul, and with all your mind. This is the first and great commandment" (Matt. 22:37–38). We see from these verses that the Holy Spirit's first agenda is to establish the first commandment in first place in us. This is the highest priority of God's activity in His kingdom. It is the first call for every believer.

The Lord loves us with all His heart and wants us to respond to Him with all our love. He wants us to bring our "all" into the relationship not because He feels lonely and rejected when we love others, but because He *is* wholehearted love. He is worthy of our wholehearted love.

It is His inheritance to receive all our love. Note that the command to love God with all our hearts does not begin with us. It is one expression of the ultimate reality of the kingdom that existed long before the creation of the world—namely, that God's heart burned with love within the fellowship of the Trinity.

We must see the first and great commandment in its eternal context of the fellowship in the Godhead. God created humans not merely to be passive recipients of His holy love but to be active participants in loving Him.

Our love for ourselves

The redeemed are to love themselves in God's love and for God's sake. We love ourselves through the lens of the revelation of Jesus, His cross, and our great worth to Him.

In His reply to the Pharisees about the greatest commandment, Jesus told them that the second commandment was like the first: "And the second is like it: 'You shall love your neighbor as yourself'" (Matt. 22:39). Clearly we must love ourselves in order to fulfill this command. In fact, we will never love others more than we love ourselves in the grace of God. The task is made easier when we are able to see ourselves as God sees us.

We have indescribably great value and worth to Jesus. He desired us so much that He gave His life for us and has crowned us with glory and honor (Heb. 2:7–8). We have received the gift of God's own righteousness (2 Cor. 5:21). Understanding this changes the way we feel about God, our life, and others. Seeing ourselves and our new identity, destiny, and worth in the light of God's love empowers us to love ourselves in God.

The Bible calls us both to love ourselves (Matt. 22:39) and to hate our lives (Luke 14:26). These two commands may seem to be contradictory. What they mean is that we are to love who we are in Christ—our new identity in Him—and what we do in God's will; yet we are to hate who we are outside Christ and what we do outside God's will.

Bernard of Clairvaux (1090–1153) wrote of loving ourselves for God's sake.[2] This includes being jealous for all He called us to be. Jesus does not want us to walk in a false humility that minimizes how much He enjoys loving us or how much He wants us to enjoy being loved by Him. We magnify Jesus and honor His "investment" in us when we love ourselves in agreement with His love for us. The Lord wants us to enter into the deep feelings He has for us in Christ.

When we hate ourselves because we don't see who we are in Christ, we experience deep rejection that damages our ability to love and receive love. God desires to liberate our hearts from self-hatred. He knows that when we love ourselves we will stop wishing that we were someone else and be genuinely thankful to be the glorious people He made us to be, with our specific callings. Then we will be able to accept ourselves as we are in Christ because He accepts and loves us as we are in His grace.

We are to love ourselves in Christ and not despise our appearances, gifts, or ministry assignments. We are to thank Jesus for who we are in Him as well as for the unchangeable aspects of our lives—our appearances, natural abilities, personalities, families, parents, nationalities, and so on. They are God-given, and we are to thank God for them.

If you have secretly wished you were like someone else or had another's calling, gifts, or family background, you must repent for hating the person God created you to be and begin to thank Him for those aspects of your life. As you agree with the will and heart of God, thank Him for who He made you to be, and praise Him that you are precious and valuable to Him exactly as He made you and sees you in Christ, over time you will begin to feel differently about yourself. The truth will set you free!

Our love for others

If we receive God's love and love Him in return, then it is only a matter of time before we will begin loving people more deeply. The same love that burns within the fellowship of the Trinity will flow from us toward others. We are to love others in the overflow of God's very own love. Jesus Himself gave us the command to "love one another as I have loved you" (John 15:12). Our loving others as Jesus loves us is a dynamic expression of the fellowship of the burning heart.

The Lord wants us to enter into how He feels about others because He knows having His heart will change the way we see people and how we respond to them. We can love even fellow believers who mistreat us because God loves them just as He loves us (John 15:9). We will delight in one another in the same way in which God loves and delights in all His people. Moreover we will be empowered to extend our love for others beyond the people who enjoy the same things we do, beyond those who are popular, and beyond those who are powerful and can enhance our status. We will love all God's people with His love.

Understanding the five expressions of God's love will change the way we view God, ourselves, and other people and will help us to pray more effectively. As we will see in the next chapter, that's our goal—to pray effective prayers that allow us to partner with God in bringing His kingdom to Earth.

The Importance of Gazing on God's Beauty

Before we move on, however, I want to emphasize why it is so important to participate with the Godhead in the fellowship of the burning heart. The reason has to do with the way God made us. He created human beings in such a way that we crave fascination, wonder, and awe—and our craving is best fulfilled by beholding God's beauty—the beauty that He possesses in Himself and expresses in creation.

King David understood this truth so well that he declared beholding God's beauty was the solitary goal of his prayer life.

> One thing I have desired of the LORD, that will I seek...to behold the beauty of the LORD.
>
> —Psalm 27:4

Because the Bible describes David as "a man after [God's] own heart" (1 Sam. 13:14), we should pay close attention to his understanding of prayer, which emphasizes gazing on God's beauty. The beauty of God is a very big subject and extends beyond the purpose of this book, but let me make a few short comments about it.

Jesus is filled with love, beauty, wisdom, joy, and ultimate goodness. One way we gaze on God's beauty is by thinking much about the details of Jesus's life, ministry, death, resurrection, ascension, and eternal reign as the King of kings over all the earth. We can live fascinated by Jesus as we ponder the many truths about Him and our relationship to Him.

By fellowshipping with Jesus, we are connecting with the Man who is ultimate beauty (Ps. 27:4). Therefore, as we grow in prayer, our capacity to enjoy beauty increases. Seeing the beauty of Jesus's person enables us to more clearly see His beauty in creation and redemption and His leadership of history. It also works the other way around. Seeing Jesus's beauty through Scripture, nature, and His sovereign leadership over the church, the nations, and history helps us to see the beauty of His person.

The best book I have ever read on the beauty of God is *The Evidential Power of Beauty* by Thomas Dubay.[3] I highly recommend it to you. Dubay teaches us to fill our minds with God's beauty from His books of creation and redemption. He encourages us to ponder how spectacular the universe is and to consider God's creation in great detail. A drop of water, the ocean, a star, a flower, an atom, a leaf, and a bird all possess vast beauty, but we miss much of their beauty when we give them only a passing glance or look at them with a dull heart. Boredom is not the result of seeing what is real but the result of seeing with a dull heart. Our communion with God, or lack of it, greatly affects our perspective on life. Prayer is immersion in beauty—God's beauty. Talking to Him regularly allows us to see His beauty in many places.

Dubay teaches that prayer is the primary, God-ordained way in which we encounter Jesus, who is in Himself love, reality, and beauty. Jesus is everything! He must be our consuming goal because anything less than everything is not enough.

The many facets of God's beauty are summed up in one reality—wholehearted *love*. Our lifelong search is really the search for deep relationship, lasting purpose, delight, and beauty. Our search ends not in things but in a person—in God's presence. The Russian novelist Dostoevsky wrote that "to live without God is nothing but torture."[4]

Our hearts thirst for the eternal, for transcendence, and they can be filled only by participating in the fellowship of the burning heart with the Father, Son, and Holy Spirit. Many people seek to quench their eternal thirst with temporal experiences, pleasures, and accomplishments. The observant person eventually discovers that everything "new and exciting"—new places, new relationships, new experiences—always leaves him needing more. The writer of Ecclesiastes noted that "the eye is not satisfied with seeing, nor the ear filled with hearing.... Is there anything of which it may be said, 'See, this is new'?" (Eccles. 1:8–10).

The worst tragedy in life is to live in continual boredom without interacting with the divine. Bored people are compelled to search for different pleasures to fill their spiritual emptiness and loneliness. If we are not growing in our understanding of the beauty of Jesus and His purpose, then we will inevitably spend our free time and resources seeking fame, fortune, pleasure, entertainment, and recognition from others, which do not satisfy. They may temporarily deaden the pain of emptiness and loneliness, which stems from not having a growing relationship with God, but encountering beauty is the only real and lasting solution to overcoming boredom.

We will never be completely satisfied by our achievements, skills, wealth, fame, pleasures, or possessions. Why? Because the human heart was created to need more than what is available to us in the natural realm. Only the eternal, supernatural God can fill our longings. We are created by God's design to need deep connection with Him in order for our deepest longing to be satisfied. Saint Augustine prayed: "You have made us for yourself, O Lord, and our hearts are restless until they rest in You."[5] Human beings are unique in all of creation in that we are satisfied only by becoming more than what our human nature defines. We are spiritual beings who need something beyond what we received in our natural makeup. This "something" is best found in our interaction with God, who is ultimate beauty—thus, through prayer. The more we grow in prayer, the more we will have the capacity to enjoy God's beauty as we were created to.

Chapter 3

CHARACTERISTICS *of* EFFECTIVE PRAYER

It is not enough to begin to pray...but we must patiently, believingly continue in prayer until we obtain an answer.[1]
—GEORGE MÜLLER

WE WILL LEARN in subsequent chapters different ways to pray, but first we must look at the characteristics of the type of prayer we are seeking to engage in: prayer that actually makes a difference and accomplishes its intended goal. Prayer is first of all about relationship, but it is also about results—results that help to fulfill God's will on the earth.

The apostle James, who was known in the early church as a great man of prayer, gave the church invaluable insight into this subject. His letter in the New Testament includes his teaching on effective prayer and what it accomplishes.

> And the prayer of faith will save the sick, and the Lord will raise him up...Confess your trespasses to one another, and pray for one another, that you may be healed. The effective, fervent prayer of a righteous man avails much. Elijah was a man with a nature like ours, and he prayed earnestly that it would not rain; and it did not rain on the land for three years and six months. And he prayed again, and the heaven gave rain, and the earth produced its fruit.
>
> —JAMES 5:15–18

According to this passage, God calls us to offer holy, believing, persevering prayer that flows from relationship in His family—this is the kind of prayer that accomplishes much.

It is the destiny of every believer to release the power of God through his simple prayers. James 5:15–16 says that the prayer of faith will deliver the sick and that our prayers can "[avail] much." Our prayers accomplish much more than we can gauge with our five senses, and the reality that they effect change gives our lives and our prayers great value. Our perspective on life changes dramatically when we believe that our prayers really make a difference. Let's look at the four characteristics of effective prayer James wrote about: prayer rooted in faith; prayer in the context of good relationships; prayer of the righteous; and prayer that is earnest.

PRAYER ROOTED IN FAITH

The prayer of faith mentioned in James 5:15 is prayer that is rooted in a three-fold confidence in God. First, it is prayer with confidence in the authority of Jesus over sickness and the works of darkness. Jesus affirmed a Roman centurion for having great faith in His authority over sickness (Matt. 8:5–13). Jesus also declared, "All authority has been given to Me in heaven and on earth" (Matt. 28:18). Our faith is to be anchored in the knowledge of His authority over every other power that exists.

Second, it is prayer with confidence in the blood of Jesus that qualifies weak people such as us to be vessels that release His power and receive His blessings. In the Book of Hebrews we learn that we have "boldness to enter the Holiest by the blood of Jesus" (Heb. 10:19). We are not to shrink back due to shame or guilt, for He has given His own righteousness to us as a free gift (2 Cor. 5:21). Therefore, we may state our requests boldly before God's throne, knowing that He has made a way for us to stand there.

Third, it is prayer with confidence in the desire of Jesus to bless. He deeply desires to heal, set free, and bless His people. God is our Father; He is eager to hear the prayers of His children. In Luke 11 Jesus concluded His teaching on prayer, saying, "If a son asks for bread from any father among you, will he give him a stone? Or if he asks for a fish, will he give him a serpent instead of a fish?...If you then, being evil, know how to give good gifts to your children, how much more will your heavenly Father give the Holy Spirit to those who ask Him!" (vv. 11–13). We pray in faith, knowing that God, whose heart burns with passion for us, really does desire to bless us.

PRAYER IN THE CONTEXT OF GOOD RELATIONSHIPS

In teaching on effective prayer, James exhorted us to confess our sins to one another: "Confess your trespasses to one another, and pray for one another, that you may be healed" (James 5:16). We are inclined to follow his advice only when we are in strong relationship with one another.

Some believers are committed to growing in relationship with others but are content to have a weak prayer life. Others are committed to growing in their prayer lives but are content to have weak relationships. The Bible sets these two values together as complementary, not competing. They are not to be separated because effective prayer flows best from those who are in strong kingdom relationships—sharing deeply with one another, partnering together in kingdom activities, and relating to one another in humility, honor, and forgiveness in the grace of God. Paul admonishes us in Colossians to "put on tender mercies, kindness, humility, meekness, longsuffering; bearing with one another, and forgiving one another." Then he adds, "But above all these things put on love, which is the bond of perfection" (Col. 3:12–14).

A strong prayer life will eventually lead to strong relationships with people.

Those who sincerely value their relationship with Jesus are energized to love people more deeply. Prayer is not about being anti-relational or antisocial. True prayer has the opposite effect. It is all about love—loving God and people. People of prayer should be the most energized in love.

The Lord cares so much about relationships that the Scripture exhorts husbands to honor their wives so that their prayers will not be hindered.

> Husbands, likewise, dwell with them with understanding, giving honor to the wife, as to the weaker vessel, and as being heirs together of the grace of life, that your prayers may not be hindered.
>
> —1 PETER 3:7

A man's prayers will be hindered if he does not treat his wife with honor, both publicly and in secret. The scripture makes it clear that the measure of a husband's effectiveness in prayer is connected to the measure with which he honors his wife. He can pray with eloquence and energy in public, but if he speaks in unkind ways to his wife in private, without repenting of it to her, then his prayers are hindered. The Lord insists that men treat their wives with understanding and honor. Husbands must take the lead in humility in their marriages.

I have known men who want to be faithful in prayer but are not faithful to honor their wives. They complain that they don't "like" their wives anymore and want to get new ones. But God places great value on the marriage covenant. Therefore, a Christian man who does not "like" his wife anymore must still serve and honor her if he desires to please God and have an effectual prayer life. Obviously it is best if a husband likes his wife, but there is something bigger at stake. It is about honoring the marriage covenant because God is a God of covenant.

The Lord can restore positive emotions in a marriage regardless of how bad things may be. I have seen the Lord bless men who chose to serve and honor their wives even in a season when they did not have romantic feelings for them. The Lord blessed these men by eventually turning their emotions toward their wives again. God so honors the covenant of marriage that He awakened the former emotions these husbands had for their wives.

The command issued in 1 Peter 3:7 is of great significance for the global prayer movement that the Holy Spirit is raising up in this hour, which we'll talk more about in later chapters. As the prayer movement matures across the earth, so the emphasis on honor in marriage will increase, especially honor for the wife. As the Spirit brings the prayer movement to a crescendo, He will also bring honor to women in their homes.

PRAYER OF THE RIGHTEOUS

One very important condition for effectual prayer is to be committed to walking out a lifestyle of righteousness before God and people, as indicated in James 5:16:

"The effective…prayer of a *righteous* man avails much." This biblical condition is often minimized or totally ignored, even by people who are deeply involved in the prayer-and-worship movement today.

A righteous person is any believer who sets his heart to obey Jesus as he seeks to walk in godly character with a lifestyle of practicing the truth (1 John 1:6). Setting our hearts to obey is very important, even if we fall short of mature, consistent obedience. There is no such thing as a person who is so mature in righteousness that he is above all temptation and never falls short in his walk with God. In other words, the prayers of a "righteous person" include the prayers of imperfect, weak people—such as you and me—who sincerely seek to walk in righteousness even as we stumble in our weakness. I am so grateful for the gloriously reality of the grace of God!

The apostle John declared that the Lord hears and responds to us because we keep His commands and do the things that are pleasing to Him: "Whatever we ask we receive from Him, because we keep His commandments and do those things that are pleasing in His sight" (1 John 3:22). Prayer is no substitute for obedience. I have met those who imagine that if they pray and fast more, they can walk in a little immorality or be dishonest in their finances or slander the people who cause pressure in their lives. They think that being extra zealous in the spiritual disciplines will balance out areas of persistent compromise. But praying more does not compensate for unrepented sins that we deliberately continue to commit, as this verse from Isaiah makes clear: "Your sins have hidden His face from you, so that He will not hear" (Isa. 59:2).

Prayer is far more boring and difficult if we seek to live one part of our lives as if it belonged to God and another part as if it belonged to us. There is a dynamic relationship between our lifestyle and our ability to enjoy prayer. Our spiritual capacity to experience and enjoy God increases as we walk in purity. Jesus emphasized this truth in the Sermon on the Mount: "Blessed are the pure in heart, for they shall see God" (Matt. 5:8).

Where there is ongoing, willful compromise in our lives, it will greatly hinder our spiritual growth and our capacity to agree with God in prayer. Sin hinders our love for Him. We must sincerely seek to live in wholehearted obedience because obedience is not optional in the kingdom life.

When we come up short in our obedience, we must acknowledge it and confess it rather than seeking to rationalize it. We call it sin, we repent of it, and we freely receive God's forgiveness. Then we "push delete" and immediately stand, once again, with confidence in God's presence. Walking in obedience is not about seeking to earn the answers to our prayers; it is about living in agreement with love because God is love.

The truth of the necessity of keeping God's commandments is overlooked by some who teach on prayer. It is more popular to emphasize our authority in Christ. That is also an essential truth, but the lifestyle of the one praying does matter. What we do negatively and what we neglect to do positively deeply affect our prayer lives.

PRAYER THAT IS EARNEST

Using the prophet Elijah as an example, the apostle James taught that one characteristic of effective prayer is earnestness in prayer: "Elijah...prayed earnestly that it would not rain; and it did not rain" (James 5:17). What does it mean to be earnest? It is important to understand what earnest prayer is because it is one of the primary conditions of effective prayer as set forth in the Scripture.

Two aspects of earnest prayer

First, earnest prayer comes from a heart that is engaged with God. To be earnest implies that we are not praying by rote or just going through the motions. Being earnest is the opposite of speaking our prayers mindlessly into the air. We are to focus our minds and attention toward the Lord when we pray.

Second, earnest prayer is prayer that is persistent (Matt. 7:7–8; Luke 11:5–10; 18:1, 7). The Greek word *proseuche* translated as "earnestly" in James 5 literally means "he prayed with prayer," which is an idiom expressing persistence in prayer. Hence, the translators said of Elijah that he "prayed earnestly."

We must refuse to be denied answers to prayers that are in agreement with God's will. We must not stop asking and thanking God for the answers until we see them with our eyes. We must not be casual about our prayer requests but persistent and tenacious.

Jesus taught a parable about the Father's willingness to answer prayer that is recorded in the Gospel of Luke. His message was that because of our persistence, the Father answers. He applied the parable by exhorting us to ask, knowing that the request will be fulfilled; to seek, knowing that we will find; and to knock, knowing that the door will open (v. 9). The Greek verbs for "ask," "seek," and "knock" are in the continuous present tense. In other words, we are to ask and keep on asking, seek and keep on seeking, knock and keep on knocking. The message is a call to perseverance.

> Because of his persistence he will rise and give him as many as he needs. So I say to you, ask, and it will be given to you; seek, and you will find; knock, and it will be opened to you. For everyone who asks receives, and he who seeks finds, and to him who knocks it will be opened.
> —LUKE 11:8–10

The apostle Paul called us to pray "with all perseverance" (Eph. 6:18) and to labor fervently (Col. 4:12) in prayer. When we ask casually, with little effort to focus our minds on the Lord, or when we stop praying for something that is in God's will, we show that we do not value what we are praying for. As we see in Jeremiah's prophecy, when we highly prize something, we will seek the Lord for it with all our hearts: "'You will seek Me and find Me, when you search for Me with all your heart'" (Jer. 29:13).

Earnest prayer doesn't have to be loud.

Earnestness in prayer is not measured by the volume of our prayers. This may seem obvious, but some assume that shouting a prayer proves they are earnest about it. Some people show that they "really" want the answer to a prayer by offering the prayer loudly.

Allow me to make a pastoral observation. During many years of leading in prayer, I have come across numerous people who devalue their prayers because they feel the prayers are not offered with enough emotion and energy. They misunderstand the nature of passionate or earnest prayer. It is mostly about being persistent and engaging with God from the heart. It is not about our prayer style in a public prayer meeting. But some conclude that they lack the necessary "passion" for God to answer them because they compare the way they pray to the way those who lead out in public prayer express themselves with great emotion or volume.

The majority of us do not speak our prayers with intense emotion and volume in public, but we should not conclude that our prayers are ineffectual or second-class. If shouting is what defines earnest prayer, then the prayer lives of about 99 percent of us would be classed as non-passionate and lacking earnestness. Why? Because most of our prayers are offered as whispers from our hearts throughout the day. Even the most energetic prayer warriors probably offer less than 1 percent of their prayers in a public prayer meeting where they shout their prayers. Yet their private prayers, which are often mere whispers of the heart, are still earnest prayers.

In the New King James Version of the Bible, the translators used the word *fervent* in James 5:16 to convey the concept of earnestness in prayer. This word is not found in the verse in Greek manuscripts. It was inserted because the translators sought to emphasize the strength of the word "earnestly" in the following verse, James 5:17.

> The effective, *fervent* prayer of a righteous man avails much. Elijah was
> a man with a nature like ours, and he prayed *earnestly* that it would not
> rain; and it did not rain on the land for three years and six months.
> —JAMES 5:16–17

Notice that neither *fervent* nor *earnestly* refers to the volume of a prayer. Quiet prayers can be passionate and earnest. In First Samuel we read of Hannah, who was praying for a child and was filled with anguish in her soul over her barrenness. She was weeping and speaking from her heart so softly that Eli the priest could not hear her. The Lord answered her prayer, and she became the mother of the prophet Samuel (1 Sam. 1:13, 27)—as well as five more children.

Once when I was in a store, a woman bent down and whispered to her young child, "Billy, if you don't stop it, I'm warning you that you will be in big trouble." She was very engaged and passionate as she whispered her warning to little Billy, but she never lifted her voice, and nobody heard her except little Billy and me.

The point is, we should not conclude that our prayers are ineffective or that we lack earnestness simply because we do not have a loud, aggressive prayer style. Passion is not about energy and volume; it is about being engaged from the heart with the Lord while praying and persevering in faith without quitting. So keep at it, and do not draw back, even if your prayer style is softer than that of others. I encourage you not to compare your prayer style to that of others and conclude that you are deficient in prayer simply because you do not shout your prayers.

Earnest prayer doesn't depend on what we feel.

Some draw back in their prayer lives because they embrace another wrong idea about earnest or fervent prayer. They believe they must *feel* God's presence when they pray. Thus, when they are discouraged or tired, they assume their prayers will be of no effect, and they stop praying. I have good news—our prayers are effective even when we are tired, discouraged, or not in a good mood. Remember that we offer our prayers to the Lord, who is in a good mood and is not tired. We don't have to be happy and energetic for our prayers to be earnest and to avail much.

The work of the kingdom is based on who Jesus is and what He did on the cross, not on how we feel. God answers our prayers because of the blood of Jesus and His desire to partner with His people. If we measure ourselves by a wrong idea of what passion or earnestness in prayer is, then we will be tempted to pray much less.

Prayer is not about informing or persuading God but about connecting with Him in relationship. He is looking for conversation and dialogue with us. Some believers think that by praying more they *earn* the answers to their prayers. God wants us to talk with Him more because He loves relating to us. We do not earn answers to prayers by our persistence or obedience.

God knows our needs before we do, so we are not informing Him of anything by our prayers. Rather, He uses our needs to call us into a dialogue of prayer so that we connect with Him. Why? He so values relationship with us that He links the release of some of His blessings to our prayers, our conversations with Him. Then when He answers our prayers, we rightly conclude that He listens to us and that we move His heart. That is one of the main reasons the Lord requires His people to pray consistently. It is a statement of His heart for us.

The Lord wants to converse with us far more than we want to talk with Him. This is a mystery to me. He is so interesting, and we are not very interesting. Why does He care so much about our praying more? Because at the core of His being, He is infinite love, and He loves conversation with His people.

Weak people can pray earnestly.

Elijah was a weak man with a nature like ours. He was prone to fear and discouragement, and he had the same weaknesses and temptations we face; yet his prayer life was still very effective (1 Kings 17–19). James emphasized this point to give us courage to pray, even in the face of our weaknesses.

> Elijah was a man with a nature like ours, and he prayed earnestly that
> it would not rain; and it did not rain...for three years and six months.
> And he prayed again, and the heaven gave rain.
>
> —James 5:17–18

The story of Elijah is the story not of a great prophet of God but of the
great God of the prophet. We may be surprised when we meet Elijah in the
age to come. We may picture him as physically strong, with a dynamic person-
ality, something like Charlton Heston when he played Moses in the famous
movie *The Ten Commandments*. But he may in fact have been a physically weak
and unimpressive man according to human standards. When we meet the great
men and women of the Bible face-to-face, we may be surprised to discover just
how much like us they are. It is faith in a great God that makes a great man or
woman of God.

During the reign of King Ahab, Elijah called the people of Israel to repent of
their backsliding. His prayers led to the healing of a nation when Israel turned
back to God. Elijah prayed for a drought, and a drought came. Then three and a
half years later, he prayed for rain to fall and break the drought. He prayed earnestly, with persistence. Seven times he prayed for the drought to break and the
rains to come. Even though the Lord had told Elijah that He would send rain
and had commanded Elijah to tell Ahab that rain was coming, the Lord required
Elijah to pray until the rain actually came.

> Elijah said to Ahab, "Go up, eat and drink; for there is the sound of
> abundance of rain." ...Elijah went up to the top of Carmel; then he
> bowed down on the ground, and put his face between his knees, and
> said to his servant, "Go up now, look toward the sea." So he went up
> and looked, and said, "There is nothing." And seven times he said, "Go
> again." Then it came to pass the seventh time, that he said, "There is a
> cloud, as small as a man's hand, rising out of the sea!" ...Now it hap-
> pened in the meantime that the sky became black with clouds and wind,
> and there was a heavy rain.
>
> —1 Kings 18:41–45

The point James makes is that God used Elijah, a man not unlike us, to cause
the nation of Israel to return to Him by releasing supernatural miracles of fire,
drought, and rain (1 Kings 17:1; 18:1, 38). In other words, if God answered the
prayers of a weak man like Elijah, prayers that led to the healing of a nation, then
how much more will He answer the prayers of weak people like us that will lead
to the healing of individuals? Remember, the context of the passage in James we
are referring to is prayer for physical healing (James 5:15–17). The point is that
God is committed to healing hearts, bodies, and nations using the prayers of
weak people, and these weak people accomplish much with their prayers when
they are in agreement with God.

GOD ANSWERS OUR PRAYERS

The apostle John assured us that if we ask anything according to God's will, no matter how difficult it is, God will hear and answer us: "Now this is the confidence that we have in Him, that if we ask anything according to His will, He hears us" (1 John 5:14). For God to "hear" our prayers means that He approves of them. No matter how impossible it seems, the Lord will answer prayers that are according to His will.

Effective prayer is answered prayer. However, we must not assume that a particular prayer is outside His will simply because we don't receive an immediate answer to it. There are certain qualifiers even for prayers that are in God's will. For example, God may answer in a different way than we expect. Or He may answer the prayer at a different time. On some occasions a prayer that is actually in God's will is delayed until the intercessor walks in righteousness—until an area of compromise is repented of. As I have said, we cannot "earn" the answer to a prayer by good behavior, but godly character is required so that we are able to steward the answer in a way that brings benefit to us and to others in the kingdom. Many believers overlook the biblical connection of effective prayer to the righteous lifestyle of the person praying. However, the Scripture emphasizes this point over and over.

It is important to remember that God answers in His way—which is often different from the one we would choose—and in His timing. His ways are so different from ours! (See Isaiah 55:8–9.) We must be careful not to become offended with Him when He delays the answer to a prayer. Those who become offended with God often conclude that prayer is not effective and is therefore worthless. But we must trust His leadership in the manner and timing in which He answers our prayers. The delay of answered prayer is designed to provoke earnestness in us.

Some people who are reading this book are in situations in which there is no human remedy to the obstacles they are facing. Jesus has power over any problem that may rise up against us. The Lord will do the impossible through those who dare to believe Him in persistent prayer, for "with God all things are possible" (Matt. 19:26; Mark 10:27).

The Bible sets forth important conditions for effective prayer. These conditions include those we have discussed in this chapter—faith, good relationships, righteous living, and earnestness—as well as knowing our authority in Christ and perseverance. However, the conditions that are most emphasized today are faith and our authority in Christ. The biblical conditions most neglected are expressions of loving God as seen in kingdom relationships, a godly lifestyle, and perseverance in prayer.

We must remember that the purpose of salvation is to walk in a deep relationship with God. Though God desires partnership with us, we are much more to Him than merely His kingdom workforce! We established in chapter 1 that salvation is a call to relate to Him with obedient love and not just to work for Him and gain more blessing on our circumstances.

Neither perseverance nor obedience earns us answers to our prayers. But obedience brings us into agreement with God's heart and thus into a stronger relationship with Him, which reaps abundant blessing in our lives. Jesus so desires relationship with us that He calls us to resist the compromise that injures our hearts and our ability to love Him. The ultimate point of prayer is not to "get things" from the Lord but to live as close to Him as we can. Jesus connected our prayers and our love for God with our obedience when He said, "Whatever you ask in My name, that I will do, that the Father may be glorified in the Son. If you ask anything in My name, I will do it. If you love Me, keep My commandments" (John 14:13–15).

In other words, loving God, obeying God, and having an effective prayer life are different aspects of the one subject of living in such a way that His glory may be seen in our lives. If we love Him, we will keep His commandments. The Bible does not describe a category of sincere believer who is casual about sin in his life. Jesus will relate to us only on His terms, not on ours. He is full of grace, but His terms are clear, and they are established on His definition of love, righteousness, and godliness.

THE HUMAN AND DIVINE SIDES OF EFFECTIVE PRAYER

The human side of effective prayer, as we have just seen, is coming into agreement with God—living and praying in accordance with His will, heart, and priorities. God is looking for our agreement with Him because it strengthens our relationship with Him. As we pray with faith, we pray in agreement with God's authority and Jesus's finished work on the cross. As we live righteously, we live in agreement with God's character. As we pray earnestly and persistently, we live in agreement with God's priorities. The Lord is zealous for certain things, and He does not want us to be casual about them and draw back from focusing on them in prayer.

The divine side of effective prayer is Jesus's work on the cross and His power's being released through us. We receive God's favor as a free gift because of Jesus, and when we combine agreement with God, as seen in our believing, righteous, earnest prayer, then we will experience more of what is freely given to us by Jesus. God doesn't love us more when we live in greater agreement with Him, but He is able to use us more, and we are able to experience a greater measure of blessing in our experience.

To summarize, effective prayer is earnest prayer that is in agreement with God's will and that is offered in faith in the context of our commitment to building strong kingdom relationships and walking in righteousness. It is prayer that is prayed under the following ten conditions, some of which I have only touched on in this chapter. I encourage you to study all of them further using the references provided:

- Faith (Matt. 21:21–22; Mark 11:23–24; 1 John 5:14–15)

- Right relationships, particularly husbands honoring wives (1 Pet. 3:7)

- A righteous (holy) life (Ps. 66:18; Isa. 59:2; 1 John 3:19–22)

- Earnestness (persistence) (Isa. 30:18–19; 62:6–7; Matt. 7:7–11; Luke 11:5–13; 18:1–8; James 5:17)

- In accordance with the will of God (1 John 5:14–15)

- In the name of Jesus (John 14:13–14, 26; 16:23–24)

- Pure motives (James 4:2–3)

- Boldness (Heb. 4:16)

- Forgiveness (Matt. 6:15; 5:23–24)

- Prayer of agreement, in unity (Matt. 18:19–20).

OUR PRAYERS REMAIN EFFECTIVE FOREVER

James assured us that our prayers avail much, that much can be accomplished through the prayers of a righteous man (James 5:16). Indeed, our prayers accomplish much in this age *and* in the age to come. The challenge is in not being able to fully measure right now the extent to which our prayers impact us, other people, and the nations.

In Revelation 5 we learn that all the prayers prayed in God's will throughout history are stored in golden bowls near the throne: "The twenty-four elders fell down before the Lamb, each having a harp, and golden bowls full of incense, which are the prayers of the saints" (Rev. 5:8; see also Rev. 8:1–6). Notice that the bowls will one day be "full." The fact that the bowls of prayer in heaven fill up implies that God does not forget our prayers. He still remembers our prayers from five years ago or even twenty years ago. We may have forgotten them, but God has not. They are in a golden bowl near to His throne and near to His heart.

In the vision recorded in the Book of Revelation, the apostle John saw the prayers of all the saints, not just those of the end-time saints. An angel was given incense to offer with the prayers of all the saints upon the golden altar before God's throne (Rev. 8:3).

Our prayers avail so much that they remain effective, or "alive," in God's sight long after this life, and I assume that they "live" forever in God's heart. Even the prayers from the distant past—from three hundred years ago or three thousand years ago—are still effective in God's presence. I believe that the prayers we offer today will still be effective in the distant future—five hundred or five thousand years from now. What we accomplish in prayer affects events on the earth today and also those in the distant future. Our prayers now for cities and nations will continue to have an impact in the age to come.

The prayers for revival and justice offered by *all the saints* from the whole of history will be fully answered together at the end of the age. These prayers did not "die out" after they were partially answered by the revivals in history, which we'll learn more about in a later chapter. Our prayers have a significant, partial release in our generation and a greater, more complete release in the future—even in the age to come.

As we gain greater understanding that our weak, simple prayers are not forgotten, we are motivated to persevere in prayer, even when we feel discouraged. The Word reminds us that the Lord will not forget one act of obedience done in love for Him: "God is not unjust to forget your work and labor of love which you have shown toward His name, in that you have ministered to the saints" (Heb. 6:10).

Our love in this age is weak, but God is still moved by it. He will never forget the love we show toward Him in ministering to others in prayer or performing other acts of service. We may forget our small acts of service, but He doesn't. None of the prayers we offer or the actions we take in the will of God is wasted. The Lord would consider it an "injustice" if He forgot anything we do in love for Him.

Remember Cornelius? According to the account in Acts 10:4, an angel appeared to this Gentile, a Roman soldier, to let him know that his prayers and financial giving would be remembered *forever* as a memorial before God. Now, if the Lord eternally remembers the prayers of a Roman soldier who did not yet have the Holy Spirit because he was not yet born again, how much more will He remember the prayers of born-again believers? This verse helps us to understand that there is continuity between what we do now and what happens in the age to come.

Knowing the characteristics of effective prayer will help us understand what it takes to pray prayers that are in agreement with God's will and that make a difference for eternity. But in order for such prayers to flow out of us, we must adopt a lifestyle of abiding in Christ.

Chapter 4

ABIDING *in* CHRIST

The battle of prayer is against two things in the earthlies: wan-
dering thoughts, and lack of intimacy with God...neither can
be cured at once, but they can be cured by discipline.[1]
—OSWALD CHAMBERS

WHILE ON EARTH Jesus taught us how to live in dynamic union with God. He said, "I am the vine, you are the branches. He who abides in Me, and I in him, bears much fruit....I chose you and appointed you that you should go and bear fruit, and that your fruit should remain" (John 15:5, 16). These verses are the essence of His foundational teaching on prayer.

Jesus declared that He is the vine, the source of life, and that we are the branches, the expression of His life. In this statement Jesus gave us one of His primary exhortations on living a kingdom lifestyle, which is to "abide in Christ" so that we may bear fruit that remains forever.

A person who cultivates a lifestyle of abiding in Christ is one who bears fruit that remains. God remembers our fruit forever because it lasts forever. In his first letter to the Corinthians Paul links the subject of lasting fruit—work that remains—to eternal rewards (1 Cor. 3:9–15). Jesus will give eternal rewards in the age to come as an expression of how He feels about the way we love Him in this age. How glorious it is that He remembers and esteems our small acts of obedience! Others may not see or appreciate them, but God notices and values them.

We bear fruit in two ways: inwardly in our character and outwardly in our ministry and service to others. Thus our fruit consists of godly character[2] as well as ministry and service.[3] It is made up mostly of small things—for example, humbling ourselves in our marriages and family relationships or doing small acts of obedience, such as giving someone a cup of cold water. Choosing humility, purity, and kindness leads to fruit that lasts forever.

Through the activity of the Spirit in us and through us, we can do things that bear lasting fruit that God esteems forever. Our life becomes epic as we grasp the implications of this truth.

Fruit-bearing that lasts forever is for anyone who will cultivate a life of abiding in Christ. Maybe you have no education, no money, no gifting that you can see, and no friends. Maybe you feel unloved and believe that you are not beautiful. No matter what your circumstance or status is, you can still bear lasting fruit if you abide in Christ. Jesus essentially said, "Anyone who abides in Me can bear fruit" (John 15:5).

Three Aspects of Abiding in Christ

The most important activity related to growing in prayer is abiding in Christ. It is one of the most neglected activities in the kingdom, yet it involves only three simple aspects—talking to Jesus, applying His promises, and obeying His leadership. These activities overlap, but they are not the same.

1. Talking to Jesus

The core task of abiding in Christ is talking to Jesus. It is so simple that anyone can do it but so simple that many do not do it. I often exchange the phrase "abide in Me" for the phrase "talk to Me"—I use them interchangeably.

The Christian life is an ongoing dialogue with a real person. In fact, the essence of Christianity is living in an ongoing dialogue with the most glorious Man who ever walked the earth. He is fully God and fully man, and we get to talk to Him!

Jesus has much to say to us, but He allows us to set the pace of the conversation. If we start, He will continue the conversation as long as we do. When we stop, He stops and waits until we begin again. He responds in the degree to which we communicate with Him.

Over the years I have heard some say, "I just pray on the run." I have found that if we will pray in a focused way in regular, near-daily prayer times, then we will "pray on the run" far more often and far more consistently. We abide in Christ more consistently by having many short ten- to twenty-second exchanges with the Lord throughout each day, in addition to having longer, focused prayer times that we put into our regular routine or schedule.

2. Applying His promises

The second aspect involved in abiding in Christ is applying the promises in His Word to our hearts. Emotions such as shame, guilt, fear, or rejection often rise up in us to challenge what God says in His Word about His loving us, forgiving us, and providing for us. The enemy challenges these truths in the Word and accuses God continually (Rev. 12:10).

We apply the promises in His Word to our hearts by confessing the truths and resisting the devil's lies (Rom. 10:8–10). We take a stand for what the Word says is true about us by speaking the Word over the negative emotions that rise up in us. The lies will not go away by themselves; they must be actively resisted as we confess the truths of the Word.

If we feel shame, guilt, fear, or rejection by God, we are to apply the truth of Romans 8:1: "There is therefore now no condemnation for those who are in Christ Jesus." We can stand with confidence in God's sight because Jesus paid the price for our sin and took our condemnation. So we confess, "We are the righteousness of God in Christ, and therefore, there is no condemnation" (2 Cor. 5:21). Or in the face of fear we confess, "God will supply all our needs according to His riches in glory by Christ Jesus" (see Phil. 4:19).

Many believers are still living under the tyranny of Satan's lies twenty or thirty years after they have been born again, believing that their lives are worthless and that God has forgotten and rejected them. Others choose to ride out the storm of the negative emotions that rise up in them. But there is great power in the Word, and we must not neglect to apply His promises in the face of fear, condemnation, or other negative emotions.

3. Obeying His leadership

The third aspect related to abiding in Christ is obeying His leadership, and we must not minimize this vital part of abiding. Jesus clearly stated that our obedience and our love for Him are closely connected:

> He who has My commandments and keeps them, it is he who loves Me....I will love him and manifest Myself to him....If anyone loves Me, he will keep My word; and My Father will love him, and We will come to him and make Our home with him.
> —JOHN 14:21–23

From these words, we understand that those who set their hearts to keep Jesus's commands are the only ones who truly love Him. Obedience is an expression of our love for Jesus, and we are to set our hearts to love Him with a spirit of obedience.

Jesus promised to manifest His presence to those who obey Him: "He who loves Me will be loved by My Father, and I will love him and manifest Myself to him" (John 14:21). He was saying He will release the grace of His presence to our minds and emotions in such a way that we can feel it. Only in the context of obedient love does He reveal the deeper things of His heart.

It is popular today to minimize obedience in the name of magnifying God's grace. Some preach a distorted grace message that emphasizes the freeness of forgiveness while undermining the necessity of loving Jesus in a spirit of obedience. But the biblical grace message never minimizes obedience. God's wholehearted love for us always calls for a response of our wholehearted love for Him, as evidenced by our seeking to walk in obedience to Him.

God's grace is sufficient when we come up short in our obedience, but it is important to call sin "sin" and declare war on it. Those who love God in truth will set their hearts to live in a spirit of obedience in every area of their lives— including their use of time, money, and words, and in what their eyes look at.

Many in the church today believe it is acceptable to disregard God's commandments. This is a grave error. We are in a covenant relationship in which we receive God's love, and the only acceptable response that is worthy of Jesus is for us to love Him in return. He loves us with all His strength. He wants us to love Him with all our strength. Yes, our "all" is small compared to His "all," but it is a covenant relationship of love in which both parties give their all.

The Bible tells us that it is the obedient, or the pure in heart, who will see God (Matt. 5:8). What this means is that they will experience God more. The result of walking in purity is that our spiritual capacity to feel or experience the love of God increases. We do not earn God's love by obeying His commands; rather, we express our love to Him through our obedience. Furthermore, God does not love us more when we obey Him; He already loves us completely and fully because of who He is—He is love. However, we do experience His love more. We feel it. We are inspired by it more.

In summary, abiding in Christ involves three aspects—talking with God, applying His promises, and obeying His leadership. Some talk to Jesus regularly yet do not apply His Word to their hearts. Others apply the Word but neglect to talk to Jesus regularly. Some seek to obey Him but do not apply His Word. Others claim His promises but do not set their hearts to obey Him. Abiding in Christ requires all three of these activities, and it results in God's people being empowered to bear fruit that remains and to live a transformed life.

CHRIST'S ABIDING IN US

Jesus spoke in detail about our union with God (see John 15), which leads to our transformation. Cultivating union with God results in transforming our minds and emotions by allowing us to participate in the family dynamics of the Trinity; it transforms our deeds from insignificant, small acts to those that are remembered forever in God's sight.

We see two elements of this transforming union in John 15:1–11—we abide in Christ, and Christ abides in us. The first idea, that our life is in Christ, is familiar to most of us, and we have just seen what it takes to make this a reality. But the truth that Christ lives in us is often overlooked, and few emphasize its implications. It is important to live in the light of both truths because doing so makes it possible for us to bear lasting fruit for the kingdom. Jesus said, "He who abides in Me, and I in him, bears much fruit" (v. 5).

There are two aspects of Christ's abiding in us. First, He abides—lives—in our spirits *instantly* when we are born again. Second, He abides in our hearts *progressively* as He manifests His presence in our minds and emotions. In John 15 Jesus was referring to this second aspect of abiding.

The apostle Paul wrote of Jesus's "dwelling in believers' hearts," which refers to His abiding in us by His manifest presence, when he prayed "that He [Jesus] would grant you [the believers at Ephesus], according to the riches of His glory, to be strengthened with might through His Spirit in the inner man, that Christ may dwell in your hearts through faith" (Eph. 3:16–17).

Paul was praying that Jesus would abide, or dwell, in their hearts. Jesus dwells in our spirits on the day we are born again, but in this verse in Ephesians, Paul is referring to our souls, or our hearts—our minds, wills, and emotions.

Paul also wrote of Christ's being formed in our hearts (souls): "My little children, for whom I labor in birth again until Christ is formed in you" (Gal. 4:19). The Holy Spirit wants to form Jesus in our hearts—in other words, in our personalities.

Many know the verse, "Behold, I stand at the door and knock" (Rev. 3:20). Jesus is presented as knocking at the doors of hearts, and we are to open the doors and let Him in. We often use this verse with unbelievers. We ask them, "Do you want to invite Jesus into your heart? He stands at the door and knocks." This verse can be applied to unbelievers, but written as it was to the church of Laodicea, it is not addressing primarily unbelievers but believers. Jesus wanted deeper fellowship with them and desired to move in their lives in a greater way as they opened the doors of their hearts to Him. During His earthly ministry, Jesus promised that the Holy Spirit would flow like a river out of the hearts of His people to inspire, direct, and transform their minds and emotions and to minister in power through them to others:

> He who believes in Me…out of his heart will flow rivers of living water.
> —JOHN 7:38

THREE RESULTS OF CHRIST'S ABIDING IN US

Christ's abiding in our hearts is a glorious promise. It has at least three results. First, the indwelling Spirit *teaches* us about Jesus's heart, Word, and will. Second, He *inspires* us with courage to keep diligently seeking God. And third, He *empowers* us by renewing our minds, wills, and emotions to live in obedient love, and then releases His power through us to touch others.

1. The Spirit teaches us.

The Father sent the Holy Spirit to us to teach us all things (John 14:26). The Spirit is the great teacher, and He dwells within us. He desires to teach us many things about Jesus's heart, Word, and will. It is a most glorious privilege to have the teacher living in us. If we ask the Spirit, He will teach us about God's Word, will, and ways by giving us wisdom and creative ideas for every area of our lives, including how to steward our money, manage our schedules, prosper in relationships, function in ministry, and walk in purity and health, physically and emotionally.

2. The Spirit inspires us.

The Holy Spirit inspires our hearts by regularly renewing our courage. He will woo us and motivate us not to draw back or quit. One of the greatest needs in the body of Christ is the continual motivation that the Spirit gives us. Why? Because one of the most common temptations is to draw back from pressing in hard after God. I am not referring to being tempted to quit the faith but of being tempted to quit pressing in hard after Jesus and to just "coast" spiritually for a few years. The Spirit inspires us to recommit again and again to live in wholeheartedness and to never let go of our vision to walk in the fullness of God in our lives.

3. The Spirit empowers us.

The Holy Spirit empowers our hearts and our hands. He renews our minds, wills, and emotions so that we live in obedient love, and He releases His power through us to touch others. The essence of the new covenant is that the Spirit writes God's Word on our hearts and minds.

> This is the covenant that I will make with them…I will put My laws [Word] into their hearts, and in their minds I will write them.
> —Hebrews 10:16

God's writing His Word on our hearts includes the Spirit's empowering our emotions with new, holy desires so that we love what God loves and hate what He hates. God's writing His Word on our minds includes the Spirit's giving us insight into His heart. It is the spirit of revelation (Eph. 1:17), and it causes our cold and dull hearts to become fiery and alive.

How glorious to have our hearts and minds renewed by the Spirit so that we see and feel more of God's heart! The prayer I use most often is to ask the Spirit to let me see what He sees and feel what He feels—about my life, my family, and others, as well as what He sees and feels about Jesus, the church, the harvest, the nations, the end times, and so on. You can put a thousand different subjects at the end of this, my favorite prayer.

In summary, our abiding in Christ means that we have daily conversations with God, apply the promises of His Word to our hearts, and obey His commands. Christ's abiding in us results in the Holy Spirit's revealing more to us about Jesus's heart, giving us resolve to keep seeking God diligently, and empowering our hearts to live in obedient love and our hands to bless others.

Abiding in Christ is the foundation of our prayer lives and the lifestyle that is necessary if we are to bear much fruit that remains forever. As we read before, "He who abides in Me, and I in him, bears much fruit" (John 15:5).

Chapter 5

A PRACTICAL PLAN *to* GROW *in* PRAYER

Don't pray when you feel like it. Have an appointment with the King and keep it.[1]
—CORRIE TEN BOOM

THERE IS MORE to developing a consistent prayer life than loving God, knowing what constitutes effective prayer, and abiding in Christ; it also involves practical matters such as establishing set times for prayer and developing prayer lists that help us to be focused in prayer. I understand the difficulties you may experience in developing a consistent prayer life because I too have struggled through many of the same difficulties. But by the grace of God, I have been able to maintain a consistent prayer life for more than thirty-five years. In this chapter I will share a simple but practical plan to help you grow in prayer, a plan that has helped me for many years. I still use this three-part plan today:

1. Set a schedule for regular prayer times. A schedule establishes *when* you will pray.

2. Make a prayer list. A prayer list helps you to focus on *what* to pray.

3. Cultivate a right view of God. A right view of God causes you to *want* to pray.

If you will take these three simple steps, I boldly declare that over time both your consistency in and your enjoyment of prayer will increase dramatically. When I was struggling in college to establish my prayer life, a leader suggested that I schedule a time each day and make a prayer list. He assured me that doing these two things would change my prayer life over time. He was right! I was hesitant at first, but his counsel to me worked.

If you schedule time for prayer and make a prayer list, you will pray ten times more than you do now. I have made this statement for more than thirty years. People usually do not believe it, and some even argue against it. Nevertheless, I am sticking by it because I have proved the truth of it in my own life and witnessed the results of others' applying the plan in their lives. It will work for you, and then you will wonder why you did not start this practice much sooner.

SCHEDULE A PRAYER TIME

Life is busy, and there are many demands on our time. For this reason we must be intentional about developing consistent prayer lives. If we do not set our schedules ourselves, others will set them for us, and the result will be very little time for prayer. It is of the utmost importance that we schedule time for prayer. It sounds simple, but setting a regular time will profoundly impact our prayer lives.

Of course, we will not keep our schedules 100 percent of the time, but we will keep them more often than we do not. I feel pretty successful if I keep my scheduled prayer time 85 percent of the time. I aim to keep it 100 percent of the time, however, and I treat my prayer time as a sacred appointment that I try not to miss except for an emergency. I encourage you to do the same.

I do not limit my prayer life to my scheduled prayer times; I pray "on the run" a lot during the day. Praying on the run is part of abiding in Christ and will help you to abide in Him also, as we learned in the previous chapter. But you will pray and abide in Him much more consistently if you have regular times to talk to God set into your weekly schedule. If you do not intentionally set apart time to pray, you will not pray nearly as much.

We cannot consistently misuse hours each week and still have strong prayer lives. Growing in prayer takes time. It is normal for unexpected events and emergencies to interrupt our schedules. But we must aim to stick to our plan for prayer at least 85 percent of the time.

You may have to occasionally reevaluate your set or scheduled prayer times. It may be necessary to tweak your schedule to keep it working with other things happening in your life.

We each have one hundred sixty-eight hours each week to use. If we take ten hours a day to sleep, eat, and get dressed (seventy hours a week), that will leave us about a hundred hours a week for work and other things. With creative scheduling and a hundred hours a week, most people can find one hour or more a day for prayer if they really want to. We have time for what we truly care about.

Without scheduling prayer as part of our regular activities, we may sincerely intend to have an hour of prayer a day, but we will often not get around to it. As we make prayer a part of our planned routines, we will pray much more consistently.

MAKE A PRAYER LIST

I recommend that in addition to scheduling daily prayer times, every believer prepare a prayer list—or several lists. A prayer list is a simple tool that can help keep you focused during your prayer times.

Often when I sit down to pray, my mind is blank. I need a little "jump start" to help me focus, especially when I feel tired or distracted, so I use prayer lists. I have found them invaluable. I was eighteen years old when I made my first prayer list, and forty years later I am still using lists because I still need them.

By no means do I limit my prayers to the things on my lists. Using my prayer lists as a guide, I am free to depart from them at any time. I often feel a desire to pray in a different direction, and I enjoy praying with the inspiration that comes from the leading of the Holy Spirit. When I follow His prompting, I may not finish praying through my lists. But the lists are always there as a "pump primer" if I need them.

The more we pray, the more our prayer lists will grow and change over time. The Lord will lead us to change the focus of our prayers in the different seasons of our lives. So I add prayers and people to my prayer lists any time I need to.

Paul called us to pray always "with all prayer"—with all types of prayer and with supplication—in the Spirit "for all the saints" (Eph. 6:18). "To make supplication" simply means "to make a request." Our supplication can include praying for many different people and places.

I have three prayer lists: one for my personal life, one for people and places (ministries, businesses, cities, nations), and one for justice issues, including governments and social problems. I pray for the release of the gifts, fruit, and wisdom of the Spirit in each of these areas, as you will see in the next chapter. Below is a brief rundown of some of the content of my lists.

For my personal life

This list includes several categories, such as praying for my inner man, my ministry, and my circumstances (physical, financial, and relational). Some years ago I developed a list of ten prayers focused on strengthening my inner man, using the acronym FELLOWSHIP. I share these prayers in detail in chapter 14. I also use the acronym TRUST to remind me of five short phrases that help me commune with the Holy Spirit, who dwells within me (see chapter 15).

For people and places

I keep an updated list of individuals, ministries, and cities that I pray for on a regular basis. I pray for individuals (family and friends), ministries (including my local church), missionaries and missions endeavors in particular parts of the world, and so on. I also pray for the destinies of specific cities—Jerusalem, for example, and Cairo, because the Lord laid this city on my heart—and for nations in great need such as Egypt, Syria, Haiti, Russia, North Korea, Israel, and so on. I spend extra time praying for the city of Jerusalem and the nation of Israel because Scripture exhorts us to pray for Jerusalem (Ps. 122:6; Isa. 62:6–7) since it has a special place in the Lord's heart and His end-time purposes.[2]

Finally, I intercede for those in authority in my city and nation, according to Paul's urging in his first letter to Timothy:

> I exhort first of all that supplications, prayers, intercessions, and giving of thanks be made for all men, for kings and all who are in authority, that we may lead a quiet and peaceable life in all godliness and reverence.
> —1 TIMOTHY 2:1–2

For justice

This is a broad topic that includes governmental and social issues such as the ending of abortion and human trafficking and unfair educational systems. My list sometimes includes situations related to economic injustice, water rights, civil unrest (terrorism, riots, and so on), natural disasters (hurricanes, tsunamis, tornadoes, drought), disease (AIDS, tuberculosis, and so on), social crises (for example, famine and genocide), and more.

As I mentioned earlier, I believe most of us will pray ten times more if we will use these two practical tools of establishing a schedule for daily prayer times and developing prayer lists. By putting these practical tools in place, you will be better equipped to pray with focus and consistency in the years to come. Why not put it to the test in the next year and see how much more you will pray by having a set time for prayer and using prayer lists?

Discipline in Prayer Is Not Legalism

Some people protest that it is legalistic to schedule time for prayer or use a prayer list. I disagree. We step into legalism when we seek to *earn* God's love by praying or obeying rules. The good news of the gospel is that we don't have to earn it; God offers His love and grace freely. Consistency in prayer—talking to the Lord regularly and with focus—simply positions us to sit before Him more often so that we can receive more of His free grace in our daily experience.

Setting a regular time for prayer is not an attempt to earn God's love; it is a reflection of our desire to take control of our schedules so that we can make prayer a priority. I urge you not to fall for the age-old lie that automatically calls all discipline "legalism." This lie has robbed many of the blessing of a consistent prayer life. Being aimless or passive and thinking only of the present moment is not what liberty in grace is about.

> For you, brethren, have been called to liberty; only do not use liberty as
> an opportunity for the flesh.
> —Galatians 5:13

God's grace empowers us to discipline our time, money, and appetites in a way that fulfills His will for our lives, positions us to experience more of His grace, and enables us to encounter Him in a greater way. What Jesus freely offers in grace and what we actually experience are often two very different things. I want to practically experience in my everyday life all He freely offers me! I am able to best do this as I make it a priority to talk to Him. Scheduling time for Him is an expression of both my love for Him and my hunger for more. It is in no way an attempt to earn love from the One who gives His love freely and abundantly.

Cultivate a Right View of God

Cultivating a right view of God, the third step in my practical action plan, is another essential aspect of growing in prayer. Too many believers have a wrong view of God. For example, many live under the all-too-common and completely wrong assumption that God is either an angry taskmaster who forces us to pray or endure conversation with Him to prove our devotion to Him or a stoic God who has no interest in our lives. Nothing could be further from the truth! God is a tender Father who deeply loves His children, and Jesus is a Bridegroom King filled with desire for His people.

On our journey to grow in prayer, it is essential that we establish a strong biblical foundation in our lives in order to have a right view of God. The Word of God tells us the truth about who God is. Without this foundation, it is difficult to sustain our prayer lives.

As we come to know God as our tender Father and Jesus as the Bridegroom King, we are energized to seek God with all our strength and to experience new delight in our relationship with Him as we grow in prayer. Our prayer lives are very different when we come confidently to God with the assurance that He enjoys us and is actually glad in His relationship with His people.

My earthly father and I were good friends. He was my number one cheerleader, and during my childhood he affirmed me consistently. For this reason there was no one I liked being around more than my dad. I liked being with him because I knew he enjoyed being with me, and I felt it.

I remember when I first discovered that the Lord likes me even more than my dad did. When I saw that truth, I wanted to be with the Lord and talk to Him much more than I had desired to before. It is enjoyable to talk to someone who really likes you!

Several years ago I wrote a book focused on this truth titled *Passion for Jesus*.[3] People often ask me, "How do you get passion for Jesus?" I can tell you the key, and it is simple. As we grow in our understanding of *His* passion for *us*, it awakens passion in *our* hearts for *Him*. Encountering the Father-heart of God is foundational to growing in prayer.

Just before Jesus died, He made an astounding request of His Father. He asked "that the world may know that You [the Father] have sent Me, and have loved them [God's people] as You have loved Me [Jesus]" (John 17:23). Jesus wants us to know that His Father loves us just as He loves Jesus! Jesus's prayer for us gives us insight into the great value we have in God's eyes. The revelation that the Father loves us as He loves Jesus is a profound statement of our worth to Him.

Paul tells us that we have "received the Spirit of adoption by whom we cry out, 'Abba, Father'" (Rom. 8:15). In Hebrew *Abba* is a term of endearment for a father, much like "Papa" in our culture; it indicates respect but also affection and intimacy. The understanding of God as "Abba" and the knowledge of our identity as His adopted children equip us to reject Satan's accusations that we are hopeless failures.

This truth, that Abba-God enjoys us, even in our weakness, is a stabilizing anchor that gives us confidence in prayer. As sons and daughters of God we are able to approach His throne with confidence and without shame or hesitation. Our prayer lives will not grow properly until we come to a place of confidence in God, knowing we are loved and enjoyed by Him even in our weakness.

In the context of exhorting husbands to love their wives, Paul described the great mystery of redemption as a marriage between Christ and the church (Eph. 5:29–32). Before the Lord returns, the church will see herself as a bride crying out to her Bridegroom King to come to her, as John writes in the Book of Revelation: "And the Spirit and the bride say, 'Come!'" (Rev. 22:17). Even now, the Holy Spirit is emphasizing the church's identity as His cherished bride.

As sons of God we are positioned to experience God's *throne*—we are heirs of His power (Rev. 3:21; Rom. 8:17). As the bride of Christ we are positioned to experience God's *heart*. The Bridegroom message is about Jesus's fiery emotions for His people and His commitment to share His heart, home, throne, secrets, and beauty with them.[4]

In November 1995 I had a prophetic dream about this biblical truth. In the dream the Lord spoke audibly to me as I stood on the stage in a large auditorium filled with young adults. He said, "Call the people 'Hephzibah.'" This word was reminiscent of a passage in Isaiah:

> You shall be called Hephzibah...for the LORD delights in you...and as the bridegroom rejoices over the bride, so shall your God rejoice over you.
>
> —ISAIAH 62:4–5

The Lord continued to instruct me in this dream, saying with a loud voice, "Tell the people that I delight in them and rejoice over them like a bridegroom rejoices over a bride." In the dream, as soon as I called His people "Hephzibah" and declared, "And the Lord delights in them," the power of God touched them and changed their lives dramatically. I woke up from the dream and turned to Isaiah 62:4.

This Hebrew name, *Hephzibah*, carries the meaning "the delight of the Lord." We can be confident in God's love because we know that God delights in His people and His relationship with them even as a bridegroom delights in his bride (Isa. 62:4–5).

The Lord is raising up a multitude of men and women—singers, preachers, evangelists, writers, intercessors, people in the workplace—all over the world who will proclaim that God delights in His people. Then it will become normal for God's people to grow confident in His affections for them instead of drawing back in shame as many do today.

How we view God determines how we approach Him in prayer. If we view Him as aloof or angry, we will not want to pray very much. When we see Him as a tender Father and passionate Bridegroom who desires for us to come to Him, then we will pray much more.

Many Christians do not have a picture of God as a person who delights in His people with a heart of gladness. In fact, I believe that many view God as mostly mad or sad. But the truth is that His heart is filled with gladness over us (Zeph.

3:17), and appropriating this powerful truth will help us to grow in prayer with great confidence.

TOO BUSY TO PRAY?

One challenge we all face on our journey to grow in prayer is the necessity of managing our time in handling our work and life responsibilities. Most of us feel that we are too busy to pray, but the truth is that we are too busy *not* to pray. We cannot afford to carry out our responsibilities while living spiritually burned out.

As I have stated before, the call to prayer is for *every* believer. The Lord calls each one of His children, no matter what his occupation—lawyer, doctor, maintenance man, carpenter, accountant, athlete, musician, teacher, homeschooling mom, and so on—to have a real prayer life.

Some believers worry that if they take time to pray, they will lose valuable time to love and serve their families, friends, churches, or businesses. I assure you that people who pray regularly will love their families, friends, neighbors, and even their enemies more because their hearts will be energized by the Holy Spirit, and their negative emotional traffic will be diminished, leaving them able to love more deeply and more consistently.

The best thing husbands and wives, dads and moms can do for their marriages and families is grow in prayer. The same is true for pastors and godly leaders in the marketplace. It is not a question of choosing *either* work or prayer; we are to engage in both in proper balance and in the right order. Jesus is our example, and He did not permit His ministry to others to interfere with His prayer life, nor did He allow His prayer life to hinder His ministry to others.

The Gospels show us how much Jesus valued prayer: Even after He had ministered long hours in preaching and healing the sick, He still departed to a lonely place to pray—to commune with His Father and be strengthened.[5]

> And when He had sent them away, He departed to the mountain to pray.
> —MARK 6:46

Jesus emphasized the importance of prayer in His teaching and in His personal life both in this age and in the age to come. Indeed, He will forever continue to intercede at the right hand of the Father (Rom. 8:34; Heb. 7:25). During His earthly ministry, Jesus often spent long hours in prayer.[6]

> So He Himself often withdrew into the wilderness and prayed.
> —LUKE 5:16

> He went out to the mountain to pray, and continued all night in prayer to God.
> —LUKE 6:12

If prayer on a regular basis was important to Jesus, then how much more important should it be to us? If Jesus prayed often, how much more must we do so? In other words, prayer is not just one activity among many other good spiritual activities. It is the *core* activity for a deep and full life that glorifies God and enables us to walk in the fullness of our destiny in God.

Time for both God and people

We really do have enough time both to go deep in God and to relate well to people. We do not have to give up our prayer times with God to fulfill His will in our personal responsibilities related to our jobs and family lives. I have found that most of us can "steal" time for the kingdom from the time we spend on recreation and entertainment and still have time for our jobs and families. I realize that there are exceptions, but they are rare.

We must be fiercely determined to grow in our prayer lives and in intimacy with God because our culture has grown increasingly busy and noisy, crowding out the ability to create "sacred space" for fellowshipping with God. However, even with busy work and school schedules, most of us have more time than we realize. It is imperative that we seek to redeem our time instead of allowing it to be squandered, along with our destinies, for the sake of entertainment and material things.

We would be wise to downsize our lifestyles to make time to connect with God and grow in His Word. Eliminating or limiting the nonessential activities we engage in is far better than downsizing our walks with God. The choice seems clear; however, many sincere believers continue to make wrong choices day after day.

I find the task of balancing my time for work, rest, family, and relationships challenging. Therefore, I ask the Holy Spirit to help me know the best way to spend my time in each season of my life. He has the answer for each of us.

Paul gave us very good advice about taking control of our schedules in order to make the most of our time:

> Awake, sleeper, and arise from the dead, and Christ will shine on you. Therefore be careful how you walk, not as unwise men but as wise, making the most of your time.
> —Ephesians 5:14–16, nas

Paul wrote this counsel in his letter to lethargic believers in the church at Ephesus who were spiritually asleep. Paul was first exhorting them to awake and shake off their spiritual lethargy and passivity so that Christ would shine on them. What Paul meant by Christ's "shining" on them was that the Lord would release His presence to touch their hearts.

Next, Paul challenged them to spend their time wisely. Instead of saying "making the most of your time," some Bible translations say "redeeming your time." To redeem our time is to use it with the utmost care so that we may grow in God and extend His kingdom. It involves setting godly and wise priorities for the use of our time.

If we do not schedule our time, others will seize it, as I stated earlier, and we will end up living in the tyranny of the urgent, giving ourselves to whatever opportunity, social event, need, or crisis presents itself to us in the moment. I have known people who lived at the whim of everyone and everything that came their way, but when they looked back over the years, they sadly admitted that many of those pressures, opportunities, and "urgent matters" had not been connected to their destiny in God or the assignment He had given them in life. *Live by what is important, not by the tyranny of the urgent.*

By establishing a set time for our prayer lives we can redeem our time—our time can "purchase" eternal things that last forever. We can invest our time in a way that will lead to our hearts being awakened from the death of passivity and to our experiencing the light of God's presence. Then we will be equipped to love God and people in a far more consistent way. A focused use of time is critical for anyone who desires to have a strong prayer life.

Writer and philosopher Henry David Thoreau recognized the importance of using our time wisely. He wrote, "As if you could kill time without injuring eternity."[7]

In a day and an age with so much "expendable time" available to us, we must resolve to invest each moment wisely.

The godly, healthy, biblical call to "sacred aloneness" allows us to grow in love. It energizes us to love God and to love people for the long haul. Being connected to Jesus at the heart level through prayer is the lifeline that enables us to sustain ministry in healing the sick and doing works of justice and compassion for decades without burnout.

Prayer was never meant to be only about asking God to give us things. Rather, it is a place of encounter with God, where our spirits are energized as we grow to love Him more. It positions us to love God and people by receiving God's love as a Father and a Bridegroom.

We can find time for prayer by avoiding the tendency to waste time with idle talk; too much television, social media, or recreation; and an excess of networking (to help our ministries or businesses grow). We have to say no to certain things, even some good things, in order to have time to say yes to growing in prayer.

Time for prayer will not suddenly appear in our schedules. We have to seize it by saying no to some legitimate activities and pleasures. We can say no even to some important things in our lives because praying is the most important thing—even the best thing. Read what Jesus told Martha when she wanted her younger sister, Mary, to stop sitting at Jesus's feet to help her prepare the meal: "But one thing is needed, and Mary has chosen that good part, which will not be taken away from her" (Luke 10:42).

In our prayer times it is essential to turn off our phones as well as our e-mail, Facebook, Twitter, and other social media notifications. The person who is overly stimulated with information and communication will not be able to connect with God in the same way as if he turned off his devices and ignored them for a while.

Our culture is overstimulated with information and visual images. It drains us emotionally and mentally. Our emotional and mental energy is limited, just as our physical energy is, and in the same way that we need to rest after physical exertion, we also need to rest from being overstimulated emotionally.

Prayer builds strong relationships.

Prayer is very relational. A strong and vigorous prayer life will always lead to strong and healthy relationships. The people who most value their relationships with God and others, who desire to love with greater depth and consistency, are people who pray.

Prayer empowers us to overcome our natural tendencies toward laziness, grouchiness, vanity, and overindulgence with food and drink, as well as our tendency to seek recognition from people. Thomas Dubay wrote that self-denial in the grace of God is about emptying ourselves in order to become full and whole that we may love well.[8]

Prayer is not antisocial; in fact, true prayer is the opposite. It is all about love. We must draw back from the overactivity that hinders our ability to love God and people. Yes, it is a paradox because it takes time with God to grow in relationship with God and people. Only emotionally uncluttered people who cultivate a quiet heart are able to grow in relational depth.

Some blame their antisocial tendencies on their prayer lives, but this is a dangerous cop-out. A healthy prayer life will eventually result in healthy relationships. I am not saying that you will engage in every social event that comes your way. You will have to say no to some of them. But the relationships you maintain will be healthy.

When we lack quality time with God, our sincere quest for deep relationships with people often results in disappointment, frustration, and a sense of loneliness, even in the midst of many social activities. To have the highest quality of relationships, we must take time to connect with God because we simply do not have the emotional resources to relate well unless our hearts are energized and filled with peace by the Holy Spirit. It is not prayer but fear, shame, and other emotions that lead some into unhealthy isolation and avoidance of relationship.

If you will take the necessary time for prayer and will implement the three practical steps outlined in this chapter for developing your prayer life—setting a schedule for regular prayer times, making a prayer list, and cultivating a right view of God—you will find that you grow not only in prayer but also in love for God and people. The schedule will establish *when* you pray. The prayer list will help you focus on *what* to pray. And a right view of God will cause you to *want* to pray. Now let's take a brief look at the types of prayer and the themes in prayer that will help you to organize your prayer times.

Chapter 6

ORGANIZING YOUR PRAYER TIME

Therefore, whether the desire for prayer is on you or not, get to your closet at the set time; shut yourself in with God; wait upon Him and seek His face.[1]
—R. F. HORTON

I USE THREE TYPES of prayer and three prayer themes to organize my own personal prayer time. The three types of prayer are intercessory prayer, personal petition, and devotional prayer. These are very general categories and can each include many different expressions. Others use different terminology for these same general categories or types of prayer, which we will look at in more detail in subsequent chapters.

The three prayer themes are the gifts (relating to power) of the Holy Spirit, the fruit (relating to personal character) of the Holy Spirit, and the wisdom (relating to insight) of the Holy Spirit. I find it helpful to use all three themes with each of the three types of prayer. Rather than praying random requests, I find it practical to use these themes as targets, so to speak, to help focus my prayer requests and prayer lists.

THREE TYPES OF PRAYER

Generally you will engage in all three types of prayer during your prayer times. All are important, and knowing how they differ will help to ensure that you give each one the proper attention when you come before the Lord in prayer.

Intercessory prayer

Intercession is prayer for others—people, places, and organizations. God has ordained intercessory prayer as the means of releasing a greater measure of His power and blessing on individuals, families, businesses, ministries, churches, and the various spheres of society. Intercession takes on different expressions: we pray for the sick, for friends facing difficulties and families in crisis, for revival in the church, for justice, for the salvation of those who don't know the Lord, for social transformation, and so on.

Some refer to intercession as "contending in prayer." The word *contend* carries the meaning of believing God and working together with Him to bring about great change. We contend in prayer for the fullness of God's purpose and destiny for people, places, and organizations.

In intercession we are praying that people will experience more of God's power, provision, protection, and guidance in their lives. We pray for strategic issues in society, including people and policies related to the government, elections, education, the military, economic crisis, and so on. We pray for deliverance and provision for those suffering from oppression due to human trafficking, abortion, persecution, poverty, and other types of injustice. We ask for God's help in times of pressure related to natural disasters such as hurricanes, drought, disease, and other calamities. These are just a few examples of the areas in which we might engage in intercessory prayer.

Praying for the sick is one form of intercession that is not optional. Scripture commands us to pray for the sick and oppressed (Matt. 10:8; Mark 16:17; James 5:14–15). The Lord wants His people to operate in the supernatural ministry of the Holy Spirit as a lifestyle. It really matters that we take time to pray for the sick, whether in our prayer closets or when we gather.

If no one prays for the sick people in a prayer meeting, fewer of them will be healed. But if someone prays over them, more healings will occur in the body of Christ. The Spirit moves more as we take time to speak God's Word over people who are sick.

Set your heart to pray for someone who is sick every day for the rest of your life. We can do the works of the kingdom every day. We are called to pray for the sick as a lifestyle, whether in the ministry line at a church service, at a shopping mall, on campus, in our dorm rooms, in our homes, at work, or on vacation— wherever we may be.

Personal petition

Personal petition is prayer for the release of God's blessing and favor for our personal lives—our families, finances, ministries, relationships, health, and circumstances. This type of prayer includes praying for your own physical health and protection and for your ministry, as well as for financial increase and blessing, favor in relationships, the opening of new doors of opportunity to impact others, and so on. We pray that God's power and blessing will be released to us and through us to others.

Devotional prayer

Devotional prayer is related to our own spiritual renewal, growth, and communion with God. It focuses on worshipping God and asking to be strengthened by the Holy Spirit in order to love and obey God more and commune with Him in a deeper way. We ask to experience more grace on our minds and hearts as we develop an intimate relationship with God. This type of prayer includes connecting with God in worship, meditation on the Word (pray-reading it), and fellowshipping with the Holy Spirit (sometimes known as contemplative prayer).

In this type of prayer our focus is growing in intimacy with God as we connect with Him at the heart level with affection, thanksgiving, and a spirit of obedience. We ask to receive greater understanding of God, His Word, and His will for our lives. This understanding includes receiving His love and being empowered to express love to Him and others. Devotional prayer strengthens our intimacy with God, and as I have mentioned, our deep relationship with

Him protects us from burnout as we minister to people through the years. Maintaining a heart connection with Jesus is the lifeline that enables us to sustain for decades our ministry of winning the lost, healing the sick, and doing works of justice and compassion.

THREE THEMES IN PRAYER

I use three prayer themes, regardless of what type of prayer I am offering to God. The three general prayer themes are the release of the gifts, fruit, and wisdom of the Holy Spirit. The vast majority of the prayers and promises in the Bible fit into one of these three general prayer themes.

The gifts of the Spirit

Praying for a greater release of the gifts of the Spirit involves praying for the release of God's power, including His supernatural favor, provision, and protection. We ask for a greater measure of God's power to be manifest in our lives and in the people or places we pray for. In his first letter to the Corinthians Paul told the believers in Corinth that the working of the gifts of the Spirit in our lives is for the "profit of all":

> The manifestation of the Spirit is given to each one for the profit of all: for to one is given the word of wisdom through the Spirit, to another the word of knowledge through the same Spirit, to another faith by the same Spirit, to another gifts of healings by the same Spirit, to another the working of miracles, to another prophecy, to another discerning of spirits, to another different kinds of tongues, to another the interpretation of tongues.
>
> —1 CORINTHIANS 12:7–10

The fruit of the Spirit

Praying for a greater release of the fruit of the Spirit refers to asking for God's character to be formed in our lives or the lives of others. We ask that the fullness of the fruit of the Spirit (God's love, joy, peace, patience, and so on as outlined in Galatians 5:22–23) be established in us and in those for whom we pray. One of the primary ways I pray for a person to have more fruit in his character and to become more godly is to ask the Lord to release a spirit of conviction and a spirit of wisdom and revelation regarding God's person to him. I know that being convicted of sin and understanding the truth of who God is will result in an increase of the fear of the Lord and the formation of godly character in his life.

> And when He [Holy Spirit] has come, He will convict the world of sin, and of righteousness, and of judgment.
>
> —JOHN 16:8

That…the Father of glory, may give to you the spirit of wisdom and revelation in the knowledge of Him.

—Ephesians 1:17

The wisdom of the Spirit

When we pray for a greater release of the wisdom of the Spirit, we are asking
for an increase of understanding and insight into God's plans, will, and Word for
ourselves or for others. We follow Paul's example of praying for spiritual wisdom
and understanding for believers so that they walk in a way that agrees with and
pleases the Lord:

We…do not cease to pray for you, and to ask that you may be filled with
the knowledge of His will in all wisdom and spiritual understanding;
that you may walk worthy of the Lord, fully pleasing Him.

—Colossians 1:9–10

Praying for spiritual wisdom includes asking the Holy Spirit for dreams and
visions that give insight into His will for our lives as well as insight into His strategic plans for a city, nation, business, church, or other organization.

And it shall come to pass in the last days, says God, that I will pour out
of My Spirit on all flesh; your sons and your daughters shall prophesy,
your young men shall see visions, your old men shall dream dreams.

—Acts 2:17

Practical Application

These three prayer themes cover all the promises in the Scripture related to
praying for people or places. During the years, I have developed my prayer lists
by applying these three prayer themes to each of the three types of prayer. In
other words, I pray for a greater release of the gifts, fruit, and wisdom of the
Spirit when I intercede for other people or places; when I offer up personal petitions for myself; and during devotional prayer when I ask the Holy Spirit to help
me love, obey, and worship Jesus more.

For more than thirty years I have used these three themes as a "grid" to help
me focus my prayers for myself and others. I have found that nearly every prayer
request can be classified under one of these three prayer themes.

I ask for the fruit or character of God to be established in people as the Spirit
convicts them of sin and righteousness and reveals the knowledge of God to
them and then releases a great measure of the fear of the Lord on them. I ask for
the wisdom of God to be given to them so that they would walk in God's will
and plan for their lives. And I ask for the gifts—the supernatural power, favor,
and protection of God—to be released to and through their lives and ministry.

I encourage you to write out your prayer list, either in a notebook or on your
laptop, and use it during your prayer times. As I mentioned in chapter 5, we will

pray more often and with greater focus if we develop prayer lists and bring them to our prayer times.

When I pray, I usually use prayers that have been recorded in the Bible. The prayers of Jesus, Paul, Peter, and others are recorded for our benefit. I refer to them as the apostolic prayers because they are prayers prayed by Jesus and the apostles. Because God never changes, we know these prayers are in God's will. I will address the value of using biblical prayers in chapter 9.

Below is a look into my own prayer journal. It reveals the names of people and places on my prayer list and examples of how I pray for them. I provided only brief "samples" of my prayers so you can get a sense of what a more developed and complete prayer list may look like. I pray most of the prayers listed below for every individual on my longer list. In other words, as you read the prayer list below, understand that you can pray all the sample prayers for each individual on your list.

My family
For my wife, Diane, our two sons, and their wives and children:

Fruit:

> *Father, release the spirit of conviction to them in a greater measure (John 16:8) and pour out Your love into their hearts by the power of the Spirit (Rom. 5:5). Fill them with love for Jesus and for others and with the spirit of the fear of the Lord (Phil. 1:9)....*

Wisdom:

> *Father, grant my sons wisdom to know Your specific will for each area of their lives—their ministries, finances, relationships, business ventures, marriages, and in raising their children (Col. 1:9–11). Fill Diane with understanding of Your will for her ministry and business and as a grandmother (Col. 4:12)....*

Gifts:

> *Father, give prophetic dreams and visions to Diane, my sons, their wives, and their children (Acts 2:17). Release the spirit of glory and the power of God in their lives and through their words. I ask for physical health for them. Grant them favor in relationships and in the marketplace and protect them from the attack of the enemy and from all sickness and financial attacks....*

International House of Prayer of Kansas City (IHOPKC) leadership team
For Allen Hood (and others on my leadership team):

Fruit:

> *Father, impart consuming zeal for Jesus into Allen's heart and the heart of each of his family members (John 2:17). Empower him to make known the glory of Jesus. Visit his wife and family with the revelation of Your love, the spirit of conviction, and the fear of God, and cause them to rejoice in holiness and righteousness. Lead them away from temptation (Matt. 6:13)....*

Wisdom:

> *Father, fill Allen and his family with Your wisdom, and deliver them from Satan's tactics. Restrain the evil one from trapping them in any way (2 Thess. 3:3). Give them understanding of Your will for their spheres of ministry and for their family relationships, finances, and circumstances....*

Gifts:

> *Father, give Allen and his family prophetic dreams and visions that reveal Your love and glory to them (Acts 2:17–18). Cause each one to minister in all nine gifts of the Holy Spirit. Release the spirit of prayer on them (Zech. 12:10). Grant them physical health and protection. Release Your power when they speak or sing Your words to others. Let them experience what Paul experienced when the Word of God went forth from him in power (1 Thess. 1:5). I ask for unity in their family and extended family and that You fill them with peace and hinder all strife and division the enemy may seek to attack them with. Release favor as You establish strategic connections and open new doors of influence for them. Silence the assignments of the enemy and cut off all his work....*

Leaders in the body of Christ

IHOPKC is committed to praying for Youth With A Mission (YWAM), one of the largest missions organizations in the world. Therefore, I put some of the leaders of YWAM on my personal prayer list. I will give only one example, using founders and leaders Loren and Darlene Cunningham. I pray the same types of prayers for other YWAM leaders, such as John Dawson and Mark Anderson, and their families.

For Loren and Darlene Cunningham (YWAM leadership):

Fruit:

> *Father, strengthen Loren and Darlene with Your power in their inner man by Your presence (Eph. 3:16–17). Fill them with steadfastness, patience, and hope by the Holy Spirit (Col. 1:11)....*

Wisdom:

> *Father, give Loren and Darlene a spirit of wisdom for Your global purposes for YWAM (Col. 1:9). Grant them wisdom to know Your specific will for each area of their lives—their ministry, finances, and relationships—and give them wisdom in strategic alliances with leaders in the different spheres of society in the nations....*

Gifts:

> *Father, empower Loren and Darlene to minister in a new measure of Your power and all the gifts of the Holy Spirit (1 Cor. 12:7–10). Release Your favor on their circumstances and finances (Ps. 91; Deut. 28:1–14). Grant them physical heath and protection from the attack of the enemy and from all sickness and financial attacks. Let God arise and scatter His enemies (Ps. 68:1). Give direction, provision, protection, power, and unity to their natural family and to their leadership team (Ps. 91:1–13). I ask for unity in the YWAM global leadership team. Cut off all strife that the enemy may seek to hinder them with. Silence all accusing voices and cut off all the works of the enemies in their midst.*
>
> *Father, I ask for a corporate release of the Holy Spirit on YWAM's outreaches so that many people are saved, healed, refreshed by Your Spirit, touched by Your power, and set free. Cause a prophetic spirit to rest on their worship leaders and musicians. Open doors of finance and favor, releasing the wealth of the nations to the ministry of YWAM (Hag. 2:7–9; Deut. 8:18). Open the financial windows of heaven until there is no more need (Mal. 3:10–11)....*

Leaders in government

For the president of the United States, the governor of my state, and the mayor of my city:

Fruit:

> *Father, fill the president, the governor, and the mayor with the spirit of wisdom and unite their hearts to fear Your name (Ps. 86:11). Release the spirit of conviction to their hearts (John 16:8). Help them to walk in righteousness, truth, and justice. Uphold them with a steadfast and right spirit (Ps. 51:10)....*

Wisdom:

> *Father, fill them with the knowledge of Your will, with all spiritual wisdom and understanding, so that they will choose what is right and accomplish Your purposes (Col. 1:9–10). Release Your strategies with*

creative ideas to help them bring Your blessing and justice to those under their sphere of influence....

Gifts:

Father, release Your favor and power to establish Your will through them. Give them prophetic dreams that cause them to fear You and to know You. Silence the voice of the enemy and cut off demonic assignments against them. Grant them unity in their families and leadership teams by removing all strife (Rom. 15:6)....

Cities and nations

For the church in my home city, Kansas City, and in Grandview:

Fruit:

Father, grant the body of Christ in my city greater revelation of Your love and glory (Eph. 1:17–19). Pour out the spirit of the love and the fear of God on one thousand congregations in our area. Let them experience the height, the depth, the breadth, and the length of Your love for them (Eph. 3:17–19). I ask that Your blessing rest on every denomination and congregation and that You release the spirit of power and conviction through all who speak Your Word, so that Your people will walk in righteousness, peace, and joy in the Holy Spirit (Rom. 14:17). Reveal the majestic beauty of Jesus and the reality of eternity to all believers in my city (Ps. 39:4–6; 90:12)....

Wisdom:

Father, fill the leaders in the churches and the marketplace in my city with an understanding of Your will and specific direction on how to steward what You have given them. Give them creative ideas and strategies to cause Your kingdom to expand in this region and beyond through each local church and ministry in my city....

Gifts:

Father, may the believers in our city experience a greater measure of power in their lives and ministries so that more people would be saved, healed, and delivered. Cause all nine gifts of the Holy Spirit to operate in one thousand congregations across this area. Release the spirit of prayer on each prayer meeting in every congregation (Zech. 12:10). Let Your Word go forth in power, and let it spread rapidly (1 Thess. 1:5; 2 Thess. 3:1–2). Cut off the plans of the enemy in every congregation. I ask for marketplace messengers who, like Job, receive economic blessing so that they will bless the poor in Your name....

IHOPKC is committed to praying for Jerusalem, Israel, and messianic leaders. I have several messianic leaders, including Asher Intrater, Dan Juster, Eitan Shishkoff, Avner Boskey, and others—and their families—on my personal prayer list.

For Jerusalem and the nation of Israel:

Fruit:

> *Father, release the spirit of conviction on the city of Jerusalem as You did in New Testament times when three thousand people repented on one day. Reveal the beauty of Your Son to the whole nation of Israel. Raise up the church in Jerusalem and throughout Israel to walk in the love of God and in purity without any compromise (Phil. 1:9); let them be filled with zeal for Your house (John 2:17)....*

Wisdom:

> *Fill Your people in Israel with the knowledge of Your will for every area of their lives and for their national assignment (Col. 1:9–10). Release prophetic strategies and creative ideas for the church, marketplace, national problems, and international relationships so that God's will and purposes come to pass in their lives, families, and ministries....*

Gifts:

> *Father, release a greater measure of power on the saints in Jerusalem and throughout the land of Israel (1 Cor. 12:7–9). Release more of Your power through them as they speak Your Word with boldness and lay hands on the sick (Acts 19:11–12). Throughout the congregations of Israel, release Your Spirit so that people get saved, healed, refreshed by Your Spirit, touched by the power of God, and set free, even during worship. Let a prophetic spirit rest on worship leaders and musicians throughout the land and in all the houses of prayer in Israel. For the marketplace messengers in Israel, I ask for breakthrough in wisdom, finances, and favor. Open doors of finance and favor, releasing the wealth of the nations (Hag. 2:7–9; Deut. 8:18)....*

For Cairo, Egypt:

Fruit:

> *Father, cause the people of Cairo to understand Your love for them. May they be consumed with love for the Father and the Son. Release the spirit of revelation of the majesty of Jesus and conviction throughout the entire church in Cairo (John 16:8). Release the spirit of the fear of God on all of Egypt. Raise up a mighty church that walks in righteousness and*

humility. Release a spirit of unity in the church, and silence all strife so that all Your people may be of one mind in Christ, with humility (Rom. 15:6)....

Wisdom:

Father, send understanding of Your kingdom purposes and ways to the leaders in Your church across Cairo and to political and economic leaders. Release prophetic strategies with creative ideas for ministry and each sphere of society as well as for national problems. Grant the church in Cairo and throughout Egypt wisdom and strength to stand for You in the midst of persecution....

Gifts:

Father, release the power of conviction on the words of the believers in Cairo and all of Egypt so that when they speak Your words, multitudes will be convicted of sin, righteousness, and judgment (John 16:8). I ask for the corporate release of the power of the Holy Spirit on one thousand congregations in Cairo so that people get saved, healed, refreshed by the Holy Spirit, and touched by the power of God. Let a prophetic spirit rest on worship leaders and musicians in each congregation and in every prayer ministry so that the house of prayer throughout all Egypt is mighty (Isa. 19)....

You can use all these sample prayers for each individual or city you pray for. But don't be limited by them! I pray similar things for each person and city on my list, in addition to praying specific things that the Holy Spirit highlights for them. Making a list of those for whom you pray regularly and basing your prayers on the themes discussed in this chapter will make it easy for you to remember what to pray when you bring them to the throne of grace. (See Appendix B for additional guidance in praying for the release of the fruit, wisdom, and gifts of the Holy Spirit.)

Chapter 7

A BIBLICAL PARADIGM *for* PRAYER

*Before a word of petition is offered, we should have the definite and vivid
consciousness that we are talking to God, and should believe that He is listening to our petition and is going to grant the thing that we ask of Him.*[1]
—R. A. TORREY

N OW THAT WE know what prayer is, why we pray, how to ensure that
our prayers will be effective, and what the three primary types of prayer
are that we can engage in—intercession, personal petition, and devotional prayer—let's consider the five "steps" we are to take when we actually *pray*.
Taking these steps will ensure that we are following a biblical paradigm or perspective for prayer.

Though there is no place in Scripture that provides us with a one-two-three
formula of how to pray, I believe that as we study the whole teaching of Scripture,
we find that these five steps are part of the process. They will help us to grow in
prayer and to understand how perseverance relates to receiving answers to our
prayers.

Throughout our Christian lives, we will pray for various aspects of our personal circumstances—things that are not specifically promised in the Scripture
but that are not in opposition to the Word of God. For example, a person may
pray that it will not rain on his wedding day or that he will be accepted as a student at a prestigious university or that he will make the football team or get the
job he applied for. Circumstantial prayer requests such as these do not appear
as promises in Scripture, but neither do they contradict God's Word. The Holy
Spirit may impress on your heart that He will in fact grant a specific request.
Remember, though, that impressions are subjective, so you must be careful about
concluding that the Holy Spirit has promised you something simply because you
desire it.

STEP ONE: VERBALIZE YOUR REQUESTS TO THE FATHER

The first step in praying is to identify a specific prayer request and verbalize it to
God. Many times people think about all the things they need or want but never
actually *pray* about them. For such people, the words of the apostle James are
apt: "You do not have because you do not ask" (James 4:2).

Another foundational principle in the kingdom is that we must be specific
when we present our requests to God. God knows all our needs—"your heavenly
Father knows that you need all these things" (Matt. 6:32)—but He requires that

we make specific requests because doing so causes us to interact with His heart and grow in relationship with Him.

At times God will answer our vague thoughts without our asking, but Scripture teaches us to make specific requests to our Father.

> Be anxious for nothing, but in everything by prayer and supplication, with thanksgiving, let your requests be made known to God.
> —Philippians 4:6

The benefits of verbalizing our prayers include clearly identifying our requests, strengthening our faith and our sense of partnership with God, helping to keep our minds from wandering, and staying focused in our prayer times.

Step Two: Receive Your Requests in the Spirit Realm

When Scripture states that God "hears" our prayers, it means that He approves of our requests.

> Now this is the confidence that we have in Him, that if we ask anything according to His will, He hears us.
> —1 John 5:14

When we pray according to God's will, we know that He hears and approves of the request, so we are to *receive it in the spirit realm* with confidence. We receive our prayers in two ways. First we receive them in the spirit realm, and later we have them in the natural, when we see them with our eyes. However, before we receive them in the spirit, God must hear and approve of our prayers. Remember, many circumstantial prayer requests are not promised in Scripture, so sometimes we cannot be sure that the Lord has approved our request until He answers it.

Step Three: Believe That You Receive What You Ask For

Jesus spoke of the necessity of first believing that we receive the things we ask for (in the spirit realm) as the condition for receiving them in the natural, earthly realm. "Therefore, I say to you, whatever things you ask when you pray, believe that you receive them [in the spirit], and you will have them [in the natural]" (Mark 11:24).

When we ask something in God's will, we must believe that we have the "title deed" to our answer (we receive it in the spirit realm) and that in due time the answer will be manifest in the natural realm. Because of Jesus's work on the cross, the Father has already given us every spiritual blessing that exists in the heavenly realm (Eph. 1:3).

The spiritual blessings include the indwelling Spirit; the right to use Jesus's authority; the promise of God's provision, protection, and direction to do His will; and more. In the spirit realm God has already given us all things that pertain to life and godliness (2 Pet. 1:3).

We must be aware of the distinction between the spiritual and the natural realms to understand how prayer works. How do our requests move from the spiritual realm to the natural realm? Through holy, persevering, believing prayer. Again, we acknowledge that we may not be certain about receiving some requests related to our personal circumstances until we see the answers to our prayers.

STEP FOUR: REMIND GOD OF HIS WORD

This fourth step is essential. We are to consistently remind the Lord of what He promised us and of what He has already given us in the spirit realm, as the prophet Isaiah makes clear: "You who remind the LORD, take no rest for yourselves; and give Him no rest until He establishes [what He promised]" (Isa. 62:6–7, NAS).

Biblical promises in the Scripture are like a legal document, "the title deed" to what we already possess in the spirit. This is also true of the promises of blessing on our circumstances that the Holy Spirit speaks to our hearts. However, as mentioned previously, circumstantial blessings are subjective rather than directly promised in the Word, so we must be careful not to be presumptuous, and many times we must wait until the Lord answers a request to know whether He approves of it. I know I'm repeating myself on this score, but I want to be certain not to mislead anyone.

In prayer we state our cause and put Him in remembrance of His Word and what He has already given us in the spirit realm in Christ or of what He has promised to give us related to our personal circumstances.

> Put Me in remembrance; let us contend together; state your case.
> —ISAIAH 43:26

We remind God of His promises and thank Him for having already given them to us in the spirit and for the certainty of their being manifested in the natural in God's timing. As we continually remind God of His promises with thanksgiving, we position ourselves to receive them in the natural realm.

Jesus emphasized the value of perseverance and persistence in asking Him to release His blessings (Matt. 7:7–8; Luke 11:5–10; 18:1, 7). The verb He used is in the present continuous tense, meaning that we are to ask and keep on asking.

Because of his persistence he will rise and give him as many as he needs.
So I say to you, ask, and it will be given to you.

—Luke 11:8–9

Luke 11:5–10 records a parable Jesus told the disciples as a means of teaching them about the Father's willingness to answer prayer. His message was that the Father is moved by persistence. In this parable Jesus exhorted the disciples to continually ask.

The idea is for us to ask for the request to be manifest in the natural realm. We do not ask God to give us the spiritual blessings that He has already given to us in the spirit realm (Eph. 1:3); rather, we ask Him to release them to us in a greater measure in the natural realm. So we ask for the release in the natural of the things that we already have in the spirit. If we do not see the distinction between these two realms, then the truth of persevering, believing prayer can be confusing.

Paul called us to pray "with all perseverance" and "laboring fervently" in prayer.

Praying always…being watchful to this end with all perseverance and supplication for all the saints.

—Ephesians 6:18

Epaphras…greets you, always laboring fervently for you in prayers.

—Colossians 4:12

We must persist until we receive the requests that are according to God's will. We should never stop asking, reminding, and thanking God until we see the answers with our eyes.

Step Five: Receive Your Requests in the Natural Realm

Prayers that are in God's will are always answered in God's timing and in God's way, so do not give up too quickly or become discouraged if the answer to your prayer is delayed. There are reasons God delays answers, as we will see.

Again, we must receive every request *twice*. First we receive it in the spirit, and then eventually we will receive it in the natural. Often what we receive in the earthly realm is given progressively in increasing measure. God does not always give His answer as one big downpour of blessing. Sometimes the answer comes in stages over months, years, or even decades.

We can trust His amazing leadership in the timing and method in which He answers our prayers. It is not our responsibility to fix the timing or the circumstances of our expected blessing; we are simply to be faithful and patient in prayer.

WHY DOES GOD DELAY ANSWERS?

One of the most common questions Christians ask about prayer is why God delays answers to prayers, especially when they seem to be clearly in accordance with His will. Several factors may contribute to a delay, including God's timing, demonic resistance, man's free will, the Lord's desire for partnership with His people, and the value the Lord places on our being in unity with His heart and with one another. Other factors also contribute to the timing in which our prayers are answered. Let's very briefly consider a few of these factors:

+ God's timing is often very different from ours. We may want an answer right away, but God has a purpose and a plan in providing the answer at a different time and in different stages than we were expecting.

+ Demonic resistance can cause a delay in our receiving an answer to prayer. The resistance is removed as we persistently wrestle against demonic powers (Eph. 6:12; Dan. 10:13).

+ Man can use his free will to do evil, and God may allow it for a season.

+ The Lord desires partnership with His people, so He encourages us to persevere in prayer or "extended conversation" with Him.

+ The Lord places a high value on our living in unity with His heart and with one another. Therefore, He sometimes waits to release the answer to a prayer until His people are in unity with Him in righteousness and in unity with one another in humility and love.

The exact combination of these factors is somewhat mysterious, so we must trust Jesus's wise and loving leadership regarding the reason prayers that are according to God's will are delayed or seemingly not answered at all. For example: Why are all believers not healed physically? Why is the marriage of a Christian's divorced parents not restored? Why is a family member not saved? There are numerous examples I could elaborate on here.

When we pray for a loved one to be healed, it is important to understand that Jesus has already provided for our complete healing in spirit, soul, and body (Isa. 53). The fullness of our physical healing is guaranteed in the age to come, and yet we are also to believe Him for a "measure" of physical healing in this age (I say a "measure" because even for those who receive a physical healing in this life, the healing is incomplete because the aging process continues to work in their lives, and they will eventually die). Many believers are healed physically in this age, but all believers will be healed physically in the most complete way in the age to come. Meanwhile we press in and pray in faith for physical healing, just as the Word encourages and instructs us to do.

We are not always sure about what God has promised to fully release in this age related to our circumstances—what He will partially and progressively release now and what He will fully release in the age to come. However, we can be sure of this: God is loving and faithful, His Word is true, and He answers prayer. Therefore, we must guard against giving up and falling into unbelief when our prayers are not answered in the time frame that we would choose.

Examples of delayed answers to prayer abound in the lives of all believers, including heroes of the faith such as E. M. Bounds, Hudson Taylor, Andrew Murray, William Carey, and Charles Spurgeon. One great man of God, George Müller, prayed daily for fifty-two years for one loved one to be saved. The answer to his prayer came shortly after Müller died.[2]

Our prayer requests move from the spiritual realm to the natural realm through holy, persevering, believing prayer, as I pointed out in chapter 3. Many people give up too quickly. They offer their prayers a few times and then lose heart, moving on to other things rather than persevering. Persevering prayer is continually reminding God of what He has already given us and what He promises to yet give us and continually asking Him to manifest the full measure of each blessing in the natural.

If we understand the distinction between receiving our requests in the spiritual and the natural realms, then we will see the value of persevering prayer. Knowing how prayer works will give us the courage to rise up and ask and keep on asking until we receive all that the Lord has for us. Perseverance will be especially important as we begin to engage in intercessory prayer, which I discuss in the next section.

PART II

INTERCESSORY PRAYER

Prayer opens the way for God Himself to do His work in us and through us. Let our chief work, as God's messengers, be intercession, for in it we secure the presence and power of God to go with us.[1]
—ANDREW MURRAY

Chapter 8

RELEASING GOD'S POWER
THROUGH INTERCESSION

*We must begin to believe that God, in the mystery of prayer, has entrusted us with
a force that can move the heavenly world, and can bring its power down to earth.*[1]
—ANDREW MURRAY

IT WOULD BE impossible for me to overemphasize the importance of intercessory prayer. Why? Because God has chosen intercession as the primary
means of releasing His power in the earth. Scripture makes it clear that
intercession is one of the central activities in God's kingdom, both now and in
the age to come.

As I stated in chapter 6, intercession is prayer for others—the lost, the
oppressed, missions, families, friends, the church, leaders in government and in
every sphere of society, and so forth. Intercession is prayer that is in agreement
with what God promises to do. Seeing the value of intercession from God's point
of view gives us the impetus to make prayer a high priority in our lives.

The fact that Jesus, the divine Son of God, intercedes reveals how important
intercession is. The Bible tells us that "He always [forever] lives to make intercession for [us]" (Heb. 7:25; see also Rom. 8:34).

Jesus is fully God and fully Man, the second person of the Trinity, and yet He
intercedes and releases the Father's power. He will still be making intercession
a million years from now. Prayer will not be obsolete in eternity but will still be
central in our lives in the age to come.

God the Father told Jesus to ask Him (the Father) for the nations: "Ask of Me,
and I will give You the nations for Your inheritance, and the ends of the earth
for Your possession" (Ps. 2:8). Jesus will continue to govern the nations in the
Millennium[2] through intercession as He asks the Father to let Him fully possess the nations.

THE POWER OF JESUS'S WORDS

At the beginning of Creation, all three members of the Godhead worked together.
The Father's plan was to create the heavens and the earth. The Spirit was present
in power, hovering, or brooding, over the face of the earth, yet the earth continued formless, void, and in darkness. Then Jesus spoke the Father's plans and
the Spirit moved in power at His word.

The earth was without form, and void.... And the Spirit of God was
hovering over the face of the waters. Then God said, "Let there be light";
and there was light.

—GENESIS 1:2–3

The Spirit waited for the Father's plans to be spoken before He released His
power in the earth. When Jesus declared, "Let there be light," the Spirit released
light. The Spirit would not release the light until Jesus actually spoke it. The
darkness remained until Jesus "interceded" and spoke God's word over the darkness to release the Spirit's creative power. The apostle Paul affirmed that God
created all things through Jesus Christ (Eph. 3:9), so we know that it was Jesus
who spoke creation into being as recorded in Genesis 1.

We see Jesus's work in the phrase "and God said" ten times in Genesis 1 (KJV).
The foundational principle of intercession is that the Father's plans were spoken
by Jesus, and then the Holy Spirit released power. David wrote that "by the
word of the LORD the heavens were made" (Ps. 33:6). The apostle John confirmed Jesus's role in Creation when he wrote, "All things were made through
Him [Jesus], and without Him nothing was made that was made" (John 1:3).

John also revealed in his Gospel that Jesus is the Word of God: "In the beginning was the Word, and the Word was with God, and the Word was God" (John
1:1). The Book of Revelation echoes this truth: "His name is called The Word
of God" (Rev. 19:13). Most of us are familiar with this concept, but what does it
mean? One reason Jesus is called the "Word" is that He brings God's ideas into
existence in the natural world by speaking them. When Jesus articulates the
Father's thoughts to release His power into the earthly realm, He functions as
the living Word (*logos* in Greek).

Even now Jesus sustains creation by speaking God's word, "upholding all
things by the word of His power" (Heb. 1:3). He is holding the universe in place
in the same way that He created it—by speaking the Father's Word back to Him.
Note the use of present-tense verbs in Colossians 1:17:

He is before all things, and in him all things hold together.

—NIV

If Jesus the living Word stopped speaking the word, all of created order would
cease to exist, literally. The planets, the sun, our physical bodies, and all the
myriad processes of life hold together because Jesus continues to speak the word
of His power to uphold them.

THE SPOKEN WORD RELEASES POWER

The Father has ordained that His ideas must be spoken, and when they are
spoken, the Spirit releases power. A foundational law of the kingdom is that the
Spirit moves in response to God's Word being spoken by His people. Whether

Jesus is speaking over the formless heavens and the earth at Creation or we are interceding for revival at a prayer meeting, God's power is released through the principle of intercession, speaking God's Word back to God.

For example, the Lord ordained that healing would flow as God's people lay hands on the sick and speak God's Word over them. How many healings that might have occurred are not manifested because we do not speak God's Word? In other words, if we do not speak God's Word, we will miss out on some of the blessings we would otherwise have experienced.

As part of our spiritual armor, we have the sword of the Spirit, which is God's Word. It is a powerful weapon when spoken and released against darkness. In Paul's encouragement to the Ephesians to be strong in God and in the power of His might, he wrote, "Put on the whole armor of God, that you may be able to stand against the wiles of the devil.…Take…the sword of the Spirit, which is the Word of God; praying always" (Eph. 6:11, 17–18).

When tempted by Satan, Jesus spoke the Word of God, which went forth like a sword striking Satan's domain (Matt. 4:3–7). At the time of His Second Coming, Jesus will judge the nations by speaking the Father's words over them. His intercessory decrees will go forth like a sword to remove all resistance to His loving and righteous rule.

> Out of His mouth goes a sharp sword, that with it He should strike the nations.
>
> —Revelation 19:15

> He shall strike the earth with the rod of His mouth.
>
> —Isaiah 11:4

As we speak God's Word, we can release strength to a friend's heart. We call it "encouragement" because it gives him courage, or strength. Our prayer is God's way of releasing His power so that the friend can overcome condemnation or discouragement or other trials in his life. One way we grow in prayer is by speaking God's Word against Satan's lies that assault our hearts.

Much can be achieved in the Lord's purposes when we declare His Word. The Lord put His words in the mouth of the prophet Jeremiah to bring about His desired changes in the nations.

> I have put My words in your mouth. See, I have this day set you over the nations and over the kingdoms, to root out and to pull down…to build and to plant.
>
> —Jeremiah 1:9–10

The Lord has ordained that for all eternity He will put His words into our mouths so that we are able to intercede and release His power on the earth.

"As for Me," says the LORD, "this is My covenant with them: My Spirit who is upon you, and My words which I have put in your mouth, shall not depart from your mouth, nor from the mouth of your descendants, nor from the mouth of your descendants' descendants," says the LORD, "from this time and forevermore."

—ISAIAH 59:21

Why does He put His words in our mouths? Because He governs the universe in partnership with His people through intercession. The governmental center of the universe lies in the ministry of prayer, which includes all the Spirit-inspired prayers on the earth and in heaven that converge before God. The Book of Revelation gives us a picture of our intercessory prayers coming together in heaven: "Another angel…was given much incense, that he should offer it with the prayers of all the saints" (Rev. 8:3; see also vv. 1–6).

God has given the human race great dignity by offering us the opportunity to co-labor with Him in bringing His will to pass on the earth. And it is so easy! We simply use God's words to tell Him what He tells us to tell Him. Intercession makes God's power easily accessible to everyone through simple prayers of agreement with His will.

Intercession is God's brilliant strategy to include all His people in ruling with Him in power. It is so simple that anyone can do it, and yet it releases more power than any other activity in which human beings can engage. In the early days of my journey to grow in prayer, I stumbled over the simplicity of intercession, but through the years I have come to better understand and appreciate why God values it as He does.

It is important to remember that we cannot do God's part, and He will not do our part. Some wrongly assume that if God wants something, He will do it. This is true in terms of the broad strokes of His salvation plan in history. God has already determined the primary events in His eternal plan: the Second Coming of Jesus to reign over the earth as King, Satan's being cast into the lake of fire, the establishing of the new heavens and the new earth, and so on. Regardless of what any particular generation of believers do, God will eventually accomplish the primary events in His sovereign plan for human history.

But there is so much more He longs to do *with* us and *for* us, when we take action and ask Him! We each have a free will, which means we have been given the ability to make choices that make a real difference. He has chosen to give His people a dynamic role in determining some of the measure of the "quality of life" we experience.

Some "trust" the sovereignty of God in a nonbiblical way by "trusting" God to do the role that He has assigned to us. This is an abdication of our God-given responsibility and is presumption before Him.

We may be tempted to question God's wisdom in allowing weak and sinful human beings to bring about His will on the earth through intercessory prayer. But Scripture reminds us that God has a purpose in doing so:

> God has chosen the [so-called] foolish things of the world to put to shame the [so-called] wise, and God has chosen the [so-called] weak things of the world to put to shame the things which are mighty…that no flesh should glory in His presence.
>
> —1 Corinthians 1:27, 29

He uses the things that men call weak to put to shame, or triumph over, those things that men consider mighty or powerful, thus sharing His government with His people in a way that leaves no room for man to boast.

The things of God are not weak in reality, but they are seen as weak in the eyes of unbelievers. These things include prayer and fasting and declaring His Word over seemingly hopeless situations. The reality is that the so-called "weakness" of agreeing with God's Word and promises in intercession releases power into the earthly realm to triumph over darkness in people's lives. We offer our prayers in human weakness, but because of the blood of Jesus our prayers ascend before the Father in power.

The Focus of Our Intercession

Two of the primary requests Jesus exhorted us to make of the Father when we intercede are for the release of a greater measure of the Holy Spirit and the release of a greater measure of justice.

> …how much more will your heavenly Father give the Holy Spirit to those who ask Him!
>
> —Luke 11:13

> And will not God bring about justice for his chosen ones, who cry out to him day and night?
>
> —Luke 18:7, niv

As believers under the new covenant, we already have the Holy Spirit. We received the indwelling Spirit at our new birth (John 3:3–5; Rom. 8:9–11). Therefore, we do not pray for the Lord to give us the Holy Spirit in the sense of the indwelling Spirit; rather, we ask Him to release a greater measure of the *ministry* of the Spirit in and through us. The New Testament refers to a greater measure of the Spirit that is released on the church as a "greater measure of grace."

> But He gives a greater grace.
>
> —James 4:6, nas

In different verses, it is called "a greater grace" (James 4:6, nas); "great grace" (Acts 4:33); "grace…abundant" (related to Paul; 1 Tim. 1:14); "full of grace" (related to Stephen; Acts 6:8, nas); "[growing] in grace" (2 Pet. 3:18); and "grace…multiplied" (2 Pet. 1:2). I encourage believers to use the apostolic prayers to pray for this grace to be released in the church (see chapter 9).

We also pray for the release of a greater measure of justice. Justice can be defined simply as God's making wrong things right. There are two sides to justice—salvation and judgment. We see the salvation side of justice when God's people are delivered and vindicated. We see the judgment side of justice when the wicked, those who rebel against God's righteous ways, are stopped, removed, and even punished.

Justice is expressed through soul-winning, healing, revival, unity, and impacting society for the kingdom. Evangelism is an expression of justice because it is a judgment on darkness in the hearts of unbelievers. God judges the darkness in the heart of an unbeliever every time someone is born again. Healing expresses justice in releasing judgment on sickness. Revival is judgment on compromise in the church. Each of these is an expression of God's justice.

Justice may come in small measures, but it is nevertheless released when we pray. Every time we have a prayer meeting or speak the Word over someone, a measure of justice is released.

When I first began the practice of daily prayer meetings, I thought of intercessors as people who were wasting their time in a prayer room when they could have been evangelizing the lost. I saw them as disengaged from the real war of winning unbelievers to Jesus while they sat idly in a prayer room, isolated from the battle for souls.

I soon learned that I was completely wrong. I came to understand that it was Jesus who called forth prayer for justice (see Luke 18) and saw that it would increase the effectiveness of our evangelistic efforts. In fact, Jesus has made prayer—specifically night-and-day prayer—the condition for releasing His justice to the *full* measure that He has ordained.

Night-and-day prayer, which I will talk more about later in this book, is a practical expression of the commandment for us to love one another. It results is an increase of the measure of justice—God's blessing—that is released in a generation. Many miracles and healings occur outside the context of night-and-day prayer; however, I believe that even more will be manifest as the saints are intentionally mobilized in geographic areas around the world to offer night-and-day prayer.

Those who labor in intercession are not isolated from the battle as I once thought but are actively expressing love for the people for whom they pray. They are truly helping them in a practical way. Prayer is a practical expression of the commandment to love one another because it is part of the process that brings deliverance to those in need of it (2 Cor. 1:11; Phil. 1:9).

The Benefits of Intercession

The activity of intercession has many benefits beyond a greater release of God's power to others. Intercession draws us into intimacy, transforms our hearts, unifies us in community, renews our faith, multiplies blessing back on us, and gives us an inheritance in the people and places we pray for.

Deepens intimacy and encourages transformation

Intercession helps us to grow in intimacy with God and transforms our hearts by causing us to internalize God's Word as we pray it back to Him. Because Jesus's words are spirit and life (John 6:63), they have the power to impart life to us as we speak them. Each time we say what God says, it "marks" our hearts and changes us in a small measure because we receive a small impartation of His life. This progressively renews our minds and tenderizes our hearts.

Think of a computer programmer who writes many lines of code while developing a computer program. Spiritually we are doing something comparable to this. We "write a line of code" on our hearts every time we speak God's Word back to God in prayer. Everything we say that is in agreement with God is like "code" being written on our hearts. It marks our hearts even though we cannot accurately measure the change in weeks or months. Over the years the change inside us is profound.

Our prayers for others affect our own hearts more than we know. We may not feel anything when praying for a nation that is remote and far away. However, there is an accumulated impact on our lives that often goes unnoticed.

The fact that we have been engaged in prayer for revival and justice changes many things in us that we often overlook and cannot easily measure. Think about it for a moment: we simply do not know where we would be today if we had neglected prayer through the years. Where would we be in our mind-sets? What negative emotions might we have developed if we had been living in a spiritual vacuum of prayerlessness? What might the difference be in our friends and our conversations had we not pressed into prayer for revival and for others?

We cannot know what evils we have avoided in our inner lives simply as the result of consistent intercession for others. The opposite is equally true: if prayer has not been a regular part of our lives, then some of the difficulties and negative emotions we experience may well be attributed to the lack of a growing relationship with God through prayer. I encourage those who are beginners in prayer or who have not been consistent in prayer to start today—take small steps on your journey to grow in prayer, and watch what God will do in your life.

Unites us in community

Intercession also unites our hearts to the people and places we pray for. We will grow to love who and what we pray for. In addition we will love those we consistently pray *with*. It is impossible to pray for or with anyone regularly without eventually feeling love for him.

Renews our faith

Intercession renews our faith as we speak God's Word back to Him in prayer. Praying biblical prayers builds our faith for revival. The very act of praying the Word results in strengthening our faith for the promises we pray for. You will find that your faith grows stronger and stronger as you develop the practice of speaking the Word back to the Father in intercession.

Multiplies blessing

Intercession for others causes multiplied blessings to return back on the life and family of the intercessor. Every prayer of blessing for another is a prayer that God returns back on you and your loved ones. Jesus promised:

> Give, and it will be given to you: good measure, pressed down…will be put into your bosom. For with the same measure that you use, it will be measured back to you.
>
> —LUKE 6:38

The law of the kingdom requires that we always receive more than we give away. The measure that we give in prayer for others will be measured back to us. This is one of my favorite promises about prayer. It does not matter for whom we pray. Even when we pray for our enemies as we were commanded by Jesus to do, we end up being blessed by the prayers we pray on their behalf.

> I say to you, love your enemies, bless those who curse you, do good to those who hate you, and pray for those who spitefully use you and persecute you.
>
> —MATTHEW 5:44

When we pray for our enemies, we are forced to deal with our own bad attitudes and to get our spirits right. But we also become the recipients of our prayers. For example, when we pray for the release of the spirit of wisdom on our enemies, we receive wisdom as well.

The principle of multiplied blessings applies to all we do in God's will, whether we are offering prayer, giving money or mercy, or serving people in small ways. The Lord multiplies blessing back to us in a hundredfold way. Jesus assured the disciples, "There is no one who has left house or brothers or sisters or father or mother or wife or children or lands, for My sake and the gospel's, who shall not receive a hundredfold now in this time…and in the age to come, eternal life" (Mark 10:29–30).

We will never, ever "out-give" God. Every Spirit-inspired prayer we pray will be "turned back" on us and our loved ones. For example, if you pray for the church in Egypt, your prayers will release God's blessing on the believers there, and the content of the prayers will also be released on you and your family in this age and in the age to come.

Clearly we do not earn multiplied blessings by interceding. But God is magnified when He shows His extravagant generosity by giving His people a hundredfold return. He possesses infinite wealth; thus, it is never diminished when He manifests great generosity.

Gives us an inheritance

The Father told Jesus to pray for the release of His full inheritance in the nations: "Ask of Me [in prayer], and I will give You the nations for Your inheritance" (Ps. 2:8). Part of Jesus's ministry of intercession includes the prayers that He inspires in the saints under His leadership throughout this age. These Spirit-inspired prayers contribute to Jesus's inheritance in the nations. Just as we reign with Jesus over the nations partially in this age and in fullness in the age to come (Rev. 3:21; 5:10; 20:4–6), so we also join Jesus in intercession for the nations in this age and in the age to come.

Intercession gives us an "inheritance" in the people and places we pray for. This inheritance begins in this age and continues in the age to come. When we pray for Egypt, Japan, Iran, or another nation, our prayers release blessing on that nation. They release blessing on us and our families as well, and we receive an inheritance in what happens in that country, in this age and in the age to come.

As I mentioned previously, intercession is God's brilliant strategy for including the saints in ruling with Him in power. Moreover, it has a great impact on those of us who pray because it draws us into intimacy with God, transforms us with holiness, unifies us in community, multiplies our blessings, and increases our inheritance—all the while training us to rule the nations in partnership with Him. Knowing the capabilities and benefits of intercession for both the intercessor and those for whom he prays, who *wouldn't* want to invest time growing in this type of prayer?

Chapter 9

THE VALUE *of* USING BIBLICAL PRAYERS

To make intercession for men is the most powerful and prac-
tical way in which we can express our love for them.[1]
—JOHN CALVIN

IN THE PREVIOUS chapter I discussed using the words of Scripture during intercession to tell God what He tells us to tell Him. When I intercede, I almost always use the prayers of the Bible. Some of the prayers that Jesus, Paul, and Peter prayed are recorded for our benefit. I refer to them as the "apostolic prayers" because they are the prayers that Jesus prayed as our chief apostle (Heb. 3:1) and that the Holy Spirit gave to the apostles who were His followers. Below are some examples:

+ **Acts 4:24–31** (A prayer for impartation of Holy Spirit boldness through the release of signs and wonders)

+ **Romans 15:5–7** (A prayer for unity in the church across a city)

+ **Romans 15:13** (A prayer to be filled with supernatural joy, peace, and hope)

+ **Romans 10:1** (A prayer for Israel to be saved through Jesus)

+ **1 Corinthians 1:4–8** (A prayer to be enriched with the supernatural gifts of the Holy Spirit, leading to righteousness)

+ **Ephesians 1:17–19** (A prayer to receive the revelation of Jesus's beauty, to see how greatly He values His people as His inheritance, and to walk in a greater measure of the power of God)

+ **Ephesians 3:16–19** (A prayer for the supernatural strengthening of the heart and a deeper experience of God's love)

+ **Philippians 1:9–11** (A prayer for God's love to abound in our hearts, resulting in discernment and a deep commitment to righteousness)

+ **Colossians 1:9–12** (A prayer to know God's will, to be fruitful in ministry, and to be strengthened by intimacy with God as we do the work of the kingdom)

- **1 Thessalonians 3:9–13** (A prayer for the release of effective ministry to strengthen believers so they will abound in love and holiness)

- **2 Thessalonians 1:11–12** (A prayer to be equipped and prepared to walk in the fullness of God's destiny for the church and its people)

- **2 Thessalonians 3:1–5** (A prayer for the Word to increase by the release of Holy Spirit power and to encounter the love of God in a greater way)

When I first began to lead prayer meetings, I used the apostolic prayers simply because I didn't know what else to do, as you will see in the following story from my book *After God's Own Heart* about my early days as an intercessor. Perhaps it will make you feel better about your own initial steps into this calling!

In that book I wrote about the time God called me to be an intercessor in May 1979. It was one of those real-life encounters when God grabbed hold of my life and apprehended me and said, "You are an intercessor." I got up in front of my church and said, "I am an intercessor." They said, "What's that?" I said, "I don't have a clue." I truly had no idea what an intercessor was! I went to the bookstores in town and bought books on intercession. There were hardly any—just a few of the standard books on prayer, such as those by Andrew Murray, Watchman Nee, Dick Eastman, E. M. Bounds, and Leonard Ravenhill. I also obtained a life-changing tape series on prayer by Joy Dawson.

In spite of my lack of knowledge and experience, I tried to move ahead in intercession anyway, and I began daily prayer meetings, which I've continued by the grace of God on a near-daily basis since that time. I was so clueless at first about what to do in a prayer meeting that I didn't even know what we would pray, so I wrote out by hand the apostolic prayers. I photocopied the handwritten prayers and gave them to both guys who showed up for the first prayer meeting. That was the beginning of my education in prayer and intercession.[2]

I have since learned that the apostolic prayers in the Bible are a valuable gift to the church: they are the prayers that burned in God's heart for His people. They give us the language of His heart, and because God never changes, we can be assured that they are still burning in His heart. These prayers are guaranteed! They are like checks already signed in heaven and waiting only for a cosigner on the earth before they are cashed. And they are as relevant today as they were in the early church.

If you include the doxologies, there are about thirty apostolic prayers in the New Testament (see Appendix C for a complete list of these prayers). As you begin to pray them during your prayer times, you will see that each of the apostolic prayers is God-centered and positive and that most of them are focused on believers rather than on the lost.

APOSTOLIC PRAYERS ARE GOD-CENTERED

All the prayers in the New Testament are God-centered prayers: each one is addressed to God. Not one apostolic prayer is addressed to the devil. God-centered prayer, including spiritual warfare prayer, is the model set forth in the New Testament, as we will see in the next chapter. It is the model the early church used in resisting and dislodging demonic spiritual forces and cultural strongholds (Eph. 6:12; 2 Cor. 10:3–5).

All the prayers of Jesus that are recorded in the Scripture were directed to the Father (John 14:16; 17:5, 11, 15, 25). Jesus taught His disciples to direct their prayers to the Father as well (Matt. 18:19; Luke 11:2, 13). The apostles' prayers followed Jesus's example, and they also teach us to address the Father when we pray. In the great "warfare epistle" Paul wrote to the Ephesians, he addressed all his prayers to the Father (Eph. 1:16–17; 3:14, 16, 20).

APOSTOLIC PRAYERS ARE POSITIVE

The apostolic prayers are "positive" prayers: they ask God to release good qualities rather than asking Him to remove negative qualities. They focus on the impartation of something positive, not on the removal of something negative. For example, the apostle Paul prayed for love to abound rather than asking the Lord to remove hatred (Phil. 1:9). He prayed for unity instead of praying against division (Rom. 15:5–7). He asked for an increase of the spirit of peace rather than the removal of the spirit of fear (Rom. 15:13). He did not pray against sin but asked for an increase of holiness, purity, and love (1 Thess. 3:12–13). Even Paul's requests to be delivered from evil men are positive in that they focus on the deliverance of God's people rather than on exposing or bringing down the evil men who were persecuting him (2 Thess. 3:2–3).

I believe that one reason the Father established "positive prayers" as the norm in the New Testament is to enhance unity and love in the church. Why? Many times I have heard people pray "negative prayers" in a prayer meeting that focused on sin in the church or its leadership and that became judgmental and angry. Others in the meeting did not agree with the view or tone that was expressed in the negative prayer, so the prayer against division actually created division among some of the people at the meeting.

The Father knew that praying for the impartation of positive virtues instead of focusing on removing negative characteristics would *unify* intercessors and *heal* some of the negative emotions against the church in the person who is praying. Our emotions are impacted as we come before our loving Father day after day to pray for His goodness to increase in the church.

I noticed change in my own life in the early days as I regularly prayed the apostolic prayers with their positive language. Little by little I became more positive in my emotions and developed more mercy and kindness in my heart toward the weaknesses in the church.

The positive focus of the apostolic prayers is also essential in helping us to operate in faith. The apostolic prayers in the New Testament provide us with good theology for a victorious church. Praying these prayers builds our faith for revival.

A man once asked me, "Why do you believe the church will be victorious at the end of the age?" I told him to look at the prayers of Jesus and the apostles for the church. My theology on a victorious church and revival was formed partially by praying the New Testament prayers repeatedly. These prayers were given by the Holy Spirit, and though they have not yet been fully answered, they surely will be. The church will walk in great victory, power, purity, unity, and love before Jesus returns.

Positive prayers facilitate unity, impact our emotions, and build our faith. The Father is the "Great Psychologist." He designed these prayers to make human hearts work right and work together in unity with a spirit of encouragement.

APOSTOLIC PRAYERS ARE FOR THE CHURCH

It is important to note that the vast majority of the apostolic prayers are focused on the church, not on the lost or the transformation of society. This does not mean that God is ambivalent about the lost or society or that we are not to pray for these things. However, the only prayer in the New Testament that is specifically focused on the lost who are in need of salvation is found in Romans 10:1, where Paul entreats, "Brethren, my heart's desire and prayer to God for Israel is that they may be saved."

It is significant that the vast majority of the apostolic prayers are for the strengthening and reviving of the church. Why? Because God's primary strategy and plan to reach the lost or to impact a city is by anointing His church with power, love, and wisdom. When we pray for the whole church in a particular city to be revived in love and power, the answer to these prayers will have an immense impact on the lost in that city. Many unbelievers will inevitably come to Jesus, and society will be changed as the church walks in the power of the Holy Spirit.

We see this principle at work through the prayers in Ephesians 1:17–19 and Ephesians 3:16–19. They are for the whole church in the city of Ephesus, not for the lost or the transformation of society. The prayer in Philippians 1:9–11 is for the whole church across the city of Philippi, that in Colossians 1:9–12 is for the whole church in Colossae, and so on.

What was the result of the prayers for the church in Ephesus? The preaching of the Word of God was so powerfully anointed that its influence "grew mightily and prevailed" across the entire city of Ephesus (Acts 19:20). God's strategy was to raise up a large anointed church there that would win a great harvest all across Asia. What happened in Ephesus was so powerful that everyone who lived in Asia "heard the word of the Lord" from Paul and others in this church.

All who dwelt in Asia heard the word of the Lord Jesus, both Jews and Greeks.... So the word of the Lord grew mightily and prevailed.
—ACTS 19:10, 20

Considering the limited communication and transportation systems of the day, it seems likely that for all the Jews and Greeks in Asia to hear the Word, they had to hear it not only from Paul but also from *many believers* who were a part of the large church at Ephesus that was inspired by Paul's anointed preaching.

When preachers are anointed and the church is revived, the saints will speak the Word and do the works of the kingdom with great consistency, and a multitude of unbelievers will come to Jesus. Therefore, we do well to labor in prayer for an increase of the measure of the anointing of the Spirit on the church, knowing that a harvest will surely result. No power can prevent the lost from coming to Jesus in great numbers when the church is revived and operating together in the anointing of the Spirit.

At the International House of Prayer of Kansas City (IHOPKC) we regularly pray for the whole church in our area. Thus, we ask the Lord to visit a thousand congregations with His power in the region of Kansas City. In addition to praying, I encourage our staff to love the whole church. I encourage you to do the same. Pray much for the body of Christ in your city. Do not write off any group, but serve them, love them, and pray much for them. The Lord loves the whole church—every denomination and congregation that proclaims Jesus and His grace. He will surely visit your city in His timing and His way as you love and pray for His people.

As I mentioned before, we will love those whom we pray for consistently. One reason God requires us to bless our enemies is because in doing so, we begin to love them. And that is what He is looking for—a heart of love, compassion, and forgiveness, even for those who offend us. If we pray for our enemies, our hearts will eventually become tender toward them. In other words, it is impossible to pray for anyone regularly without eventually loving him.

God knows that we will love the church more as we pray for it regularly. God wants the hearts of the intercessors to connect with the church in the city for which they consistently pray. This is His divine strategy of love.

It is easy to love the lost in a city or nation because we do not know most of them. But we are often quick to become frustrated and impatient with the churches in our own cities because we know the believers in them. Therefore the Lord calls us to pray for the church so that we will love it while we are working to bring the lost to Jesus and impact society. He doesn't want us to despise the church in our areas because of the weaknesses we see in the people in various congregations or the way their leaders do things; He wants us to love both the church and the lost.

God is a brilliant strategist! He directs us to pray for the harvest by asking Him to visit the whole church—the local churches—in our area with His great power. It is no coincidence that most of the New Testament prayers are for the church!

Suggested Ways to Pray for the Church Using the Apostolic Prayers

As a rule our prayers should be God-centered prayers, rather than demon-centered or sin-focused prayers. This is the New Testament model of prayer, set forth especially by Paul. The major thrust of our prayers should be for a greater release of the ministry of the Holy Spirit on the whole church in our city and for the impartation of positive kingdom virtues such as love, holiness, unity, hope, and peace. Below are suggested ways to pray for the church using the apostolic prayers.

Pray for the presence of God to be powerfully manifested in church services and for people to be saved, set free, healed, and refreshed by the Spirit during the worship, preaching, and ministry times.

Pray that love will abound and that believers will approve the things that God calls excellent (Phil. 1:9–10).

Pray that the anointing of conviction will rest on the preaching of the Word so that both believers and unbelievers are impacted greatly (John 16:8). Pray for a spirit of holiness and love to prevail in the congregation.

Pray for a great increase of the gifts of the Spirit in the church and the manifestation of these gifts through words of knowledge, words of wisdom, discerning of spirits, healings, miracles, and so on.

Pray for a prophetic spirit to rest on preachers, worship teams, and ministry leaders, according to Acts 2:17.

Pray that the Spirit will open more doors to minister to unbelievers and that He will prepare them to receive the gospel (Col. 4:3; 2 Thess. 3:1).

Pray that the Spirit will motivate more believers to share the gospel and give more believers a burden for evangelism (Matt. 9:37–38).

Pray for the spirit of wisdom and revelation in the knowledge of God, His will, and His ways to be given to leaders of churches and the individual members (Eph. 1:17).

Pray that believers will be strengthened with might by the Spirit in their inner man (Eph. 3:16).

Pray for unity among all the believers and all the families in the church (John 17:21–23).

Pray for an increase of the spirit of prayer to be released in the church (Zech. 12:10).

Pray for every family member to be saved and healed, and for every family to prosper with secure, steady jobs (3 John 2).

If we pray consistently and faithfully in this manner for the church in our cities, over time we will see both the church and the cities transformed before our eyes. One particular apostolic prayer with which we are all familiar and that I'll discuss in the next chapter is an especially effective cornerstone for our intercession.

Chapter 10

THE MOST FAMOUS APOSTOLIC PRAYER

Prayer surely does influence God. It does not influ-
ence His purpose. It does influence His action.[1]
—S. D. Gordon

The most famous, or well-known, apostolic prayer in history is probably the Lord's Prayer as recorded in Matthew's Gospel:

Our Father in heaven,
Hallowed be Your name.
Your kingdom come.
Your will be done
On earth as it is in heaven.
Give us this day our daily bread.
And forgive us our debts,
As we forgive our debtors.
And do not lead us into temptation,
But deliver us from the evil one.
For Yours is the kingdom and the power and the glory
forever. Amen.

—Matthew 6:9–13

It is actually an example of all three types of prayer—devotional prayer, intercessory prayer, and personal petition—but for the sake of simplicity we will consider it along with other forms of intercessory prayer.

What a glorious gift it is to learn about prayer from the Man who had the greatest prayer life of all time! Jesus's prayer is one of the most familiar passages in the Bible, but we can become overfamiliar with it and lose sight of what it teaches us about prayer. It is a very important passage for all who want to grow in prayer, and we need more than a superficial knowledge of the words contained in it.

How did this prayer come about? Jesus was on a hillside by the Sea of Galilee, teaching the multitudes and His disciples what it means to live a kingdom lifestyle according to His priorities, His heart, and His values. We know His teaching, recorded in Matthew 5–7, as the Sermon on the Mount, and I refer to it as the "constitution of God's kingdom." It was in this context that Jesus said to His followers, "In this manner, pray," and then gave them a model for prayer that provides insight into what God is like and into the nature of the kingdom and how it functions.

In His prayer to His Father Jesus gave us keys that we need in our quest to grow strong in prayer. In essence He was saying, "Keep these things central in your prayer life." He gave us six requests to pray regularly, each with many implications and applications. The first three focus on *God's glory* (His name, kingdom, and will); the second three focus on *man's needs* (physical, relational, and spiritual).

Seeing God as Father and King

Jesus's teaching on prayer begins by acknowledging God as our Father: "Our Father in heaven, hallowed be Your name" (Matt. 6:9). In His time the Jewish people saw the God of heaven mostly as the transcendent creator and king. The phrase "in heaven" points to God's transcendent majesty, to One who is infinitely superior in power and greatness to everything and everyone else. God's people trembled before the great power of their Creator.

Here, at the beginning of His prayer, Jesus was showing them that their creator God is also their Father. He wanted them to see His affection, tenderness, and personal involvement with His people. Jesus emphasized both dimensions of God: His *majestic transcendence* as the One who dwells in heaven and His *tenderness as a father.* He is both powerful and personal, transcendent and tender.

We end up with a wrong view of God if we separate these two aspects of His nature. Throughout history the church has laid much emphasis on the transcendent God who rules with infinite power and has largely missed the tender father-heart of God. When the truth of the Father's heart of love comes into focus alongside His majestic splendor, we gain a more accurate picture of who God is.

As we have seen before, a right view of God is foundational to prayer, and this includes knowing Him as our heavenly Father. Jesus started right where we need to start in our prayer lives, with our focus on the being of God Himself. The great evangelical teacher and one of my favorite authors A. W. Tozer held that the greatest problem in the church in every generation has been a low view of God.[2] Having a low view of either God's fatherhood or His majesty diminishes our relationships with Him and hinders our prayer lives. Therefore, we must take time to cultivate our understanding of God in these two facets of His nature. He is both powerful in His majesty and deeply personal as a Father.

Addressing God as "Father," Jesus set the context of intimacy with God within His sovereignty and majesty. If we miss either one or the other, our view of God is warped, and we will not relate to Him rightly. Those who see only His heavenly glory and fail to see His nature as a father with deep love, tend to depersonalize God; they view Him and present Him as majestic but also as distant, cold-hearted, and even harsh.

On the other hand, those who see God only as a tender father do not acknowledge His heavenly glory. They relate to a father who is kind and personal but do not tremble before His transcendence. They are apt to portray God as a familiar, fun-loving buddy, but this is bad and shallow theology. We must know God in truth—the truth of His fatherhood *and* His majestic transcendence.

Jesus's prayer emphasizes that God is not only *my* Father but also *our* Father.

Our prayer requests must convey the reality of who we are to God as one family. We are to pray inclusively for the whole family of believers, not for ourselves alone.

PRAYING FOR GOD'S GLORY (MATTHEW 6:9–10)

In His prayer model Jesus gave us six requests to pray regularly. The first three requests are for God's glory—that His name be treated as holy, that His kingdom be openly expressed, and that His will be done individually and collectively by His people.

Petition 1: Praying for God's name to be hallowed

> Our Father in heaven, hallowed be Your name.
>
> —MATTHEW 6:9

God's name refers to His person, character, and authority. His name is hallowed when we respond to Him in the way He deserves. The very thought of His name stirs awe and holy fear in any who have a little understanding. This first petition is that God's majestic name be revealed first *to* us and then *through* us. When we pray for His name to be hallowed, we are praying that the Father take the highest place in our lives, hearts, and worship, and that He work in us and in others so that we see and respond appropriately to His greatness. We are asking God to release His power to cause more people to see the truth about Him and refuse to take His name in vain or use it in jest and expressions of anger. We also revere God's name by not asking for anything contrary to His glorious name or will.

Petition 2: Praying for the kingdom to come

> Your kingdom come.
>
> —MATTHEW 6:10

This prayer request is for God's kingdom to be openly expressed on the earth. The kingdom is the place where God's Word is obeyed, His will done, and His power expressed. For example, the kingdom is manifested when the sick are healed and demons are cast out. Jesus told us, "If I cast out demons by the Spirit of God, surely the kingdom of God has come upon you" (Matt. 12:28). The kingdom is present wherever God's will is expressed under the authority of Jesus the King.

The kingdom is the sphere in which God's rule is expressed, and the church is the family and the vehicle of the kingdom. The church is the community of the kingdom but not the kingdom itself. As the church proclaims the good news of the kingdom, people come into the church, the body of Christ, and experience the blessings of God's kingdom rule.

The schoolteacher who does God's will in the classroom is expressing God's kingdom in that setting. The same is true of the one who works at the bank, the gas station, the hospital, or the courthouse. It is true for the surgeon, the ditch digger, the soldier, the homeschooling mom, and all those who do God's will. The kingdom is already here but not yet fully here. It is manifest *in part* in this age and will be manifest *in fullness* when Jesus returns to Earth.[3]

We labor in prayer for the kingdom to increase. In Revelation 2 we read that the error of the great missionary church at Ephesus was to do kingdom work without kingdom prayer—in other words, without connecting deeply with Jesus by loving Him and talking with Him (Rev. 2:4). Praying for the release of the kingdom is part of the work of the kingdom. We must not allow our service in the kingdom to take the place of conversing with the King and praying for the kingdom to come. This second petition includes being kingdom-minded in our lifestyles and in our attitudes toward others. We are to work together with other believers rather than having a territorial mind-set and focusing on only our own spheres of authority and influence.

Petition 3: Praying for God's will to be done

> Your will be done on earth as it is in heaven.
>
> —MATTHEW 6:10

The third request related to God's glory is that His people will do His will, both individually and collectively. In this prayer we set our hearts to obey His will. Obeying His will includes obeying His commands in our personal lives as well as fulfilling the ministry assignments He gives to each of us. We pray for God's will to be done *through* us (in our ministries) and *in* us (in our personal lives). Some believers are committed to changing the nations through ministry but not to living in purity; they are more captivated by growing their ministries as "agents for change" than by interacting with Jesus and obeying Him in their personal lives. However, there is no substitute for obedience and intimacy with God.

As we pray for the Father's will to be done on Earth, for the outworking of His righteousness, holiness, and love in our personal lives and in our midst, we are mindful that His will is being done perfectly in heaven. We are praying that Earth become more like heaven, where the righteous, humble King reigns in the perfection of love and all of heaven rejoices in His majestic beauty.

PRAYING FOR PERSONAL NEEDS (MATTHEW 6:11–13)

The next three requests are for our needs—physical (daily bread), relational (forgiveness), and spiritual (deliverance from evil). Jesus encouraged us to bring our personal requests to God in prayer. These prayers express our dependence on God in every area of life as well as our trust in His provision.

Our daily bread speaks of our daily, personal needs. Jesus directs us to pray for personal needs in addition to praying for God's glory. The Lord delights in meeting our needs and seeing us rejoicing in His goodness, as the psalmist Asaph wrote, "Call upon Me in the day of trouble; I will deliver you, and you shall glorify Me" (Ps. 50:15).

Some "holiness" teachers throughout history have concluded that our sole prayer focus should be worshipping God. This unbalanced approach leads to renouncing all that is personal as self-centered. It sounds noble, but it leads people to believe that praying for their own needs is always a selfish endeavor. The result is that, in their quest to be humble and holy, they neglect to make petition for personal needs.

The truth is that God deeply enjoys meeting our needs because He is our Father, and He loves to give good gifts to His children who ask Him:

> If you then, being evil, know how to give good gifts to your children, how much more will your Father who is in heaven give good things to those who ask Him!
>
> —MATTHEW 7:11

We express our dependence on Him when we ask Him to meet our needs. The Word promises that He will supply all our needs according to His riches in Christ (Phil. 4:19). As a loving Father He *delights* in supplying all our needs and in our asking and believing that He will do so. He is intimately involved with His creation, even feeding the birds of the air, who are of much less value than we are (Matt. 6:26).

Petition 4: Praying for our daily provision

> Give us this day our daily bread.
>
> —MATTHEW 6:11

The fourth request is for our daily provision, protection, and direction. We do not pray to inform God of our needs because He knows them before we ask (Matt. 6:7–8). Rather, we pray to enhance our relationship with Him by connecting and dialoguing with Him. Though He already knows our needs, He often withholds some of our provision until we talk to Him about it by making requests in prayer.

Asking God to meet our needs does not free us from the responsibility of working. He meets our needs partially by giving us the ability and opportunity to earn a living. But He delights in meeting all our needs because He is our Father.

Please note that Jesus taught us to ask for our "daily" bread. Most of us would prefer for the Lord to give us monthly bread or yearly bread, but He promised to give us bread only one day at a time.

Petition 5: Praying for forgiveness

> And forgive us our debts, as we forgive our debtors.
> —MATTHEW 6:12

The fifth petition deals with our relationships with God and people. The evidence that we have been freely forgiven is that we gladly forgive others. The man who knows he has been forgiven is compelled to forgive others.

Because Jesus is speaking to believers here, the question is often asked, "Why must a born-again believer pray for forgiveness?" Certainly we have fully and freely received the righteousness of God in Christ as a gift (2 Cor. 5:17–21), so when we ask God to "forgive us our debts," we are not asking to be saved or delivered from hell. We have already been freely forgiven and justified by faith (Rom. 3:21–31). Prayer for our debts to be forgiven speaks of restoring our fellowship with God. The apostle John explained this principle clearly in his first letter:

> If we say that we have no sin, we deceive ourselves, and the truth is not in us. If we confess our sins, He is faithful and just to forgive us our sins and to cleanse us from all unrighteousness.
> —1 JOHN 1:8–9

We do not lose our standing with God when, as sincere believers, we stumble in sin, but sin defiles our minds and quenches our hearts, thus hindering our ability to enjoy the presence of God. So we understand that this petition to "forgive us our debts" is to restore communion with Jesus. Again, John tells us, "If anyone sins, we have an Advocate with the Father, Jesus Christ the righteous" (1 John 2:1). This fifth petition is asking that we would be cleansed from the defiling effects of sin on our hearts.

Some believers have misinterpreted the second part of this petition, "as we forgive our debtors," to mean that we earn our forgiveness on the basis of forgiving others. That is not at all what Jesus is saying here. Rather, the evidence that we have been freely forgiven is that we are compelled by gratitude to extend that forgiveness to others.

Petition 6: Praying for deliverance from evil

> And lead us not into temptation, but deliver us from the evil one.
> —MATTHEW 6:13, NIV

The sixth petition is what I refer to as a "pre-temptation prayer." Jesus called us to pray for the Lord's help to avoid and escape "intensified" temptations before they even occur. This is a very important prayer, yet it may be one of the most neglected prayers in the Bible. In it Jesus expressed one petition in two ways: "lead us not into temptation" and "deliver us from evil." The second half of the request defines positively what the first half expresses negatively.

God never tempts anyone with evil (James 1:13), so why ask Him to "lead us not into temptation"? In the garden of Gethsemane Jesus urged the disciples to pray that they would not enter into temptation:

> Watch and pray, lest you enter into temptation. The spirit is willing, but the flesh is weak.
>
> —MATTHEW 26:41

To "enter into temptation" is to fall into something far more intense than the general temptations we face each day in a fallen world. It points to a specific "storm of temptation" that occurs when three components come together—demonic activity is heightened, our lusts are aroused, and circumstances are "optimum" for sin. By praying, we can avoid or minimize the intensity of a heightened temptation.

I see Jesus's petition in the Lord's Prayer as being focused on escaping the storms of temptation, which include more than general temptations that occur in everyday life. I think of "general" temptations as temptations to be proud in our attitudes, lack patience in our communication styles, act selfishly in our decisions, and be less than honest with our finances or in our communication with others. I think of the "storm" of temptations as acts such as committing adultery or participating in activities that cause serious harm to others or to society itself. I see the most serious temptation as the temptation to deny Christ.

The Scripture tells us that after he tempted Jesus, Satan departed until a more "opportune time" (Luke 4:13). Satan always looks for opportune times when demonically energized temptations will hit us like a storm and cause us to fall in a great way. He seeks to lure us into a trap "at an opportune time" to destroy our faith.

He did this to the apostle Peter, creating a "perfect storm" of temptation in the form of a heightened demonic attack combined with the circumstance of soldiers coming for Jesus with swords and causing fear at a time when Peter was very fatigued. (See Matthew 26:43.) It was the "optimum" setting for Peter to be tempted in a heightened way. The Lord warned Peter about this perfect storm, but he was not able to stand in the midst of it.

> Satan has asked for you [Peter], that he may sift you as wheat. But I have prayed for you, that your faith should not fail.
>
> —LUKE 22:31–32

"Pre-temptation prayers" ask the Lord for help in advance and remove or diminish a storm of temptation. Praying before temptation occurs expresses our humility because we are acknowledging our weakness and our dependence on God's strength when we ask Him to lead us away from various temptations so that we do not become trapped by them. Paul said that we must be aware of Satan's deceptive devices against us to prevent him from taking advantage of us (2 Cor. 2:11).

Paul encouraged us to be alert to our situations, so we can pray, "Lord, keep me from situations in which temptation is heightened" or "Lead me not into temptation but into full deliverance." David prayed for deliverance from sinful situations even before they occurred:

> Cleanse me from secret [unperceived] faults. Keep back your servant from presumptuous sins; let them not have dominion over me. Then I shall be blameless.
> —Psalm 19:12–13

Paul exhorted us, "Let him who thinks he stands take heed lest he fall." He was talking about believers who think they will always be strong. They have false confidence in their ability to walk in continual victory without praying and regularly asking Jesus for help. This is not the biblical approach to temptation. We "take heed" by keeping our relationships with Jesus strong through a consistent prayer life and abiding in Christ.

> Let him who thinks he stands [without prayer] take heed lest he fall....God is faithful, who will not allow you to be tempted beyond what you are able, but with the temptation will also make the way of escape, that you may be able to bear it.
> —1 Corinthians 10:12–13

In these last days, as the pressures of society increase and sin becomes more and more universally accepted, the request "Lead us not into temptation, but deliver us from evil" is becoming all the more significant for us in our prayer lives. Jesus calls us to "pray always" to prepare for the snare of temptation in the end times.

> Take heed to yourselves, lest your hearts be weighed down with carousing, drunkenness, and cares of this life, and that Day come on you unexpectedly. For it will come as a snare on all those who dwell on the face of the whole earth. Watch therefore, and pray always that you may be counted worthy [found prepared] to escape...and to stand [victorious] before the Son of Man.
> —Luke 21:34–36

One prayer, six requests. Jesus could not get more concise in giving us the prayer requests to unlock all that God wants to do in us, for us, and in our world. Let us not neglect to "in this manner, pray."

Chapter 11

PRAYER *and* PROPHETIC PROMISES

Prayer is not overcoming God's reluctance but laying hold of His willingness.[1]
—MARTIN LUTHER

A S WE HAVE seen, part of our responsibility as intercessors is praying for the release of the kingdom—the increase of God's kingdom on Earth. Whenever we pray the Lord's Prayer, we are asking for His kingdom to come (Matt. 6:10). Another way to intercede for the manifestation of the kingdom is to contend for the fulfillment of prophetic promises—biblical prophetic promises, contemporary prophetic promises, and personal prophetic words—particularly those related to revival. (See chapter 20 for more about revival and what I mean by the term.)

The more you intercede, the more you will become aware of the dynamic relationship between prophetic promises and persevering prayer. As our faith is stirred by prophetic promises, we are energized to sustain prayer for the full release of those promises. Indeed, prayer and the prophetic are inseparable. Prophetic promises fuel the work of intercession, purity, and more effective outreach to others. They help us persevere in our faith and obedience so that we do not draw back in times of pressure and difficulty.

Prophetic promises are often invitations rather than guarantees. God speaks prophetically to equip us to more fully cooperate with the Holy Spirit as we intercede for the full release of what God has promised.

We value prophetic promises especially from the Scriptures, but we should not neglect personal prophetic promises given to us by the Holy Spirit. Paul exhorted Timothy to fight the fight of faith according to the prophetic words that were given to him: "This charge I commit to you, son Timothy, according to the prophecies previously made concerning you, that by them you may wage the good warfare" (1 Tim. 1:18). Prophetic words help us to persevere in faithfulness in our assignments from the Lord, especially difficult ones.

Biblical and contemporary prophetic promises and personal prophetic words are important aids in sustaining persevering prayer over many years. Of course, we should never receive prophetic promises that do not honor the written Word or that contradict it. The Scriptures are the final authority on all matters of faith, including prophetic promises. Our ministries must be established on the Scriptures, not on prophetic words. Prophetic words are given not to direct us to do something that is foreign to the Scriptures but to help us to faithfully persevere and not quit when our ministry assignment is difficult.

I think of three stages in our partnership with God. First, God initiates what He wants by declaring it in His Word and stirring our hearts to believe for it.

Second, we respond in obedience with prayer, speaking God's will back to Him. Third, God answers our prayer by releasing what we pray for.

In other words, the Lord is over the whole process of releasing revival. He sends prophetic encouragement to stir us to persevere in prayer, and then the Holy Spirit helps us to pray. Then God answers the prayers by releasing His power and blessing in a greater measure. A glorious cycle! He starts, sustains, and finishes His work of revival. Paul said it best: "From Him and through Him and to Him are all things. To Him be the glory forever" (Rom. 11:36, NAS). Both prayer and revival start with Him and are sustained through Him, and then the glory goes back to Him.

BIBLICAL PROMISES FOR A GREAT OUTPOURING OF THE HOLY SPIRIT

I am convinced that the greatest outpouring of the Holy Spirit in all history will be released just before Jesus's Second Coming. The body of Christ will participate in the greatest revival ever to occur in the generation in which the Lord returns. In this great revival the Holy Spirit will release the types of miracles recorded in Acts and Exodus, combined and multiplied on a global scale.

How do I know? Because the Bible contains many promises related to the end times. And it tells us that Jesus is coming back for "a glorious church, not having spot or wrinkle or any such thing, but that she should be holy and without blemish" (Eph. 5:27).

Before we continue, I want to take a moment to define what I mean by the two terms "the last days" and "the end times." The last days began on the Day of Pentecost and will continue until the second coming of Jesus. The phrase "the end times" refers to the final decades of the "last days." I use the term "the end times" synonymously with the phrase "the generation in which the Lord returns."

The biblical promises show us that we can expect to witness various expressions of revival in the end times. I will identify five:

1. We will see the emergence of a victorious, unified, anointed church that is full of God's glory. Jesus prayed "that they [the church] may be made perfect in one," so that the world may know that the Father sent Jesus (John 17:22–23).

2. The church will live in love, humility, and purity as believers live their lives according to Jesus's Sermon on the Mount (Matt. 5–7).

3. We will see a great end-time harvest from every nation, tribe, and tongue. I expect this great ingathering of souls to exceed one billion new souls coming to Jesus.

I looked, and behold, a great multitude which no one could number, of all nations, tribes, peoples, and tongues, standing before the throne and before the Lamb.... "These are the ones who come out of the great tribulation, and washed their robes and made them white in the blood of the Lamb."

—REVELATION 7:9, 14

4. The spirit of prophecy will operate in the church and rest on every believer.

And it shall come to pass in the last days, says God, that I will pour out of My Spirit on all flesh; your sons and your daughters shall prophesy, your young men shall see visions, your old men shall dream dreams.

—ACTS 2:17

5. The church will fulfill its primary calling to win the lost and build His church—a kingdom community expressing the two great commandments to love God and people and fully engaging in the Great Commission.

"You shall love the LORD your God with all your heart, with all your soul, and with all your mind." This is the first and great commandment. And the second is like it: "You shall love your neighbor as yourself."

—MATTHEW 22:37–39

Go therefore and make disciples of all the nations...teaching them to observe all things that I have commanded you.

—MATTHEW 28:19–20

We must embrace a tension as we contend in prayer for the full release of these prophetic promises of revival: we are to operate in a *partial* release of God's power *now* while also continuing to earnestly pray for a historic breakthrough of the *fullness* of the Spirit.

Some who pray for a historic outpouring lose sight of ministering in the power of God in the present. And some who are currently ministering to people on a regular basis lose sight of contending in intercession for a historic breakthrough of the fullness of all God has planned. They pour out all their energy in the present and do not have the faith, energy, or desire to contend for a greater breakthrough in the future.

We can walk in the measure that God has ordained for us now as well as seeking for the fullness of what He has in store. We can heal the sick and win many to Jesus now, even before the time when great multitudes will come to Jesus in the end-time revival.

We are to take hold of God's power today while we contend for the fullness for tomorrow. In other words, we can have a "present-tense relationship" with

Jesus and at the same time pray for and anticipate the fullness of what God promised.

GOD'S WORD TO ME

For many years I read about the revivals that accompanied the ministry of heroes of the faith such as Jonathan Edwards, John Wesley, George Whitefield, David Brainerd, and Charles Finney (see chapter 20 for more about these great men of God and their roles in revival). I read their teaching alongside that of Martyn Lloyd-Jones and the Puritan writers—those who had a grasp of the biblical promises about revival—and I adopted their theology of an unprecedented ingathering of souls at the end of the age.

Much later my confidence in an end-time outpouring of the Spirit became a very personal issue. One night in September 1982, in a rather shabby hotel room in Cairo, Egypt, I experienced a life-changing encounter in the Holy Spirit. I would like to share part of that glorious encounter with you.

The eight-by-eight-foot room was equipped with a small bed, squeaky ceiling fan, stone-age plumbing, and an assortment of crawling things that periodically scampered across the concrete floor. It was decidedly primitive by Western standards. I was alone and had set aside the evening to spend with the Lord in prayer. I had been kneeling on the cement floor by the rickety bed for about thirty minutes when I suddenly had one of the most incredible encounters with the Lord I've had in all my years of being a Christian.

I didn't see a vision, and I wasn't caught up into heaven. I simply heard God speak to me—not in an audible voice that I could perceive with my natural ears but in what I call the "internal audible voice" of the Lord. I was instantly overwhelmed with a sense of God's presence. It came with a powerful feeling of cleanness, power, and authority. I wanted to leave, but I didn't want to leave. I wanted the experience to be over, but I didn't want it to be over.

I received only a few sentences, but every word had great meaning. The awe of God flooded my soul as I felt a bit of the terror of the Lord. I literally trembled and wept as God Himself communicated to me in a way I had never experienced before and have not experienced since.

The Lord simply said, "*I will change the understanding and expression of Christianity in the earth in one generation.*" It was a simple, straightforward statement, but I felt God's power with every word as I received the Spirit's interpretation: God Himself will make drastic changes in Christianity across the whole world, and this reformation-revival will be by His sovereign initiative and for His glory.

I knew by the Holy Spirit that the phrase "the understanding of Christianity" meant the way Christianity is perceived by unbelievers. In the early church people were afraid to associate casually with believers, partly because of the displays of supernatural power (Acts 5:13). Today most unbelievers consider the church antiquated and irrelevant to their lives. God is going to change the way unbelievers view the church. Once again they will witness God's wonderful yet terrifying power in His body. They will have a very different understanding of Christianity before God is finished with this generation.

I also knew by the Holy Spirit that the phrase "the expression of Christianity" meant the way the body of Christ expresses its life together under Jesus's leadership. God will bring about dramatic change so that we function as a unified, holy people in the power and love of God. What happens when we gather together as the body of Christ will change. We will see unparalleled power, purity, and unity in the end-time church.

God Himself will radically change Christians' relationships with God and with one another, the way we are perceived by unbelievers, and even the structure and functioning of the church across the whole earth. He will do it not in a month, a year, or a few years, but over a generation. He will use His people who are serving in many different denominations and ministry streams in the body of Christ. He loves the whole church and will use all who want to be used by Him.

The understanding and expression of Christianity will be changed by a great, sovereign outpouring of the Spirit that will cross national, social, ethnic, cultural, and denominational barriers. It won't be just a Western revival or a third-world revival. The prophecy in Joel 2:28–32, reiterated by Peter in Acts 2, says that in the last days God will pour out His Spirit on "all flesh" (v. 17).

Much will change as a result of the progressive outpouring of the Spirit. It will have multidimensional expressions so that it will be seen not as only one type of movement—an evangelism movement, a healing movement, a prayer movement, a unity movement, or a prophetic movement. It will be all of these and more. Above all, this outpouring of the Spirit will impart deep passion for Jesus in the hearts of men and women. The first commandment to love God will be established in first place in the church, which will lead to the church's walking in the second commandment to love others and engaging in the Great Commission in an unprecedented way. The Holy Spirit longs to glorify Jesus in the body of Christ throughout the nations. (See John 16:14.)

My experience in the Cairo hotel room lasted less than an hour, though it seemed much longer. I left the room and walked around the streets of downtown Cairo alone until about midnight, committing myself to the Lord and His purposes. The awe of God lingered in my soul for hours. I woke up the next day still feeling its impact.

This experience was evidence to me that I must value the prophetic ministry, realizing that it is essential to "fueling" the end-time prayer movement. The prophetic ministry in the local church will involve more than verbal, inspirational prophecies. It will include angelic visitations, dreams, visions, signs and wonders in the sky, and more. The Holy Spirit will be poured out on all flesh as foretold in Joel 2 and cited in Peter's first sermon on the Day of Pentecost.

> And it shall come to pass in the last days, says God, that I will pour out
> of My Spirit on all flesh.
>
> —Acts 2:17

Many Old Testament prophecies about God's kingdom are fulfilled in two
ways and two time frames. First, a *partial*, local fulfillment like that which
occurred in the early church and is described in the Book of Acts will take place.
Second, a *total*, *global* fulfillment will occur on a worldwide scale in the generation in which Jesus returns. Jesus spoke of the kingdom not only as if the
kingdom had fully come but also as if it was still yet to come. As George E. Ladd
puts it, the kingdom of God is both *"already"* but *"not yet"*—it is already here
but not yet fully here. The Bible teaches that the kingdom came to earth in part
with the advent of Christ but that the complete manifestation of biblical prophecies concerning the kingdom of God will occur at the end of this age when Jesus
Christ returns again.[2]

This aspect of already but not yet is a theme throughout the Bible. For example,
in the penultimate verse of the Old Testament, Malachi prophesied:

> Behold, I will send you Elijah the prophet before the coming of the great
> and dreadful day of the LORD.
>
> —MALACHI 4:5

Jesus identified John as Elijah (Matt. 11:14) and later said of him:

> Indeed, Elijah is coming first and will restore all things. But I say to you
> that Elijah has come already, and they did not know him but did to him
> whatever they wished.
>
> —MATTHEW 17:11–12

We see an immediate, partial, local fulfillment of "Elijah's coming" in John
the Baptist's ministry in Judea. However, we will also see a future, complete fulfillment when "Elijah" comes to restore all things at the end of the age.

In the same way, the Joel 2 prophecy concerning the outpouring of the Holy
Spirit was partially fulfilled in Jerusalem on the Day of Pentecost. Peter quotes
the prophecy and says:

> But this is what was spoken by the prophet Joel...
>
> —Acts 2:16

But although the outpouring at Pentecost was "that which was spoken
through the prophet Joel," it was not *all* of that which was spoken of by Joel. The
Spirit fell on one hundred twenty people in a small room in Jerusalem and then
touched three thousand people (Acts 2). But Joel spoke of much more than that.
He said, "I will pour out My Spirit on *all flesh*" (Joel 2:28). One of the unique

things about the last great revival will be the signs and wonders described in Acts 2:19 that will be displayed in nature, both on the earth and in the sky.

> I will show wonders in heaven above and signs in the earth beneath: blood and fire and vapor of smoke. The sun shall be turned into darkness, and the moon into blood, before the coming of the great and awesome day of the LORD.
> —ACTS 2:19–20; SEE ALSO JOEL 2:30–31

At the time that Joel gave this prophecy, many of the ideas in it were new to Israel. The anointing of the Spirit had been given to only a few people in the Old Testament era, usually older Jewish men who were kings, judges, or prophets. However, Joel prophesied that the Spirit would be poured out on *all flesh*, Jew and Gentile, men and women, young and old. Paul confirmed Joel's word in 1 Corinthians 14:31 when he indicated that all believers can prophesy: "For you can all prophesy one by one, that all may learn and all may be encouraged."

The only qualifier Joel made to this all-inclusive promise that the Spirit would be poured out on "all flesh" is the phrase "on My menservants and on My maidservants I will pour out My Spirit in those days" (Joel 2:29). Therefore, "all flesh" refers to those who are servants of God. "My servants" speaks not of those who casually profess their faith but of those who genuinely serve God.

Joel's prophecy gives us great confidence for a global outpouring of the Spirit, as do many other prophetic Bible passages. They inspire our faith and equip us to persevere in prayer and service over the course of many years. The prophetic promises of the Scriptures also focus our intercession by revealing the will of God as an invitation for us to receive through persistent, believing prayer. Let us continue in the pursuit of both the ministry of intercession and the ministry of the prophetic as we wait in joyful expectation for the return of Jesus as the Bridegroom, King, and Judge.

Chapter 12

THE NEW TESTAMENT MODEL
for SPIRITUAL WARFARE

Satan trembles when he sees the weakest Christian on his knees.[1]
—WILLIAM COWPER

As we pray in faith for the fulfillment of prophetic promises, we may have a need to engage in a form of intercession known as "spiritual warfare." Some people have a misunderstanding about this type of prayer. In most cases spiritual warfare is not to be carried out by directly confronting the powers and principalities over cities and nations. The New Testament model for spiritual warfare is to direct our prayers to God, proclaim His name and promises, and do His works as the primary way to wrestle with the disembodied evil spirits in the heavenly places. These evil spirits are called principalities, powers, rulers of the darkness of this age, and spiritual hosts of wickedness (Eph. 6:12). Of course, there are exceptions to this general rule, in which case we address our proclamations directly to the enemy. On specific occasions the Spirit may lead someone to speak directly in intercession to a demonic principality. However, this is not the primary prayer model presented by the New Testament apostles.

Jesus and the apostles spoke directly to the demons that dwelt *in* a demonized person—in other words, to "embodied" demonic spirits—but what they did is not the same as speaking to "disembodied" demonic principalities that dwell in heavenly places. We do wrestle with them (Eph. 6:12) but usually by praying to the Father, not by speaking to them directly. The prophet Daniel dislodged the powerful demonic principality of Persia (Dan. 10:12–13) as he fasted and prayed, focusing on the God of Israel (Dan. 9:4–23), not on the demonic being itself.

Spiritual warfare prayer requires a three-pronged approach. First, we proclaim God's victory by agreeing with the supremacy of Jesus, His power, promises, and will. We pray the prayers of the Bible, remind God of His promises, and make prophetic decrees related to the certainty of the supremacy of God and His kingdom purposes. Second, we confess sin and renounce the works of darkness. In other words, we break our agreement with the enemy. In this way, we resist Satan: "Submit to God. Resist the devil and he will flee from you" (James 4:7). Third, we do the works of the kingdom, acting in the opposite spirit of the evil characteristics that permeate a specific city or region.

THREE TYPES OF STRONGHOLDS

The Scripture speaks of spiritual "strongholds": "For the weapons of our warfare are not carnal but mighty in God for pulling down strongholds, casting down arguments and every high thing that exalts itself against the knowledge of God" (2 Cor. 10:4–5). A stronghold is a collection of ideas that are in agreement with Satan's lies and accusations against the truth of God (v. 5). They are lies about God, who He is, and what He says He will do, and when we receive them, they bind our hearts in darkness.

Whole geographic regions can be affected by the same lies and assaulted by the same demonic darkness that is manifest. We are to pull down and dismantle spiritual strongholds by agreeing with God and His Word and by "casting down arguments"—renouncing the lies—that are against the knowledge of God, His Word, and His will. In this way we break any agreement with Satan.

There are three types of spiritual strongholds:

1. **Personal strongholds** of the mind that bind people in sinful mind-sets and lifestyles.

2. **Cultural strongholds**, or values in our society, that are in agreement with darkness. Cultural strongholds are agreements with Satan's values in our society at large. There are many ways in which we agree with him and keep those evil values entrenched. (For prayers to gain victory over cultural strongholds, see Appendix D.)

3. **Cosmic strongholds**, which are demonic powers and principalities in the air, are demonic angels or demonic hosts. Paul describes them in his letter to the Ephesians: "For we do not wrestle against flesh and blood, but against principalities, against powers, against the rulers of the darkness of this age, against spiritual hosts of wickedness in the heavenly places" (Eph. 6:12).

We dismantle each of these strongholds by *agreeing* with God and *renouncing* the enemy's lies through our prayers and actions.

THE PRINCIPLE OF AGREEING WITH GOD

Engaging in spiritual warfare is essentially agreeing with God and disagreeing with the enemy. It involves reminding God of His character and covenant promises, agreeing with His Word, and declaring the supremacy of Jesus and who we are in Christ—a new creation, the sons of God, the bride of Christ, and so on. It also involves renouncing agreement with Satan as we confess sin, reject the works of darkness, and act in the opposite spirit by doing the works of the kingdom.

Corporately we agree with God when we engage in worship and intercession. Some prayer ministries emphasize worship, and others highlight intercession. Sometimes I am asked which is the most important in spiritual warfare— worship or intercession. I encourage people not to concern themselves too much with this question. When we agree with *who God is*, we call it "worship." When we agree with *what God promised to do*, we call it "intercession." In heaven worship and intercession flow as one river and are woven together in the exercise of God's government. They overlap and are deeply related. Both are necessary, so we must value both activities in our approach to God-centered spiritual warfare.

In addition to agreeing with God through worship and intercession, we can agree with Him through holiness and healing. All four forms of agreement play a role in spiritual warfare.

Worship is agreement with who God is.

In worship we declare truths about who God is. For example, the saints and angels in heaven declare truths such as "Holy, holy, holy" (Rev. 4:8). They also proclaim, "Holy is the Lord" and "You are worthy." Throughout the Old Testament we find the declaration "The Lord is good, and His mercy endures forever."[2] This is the most emphasized declaration about who God is.

Intercession is agreement with what God promises to do.

In intercession we declare truths related to what God promises to do. For example, we pray: "Lord, release a greater measure of Your Spirit's activity to revive the church. Release the power of Your Word, confirmed with signs and wonders."

Holiness is agreement with God's heart of love.

Holiness involves repentance that breaks any agreement with sin and comes into agreement with God's standards of purity.

Healing is agreement with God's heart for life.

We proclaim the truth of Jesus as Healer, and we break all agreement with sickness.

What Happens in the Spirit Realm When We Pray?

Daniel 10 gives us a snapshot of what happens in the spirit realm when God's people pray. This is a favorite chapter for many intercessors because the veil is drawn back, allowing us to see how our prayers affect angels and demonic powers and principalities. It also reveals the intense conflict between high-ranking angels and demons that is manifest in earthly spheres of government.

Angelic and demonic authority structures exist over each city and region in the world. There are high-ranking angels that serve God's purposes, and there are high-ranking demons that fight His purposes. The conflict between these angelic and demonic beings is dynamically related to the prayers and deeds of the people in the city or region the beings preside over. If we could see into the spirit realm, I believe we would be amazed by how much the heavenly host is involved in earthly affairs and how they respond to our prayers.

There is a dynamic correlation between what people do on earth and the measure of demonic activity that is released in the areas in which they live. For example, as people sin more in a particular city or region, they give greater access to the demonic realm to increase the amount of spiritual darkness in that city or region. The same principle operates in the angelic realm—the righteous deeds and prayers of the saints affect the measure of angelic activity in a specific area.

Political leaders and the governmental infrastructures under them are deeply affected by the activity of angels and demons, though many of these leaders are completely unaware that they are wrestling against, and being oppressed and influenced by, demonic powers and principalities (Eph. 6:12). Whether they are kings, presidents, or prime ministers, they have high-ranking angels and demons related to their political sphere of authority. The result of the conflict between these good and evil forces affects many events and political decisions as well as the spiritual culture of the cities of the earth.

I believe there are demonic assignments focused on deceiving and harassing every governmental leader. When a person steps into office, he is stepping into an increased assault. For this reason we need to stand for him before God's throne—and the only way to prevail in wrestling with demonic principalities is by submitting to Jesus's leadership and exerting His authority over these evil, supernatural powers in prayer.

When we pray, the Holy Spirit and the angels increase their activity on behalf of all those for whom we pray, and the result ultimately benefits us. Paul understood this truth, so he encouraged the body of Christ to make it a priority to pray for all in authority:

> I exhort first of all that supplications, prayers, intercessions, and giving of thanks be made for all men, for kings and all who are in authority, that we may lead a quiet and peaceable life in all godliness and reverence.
> —1 TIMOTHY 2:1–2

Paul also knew from the Scripture that the heart of a king or political leader is in the hand of the Lord. The Lord can turn it like channels of water, and He can use angels in this process.

> The king's heart is in the hand of the LORD, like the rivers of water; He turns it wherever He wishes.
> —PROVERBS 21:1

Consider an example of how our prayers can affect a political leader. Sometimes when the leader of a nation feels oppressed, it is due to the influence of a demon. For example, when the president of a nation is having a difficult day, he may think he is simply in a bad mood. It may be just that, but in reality it may be that a demonic spirit is attacking him. One purpose of the oppression is to get the leader to establish new laws and decrees while under the negative, oppressive influence of a demonic power. As a result of our prayers, angels drive back demons and hinder their negative influence on a political leader.

Just as demons can influence leaders to make poor decisions, angels can influence them to make wise decisions. When an ungodly king or president feels a sudden surge of peace in his heart, often because of the prayers of the saints, he is far more likely to make good decisions for his nation. Therefore, even the tone and attitude in a president's cabinet meetings can be affected by such prayers, which release angelic activity that hinders the oppressive feeling demons can incite.

If the demonic hierarchy is not hindered sufficiently, then the human leader is influenced to make evil decisions. The leader has a free will; but if he has a happy mind-set with peace, even though he is an unbeliever, then his decisions will be different from those he may make when he is angry, fearful, jealous, bitter, and oppressed by a demon. The leader still makes his own decisions, but under a very different influence, according to the angel or the demon that may be "putting his hand on their chest," so to speak.

Our prayers for kings, presidents, and others in authority really matter, and they can affect the decisions a leader makes. His decisions can then affect our lifestyles, families, and economies. This is the reason Paul exhorted us to pray for all who are in authority "that we may lead a quiet and peaceable life" (1 Tim. 2:2).

Daniel's experience

When the prophet Daniel was probably in his mideighties, he set his heart to pray for the Jews in Jerusalem. He prayed for twenty-one days, mourning with prayer and fasting because of the resistance of the remnant back in Jerusalem.

> In those days I, Daniel, was mourning three full weeks. I ate no pleasant food, no meat or wine came into my mouth, nor did I anoint myself at all, till three whole weeks were fulfilled.
> —DANIEL 10:2–3

In response to Daniel's prayer a mighty angel came (vv. 10–14). This high-ranking, mighty angel (vv. 5–6) was similar in stature to the angel the apostle John later saw in his vision (Rev. 10:1). The angel said to Daniel:

> "From the first day that you set your heart to…humble yourself before your God, your words were heard; and I have come because of your words. But the prince [demonic principality] of the kingdom of Persia withstood me twenty-one days; and behold, Michael, one of the chief princes [archangel], came to help me."
> —DANIEL 10:12–13

This is a very important passage for understanding the biblical theology of intercession and spiritual warfare. A mighty angel told Daniel, in essence, "From the very first day, twenty-one days ago, when you set your heart to humble yourself, I was sent to you." The mighty angel made a dramatic statement: "I came because of your words." This statement makes clear that angels respond to the prayers of the saints. Gabriel had told Daniel the same thing two years earlier: "Because of your words, the Father sent me." (See Daniel 9:22–23.)

But if Daniel had not *continued* in prayer with fasting, the angel would not have come. It was important for Daniel to persevere in prayer for the full twenty-one days to get the necessary breakthrough. His experience proves that there is a dynamic relationship between what we do and how God visits a city or nation. Remember, this is not about "earning" anything but about aligning with Him by coming into *agreement* with His will. Our words are heard because of Jesus's death and resurrection.

The mighty angel pulled back the curtain in the spirit realm to allow Daniel to see a glimpse of the angelic and demonic authorities that are over the natural authority structures of the nations. He told Daniel that the "prince of the kingdom of Persia" withstood him when Daniel first began to pray. This is a reference to the demonic prince—principality or high-ranking demonic power—that was exerting his influence over the region of ancient Persia (modern-day Iran) and was affecting the human prince, or king, of Persia in a negative way. This demonic prince was warring against Israel by seeking to stir up the human king of Persia against God's people (Dan. 10:13, 20–21).

Daniel fought the demonic prince of Persia by agreeing with God in prayer and fasting. The mighty angel informed him that "Michael, one of the chief princes, came to help" (v. 13). A "chief prince" is an archangel, one who leads angels.

Jesus can easily overpower a demonic principality. However, His authority is exerted or made manifest in the earthly realm through believers who agree with Him and who persevere in obedience and prayer with faith. As I have noted in previous chapters, the reason Jesus releases His power more through prayer is because He wants partnership with His people, and prayer is one of the main ways that partnership is strengthened.

The spiritual events of Daniel 10 were recorded in the Scripture to give us a model of what God wants to do in our day to hinder the demonic principalities over Iran, Iraq, and every other nation. These principalities can be withstood as the Spirit raises up a "corporate Daniel" to pray for angelic help to overcome the demonic powers assaulting Israel.

Indeed, Daniel 10 is a model of spiritual warfare for the end-time church. Let us take our stand before the throne of God as we follow this prayer model and ask for angelic intervention in our world today.

Chapter 13

LIFESTYLE *of an* EFFECTIVE INTERCESSOR

He who has learned to pray has learned the greatest secret of a holy and happy life.[1]
—WILLIAM LAW

IN THE LAST chapter we saw the effectiveness of Daniel's prayers as recorded in Daniel 10. They resulted in an increase of activity by high-ranking angels to resist the activity of powerful demons. Daniel's prayers with fasting had a significant impact by shifting things in the spirit realm (Dan. 10:11–14).

Would you like your prayers to move angels and demons as Daniel's did? Would you like to experience similar results when you intercede? If we want a greater level of effectiveness in prayer along the lines of what Daniel had, we must live as he lived.

So what does the lifestyle of an effective intercessor look like?

We will not really understand the message related to prayer in Daniel 10 without understanding Daniel's dedication to God. His lifestyle was directly related to his effectiveness in prayer. We must consider his dedication, especially his consistency in prayer throughout his life (Dan. 6:10); his determination to set his heart to walk in wholehearted obedience to God (Dan. 1:8); and his commitment to gain understanding of God's will for his generation (Dan. 10:12).

It is important to understand that Daniel's life of faithfulness did not earn God's power or greater effectiveness in prayer; rather, it positioned Daniel to live in greater agreement with God, and it was this agreement that impacted the effectiveness of his prayers. But the Old Testament is not the only place we find examples of effective prayer. The New Testament also has much to say about the quality of our lifestyles and their relationship to effective prayer. The essence of real faith is agreement with God—in our words, hearts, *and* lifestyles.

Daniel's prayers were offered by a man who was weak in the flesh just as we are. But through the blood of Jesus and our agreement with God, our prayers offered in weakness ascend to the throne of God in power just as Daniel's did.

CONSISTENCY IN PRAYER

The Scripture tells us that Daniel prayed three times a day. This was his custom from his youth: "Daniel...knelt down on his knees three times that day, and prayed and gave thanks before his God, as was his custom since early days" (Dan. 6:10). One of the great miracles of his life was his consistency in prayer for more than sixty years. He had begun praying in his youth, probably in his teen years.

If you are a young person reading this, I encourage you to follow Daniel's example and begin, or continue, having regular prayer times. You may be in your later years and regret the many years you have wasted, spiritually speaking, and think it is too late to start. But I have good news for you. It is never too late to start! We can begin today and make it our custom to be faithful in prayer for the rest of our days.

I think of the setbacks or disappointments that a young person often has in his or her twenties and thirties. Daniel suffered the same setbacks. The details were different, but the general disappointments surely were the same as those of other young people in other nations and in other generations. He refused to be offended by what God "did not do" for him in his young adult years or to become bitter toward those who mistreated or betrayed him, and he refused to be distracted from his prayer life by the great amount of work that came his way due to the rapid promotions in his political career.

Oh, the miracle of a life that stays consistent in seeking the Lord for decades in the face of the positive and negative experiences in life we all have! He must have said a million times, "No, I will not get off course; I will stay consistent in my prayer life."

I have no doubt that Daniel also faced pressures and opportunities in his fifties and sixties. It is easy for well-meaning, middle-aged believers to drift away from the commitment they made about their relationships with Jesus and specifically their prayer lives in their youths.

But despite the setbacks, resistance, pleasures, growing responsibilities, or wonderful opportunities throughout the years, Daniel remained steady in prayer. His consistency is one of the primary reasons he had such an effective prayer life in his eighties. It is also one of the reasons God used him as an example of a righteous, faithful intercessor.

Consider what God told the prophet Ezekiel:

> When a land sins against Me by persistent unfaithfulness, I will stretch out My hand against it…Even if these three men, Noah, Daniel, and Job, were in it, they would deliver only themselves…if I send a pestilence into that land and pour out My fury on it…even though Noah, Daniel, and Job were in it…they would deliver only themselves by their righteousness.
>
> —EZEKIEL 14:13–14, 19–20

Ezekiel was also a Jewish captive who lived in the city of Babylon. He received this message from the Lord when he was living in the Jewish "work camp" that was undoubtedly in the poor part of the city of Babylon, whereas Daniel lived in the king's court. Ezekiel knew Daniel worked in the royal court. They were men of like spirit even though they lived in two very different parts of the same city.

When God spoke to Ezekiel saying, "When a land sins against Me by persistent unfaithfulness…even if these three men prayed," He picked three of the mightiest intercessors—Noah, Daniel, and Job—to use as examples (vv. 13–14). One reason God picked them was for their righteous lifestyles—each stood alone in the midst of an evil generation. God highlighted them for taking a stand for righteousness in their generations. The Lord told Ezekiel that even if Noah, Daniel, and Job prayed for Israel, He would not deliver the nation at that time because Israel persisted in unfaithfulness and refused to repent.

He said it again in verse 20: "Even if Noah, Daniel, and Job…prayed, I would not save the whole nation of Israel." Noah and Job were no longer living, but Daniel was alive. Imagine the implications of this fact: Daniel is the only man in the Bible about whom God spoke audibly from heaven *while he was still alive*. In other words, God held him up as one who was faithful in prayer while he was living; yet in the Scripture we typically find the Lord honoring a person's dedication and godliness only after he has died.

WHOLEHEARTED OBEDIENCE

The record of Daniel's story in Scripture begins when Daniel was in his teen years. In those early days he purposed not to defile himself related to food or any pleasures: "But Daniel purposed in his heart that he would not defile himself with the portion of the king's delicacies, nor with the wine which he drank" (Dan. 1:8). The main point is not what specific food he avoided but that he determined to walk in wholehearted obedience in the face of peer pressure. He saw the lifestyle of other young people around him, but he made the choice not to live the way other young people lived.

Whether you are young or old, it is not too late to start. It is never too late to start. We can set our hearts to walk in wholehearted obedience beginning today. I encourage you to make that choice and to set your heart not to be defiled by food, immorality, porn, slander, lying about finances, or any other sin; and not to be too busy to spend time with God.

Daniel set his heart to not be defiled all his days. I am sure at the end of his life, when he stood before God, he had no regrets about giving up various pleasures. I am confident that he did not wish he had spent more time in recreation. On the last day when we all stand before Jesus, no one will regret having spent too little time playing video games or watching movies.

THE REWARD OF FAITHFULNESS

The Lord revealed His love to Daniel in a deep way through an angel, who addressed Daniel as the beloved of the Lord: "He [an angel] said to me, 'O Daniel, man greatly beloved…' He said, 'O man greatly beloved, fear not!'" (Dan. 10:11, 19).

I assume that receiving the understanding of how much God loved him was one of the most powerful things that happened to Daniel personally. The angel said, "O Daniel, greatly beloved." Imagine a high-ranking angel telling you, "The Lord greatly loves you, and you are beloved by your God"; in other words, "The

Lord is moved by the way you live. He is moved by your hunger for Him and by your lifestyle choices."

We know that God loves the world. He loves unbelievers, even though He does not enjoy a relationship with them. But there are those in whom God takes special delight; that is, He delights in the choices they make for Him. In this sense His love for them is different from that with which He loves the world. He takes greater enjoyment in those who seek to love and obey Him with all their hearts. And God clearly took great enjoyment in Daniel. In essence He told Daniel, "I am moved by the way you care about My kingdom and My glory and the way you care about who I am. That touches Me."

Jesus taught that the Father loves all who obey Him. He loves the relationship He has with all who keep His commandments, and He loves their life choices.

> He who has My commandments and keeps them, it is he who loves Me. And he who loves Me will be loved by My Father, and I will love him and manifest Myself to him.
>
> —JOHN 14:21

Lest we think that Jesus loves only those who love Him, let's remember that Scripture says God loved us first (1 John 4:19). But He loves the choices of those who love Him.

Jesus made the amazing statement that He would manifest Himself to those who show their love for Him in their words, actions, and lifestyles. No one is "good enough" to deserve a greater manifestation of God's glory. It's not about being good enough but about positioning ourselves to receive more from God.

Every believer can have a close relationship with the Lord. Daniel was forcibly taken to Babylon as a prisoner of war in his youth. Yet even as a captive, far from his home in Jerusalem and in a foreign culture, he determined to seek God with all his heart for all his days. Today the Lord is looking for men and women like Daniel, who will set their hearts to live before God as Daniel did.

Some people are easily offended. If they don't get on the worship team at their church or aren't hired for the job position they were hoping for, they ask, "How could God allow this to happen to me? It's so rough." Yes, your heart hurts, and the pain is real, but your response to life's trials and disappointments is the crucial issue.

Look at Daniel. He was taken into captivity, and yet he determined not to defile himself and to be a man of prayer all his days. He did not let any person or any disappointment steal the vision of what he was determined to be from his heart. He remained steady in His love for God and lived out his commitment in his daily life until he died.

In my forty years of ministry I have seen many people go hard after God for five or even ten years. Most of them were young and in their twenties. By the time they reached thirty-five, several had "good" reasons for drawing back and being more "practical." I have seen only a few people stay consistent in seeking

God with diligence for twenty or thirty years or more. Daniel stayed consistent in seeking God for sixty years, even during his time in the pagan city of Babylon.

I want the Lord to say to me on the last day, "I loved the way you spent your time and money and the way you obeyed Me; I loved the way that you loved Me." I want Him to be able to say the things about me that He said about Daniel. I want to be steady like this great man of God, even when I'm eighty. What about you?

PART III

DEVOTIONAL PRAYER

There is not a kind of life more sweet and delightful than that of a continual conversation with God.[1]
—Brother Lawrence

Chapter 14

PRAYERS *to* STRENGTHEN OUR INNER MAN

*Prayer wonderfully clears the vision; steadies the nerves; defines
duty; stiffens the purpose; sweetens and strengthens the spirit.*[1]
—S. D. GORDON

NOW THAT WE'VE considered some of the aspects of intercessory prayer, we turn to a study of devotional prayer—prayer that, as we learned in chapter 6, is related to our own spiritual renewal, growth, and communion with God. In this type of prayer we focus on growing in intimacy with God as we connect with Him through requesting strength in our inner man, meditating on the Word (pray-reading it), fellowshipping with the Holy Spirit, and appropriating God's names. In this chapter we will focus on requesting strength in our inner man.

In his letter to the Ephesians the apostle Paul wrote the following prayer:

> I bow my knees to the Father…that He would grant you…to be strengthened with might through His Spirit in the inner man.
> —EPHESIANS 3:14–16

This prayer for the Holy Spirit to strengthen the inner man of believers is one of the most important prayers recorded in the Scripture, and it is vital that we understand it if we want to grow in prayer. Let's begin by looking at what our inner man is.

The term *inner man* refers to a person's soul—his mind, emotions, and will. It is where we are most aware of our interaction with the Holy Spirit. Our highest calling in life is our fellowship with God, and what happens in our inner man is an essential aspect of that fellowship. Therefore, our inner man is the most important part of us.

In fact, our inner man is the only part of us that we will take into eternity. For this reason, praying to strengthen it should be one of our greatest priorities. Strengthening our inner man consists of renewing our minds and emotions by the grace of God as we talk to Him. Sadly I find that for many people, praying for strength in their inner man is often the most neglected part of their prayer lives.

When people think of prayer, they often think of praying for people or places, for justice issues, or to receive more things, such as money or more blessings in their circumstances. But rarely do I hear people talk about focusing their prayers on their own inner man, or heart. Prayer for our inner man includes growing in intimacy with Jesus—focusing on giving our love and devotion to God. This kind of prayer encompasses worship, fellowshipping with the Holy Spirit, and pray-reading the Word—including appropriating the names of God.

Just as our physical strength can increase or decrease, so can our spiritual strength. We cannot always discern the specific times when the Spirit strengthens us; He usually does so in small measures. Being strengthened in our inner man is similar to being strengthened by taking vitamins. Many of us have taken vitamins for years but cannot remember the precise day when we realized they were making a difference. However, we know that if we consistently take vitamins, they will strengthen us physically over time. It is the same with our inner man. If we ask regularly, the Spirit will release His might in our inner man (our mind, emotions, and will), and over time we will experience newfound strength. This divine strengthening of our hearts equips us to live in a godly way and enables us to stand against compromise, depression, fear, rejection, spiritual lethargy, and other negative emotions and behaviors.

Even when we do not feel strength in our inner man in an overt way, the Holy Spirit's power is working to influence our thoughts and emotions. A cancer patient who receives a radiation treatment may say to his doctor, "I didn't feel the power of the radiation during the treatment," but the doctor would assure the patient that it was nevertheless effective, even though he felt nothing.

Just as we must be intentional about taking vitamins daily if we want to experience their benefit over time, so we must be intentional about praying for the strengthening and development of our hearts in God. We will experience more of God's grace that renews our minds and emotions if we ask for it on a regular basis. I want to emphasize again the simple truth I mentioned in a previous chapter—God releases more blessing if we ask for it. In James 4:2 we are told, "You do not have because you do not ask." The Lord knows that we have needs, but He withholds many things until we ask Him.

Again, I repeat that not all the promises in the Bible are a *guarantee* of increased blessings; they are *invitations* to receive blessing based on our responses, and one important response is to ask for the release of these promises. For example, the Lord promised to put the fear of God in the lives of His people (Jer. 32:39–40). The promise is sure, but it takes the supernatural activity of the Holy Spirit for the fear of the Lord to actually grow in us. The Holy Spirit waits for us to ask Him to help us to grow in the fear of God. I encourage you to pray according to David's prayer in Psalm 86: "Unite my heart to fear Your name" (v. 11).

God has made similar promises related to strengthening our inner man, yet many believers continue, decade after decade, in unnecessary deficiency, because they do not ask the Lord to release these great promises. The Spirit will release far more strength in our hearts if we consistently ask Him for it. He waits for us to ask.

As I wrote earlier, a prayer list is a simple tool that helps us to focus in our prayer times. Below is one of my prayer lists, made up of ten prayers to receive strength in my inner man, using the acronym F-E-L-L-O-W-S-H-I-P. I encourage people to pray through this ten-letter acronym on a daily basis. All ten requests are based on promises or prayers in Scripture. The foundational request for these ten prayers is Paul's prayer that the Holy Spirit would strengthen believers with might in the inner man (Eph. 3:16). I have included a breakdown of what each letter in the acronym stands for, along with an explanation of its importance, related Scripture verses, and a sample prayer to serve as a pump primer in your own times with God.

F-E-L-L-O-W-S-H-I-P

F: Fear of God

The Lord promised that He would put His fear into the hearts of His people: "I will put My fear in their hearts so that they will not depart from Me" (Jer. 32:40). He will do this much and more if we ask. As we ask the Holy Spirit to impart the fear of God to our hearts, He unites our hearts to His heart in a way that causes us to have great awe of God (Ps. 86:11). It is far easier to resist sin and compromise when we feel even a small measure of the fear, or awe, of God in our hearts. I ask Him to cause me to delight in the fear of the Lord (Isa. 11:3), and I recommend that you ask Him to strike your heart with the majesty and awesome dread of God according to Isaiah 8:13, "The LORD of hosts, Him you shall hallow; let Him be your fear, and let Him be your dread."

Scriptures

I will put My fear in their hearts so that they will not depart from Me.
—JEREMIAH 32:40

Unite my heart to fear Your name.
—PSALM 86:11

The LORD…you shall hallow; let Him be your fear, and let Him be your dread.
—ISAIAH 8:13

Prayer

Father, release the spirit of the fear of God into my heart. Strike my heart with understanding of Your majesty that I may live in awe before You. Release Your presence with holy dread that causes my spirit to tremble before Your glorious majesty. Unite my heart to Your heart and Word, and cause me to delight in the fear of God.

E: Endurance

In the New Testament the words *endurance*, *perseverance*, and *patience* are often interchangeable. These words speak of being faithful in our God-given assignments and refusing to quit even when facing great pressures. The word *patience* means more than being kind to someone who is disturbing you or patiently listening to someone. Holy Spirit-empowered endurance enables us to seek and serve the Lord faithfully with all our strength for decades without drawing back.

It takes God's power touching our hearts and minds to keep us from drawing back in our zeal and wholeheartedness, and He is willing to help us. Ask the Lord to give you endurance to be faithful even in the difficult and dry seasons of life. Remember to ask the Spirit to impart endurance to you on the days that you commit to fast. Another way to ask for endurance is by asking God to impart zeal to your heart for His heart and His house (Ps. 69:9; John 2:17). Zeal and endurance go together—they are like two sides of the same coin.

Scriptures

> Being strengthened with all power...so that you may have great endurance and patience.
>
> —COLOSSIANS 1:11, NIV

> May the Lord direct your hearts into...the patience [endurance] of Christ.
>
> —2 THESSALONIANS 3:5

> Zeal for Your house will consume me.
>
> —JOHN 2:17, NAS

Prayer

> *Father, strengthen my heart with endurance, that I may faithfully do Your will with zeal and diligence and that I may never draw back in any way in my pursuit of the deeper things of Your heart. Give me endurance to fast regularly. Direct my heart into the patience, or endurance, in which Jesus walked. Give me strength to follow through in my commitments to You and to fulfill my ministry calling even when it is difficult or small.*

L: Love

The Holy Spirit's first agenda is to establish the first commandment in first place in the church so that we will love Jesus with all our hearts and strength. The command to love with all our hearts does not start with us but with God's love for His Son and His people. In fact, the Father will impart the very love that He has for Jesus into the hearts of those who long for it (John 17:26). It "takes God to love God." The grace to receive God's love and to love Him back is the greatest gift the Spirit imparts to us.

Paul prayed that love would abound in the church (Phil. 1:9). When we ask for our hearts to abound in love, we are actually asking for the Holy Spirit to inspire us in four ways. First, we are asking for greater understanding of God's love for us to abound in our hearts. Second, we are asking the Spirit to tenderize our hearts so that we abound in love for Jesus. Third, we are asking the Spirit to cause love for others to abound in our hearts. Fourth, we are asking the Spirit to help us abound in the same love for ourselves that God has for us. Jesus commands us, "Love your neighbor as yourself" (Matt. 22:39). One reason people hate their neighbors is that they hate themselves. When we see ourselves in the way that God sees us in Christ, we can abound in love even for ourselves in the grace of God.

Scriptures

I pray, that your love may abound still more.

—Philippians 1:9

You shall love the Lord...with all your heart.

—Mark 12:30

The love of God has been poured out in our hearts by the Holy Spirit.

—Romans 5:5

May the Lord make you increase and abound in love to one another.

—1 Thessalonians 3:12

As the Father loved Me, I also have loved you; abide in My love.

—John 15:9

...that the love with which You [the Father] loved Me [Jesus] may be in them.

—John 17:26

May the Lord direct your hearts into the love of God.

—2 Thessalonians 3:5

Prayer

Father, pour out Your love in my heart by the Holy Spirit that I may overflow in love back to You and to others (Rom. 5:5). I ask that You impart Your love for Jesus into my heart (John 17:26). I ask for grace to love God with all my heart, soul, mind, and strength (Mark 12:30). Allow me to comprehend Jesus's love for me and to abide in it—to stay focused on and connected to it (John 15:9). Let me see myself through Your eyes and love who You created me to be (Ps. 139:13–15).

L: Light of glory

On the day of Paul's dramatic conversion he saw Jesus and His glory in a great light from heaven. Paul recounts the story in Acts 22:6–11. As one who zealously persecuted the followers of Jesus, even condemning them to death, he came face-to-face with Jesus on the road to Damascus, when "suddenly a great light from heaven shone around [him]" (v. 6). Moses prayed, "Please, show me Your glory" (Exod. 33:18). Afterward his face shone with the light of glory.

Like Moses, we can ask to encounter the realm of God's glory. Jesus spoke of an open heaven in which His disciples would see the angels ascending and descending (John 1:51). Ask Him to shine the light of His countenance on your heart in such a way that you experience the supernatural realm of His glory, including receiving dreams and visions and seeing angels and so on.

Scriptures

> Suddenly a great light from heaven shone around me…And since I could not see for the glory of that light, being led by the hand of those who were with me, I came into Damascus.
>
> —ACTS 22:6, 11

> His countenance was like the sun shining in its strength.
>
> —REVELATION 1:16

> And he [Moses] said, "Please, show me Your glory."
>
> —EXODUS 33:18

> You shall see heaven open, and the angels of God ascending and descending.
>
> —JOHN 1:51

> The LORD opened the eyes of the young man…The mountain was full of [heavenly] horses and chariots of fire all around Elisha.
>
> —2 KINGS 6:17

> LORD, lift up the light of Your countenance upon us.
>
> —PSALM 4:6

> And it shall come to pass in the last days, says God, that I will pour out of My Spirit on all flesh; your sons and your daughters shall prophesy, your young men shall see visions, your old men shall dream dreams.
>
> —ACTS 2:17

Prayer

> *Father, let me see the light of Your glory and give me supernatural encounters—dreams, visions, angelic visitations, manifestations of Your glory and light—even as You gave to Moses, Isaiah, Ezekiel, Paul, John, and the disciples on the Day of Pentecost (Exod. 33–34; Isa. 6; Ezek. 1; Acts 2; Acts 9; Rev. 1).*

O: One thing

It is essential to spend quality time with the Lord in His Word—to be a man or woman of "one thing" as King David was. David revealed his solitary focus when he prayed: "One thing I have desired of the LORD, that will I seek: that I may dwell in the house of the LORD all the days of my life, to behold the beauty of the LORD, and to inquire in His temple" (Ps. 27:4).

Another inspiring example is Mary of Bethany, who "sat at Jesus' feet and heard His word" (Luke 10:39), while her sister, Martha, was "distracted with much serving" (v. 40). Jesus explained to Martha, "One thing is needed, and Mary has chosen that good part" (v. 42). We must intentionally set our hearts to be a "person of one thing." Ask the Holy Spirit to help you not to lose this focus by reminding you and intervening to speak to your heart when you start to drift away from the "one thing lifestyle." Ask Him to speak to you about it using Scripture, others, dreams, or His still, small voice to your heart. I pray this prayer regularly, and I am far more sensitized to receiving the Lord's help in the times when I begin to lose my "one thing focus."

Scriptures

> One thing I have desired...that I may dwell in the house of the LORD all the days of my life, to behold the beauty of the LORD.
> —PSALM 27:4

> But one thing is needed, and Mary has chosen that good part.
> —LUKE 10:42

> One thing I do...I press toward the goal for the prize of the upward call of God in Christ Jesus.
> —PHILIPPIANS 3:13–14

> I have set the LORD always before me; because He is at my right hand, I shall not be moved.
> —PSALM 16:8

Prayer

> *Father, I commit to live as a "person of one thing." Help me to sit regularly at Your feet to behold Your beauty as King David and Mary of Bethany did. Strengthen my desire in this, and help me to maintain a lifestyle that has regular times with You in Your Word. When I lose this focus, get my attention and send Your Word to alert and deliver me of a divided heart, even as You did for the saints in the early church (Rev. 2:4–5; 3:1–3, 15–20).*

W: Worthy

Paul wrote, "We also pray always...that our God would count you worthy of this calling, and fulfill all...His goodness" (2 Thess. 1:11). Paul emphasized that he always prayed this for the saints because he understood how important it was. Walking worthy before the Lord is not the same as seeking to be worthy by earning our forgiveness. Rather, it is about having a worthy response to God that prepares us to walk in the fullness of our callings, referred to as "[fulfilling]...all His goodness."

Too many believers come up short of what God has invited them to walk in because of their halfhearted responses and choices. Jesus urged us to pray that we would receive grace to walk worthy of His calling. Walking worthy of our callings implies receiving strength to escape compromise so that we may stand in victory before Him. Jesus encouraged us to "pray always that you may be counted worthy to escape all these things that will come to pass, and to stand before the Son of Man" (Luke 21:36). Paul prayed that God would sanctify His disciples completely and that they would walk in such a way as to be preserved blameless, or without compromise, until they met the Lord (1 Thess. 5:23).

Scriptures

> We also pray always for you that our God would count you worthy of this calling, and fulfill all the good pleasure of His goodness and the work of faith with power.
>
> —2 THESSALONIANS 1:11

> Pray always that you may be counted worthy to escape all these things that will come to pass, and to stand before the Son of Man.
>
> —LUKE 21:36

> Now may the God of peace Himself sanctify you completely; and may your whole spirit, soul, and body be preserved blameless [without any compromise] at the coming of our Lord Jesus Christ.
>
> —1 THESSALONIANS 5:23

...that He may establish your hearts blameless [victorious] in holiness before our God.

—1 Thessalonians 3:13

Create in me a clean heart, O God, and renew a steadfast spirit within me.

—Psalm 51:10

Search me, O God, and know my heart; try me, and know my anxieties.

—Psalm 139:23

Prayer

Father, strengthen my heart and mind so that I walk in a measure of faith and obedience that is worthy of who You are and of Your calling on my life. Help me to walk worthy of You by escaping all compromise. Prepare me for the highest things You have called me to. Help me to live free of compromise so that I will walk blamelessly in body, soul, and spirit in this age and be able to stand before You victoriously with the testimony that I sought to obey You with all my heart.

S: Speech

Speech is a very significant issue in our spiritual lives. When our speech comes under the leadership of the Holy Spirit, our entire inner man will also come under His leadership. James tells us, "If anyone does not stumble in word, he is a perfect man, able also to bridle the whole body" (James 3:2). Paul exhorted the saints not to speak any corrupt words or to grieve the Holy Spirit by filthy or foolish speech (Eph. 4:29–30; 5:4).

The subject of speech was also on David's "prayer list"—he asked the Lord to help him control the words of his mouth so that they would be pleasing to God. I encourage you to pray David's prayer often, even on a daily basis: "Let the words of my mouth and the meditation of my heart be acceptable in Your sight, O Lord, my strength and my Redeemer" (Ps. 19:14). David purposed that he would not sin with his speech. He asked the Lord to set a guard over his mouth (Ps. 17:3; 141:3).

Scriptures

If anyone does not stumble in word, he is a perfect man, able also to bridle the whole body.

—James 3:2

Let no corrupt word proceed out of your mouth, but what is good for necessary edification, that it may impart grace to the hearers. And do not grieve the Holy Spirit…Let it not even be named among you…neither filthiness, nor foolish talking, nor coarse jesting, which are not fitting.

—Ephesians 4:29–30, 5:3–4

Let the words of my mouth and the meditation of my heart be acceptable in Your sight.

—Psalm 19:14

Set a guard, O Lord, over my mouth; keep watch over the door of my lips.

—Psalm 141:3

I will guard my ways, lest I sin with my tongue; I will restrain my mouth with a muzzle.

—Psalm 39:1

Prayer

Father, set a guard over my lips and help me to speak only words that are pleasing to You. Free me from defensive, angry, foolish, sensual, or impure speech. Keep me from quenching the Spirit with my words. I set my heart not to sin with my speech that I may sustain unbroken communion with You.

H: Humility

Jesus called us to learn from Him about walking in humility, or lowliness of heart (Matt. 11:29). He is willing to teach us about this vital subject if we ask Him for understanding. Ask Him to teach you how to walk in humility. Oh, the glory and wisdom of learning humility from Jesus!

Scriptures

Take My yoke…and learn from Me, for I am gentle and lowly in heart.
—Matthew 11:29

Let nothing be done through selfish ambition or conceit, but in lowliness of mind let each esteem others better than himself. Let each of you look out not only for his own interests, but also for the interests of others. Let this mind be in you which was also in Christ Jesus.

—Philippians 2:3–5

Prayer

Jesus, teach me how to walk in Your yoke of humility and lowliness. I set my heart to learn lowliness of heart from You, gaining insight and inspiration that will result in the transformation of my attitudes, speech, and actions. Give me wisdom about how to carry my heart in humility.

I: Insight

The Holy Spirit desires to guide us into truth—to give us insight or wisdom into His will for every area of our lives so we are able to live in intimate partnership with His heart. It is insight that leads to intimacy. He longs to teach us how to walk in agreement with His heart so that we enjoy deep friendship and partnership with Him in the work of the kingdom. He will give us creative wisdom about how to steward our time, money, careers, ministry activities, and relationships. He will guide us in the specific ways that we pursue purity and health in our bodies, and so on. He will also give us insight into what is on His heart for our cities, nations, and generations. Receiving insight into His heart for all the areas of our lives leads us to a life of greater intimacy with God that walks out real partnership with Him.

Scriptures

The Spirit of truth…will guide you into all truth…He will tell you things to come.

—John 16:13

The Holy Spirit…will teach you all things.

—John 14:26

The secret of the Lord is with those who fear Him.

—Psalm 25:14

That the God…may give to you the spirit of wisdom and revelation in the knowledge of Him.

—Ephesians 1:17

We…ask that you may be filled with the knowledge of His will in all wisdom and spiritual understanding; that you may walk worthy of the Lord.

—Colossians 1:9–10

Prayer

Father, give me insight into Your Word, will, and ways. Give me wisdom about how to walk in intimacy with You in every area of my life, including my finances, schedule, emotions, circumstances, physical body (diet, health), relationships (in the home, office, ministry), future, fears, addictions, and so on. Let me know the secrets of Your heart (Ps. 25:14).

What are You thinking and feeling about me, my life, city, nation, and generation?

P: Peace and joy

The Holy Spirit desires to guard our hearts and minds with supernatural peace; we have only to ask Him. In Philippians 4:7 the "heart" speaks of our emotions. It is the inheritance of very believer to live in peace. We do not have to live with hearts that are troubled by jealousy, rejection, anxiety, or fear, or with minds that are filled with turmoil, confusion, and indecision. If we ask for peace and joy in specific areas of our lives, we will receive more of them.

Scriptures

> The peace of God…will guard your hearts and minds through Christ Jesus.
> —PHILIPPIANS 4:7

> Now may the God of hope fill you with all joy and peace in believing, that you may abound in hope by the power of the Holy Spirit.
> —ROMANS 15:13

> Now may the Lord of peace Himself give you peace always in every way.
> —2 THESSALONIANS 3:16

Prayer

> *Father, strengthen my heart with supernatural peace in areas in which I feel rejection, fear, or anxiety; strengthen my mind so I may overcome all turmoil, confusion, and indecision.*

Prayers to Receive Strength in the Inner Man Using the Acronym F-E-L-L-O-W-S-H-I-P

F — Fear of God: Father, release the spirit of the fear of God into my heart (Ps. 86:11).

E — Endurance: Strengthen my spirit with endurance to do Your will (Col. 1:11).

L — Love: Father, pour out Your love in my heart in a greater measure (Phil. 1:9).

L — Light of glory: Father, let me see more of the light of Your glory (Acts 22:6–11; Exod. 33:18; Ps. 4:6).

O — One thing: In my life focus, I choose to be a person of one thing who sits at Your feet (Ps. 27:4).

W — Count me worthy: Strengthen me to have a worthy response to God in my life (2 Thess. 1:11).

S — Speech: Father, set a guard over my lips that I may walk free from unclean speech (Eph. 4:29; Ps. 141:3).

H — Humility: Jesus, I want to learn from You how to walk with a lowly heart (Matt. 11:29).

I — Insight (wisdom): Give me insight into Your Word, will, and ways (Col. 1:9–10).

P — Peace and joy: Strengthen my heart with peace and joy that overpower fear (Phil. 4:7).

If you use these prayers faithfully to pray for strength in your inner man, you will be blessed by how you will grow in prayer and in your ability to sustain grace for all that God has called you to do. But you will not want to stop there in your journey of devotional prayer. There is great benefit to be gained from learning to fellowship with the Holy Spirit.

Chapter 15

FELLOWSHIPPING WITH *the* HOLY SPIRIT

You might as well try to hear without ears, or breathe without lungs, as to try to live a Christian life without the Spirit.[1]
—D. L. MOODY

PAUL WROTE OFTEN of the blessing of fellowshipping with the Holy Spirit. The verses below are an indication of the importance he placed on relating to Him. The first one is the closing of his second letter to the Corinthians, in which he prays that the fellowship of the Holy Spirit would be with the whole church in Corinth. The second is from his letter to the Philippians.

> May...the love of God, and the *fellowship of the Holy Spirit* be with you all.
>
> —2 CORINTHIANS 13:14, NIV

> If there is any...comfort of love, if any *fellowship of the Spirit*...
>
> —PHILIPPIANS 2:1

The Holy Spirit is a dynamic Person who lives inside our spirits. We are to fellowship, or commune, with Him by talking with Him often. We must deeply value and cultivate our friendship with the Spirit in an intentional way. One way to do this is by speaking to Him as the God who dwells within us. Some refer to this activity as contemplative prayer, communing prayer, centering prayer, or the prayer of quiet. There are other names for this type of prayer in various religious traditions.

A vibrant walk with the Spirit is essential in our quest to experience more of God. It is futile to seek deep experiences with God while neglecting the Spirit's leadership in our lives. We cannot go deep in God with a dull spirit. It is a glorious privilege for every believer to be able to fellowship with the Holy Spirit to the degree that he desires to.

Our greatest destiny is to grow in intimacy with the indwelling Spirit and thus share in the "family dynamics" of the Trinity. We are incredibly blessed that God has opened His inner life to His people so that we may have deep fellowship with Him. This is the essence of Christianity and of true prayer.

Many think of prayer mostly in terms of seeking God's help to solve their problems, to gain more blessings in their circumstances, or to meet their needs related to sickness, finances, unsaved family members, loneliness, fear, guilt, relational conflicts, and so on. But there is so much more to growing in prayer than making requests to meet our needs! Prayer is first and foremost a call to communion with the indwelling Spirit.

Another erroneous idea is that growing in prayer means saying more words. Yet another is that praying louder and with more energy is the way to achieve passion in our prayers. I have found great value in what I call "communing prayer," which is silent. In this type of prayer we set our gaze and attention on the indwelling Spirit and use words only sparingly.

I want to be a "person of the Spirit"—to know the Holy Spirit in my interior life as well as in my exterior ministry. Knowing Him involves much more than prophesying and healing the sick. Yes, I want to prophesy, heal the sick, lead people to Jesus, and pray the prayer of faith that releases blessing on others. But I also want to be a "man of the Spirit" in my interior life. We should all aspire to know the anointing of the Spirit on our ministries and on our hearts.

GOD CREATED US WITH THREE PARTS

God created every human being with three parts: a spirit, a soul, and a body. One preacher summarized this reality: "We are a spirit, we have a soul, and we live in a body." The apostle Paul confirmed it when he wrote, "May your whole spirit, soul, and body be preserved blameless" (1 Thess. 5:23).

Clearly our bodies are our physical selves. Our souls are our personalities, which consist of our minds, wills, and emotions—sometimes referred to as our "heart" in Scripture. Our spirit is where God literally dwells in us. These are the three parts of us that make it possible for us to commune with God.

God takes up residence in the human spirit at the new birth. The central reality of the new birth is that the Holy Spirit, a real person, comes to live in our born-again spirits. The new birth is much more than being forgiven. The uncreated life of God dwells in our spirits. Being born again involves being born into a new connectedness with the Holy Spirit.

> Unless one is born of…the Spirit, he cannot enter the kingdom…
> —JOHN 3:5

At the new birth our spirits are joined to the Holy Spirit so that we are one spirit with God. Therefore, the "Holy of Holies" is now in our spirits.

> But he who is joined to the Lord is one spirit with Him.
> —1 CORINTHIANS 6:17

The Spirit flows from your heart, which is translated as "belly" in the King James Version, and, more accurately, as "innermost being" in the New American Standard Bible.

He that believeth on Me…*out of his belly* shall flow rivers of living water.
—JOHN 7:38, KJV

He who believes…*from his innermost being* will flow rivers of living water.
—JOHN 7:38, NAS

Jesus promised that the Holy Spirit would flow like a river out of our hearts to inspire, direct, and transform our own minds and emotions and to minister to others in power. God comes to live in our born-again spirits in fullness at the new birth, yet the measure with which He expresses Himself in our minds and emotions grows progressively. The more we actively engage our minds with the indwelling Spirit, the more our minds and emotions are renewed, and thus we are "transformed by the renewing of [our minds]" (Rom. 12:2). In other words, the more our minds and hearts are renewed, the more God expresses Himself in and through us.

Now back to fellowshipping with the Spirit. The language of our minds is images. When we think of anything, we think of it as an image or picture. Because the Scripture describes God as light (1 John 1:5), we can think of light as being inside our born-again spirits where the Holy Spirit dwells. Therefore, I think of the Holy Spirit as the Shekinah glory of God dwelling in our spirits.

When I talk to the Holy Spirit, I picture Him as a bright and glorious light. I picture a bright, diamondlike, glorious person shining brightly in my spirit. (I am sure that is not exactly how it is, but this image helps me to focus.) I set my mind on Him and speak to Him directly. As we see in John 16:14, focusing on the Spirit will always lead us to glorify and obey Jesus and His Word: "He will glorify Me, for He will take of what is Mine and declare it to you." Some false religions speak of gazing into a light inside all humans, but they present a counterfeit because they do not possess the indwelling Spirit and do not lead people to love and obey Jesus.

WALKING IN THE SPIRIT

In Galatians 5 Paul exhorted us to walk in the Spirit, which we do primarily by developing a dynamic friendship with Him, and then immediately gave us one of the great promises in Scripture, "you shall not fulfill the lust of the flesh."

I say then: Walk in the Spirit, and you shall not fulfill the lust [sinful desires] of the flesh. For the flesh lusts [wars] against the Spirit, and the Spirit against the flesh.
—GALATIANS 5:16–17

What Paul was saying is that walking in the Spirit is the primary way to walk in victory over our flesh.

In our war against sin and darkness we are to focus on Jesus by the indwelling Holy Spirit. We should put more focus on walking in the Spirit than on denying our sinful desires. The way to walk in freedom from the desires is by walking in the Spirit, not by focusing on the desires themselves and gritting our teeth to say no to them. Rather than putting our best efforts into resisting the darkness (denying sinful desires), we remove the darkness by simply turning on the light, by focusing on "Christ in [us], the hope of glory" (Col. 1:27).

In Galatians 5:17 Paul described the war inside every believer: the flesh wars against the Spirit, and the Spirit wars against the flesh. The "flesh" in Paul's theology includes sinful pleasures (sensuality, gluttony, alcoholism, and so on) and sinful emotions (pride, bitterness, anger, defensiveness, and so on). In all he identified seventeen expressions of the flesh (vv. 19–21). Paul did not promise us that all fleshly desires would be gone; he said we would have the power to avoid fulfilling them.

The only way to overcome the power of sinful desires is to grow in our relationship with the Holy Spirit by being actively engaged with Him. In other words, walking in the Spirit is the primary condition for overcoming these desires. The Spirit will war against them if we engage with the indwelling Spirit in a personal way. He will go to battle with power against our fleshly desires.

The way to walk in the Spirit is by fellowshipping with the Spirit. It is as simple as can be. *We walk in the Spirit to the degree that we talk to the Holy Spirit.* When was the last time you talked to the Holy Spirit as a person living in your spirit?

We will not *walk* in the Spirit more than we *talk* to the Spirit. This is so critical to understand and practice. That is why I am saying it in this chapter in different ways. Actually we will not *obey* Him more than we talk to Him. My understanding of what Jesus said in John 15:5 is, "Apart from connectedness with Me—abiding in Me—you cannot do *anything.*"

He will not force us into the conversation, but if we talk to Him, He will talk back. Once we begin the conversation, He will continue it as long we as we do. He speaks to us by giving us subtle impressions that release power in our minds and hearts.

The more we talk to the Spirit, the less we talk to people in a way that quenches the Holy Spirit, our spirits, or their spirits.

> Let no corrupt word proceed out of your mouth, but what is good for necessary edification, that it may impart grace to the hearers. *And do not grieve the Holy Spirit.*
> —Ephesians 4:29–30

As I talk to the Spirit more, I talk to others with more grace in a way that edifies them. When I talk to the Spirit less, then I talk to others less in a way that edifies them and more in a way that quenches their spirits, my spirit, and God's Spirit.

TALKING TO THE HOLY SPIRIT

Now that we know how important it is to fellowship with the Holy Spirit, let's look at how we can go about it. In prayer we can focus our minds on God in two ways—on the Father, who sits on His glorious throne (Rev. 4), and on God the Holy Spirit, who lives in our spirits (Rom. 8:9).

> In this manner, therefore, pray: Our Father in heaven…
> —MATTHEW 6:9

> The Spirit of God dwells in you…If Christ is in you, the body is dead because of sin, but the Spirit is life because of righteousness.
> —ROMANS 8:9–10

The Spirit longs for us to talk with Him, but He will not force conversation or friendship on those who are not interested. When we talk to Him, He will talk back to us. Often when He "talks," He does not use words but rather gives us impressions, sensitizes our emotions so we can feel His nearness, or speaks through His Word. God leads us by the still, small voice in our inner man—the same still, small voice He used to speak to Elijah in 1 Kings 19:11–13.

Sadly many believers do not talk to the indwelling Holy Spirit, thus depriving themselves of a most precious relationship. Saint Augustine testified that he lost much time seeking the Lord outwardly instead of turning inward. One of my favorite prayers—the one I use most often—is asking the Spirit to let me see what He sees and feel what He feels about my life, my family, and other people, as well as what He sees and feels about Jesus, the church, the great harvest, the nations, the end times, and so on.

Get started

To get started, I suggest talking directly to the Spirit three to five times a day for three to five minutes each time. If we talk to the Spirit only when we are tempted rather than as a lifestyle, then we will not sustain our dialogue with Him in a way that results in our being changed. At first it may be difficult to bring your mind to focus on the indwelling Spirit. As you do it more often, you will become accustomed to withdrawing inwardly to speak to the Spirit. If your mind wanders, simply turn it back to the indwelling Spirit again.

Linger in God's presence

In dialoguing with the indwelling Spirit, take time to linger, speaking slowly to Him. Include declarations of your love for Him. Speak slowly, with occasional whispers of "I love You, Holy Spirit," while gently and intermittently praying in the Spirit.

We practice the presence of God, knowing that it takes time to grow in our sense of connectedness with the indwelling Spirit. The more I speak directly to Him in private, the more I sense His presence in my public life with others.

I picture the Spirit shining with a diamondlike brilliance. I say, "Thank You for Your bright presence in me." Do not rush, and do not be wordy. He enjoys us when we recognize His indwelling presence. I know this because I can feel His pleasure when I acknowledge Him.

I linger with my attention turned inward to Him. As I speak to the Holy Spirit, I do not fire off my prayers in rapid succession; I speak short, simple phrases to Him, slowly and softly. It is important to wait with a listening heart. Sometimes I will gently sigh as I pray with subtle "groanings which cannot be uttered" (Rom. 8:26) in between moments of total silence. I do this much more than I speak words.

T-R-U-S-T

I regularly use five simple phrases to focus my conversation with the indwelling Spirit. The five-letter acronym, T-R-U-S-T, helps me remember the phrases. I try to pray through them on a daily basis.

T: Thank You

The first thing we do is turn our attention inward to recognize the Holy Spirit's presence and simply thank Him for His indwelling presence. I say, "Thank You, Holy Spirit, for Your indwelling presence in my spirit." Take a few minutes to do this, adding affectionate phrases such as, "I love You, Holy Spirit. I enjoy Your presence."

Scriptures

> He who abides in Me, and I in him, bears much fruit; for without Me you can do nothing.
>
> —John 15:5

Prayer

> *Thank You, Holy Spirit, for Your bright presence in me. I love Your presence. Apart from You, I can do nothing.*

R: Release revelation of Your glory

I ask the Spirit to release revelation of the realm of God's glory and heart.

> That...the Father of glory may give to you the spirit of wisdom and revelation in the knowledge of Him, the eyes of your understanding being enlightened.
>
> —Ephesians 1:17–18

This is a request with significant biblical precedents. As I mentioned in the previous chapter, Paul saw Jesus and His glory in a great light from heaven on the day of his conversion. Moses prayed, "Please, show me Your glory" (Exod.

33:18). Afterward his face shone with the light of glory. Like Moses, we can ask
to encounter the realm of God's glory.

Scriptures

> Suddenly a great light from heaven shone around me…And since I
> could not see for the glory of that light, being led by the hand of those
> who were with me, I came into Damascus.
> —ACTS 22:6, 11

> And he [Moses] said, "Please, show me Your glory."
> —EXODUS 33:18

Prayer

> *Holy Spirit, open my eyes to see the realm of God's glory and to encounter
> His heart. I ask You to release revelation of Your glory to me.*

U: Use me

Paul exhorted us to seek diligently to be used in the gifts of the Holy Spirit
(1 Cor. 12:31). The Spirit will use us more if we ask Him to.

> The manifestation of the Spirit is given to each one for the profit of all.
> —1 CORINTHIANS 12:7

> But earnestly desire the best gifts.
> —1 CORINTHIANS 12:31

> Desire spiritual gifts, but especially that you may prophesy.
> —1 CORINTHIANS 14:1

Prayer

> *Thank You for Your gifts. Release them in me in a greater measure,
> for the Word says that each person is given manifestation of the Spirit.
> Release Your impressions in me to bless people today. Holy Spirit, release
> the manifestation of Your gifts and power through me to help others. I
> desire to be a vessel of Your presence to glorify Jesus.*

S: Strengthen me

The Spirit will strengthen our inner man by touching our minds, emotions,
and speech with the might of His presence. We can draw on His strength by
thanking Him for causing it to be manifest in us. Because the Spirit lives in us,
the fruit of the Spirit—love, joy, peace, and so on—is available to us. Thus, we
can experience more of the power of this fruit by thanking Him that it is already
in us.

Scriptures

> That He would grant you, according to the riches of His glory, to be strengthened with might through His Spirit in the inner man.
>
> —Ephesians 3:16

> The fruit of the Spirit is love, joy, peace, longsuffering, kindness, goodness, faithfulness, gentleness, self-control.
>
> —Galatians 5:22–23

Prayer

> *Holy Spirit, release divine might to strengthen my mind and emotions. Thank You for the presence of Your love, peace, and patience in me.*

T: Teach me

The indwelling Spirit is the great teacher who is committed to lead us into God's will and ways so that we are able to live in deep partnership with Him. Ask the Spirit to teach you about God's Word, will, and ways by giving you wisdom and creative ideas for every area of your life, including how to steward your money, prosper in your career, manage your time and schedule, prosper in relationships (in your home, church, office, ministry), function in ministry, and walk in purity and health (physically and emotionally).

He will guide us in ways that help us walk in holiness, have health in our bodies, and so on. Receiving His insight for our lives leads to a life of intimacy with God that walks out real partnership with Him.

Scriptures

> The Holy Spirit…will teach you all things.
>
> —John 14:26

> The Spirit of truth…will guide you into all truth.
>
> —John 16:13

Prayer

> *Holy Spirit, I ask You to lead me and teach me in every area of my life. Give me new ideas, order my steps, and open doors for new relationships and new business and ministry opportunities. Teach me how to live in a manner that is pleasing to You, and show me how best to walk in Your will, blessing, and prosperity for my life.*

Having an intimate relationship with the Holy Spirit will be of value to you in numerous ways. One of the most significant will be helping you to understand God's Word and incorporate it into your prayer life.

Chapter 16

HOW *to* PRAY-READ *the* WORD

The Word of God is the food by which prayer is nourished.[1]
—E. M. BOUNDS

WHEN JESUS WAS on Earth, He rebuked the Pharisees for thinking they were experiencing God life simply because they knew the Scriptures:

> You search the Scriptures, for in them you think you have eternal…life; and these are they which testify of Me. But you are not willing to *come to Me* [talk with Me] *that you may have life.*
> —JOHN 5:39–40

He was saying, in essence, "You study and search the Scriptures, but you are not willing to come to Me in ongoing, deep relationship that you may experience God's presence."

It is not enough just to study the Word; we must talk to God and receive from Him as we read. Bible study is meant to create an active dialogue in our hearts with God. The most substantial way in which we gain strength in our prayer lives is by feeding on the Word of God. This includes engaging in conversation with God as we read His Word.

Please don't misunderstand. I am a serious advocate of Bible study. But I strongly maintain that it is not mostly about gaining information and facts; it is about having an active dialogue or ongoing conversation with Jesus.

Scripture gives us the conversational material for our prayer lives. Talking to God as we read the Word makes prayer easy and enjoyable. We speak the truths of God's Word back to God as we read.

When I look back on forty years of walking with the Lord, I realize that pray-reading the Word—using the Scripture as the "conversational material" for my communication with Jesus—*has been the single most significant activity in my spiritual life.* This simple activity is essential to abiding in Christ.

I vividly remember the day when John 5:39–40 hit me like a bolt of lightning and radically shifted my understanding of prayer. I was eighteen years old at the time and was just beginning my college years. I had been faithful to set aside time for daily prayer and Bible study, but as I said earlier in this book, my prayer times were very boring. Then I came across the passage in John that quotes Jesus as rebuking the Pharisees for searching the Scriptures trying to find life in Bible knowledge instead of in relationship with Him. They diligently studied the Bible without connecting to God. They focused on the written Word but neglected Jesus, the living Word. This passage described me perfectly.

It suddenly became clear to me that I was seeking to find life and experience the presence of God just by studying the Scripture and gaining more Bible information. I came to understand that the Scripture is like a "neon sign" pointing to Jesus. It testifies of Him. It tells us what His heart is like. Then I read verse 40: "You are not willing to come to Me so that you may have life." When I read that they would not come to Him, I instantly understood it to mean they did not talk to Him. Right then I got it—I needed to come to Jesus, to talk to Him, as I read the Bible. Coming to Jesus in this context speaks of more than having our sins forgiven. It is a call to commune with Him as we read the Bible.

In that moment I understood that as I read, I am to move from a purely "study mode" to a "dialogue mode" and begin to talk to Jesus, the Word made flesh, through His written Word. I exclaimed, "Jesus, from now on I will talk to You when I read the Bible." The light went on that day, and I began my journey into what I term "pray-reading" the Word. I started that very hour, talking to Him over each phrase as I read the Word. I could feel His presence, and I liked it. And it was amazing how things changed in my spiritual life! I began to love God's Word. This was a new feeling. I was filled with anticipation about where this practice might lead me.

It is now forty years later, and I have been on a glorious journey and adventure with Jesus and His Word all that time. I am not saying that it is glorious every time I read the Word. Some days when I pray-read the Bible it feels dull, but usually it is alive. This became my new way forward, and I stayed with it.

I believe you will have the same experience I did. Change will come, and you will begin to love reading the Word and praying. The change may not occur in a day; it will probably develop over time. But stay with it. I am certain you will be glad you did and that the effort will be worth it.

In time God's words will abide, or live, in your heart, as Jesus promised: "If you abide in Me, and My words abide in you, you will ask what you desire, and it shall be done for you" (John 15:7). In other words, the Scripture will impact your mind and emotions, and, thus, your prayer life will grow. His Word will form new desires in you as it equips you to receive direction in prayer from the Holy Spirit. Prayer will become enjoyable and more effective as you allow the Word to abide more in your heart.

Two Categories of Scripture to Pray-Read

There are two broad categories of Scripture related to pray-reading the Word: promises to believe and exhortations to obey. Scriptures that focus on *promises to believe* are passages that declare truths such as God loves, God forgives, God leads, God protects, and God provides for us. Scriptures that focus on *exhortations to obey* are passages that command us to walk in love and purity, humble ourselves to others, bridle our speech, serve others, give time and money to God, and so on.

Promises to believe

When we come across a promise to believe while reading the Word, we turn it into conversation with Jesus. There are many verses with promises to believe such as "God loves His people" or "God forgives us" or "God will provide for us or guide us."

When I come across a promise to believe, I do two things: *I thank God for that truth*, and I ask the Holy Spirit to *give me more understanding of it*. I speak to the Father, Son, and Holy Spirit interchangeably, rather than being overly concerned about which one I should address. Let's take John 15:9 as an example.

As the Father loved Me, I also have loved you; abide in My love.

First, we thank God for a particular truth—we turn it into a simple declaration of thanksgiving or trust. When reading that Jesus loves you as the Father loves Him, for example, simply pray: "Thank You, Jesus, that You love me with the same intensity with which the Father loves You." I often feel God's presence when I talk to the Holy Spirit in this way. He enjoys it when we engage in conversation with Him. Over time you will sense an increase of the presence of the Holy Spirit touching your heart as you make prayer-statements like this to Him.

We do exactly the same thing with other promises in the Word related to God's forgiving or leading or protecting or providing for us. Pray, "Father, thank You that You forgive me" or "Holy Spirit, thank You that You will lead me" or "Holy Spirit, I trust that You will provide for me and protect me."

Second, we ask God for understanding about a specific truth. While reading that Jesus loves you as the Father loves Him, for example, you can pray, "Jesus, give me more understanding about how You love me with the same intensity with which the Father loves You."

We do the same thing with other promises. We pray, "Show me more about how You forgive me" and "Holy Spirit, give me more insight into Your leadership over my life." We ask, "Jesus, reveal more to me about the certainty of Your provision in my life" and "Father, release Your promised guidance, provision, and protection."

It is so simple to do this, yet the impact on us over time is significant. Beloved, I guarantee that talking to the Father, Jesus, and the Holy Spirit in the way I just described will transform your relationship with God!

Exhortations to obey

When we come across an exhortation to obey while reading the Word, we turn it into conversation with Jesus just as we do a promise. Many verses exhort us to obey related to our time, money, speech, work, attitudes, food, drink, eyes, sexuality, service, relationships, and so on.

When I read an exhortation to obey, I do two things—*I commit myself to obey* that truth, and I ask the Holy Spirit *to help me*. Again, I speak to the Father, Son, and Holy Spirit interchangeably. Let's again take John 15:9 as our example.

As the Father loved Me, I also have loved you; abide in My love.

In this verse we are exhorted to abide in His love. This exhortation for us to obey involves several things and has specific actions for us to take. For instance, it means to live in His love and to dwell on it continually by searching it out and going deep in our understanding of it. It will take time and focus to obey this particular truth. (I personally believe that this is the most important exhortation of Jesus in the Bible.)

First, we commit to obey a particular truth—we make simple declarations of resolve to obey it. In this case we simply pray, "Jesus, I commit to abide in Your love. I will study and search out this truth from Your Word." I may take twenty or thirty seconds to recommit myself to obey this exhortation to abide in His love.

We do the same thing with other exhortations in the Word. For example, you can pray, "Father, I commit to obey You with the use of my time and money" or "Holy Spirit, I will submit to Your leadership over my sexuality, and I commit to avoid looking at anything that stirs up lust." We declare, "Jesus, I commit to serve You and Your people with diligence and humility, even when no one is looking" and "Holy Spirit, I commit to Your leadership over my speech, even with regard to blessing my enemies."

Second, we ask God to empower us to obey a particular truth. We ask Him to help us by giving us wisdom, motivation, and power to obey in specific areas. For example, when reading that we are to abide in love, simply pray: "Jesus, help me to abide in Your love."

We do the same thing with other exhortations. For example, you can pray, "Lord, help me to use my time and money in the way You desire me to" and "Holy Spirit, help me to obey Your leadership over my speech and in all my relationships."

One very important verse that I have drawn strength from throughout my life is the one that says Job made a covenant with his eyes not to look on anything that would stir up lust in his heart (Job 31:1). I have made and remade that covenant many times since my youth. I tell God, "Lord, I make this covenant with my eyes to obey You; Holy Spirit, please help me to obey consistently."

Whenever I commit my heart in a new way, I ask God to help me obey. It is just that simple, yet the impact is real. I often feel God's presence when I talk to the Holy Spirit like this.

BENEFITS OF PRAY-READING

I believe the teaching of the prophet Hosea supports the practice of pray-reading the Word. He told us to "take words with us" when we come to the Lord in prayer.

Take words with you, and return to the LORD. Say to Him, "Take away
all iniquity; receive us graciously, for we will offer the sacrifices of our
lips [words of love, trust, and obedience]."

—HOSEA 14:2

Taking words with us is an important principle to follow when we give our
hearts to God. Do not underestimate the value of taking Bible words into your
prayer times. They do not have to be in the form of a direct Bible quote, but open
your Bible and make that your conversational material. And as you bring your
short prayers to God, remember to express your affection for Him by occasionally saying, "Jesus, I love You as I seek to obey You" and other similar phrases.

As we articulate our love, gratitude, and requests to Jesus in simple phrases,
the Holy Spirit will touch our lives. By talking with God daily in this way, we
will find that the Word of God becomes a living document. Talking to God as
we pray-read the Word is a practical way to strengthen our abiding in Christ
(John 15).

In addition, when you pray the Word, you and the Holy Spirit flow together
to provide you with teaching that is tailor-made for you. The Scripture confirms
that the anointing of the Spirit in you is the best teacher:

The anointing which you have received from Him abides in you, and you
do not need that anyone teach you; but as the same anointing teaches
you concerning all things…

—1 JOHN 2:27

What do I mean? Simply that when we talk to God as I have described, we
will end up saying things to Him that will be new to us. Actually it is the Holy
Spirit speaking through us to God and giving new insights—ones that come out
of our own mouths.

I have learned many new things in the Scripture by simply praying Bible passages back to God. In the process I have seen new things in old, familiar passages.
These fresh insights have come out of my own lips as I have spoken them to the
Lord in times of prayer. The Holy Spirit in me is teaching me. He loves to teach
us, especially as we talk to Him.

PRACTICAL REMINDERS

As is the case with other forms of prayer, we will pray-read the Word much more
if we schedule time for it. If we pray-read only when opportunity presents itself,
then we will not do it nearly as much. While you are pray-reading the Word, I
encourage you to speak:

+ Slowly and softly (not shouting or preaching at the indwelling
  Spirit)

- Briefly (short phrases, not paragraphs)

- Minimally (listen more than talk)

- With many pauses (occasionally be silent)

- With gently sighing (Rom. 8:26) and praying in the Spirit (1 Cor. 14:2, 18)

Take time to linger in God's presence and to speak affectionately to Him (intermittently say to God, "I love You"). And take time to journal—to record your thoughts and prayers as you pray-read through Scripture. Journaling will help you capture the truths the Holy Spirit gives you and develop language to talk with God. I try to always have my notepad or laptop with me in my prayer times so I can journal.

Pray-Reading the Descriptions of Jesus

I especially enjoy pray-reading the passages about Jesus in the Book of Revelation, which contains thirty different descriptions of Him (see chapters 1–3). There is no place in Scripture where Jesus is revealed with more depth and diversity than in these three chapters. Here Jesus revealed Himself through His appearance and the names He used. Remember, it is not enough to study these thirty descriptions; we must talk to Jesus as we read them. In this way the Spirit will reveal more to us about Jesus.

I use the acronym A-R-K to pray through the descriptions of Jesus. I like the word "ark" because in the Old Testament it refers to the place where God's presence dwelt and also speaks of a place of safety: Noah's ark was kept safe during the Flood. By encountering Jesus in these thirty descriptions, we can experience the ark of His presence as well as the ark of His safety. Proverbs tells us, "The name of the Lord is a strong tower; the righteous run to it and are safe" (Prov. 18:10). How do we find safety in His name? One practical way is that when our hearts are strong, we are calm in the storms of pressure and temptation. Remaining calm allows us to make good decisions during these storms instead of poor ones driven by fear, panic, confusion, or lust.

A-R-K stands for "agreement," "revelation," and "keep the prophecy." These are the three aspects of the prayers we offer related to the descriptions of Jesus.

A: Agreement

First, we agree with who Jesus is in a very specific way. For example, let's take the description of Jesus as the faithful witness: "Jesus Christ, the faithful witness, the firstborn from the dead" (Rev. 1:5). We express our agreement by simply declaring to Jesus—with affection and gratitude—that He is the faithful witness. For example, pray, "Jesus, I thank You that You are the faithful witness of what the Father is like and of all truth." It is the same simple principle we covered earlier in this chapter. By speaking out our agreement with specific aspects of Jesus's personhood, we gain inspiration and insight that equip us to know and love Him more. And again, it is so simple, but the impact on our hearts is significant.

R: Revelation

Second, we ask for revelation of Jesus according to each of the thirty descriptions based on Paul's prayer that "the Father of glory may give to [us] the spirit of wisdom and revelation in the knowledge of Him" (Eph. 1:17). For example, ask the Holy Spirit to reveal Jesus to you as the faithful witness—to give you more insight into this aspect of who He is. Pray, "Holy Spirit, show me the glory of Jesus as the faithful witness." By asking for more understanding of the specific aspects of Jesus's personhood, we will continually receive more and more.

K: Keep the prophecy

Finally, we respond in practical ways as we ask for the Spirit's help to "keep the prophecy," as Revelation 22:7 encourages us to do: "Blessed is he who keeps the words of the prophecy of this book." Keeping the prophecy refers to acting on the commands and plans of Jesus described in the Book of Revelation. We apply them to our lives by responding in faith and obedience to the specific truths about His name. We keep the prophecy by responding in three ways:

+ By *obeying* the commands of God that are implied in the thirty descriptions of Jesus

+ By *saying* the message of God as we proclaim the main truths that are related to the descriptions

+ By *praying* for the power of God to empower us to follow through in obeying and saying all that is implied by the descriptions

EXAMPLES OF USING A-R-K

Revelation 1:5 contains two descriptions of Jesus that we can pray-read, "faithful witness" and "firstborn from the dead":

Jesus Christ, the faithful witness, the firstborn from the dead...

Here's how we can pray about these descriptions using the three aspects of A-R-K:

Jesus as the faithful witness

Agreement:

Jesus, I thank You that You are the faithful witness of what the Father is like and of all truth. You are the truth. I thank You that You always tell the truth. I trust what You say because You are reliable. You took a stand for truth that cost Your reputation and life. Thank You for being faithful to the end. I love You and Your faithfulness.

Revelation:

Holy Spirit, reveal Jesus to me as the faithful witness—give me more insight into this glorious truth.

Keep the prophecy:

I commit to speak the truth, regardless of what it costs me. Holy Spirit, help me to speak up for the truths that are not popular.

Jesus as the firstborn from the dead

Agreement:

Jesus, You are the firstborn from the dead. I thank You that You have supremacy over all, that You have power over death itself.

Revelation:

Holy Spirit, reveal Jesus to me as God's firstborn. Teach me more about His supremacy over all things, including death.

Keep the prophecy:

Jesus, I will serve You as the One who is preeminent, by obeying You and drawing others to You instead of to me. I set my heart to live in light of the Resurrection. Holy Spirit, please help me to walk out this commitment.

Are you beginning to see how much your relationship with God will blossom as you invest time in devotional prayer? At the same time, your power in prayer, understanding of the Word, and effectiveness in prayer will greatly increase. You can up the power level even more by learning to appropriate God's names and all that they represent.

Chapter 17

APPROPRIATING GOD'S NAMES

Shut the world out, withdraw from all worldly thoughts and occupations, and shut yourself in alone with God, to pray to Him in secret. Let this be your chief object in prayer: to realize the presence of your heavenly Father.[1]
—ANDREW MURRAY

I WAS DEEPLY IMPACTED years ago by Larry Lea's best-selling book on prayer, *Could You Not Tarry One Hour?*, in which he taught millions of people how to appropriate God's covenant names in prayer. In this chapter I will share a few insights from his book because I believe appropriating God's names is a powerful way to grow in prayer.

Jesus taught us to pray that the Father's name be "hallowed" (Matt. 6:9). *To hallow* God's name means "to sanctify or set apart or praise it." "Hallowed be Your name" means "May Your name be sanctified or praised." In prayer we sanctify God's name by declaring it with a spirit of praise for the various truths implied by His name.

So how do we appropriate God's names? We declare them with faith and adoration in prayer. This activity results in the power and blessing associated with those truths being released in our lives.

When God gave Moses a special revelation of Himself, He used the name "YHWH," or as it is sometimes written, "Jehovah." This is God's covenant name, or the name He uses to emphasize His covenant with His people. This name was first given to Moses at the burning bush (Exod. 3:13–15), where God revealed Himself as the eternal God, who is self-existent, unchangeable, and transcendent. The Lord said, "I AM THAT I AM" (KJV). The Hebrew scribes considered this name too sacred to be spoken, so they used only four letters—"YHWH" or "JHVH"—to denote this unmentionable name of God, which is written in English as either "Yahweh" or "Jehovah."

Jehovah is the Latin spelling of the Hebrew *Yahweh*, which is often translated and written as "Lord." This is the personal name of God, and it is based on the four Hebrew consonantal letters Y-H-W-H (J-H-V-H) with the vowels of *Adonai* (Hebrew for "Lord") inserted. The Jewish scribes used the vowels of the name "Adonai" to remind the readers to say "Adonai" instead of "YHWH." This name, "YHWH," is based on the verb "to be" and can be translated with the sense of "the One who eternally exists."

In other words, English Bibles use "the LORD," "Jehovah," or "Yahweh" for this name of God, "I AM THAT I AM," which can be rendered, "I am with you, ready to save and to act, just as I have always been." The name "Yahweh" or "Jehovah" implies God's intimate presence and desire to save and to act on behalf of His people. It is important to notice that many English translations of the Bible put LORD (in all caps) to indicate YHWH, and they put Lord (without caps) as a translation of *Adonai*.

In the Old Testament eight names of God are compounded with the covenant name "Jehovah" ("Yahweh"): *Jehovah-Tsidkenu, Jehovah-M'kaddesh, Jehovah-Shammah, Jehovah-Shalom, Jehovah-Rophe, Jehovah-Jireh, Jehovah-Nissi,* and *Jehovah-Rohi.* All eight compound names reveal an aspect of the character of God and correspond to promises in the New Testament.

Some translations of the Bible use the name "Yahweh" or "the Lord" in place of "Jehovah" in the following names:

+ *Jehovah-Tsidkenu*: The Lord our righteousness

+ *Jehovah-M'kaddesh*: The Lord who sanctifies

+ *Jehovah-Shammah*: The Lord is there

+ *Jehovah-Shalom*: The Lord is peace

+ *Jehovah-Rophe*: The Lord heals

+ *Jehovah-Jireh*: The Lord's provision shall be seen

+ *Jehovah-Nissi*: The Lord my banner

+ *Jehovah-Rohi*: The Lord my shepherd

The Lord Jesus is our righteousness, sanctifier, peace, healer, provider, shepherd, banner, and the present One within us. These Old Testament names of God reveal different dimensions of His character that are expressed in Jesus, including five benefits given to us through Jesus's death.

+ Sin: forgiveness of sin

+ Spirit: fullness of the Holy Spirit

+ Soundness: health and healing

+ Success: freedom from the law's curse of failure and insufficiency

+ Security: freedom from the fear of death and hell

Jehovah-Tsidkenu

The name *Jehovah-Tsidkenu* (sid-kay'-noo), "the Lord our righteousness" (Jer. 23:5–6), reveals God's character in redemption as the One who restores us to Himself. Jesus is our *Jehovah-Tsidkenu* (Rom. 5:17–19). This name reveals the truth that we become acceptable to God on the basis of His righteousness: "He made Him who knew no sin to be sin for us, that we might become the righteousness of God in Him" (2 Cor. 5:21).

As we pray "Hallowed be Thy name, *Jehovah-Tsidkenu*," we thank God that

Jesus, who is our righteousness, forgave our sin and that we stand before God possessing the free gift of the righteousness of Christ.

Jehovah-M'kaddesh

The name *Jehovah-M'kaddesh* (ma-kah'-desh), "the Lord who sanctifies" (Lev. 20:8), has not been transliterated in our English Bibles, so it can escape our notice as one of the compound names of God. The word *sanctify* means "to set apart for God's service." God sets us apart and sends His Spirit to dwell in us to empower us to live holy lives: "You were...sanctified...in the name of the Lord Jesus and by the Spirit of God" (1 Cor. 6:11; see also 1 Thess. 5:23). God Himself has set us apart for His service, and it is He who enables us to live as ones set apart for Him.

As we pray, "Hallowed be Thy name, *Jehovah-M'kaddesh*," we thank God that He sanctifies us and gives us victory over the power of sin in our lives.

> But God be thanked that though you were slaves of sin, yet you obeyed from the heart that form of doctrine to which you were delivered. And having been set free from sin, you became slaves of righteousness.
> —ROMANS 6:17–18

> Therefore Jesus also, that He might sanctify the people with His own blood, suffered outside the gate.
> —HEBREWS 13:12

Jehovah-Shammah

God's name *Jehovah-Shammah* (sham'-mah) means "the Lord is there" (Ezek. 48:35). *Shammah* carries the meaning of "ever-present," thus *Jehovah-Shammah* is "the ever-present One." He is the God who never leaves His people (Deut. 31:6, 8; Josh. 1:5).

He is God dwelling in the midst of His people (Zeph. 3:17), and His presence dwells in believers by His Spirit (Rom. 8:9, 11; 1 Cor. 3:16; 2 Tim. 1:14; James 4:5). Jesus promised, "I will never leave you nor forsake you" (Heb. 13:5).

As we pray, "Hallowed be Thy name, *Jehovah-Shammah*," we praise God that He fills us with His presence and will never leave us or forsake us. We thank Him for living in us and manifesting His presence to us.

Jehovah-Shalom

Jehovah-Shalom means "the Lord is peace" (Judg. 6:24). The Hebrew word *shalom*, translated "peace," represents the wholeness that is ours by God's grace. Jesus secured our peace with God when He reconciled "all things to Himself...having made peace through the blood of His cross" (Col. 1:20).

As we pray, "Hallowed be Thy name, *Jehovah-Shalom*," we thank God for giving us peace with God through the cross and for imparting His peace. In Philippians Paul links prayer to peaceful minds and hearts:

> In everything by prayer and supplication, with thanksgiving, let your requests be made known to God; and the peace of God, which surpasses all understanding, will guard your hearts and minds through Christ Jesus.
>
> —Philippians 4:6–7

Jehovah-Rophe

In Exodus 15:26 God reveals Himself as *Jehovah-Rophe* (ro'-phay), "the Lord who heals." The word *rophe* means "to restore or heal in the physical and spiritual sense." We thank the Lord that by His stripes we are healed (Isa. 53:5; Matt. 8:16–17). Christ redeemed us from the curse of the law in order that the blessing of Abraham might come upon us (Gal. 3:14).

As we pray, "Hallowed be Thy name, *Jehovah-Rophe*," we thank God for physical and spiritual healing; we declare our trust in Him for our well-being.

Jehovah-Jireh

The name *Jehovah-Jireh* (yeer'-ah), "the Lord who sees to it" or "the Lord's provision shall be seen," appears in Genesis 22:14 in the account of God's providing a ram for Abraham to sacrifice in place of his son Isaac. Our Father sees our needs beforehand and makes provision for them as we ask Him.

As we pray, "Hallowed be Thy name, *Jehovah-Jireh*," we praise God for providing for all our needs—whether related to our bodies, souls, spirits, or circumstances—and that we can do all things through Christ (Phil. 4:13).

Jehovah-Nissi

In Exodus 17:15 we find the compound name *Jehovah-Nissi* (nis'-see), "the Lord my banner." The word for "banner" is also translated as "pole," "ensign," or "standard." A "standard" was a rallying point to kindle hope, a signal raised on a special occasion, particularly in battle. The banner represents God's cause, His battle, and is a sign of His deliverance and salvation. Isaiah predicted that the Messiah who would come out of the stem of Jesse would be an ensign (flag or banner) for the people (Isa. 11:10). When Jesus our banner was resurrected from the dead, He "abolished death" (2 Tim. 1:10).

As we pray, "Hallowed be Thy name, *Jehovah-Nissi*," we thank God that Jesus is our banner of redemption and warfare, who was lifted up on a rugged cross, and that He went to battle for us to give us victory and make us conquerors. We give thanks to God, "who gives us the victory through our Lord Jesus Christ" (1 Cor. 15:57).

Jehovah-Rohi

Psalm 23 contains the compound name *Jehovah-Rohi* (ro'-ee), "the Lord my shepherd." *Rohi* carries the meaning of "feeding or leading to pasture as a shepherd"; it can also be translated "companion" or "friend." Jesus is our good shepherd (John 10:11; Heb. 13:20), who feeds, leads, protects, and cares for His people. Our shepherd leads us through the valley of the shadow of death to God's house forever (Ps. 23:1, 4, 6).

As we pray, "Hallowed be Thy name, *Jehovah-Rohi*," we thank God that He is our shepherd who feeds, leads, protects, and cares for us. We are thankful that He is the best traveling companion and friend that we could ever have in our journey through this life.

Proverbs 18:10 tells us, "The name of the LORD is a strong tower; the righteous run to it and are safe." When we meditate upon and pray the names of the Lord, we are declaring the truths of those names over our lives. This is how we run to His name, take refuge in it, and are safe. Better still, we come to know Him more intimately in these aspects of His character.[2]

PART IV

GOING DEEPER *in* PRAYER

The power of prayer can never be overrated....If a man can but pray he can do anything. He who knows how to overcome with God in prayer has heaven and earth at his disposal.[1]

—CHARLES SPURGEON

Chapter 18

ADDING FASTING *to* PRAYER

Fasting helps express, deepen, confirm the resolution that we are ready to sacrifice anything, even ourselves, to attain what we seek for the kingdom of God.[1]
—Andrew Murray

I DON'T KNOW WHETHER it's accurate to use the term "going deeper" with regard to prayer as I did in the section title for Part IV of this book. But there are some activities related to prayer that do seem to make a greater demand on us but also result in a deeper impact in the Spirit. One of those activities is fasting.

When I first came to know the Lord as a young man, I did not like fasting at all. Actually I was not very interested in prayer either! I loved the worship and teaching at church meetings and Bible studies, but I had no desire for prayer and fasting. As I started reading books on these subjects, I began to see that God had ordered His kingdom to work best when His people pray and fast, but I did not like this idea at all. You could not have convinced me that one day I would be preaching and writing books on these subjects.

Many times in those days I set my heart to spend the day in fasting and prayer, and within a few short hours, I was ready to quit, complaining, "Why did You set up Your kingdom this way? Why do You want me to sit here doing nothing except telling You what You already know and not eating? What is the point of this? Lord, I could be impacting many people if You would just let me do something instead of wasting my life away in prayer and fasting!" Nothing seemed more wasteful to me, but God was teaching me that His ways are higher and wiser than ours.

God has ordered His kingdom in such a way that some things that seem weak to men are actually powerful before God. In our natural minds we may argue against taking the time to pray and fast, but God wants us to understand that this is the way His power is most effectively released in our hearts and ministries.

FOUNDATIONAL PRINCIPLES OF FASTING

There are several biblical principles related to fasting for you to be aware of as you begin to engage in this discipline. These principles describe fasting as an invitation, a paradox, a grace, and an expression of humility.

Fasting is an invitation.

God does not require us to fast but rewards those who choose to fast: "When you fast…your Father who sees in secret will reward you openly" (Matt.

6:17–18). One aspect of the Father's reward includes seeing more of His kingdom expressed in and through our lives and circumstances, as well as seeing our spiritual capacity enlarged to encounter more of His heart (which of course leads to experiencing more of His blessings). Although fasting is voluntary, it was considered a normal part of a believer's life in New Testament times. Notice that Jesus did not say "if" we fast, the Father will see and reward us but "when" we fast.

Fasting is for those who are hungry—hungry to experience more in their relationship with Jesus and to see more of His kingdom expressed in and through their lives. It expresses our desire to experience more of Him. Some spiritual blessings will be released only in the context of spiritual hunger: "Blessed are those who hunger and thirst for righteousness, for they shall be filled" (Matt. 5:6).

Fasting is a paradox.

The second principle is that fasting is a paradox. When we fast, our bodies are weak and hungry, but our hearts become tender and more sensitive to the Holy Spirit. As we temporarily forego the natural things that strengthen and stimulate us, we sometimes feel "raw" before God as we become more aware of our brokenness, barrenness, sinful motives, and wrong desires. The paradox of fasting is that as we experience weakness in our flesh, we are strengthened in our spiritual lives; as we experience the pain of rawness, our hearts are tenderized before God and postured to receive more strength.

Fasting is a grace.

We will not be able to sustain a lifestyle of fasting in our own strength; it is possible only by God's grace. I encourage you to ask for grace to enter into the mystery of connecting with God through fasting. God truly does give grace to fast, even to people who live in our modern Western culture. Whenever God asks us to do something, He promises to empower us to faithfully walk it out by the grace of God.

I want to expose the lie that twenty-first-century believers cannot fast like the saints of old or that regular fasting is simply not practical in a fast-paced, modern life. This is a lie that breeds passivity toward the powerful gift of fasting. Life has never been less physically demanding on a day-to-day basis than today in the Western world! Modern conveniences assure us a comparatively sedentary and easy existence compared to that of previous generations.

We tell ourselves that fasting is too hard and that we will be too tired and uncomfortable, but, in fact, the fear of fasting is worse than the fasting itself. Our bodies were created to operate at their best with regular fasting. There are inherent physical benefits to fasting because our bodies are cleansed when we fast. I recommend what I call a "fasted lifestyle," which includes fasting one day each week rather than engaging in occasional short or long fasts. The practice of regular weekly fasting will help you develop a personal history in God in the grace of prayer and fasting.

Fasting is an expression of humility.

David spoke of fasting as humbling himself before God (Ps. 35:13; 69:10). When we fast, our bodies are easily tired, our minds may not be clear, we feel unable to function at full capacity, and weakness seems to pervade everything we put our hands to. We find ourselves unable to do our work well. It humbles us to fast, and this is how God planned it. The Bible describes it as "humbling" or "afflicting" one's soul (Isa. 58:3, 5). Only desperate people—those who recognize their own great need and want to declare it to God—fast and pray.

Seven Types of Biblical Fasting

I have identified seven types of fasting in Scripture. Please note that the categories overlap somewhat and that is it possible to categorize fasting in different ways.

1. Fasting to experience a greater measure of the power of God in personal ministry

We can fast for a greater release of God's power in our lives and ministries. Jesus referred to this type of fasting when the disciples could not set a demonized boy free. He told them, "This kind [of demon] does not go out except by prayer and fasting" (Matt. 17:21). The power of John the Baptist's preaching was undoubtedly connected to his fasted lifestyle (Matt. 11:18). The same can be said of the power in the apostle Paul's ministry. Fasting was a regular part of Paul's life.

> In all things we commend ourselves as ministers of God…in fastings…
> —2 Corinthians 6:4–5

> Are they ministers of Christ?…I am more…in fastings often…
> —2 Corinthians 11:23, 27

> And he was three days without sight, and neither ate nor drank.
> —Acts 9:9

Historians testify that the early church fasted twice a week (Wednesdays and Fridays) to experience more of God's power. Throughout church history many anointed men and women practiced regular fasting as they led great revivals. John Wesley would not ordain a minister who would not commit to fasting two days a week.[2]

Commenting on the leaders of revival through history, Andrew Murray, the famous church minister in South Africa, urged that we could learn much from these anointed leaders who dedicated themselves to God by separating themselves from the spirit and pleasures of the world through regular fasting with prayer. He was obviously speaking from personal experience when he said,

"Prayer is the one hand with which we grasp the invisible; fasting, the other, with which we let loose and cast away the visible."[3]

Charles Finney was one of the most effective evangelists in America's history. A tremendous anointing of power and conviction rested on his preaching. He reported leading more than five hundred thousand new converts to the Lord in an eight-week period during the great New York revival of 1857. Finney wrote that when the power on his preaching seemed to diminish, he would spend several days in prayer and fasting until the spirit of prayer returned and his preaching was again anointed with power. He acknowledged that the power on his preaching was connected to regular times of prayer with fasting. Finney wrote, "I was also led into a state of great dissatisfaction with my own want of stability in faith and love….I often felt myself weak in the presence of temptation, and needed frequently to hold days of fasting and prayer, and to spend much time in overhauling my own religious life, in order to retain that communion with God, and that hold upon the Divine truth, that would enable me efficiently to labor for the promotion of revivals of religion."[4]

Many well-known preachers of the past exemplified this same principle. They were blessed with an unusual anointing of the Spirit that always included special power on their preaching for soul-winning. In some cases they were also anointed with the gifts of miracles and signs and wonders. Examples include George Whitefield, Jonathan Edwards, David Brainerd, Charles Wesley, Maria Woodworth-Etter, Aimee Semple McPherson, and many more.

John G. Lake is an outstanding example of the correlation between a life of prayer and fasting and the release of signs and wonders. Ministering in the early 1900s, Lake, an insurance agent from Chicago, was stirred by the Lord to pray and fast until he experienced a major breakthrough of power in his preaching and healing ministry. God released unusually powerful miracles through him over many years. He went to South Africa from 1908 to 1913 and started hundreds of churches, seeing an estimated five hundred thousand healings, including the raising of the dead. He led untold thousands of new converts to Christ in those short five years.[5]

Mahesh Chavda, a contemporary example, undertook two forty-day fasts per year for about ten years. The Lord released unusual miracles in his ministry, using him several times to raise the dead and to open blind eyes. Chavda, particularly known for being anointed with authority over demons, told me that regular fasting was clearly related to an increased measure of God's power being released through his ministry.

2. Fasting for direction

One of our deepest desires is to know God's direction for our lives, and fasting positions us to receive more direction from the Lord. Throughout the New Testament we see that the early believers fasted for this purpose. Immediately after Paul's conversion on the road to Damascus, he fasted from food and drink for three days, waiting to receive clear direction from the Lord (Acts 9:9). A few years later Paul and the leaders of the church of Antioch fasted and prayed for direction. God spoke clearly, giving them a strategic mission assignment to reach the Gentiles by sending out Barnabas and Paul: "Now in the church that was at Antioch there were certain prophets and teachers.... As they ministered to the Lord and fasted, the Holy Spirit said, 'Now separate to Me Barnabas and Saul for the work to which I have called them'" (Acts 13:1–2). Thus the first of Paul's missionary journeys was a direct result of corporate prayer, fasting, and seeking God, and it changed history.

Paul and his team also prayed with fasting in selecting and commissioning the elders of the new churches in Lystra, Iconium, and Antioch. "When they had appointed elders in every church, and prayed with fasting, they commended them to the Lord in whom they had believed" (Acts 14:23).

3. Fasting for the fulfillment of God's promises

The Lord has plans and promises for each city on earth. He has given the church in your city and region certain promises. We must not simply wait passively with our faith idle for these promises to manifest. The Lord intends for us to actively petition Him for their fulfillment.

Scripture recounts many stories of men of faith whom God used to usher in the completion of His promises. For example, God had spoken through the prophet Jeremiah that He would deliver the Israelites from their seventy-year captivity in Babylon (606–536 BC). Daniel prayed and fasted for the fulfillment of the prophecy, reminding God of His promises: "I set my face toward the Lord God to make request by prayer and supplications, with fasting, sackcloth, and ashes" (Dan. 9:3). As a result, the people were released from captivity and allowed to return to their land and rebuild their nation.

A few years later Nehemiah, while still in the Persian capital, Shushan, heard reports of the terrible struggle his fellow Jews were having back home in Jerusalem. The walls and gates of Jerusalem were still broken down from the devastating siege and destruction of the city by Nebuchadnezzar of Babylon, so the Jews who had returned had no protection from their surrounding enemies. Nehemiah, like Daniel before him, sought the Lord with fasting and prayer, asking God to fulfill His promises to his generation in Israel. He fasted, wept, and confessed Israel's sins, praying that God would release His promises for Israel (Neh. 1:1–11; 9:32–38). God answered Nehemiah and blessed Israel at that time.

In the New Testament we find the prophetess Anna, who "served God with fastings and prayers" for over sixty years (Luke 2:36–38). The apostle Paul fasted regularly as a key to releasing God's promises for his ministry (2 Cor. 6:5; 11:27; Acts 9:15; 22:21; 26:17–18). At his conversion, he received his appointment from the Lord to take salvation to the Gentiles. Jesus spoke to him and said:

> I have appeared to you for this purpose.... I will deliver you...from the
> Gentiles, to whom I now send you, to open their eyes, in order to turn

them from darkness to light, and from the power of Satan to God, that they may receive forgiveness of sins and an inheritance among those who are sanctified by faith in Me.

—ACTS 26:16–18

Even with such a great and dramatic commissioning from Jesus, Paul sought the Lord for the fulfillment of this promise. He petitioned the Father with much prayer and fasting rather than just waiting passively for God to do what He had promised to do through Paul's ministry.

When the Roman centurion Cornelius fasted and prayed, God sent an angelic messenger and the apostle Peter to him, and his whole household was saved (Acts 10). The spirit of revival was subsequently poured out on the region, and a door of grace was opened for the Gentiles.

Today, as we see multitudes headed for hell and the church struggling with spiritual barrenness, the biblical solution is clear. We must pray and fast until we see a breakthrough regarding the things God has promised our cities and nations.

4. Fasting to stop a crisis

Fasting to avert a national or individual crisis was a regular practice in Old Testament times. Over and over God reversed Israel's desperate situation when they turned to Him in corporate prayer and fasting.

In Joel's day Israel faced several divine judgments. First, locusts and drought brought an agricultural crisis (Joel 1), and then the Babylonian army prepared to invade the land (Joel 2:1–9). Joel called for a national solemn assembly, proclaiming that God would reverse His decision to judge them if the people humbled themselves and repented with fasting and prayer (Joel 1:13–14; 2:12–15).

"Now, therefore," says the LORD, "Turn to Me with all your heart, with fasting, with weeping, and with mourning." So rend your heart, and not your garments; return to the LORD your God.

—JOEL 2:12–13

Jonah was sent to warn the wicked Assyrian city of Nineveh that the God of Israel was going to destroy them. When the inhabitants of Nineveh humbled themselves and repented with fasting, the Lord showed mercy and spared the city (Jon. 3:3–9).

When Moses came down from being on the mountain with God, he found the people of Israel worshipping idols. God was ready to destroy Israel, but Moses entered into a forty-day fast with prayer (Deut. 9:7–21). God spared Israel because of Moses's intercession.

In the same way, Ezra the priest mourned over the compromise he found in the Jews who had returned from captivity. When he arrived in Jerusalem, he found they had intermarried with the pagans, knowing that marrying outside the Jewish faith was expressly forbidden in Scripture. Ezra fasted with great grief, knowing that their compromise deeply displeased God and would lead to further idolatry in Israel (Ezra 9:1–6). Ezra's prayer and confession resulted in many being convicted of their sin. They gathered to confess and stop their compromise (Ezra 10:1–6). God's favor was restored to Israel, and judgment was averted.

Fasting for national deliverance has been practiced throughout history. England's leaders called national days of prayer and fasting at times of crisis. In 1588 the nation fasted when the Spanish Armada threatened England with invasion. Later they fasted for God's help as Napoleon prepared to invade. Then again, during World War II, George VI called a day of prayer and fasting while the Battle of Britain raged, asking God to stop the Nazis from invading.[6] On each occasion God spared England from impending disaster. The early leaders of America in the Continental Congress and Abraham Lincoln also called for national days of prayer and fasting during calamitous times.[7]

Examples of humbling oneself with fasting during a time of personal crisis appear throughout Scripture. Hannah, the wife of Elkanah, a man in the Old Testament, was so distressed by her physical barrenness that "she wept and did not eat" (1 Sam. 1:7) as she poured out her soul to God in prayer for a son. God answered her cry and lifted her barrenness by giving her a son who grew up to become a mighty prophet: "So it came to pass in the process of time that Hannah conceived and bore a son, and called his name Samuel" (1 Sam. 1:20).

During the reign of young King Josiah, a prophetess named Huldah sent word to the king that God was preparing to send judgment on the nation of Judah because of their sin. Josiah responded with prayer and probably with fasting as well (2 Chron. 34:23–28). Fasting is not mentioned specifically, but we understand that he fasted because the Word says he humbled himself and tore his clothes (v. 27). God saw Josiah's sincere heart and delayed the judgment of the Babylonian invasion until after Josiah's lifetime.

King Ahab was one of the most wicked kings in Israel's history. Yet he humbled himself with prayer and fasting, and God stopped the judgment that was set against him. In 1 Kings we read:

> There was no one like Ahab who sold himself to do wickedness in the sight of the LORD.... So it was, when Ahab heard those words that he tore his clothes and put sackcloth on his body, and fasted...."See how Ahab has humbled himself before Me?...I will not bring the calamity in his days."
>
> —1 KINGS 21:25–29

The same was true of King Manasseh, a very evil king in Judah, who "seduced Judah and the inhabitants of Jerusalem to do more evil than the nations whom the LORD had destroyed before the children of Israel" (2 Chron. 33:9). Eventually he was carried off in captivity to Babylon, where he repented and humbled himself through fasting. God heard his prayer and "brought him back to Jerusalem into his kingdom" (2 Chron. 33:13).

5. Fasting for protection

The Scripture also gives examples of prayer with fasting for personal protection. After the Jewish captives from Babylon returned to Israel to begin rebuilding their nation, they were in need of help. So Ezra the priest led a group of Jews back to Israel to help them rebuild Jerusalem. While they were still making preparations to travel, they took time to fast and pray, asking God for protection because the journey was dangerous.

Travel in the ancient world was unsafe because bands of thieves attacked groups of travelers to seize their gold and supplies. They usually killed the people and sold their possessions. Ezra did not want to request an escort of soldiers from the Persian king, for he had told the king that God's blessing would be on them (Ezra 8:21–23). Instead, he fasted and prayed, asking God for supernatural protection through foreign lands. God answered Ezra, and the entire caravan arrived safely.

When King Darius was tricked into throwing Daniel into the lions' den, the king himself fasted and prayed for Daniel's protection (Dan. 6:18). In response "God sent His angel and shut the lions' mouths" (v. 22).

Esther, a Jewish woman in the Persian court, needed divine protection when she came before King Ahasuerus (Xerxes) without a royal summons because the penalty for approaching the king without an invitation was death. After Haman set into motion a plan to annihilate all the Jews and take their possessions (Esther 3:13; 4:7), Esther called the Jews in Persia to fast for three days, and they cried out in prayer with fasting (Esther 4:16). The Lord spared Esther's life and used her to reverse the situation among the Jews; thus He saved them from Haman's evil plan (Esther 9:1).

Church history is filled with examples of God's servants being delivered from peril and danger in response to prayer and fasting. The church today should be compelled to engage in these disciplines all the more, as the days grow more evil. (See Luke 21:34–36.)

6. Fasting for insight into God's end-time plan

The Holy Spirit is raising up forerunner messengers who will have an increased measure of insight into what the Scripture says about Jesus's end-time plan. As we have already noted from Acts 2, there will be a release of prophetic activity in the church before Jesus returns (vv. 17–21). Daniel prophesied that in the end times, God would raise up people with prophetic understanding who would teach multitudes (Dan. 11:33–35; 12:4, 10).

> And those of the people who understand shall instruct many.... And
> some of those of understanding shall fall [martyrdom], to refine them,

purify them, and make them white, until the time of the end; because it is still for the appointed time.

—DANIEL 11:33–35

In the end times God's servants will stand in the counsel of the Lord to receive greater understanding of what He is doing in context to His judgments.

For who has stood in the counsel of the LORD, and has perceived and heard His word?...The anger of the LORD will not turn back until He has executed and performed the thoughts of His heart. In the latter days you will understand it perfectly.

—JEREMIAH 23:18–20

God answered Daniel's determination to gain prophetic insight into God's plans. When the prophet set his face toward God with fasting and prayer, he was given revelation of Israel's destiny at the end of the age (Dan. 9:1–3, 20–23; 10:1–3, 12–14). After he had prayed and fasted for twenty-one days, he was visited by an angel who told him that his prayers had been heard from the first day that he had set his heart to understand and to humble himself before God (Dan. 10:10–12).

Then he said to me, "Do not fear, Daniel, for from the first day that you set your heart to understand, and to humble yourself before your God, your words were heard; and I have come because of your words."

—DANIEL 10:12

While Daniel was in prayer, the angel Gabriel came to give him "skill to understand" (v. 23).

I set my face toward the Lord God to make request by prayer...with fasting, sackcloth, and ashes...while I was speaking in prayer...Gabriel ...talked with me, and said, "O Daniel, I have now come forth to give you skill to understand...consider the matter, and understand the vision."

—DANIEL 9:3, 21–23

It takes God's help to have the skill to understand some of the deeper things that are in His heart and some of His plans for the end times. I believe the Lord will send angels to some of His end-time prophets as He did to Daniel to give increased insight into what is coming. Like Daniel, such people will have to set their hearts to gain more understanding through prayer and fasting.

7. Fasting for intimacy with God (the Bridegroom fast)

> The disciples of John came to Him, saying, "Why do we and the Pharisees fast often, but Your disciples do not fast?" And Jesus said to them, "Can the friends of the bridegroom mourn as long as the bridegroom is with them? But the days will come when the bridegroom will be taken away from them, and then they will fast."
> —MATTHEW 9:14–15

John the Baptist's disciples came to Jesus with a sincere question. They were confused by the lack of fasting among His disciples. Jesus answered them with a question, "Can the friends of the bridegroom mourn as long as the bridegroom is with them?" Then He spoke of the days when He, the Bridegroom God, would be taken from them through His death on the cross and return to His Father in heaven. Then His disciples would fast with the same intensity that John's disciples did. Yet their fasting would be different for it would flow out of longing or mourning for God as their Bridegroom.

Remember, while Jesus was on Earth, His disciples had grown accustomed to His presence with them. They felt cherished and loved by Him, and they rejoiced in His closeness and the intimacy of His friendship as they walked and talked together during His earthly ministry. They did not understand what it meant to have intense longing for more of His presence—He was right there! But things changed dramatically after Jesus died and then later ascended into heaven. When He was physically absent, they mourned to experience more of His manifest presence in their lives and ministries.

In these verses Jesus spoke of a new kind of fast based on His identity as the Bridegroom God and their desire to be with Him. They would fast in mourning for His physical absence, longing to experience an increase of His spiritual presence and to receive greater revelation of His beauty and affection for them. Fasting for this purpose is engaging in what I call a "Bridegroom fast." It is a fast motivated primarily by one's desire for Jesus rather than by a need for more power, direction in ministry, divine intervention or protection, and so on.

The Bridegroom fast is based on desire. We engage in it to grow in our understanding of God's desire for us and to have Him awaken our desire for Him. God imparts new desires to us as He answers existing ones. Jesus promised that we would be satisfied as we mourn for more of Him. Two of the eight Beatitudes in Jesus's Sermon on the Mount speak of our longing and God's fulfillment of our longing:

> Blessed are those who mourn, for they shall be comforted.... Blessed are those who hunger and thirst for righteousness, for they shall be filled.
> —MATTHEW 5:4, 6

Spiritual hunger is a divine gift that leads us to seek greater experiences in His love, regardless of the cost. Those who are spiritually hungry agree to whatever changes are necessary in their hearts for love to have its full way. We were made to love and be loved by God, and He has made us to crave Him until our hearts' cries are answered. He increases our experience of Him through the process of both awakening and answering desires within us.

THE BRIDEGROOM FAST

Why would the disciples "mourn" while Jesus was away? We were made to live in joy, but that joy is found only in Jesus and His presence. Joy separate from Him is not real joy. Mourning for the Bridegroom, with fasting, positions our hearts to experience more of His presence.

The Bridegroom fast is a paradigm of fasting that expands our hearts as we encounter the beauty of Jesus as our Bridegroom God. God has designed us in such a way that when we give ourselves to Him through praying the Word and fasting, the capacity of our hearts to receive more of Him increases.

No other dimension of the grace of God opens wide the deep places of our beings as fasting does. When we pray and fill our hearts with the Scriptures, focusing on the truths of Jesus as our Bridegroom God, our spiritual capacity to receive from God increases. Fasting before the Bridegroom is a catalyst to speed up the depth of our encounter and the measure in which we receive from the Lord. We receive greater measures of revelation at an accelerated pace and with a deeper impact on our hearts.

One of the primary purposes of the Bridegroom fast is to cause our hearts to grow in greater love and longing for God. We do not fast in an attempt to make God pay attention to us but rather to enter fully into the affection and presence of God that is already ours in Christ. The goal is not to move *His* heart but to move *ours*.

Our hearts are prone toward spiritual dullness and lethargy. Unless we deliberately confront the dullness, we become hardened without realizing it. The Bridegroom fast softens our hearts in the grace of God in such a way that spiritual dullness is diminished, and we are able to experience the affection of God in a greater measure. Our hearts become tender as we experience the pleasures of knowing Him. Then we long for more.

Our longing has a purpose. Spiritual hunger is a divine agent that leads us to greater love. It is an instrument that makes room for love and purity to have its full way in our hearts. Our desire for Him creates the mourning or the pain of lovesickness that compels us to make changes in our lives so that we may have all that is ours in God. We are wounded in love because God intentionally withholds a measure of His presence in order to draw us forth into greater intimacy with Him as He works humility in us. The mourning produces meekness in us, which results in His nearness being sustained in us long term.

The one who fasts has an understanding of the gap between what God wants to give and what he actually experiences. The lack in our experience causes discontentedness and mourning. When we recognize that there is a greater realm in God to which we are invited, then we become ruined; we must have this fullness. Therefore we fast because we refuse to live in spiritual dullness and barrenness.

The grace of fasting is a gift from God that leads our hearts and spirits into fascination and exhilaration with Jesus. This gift results in a tenderized heart and great change in our lives. Fasting expresses our vision and determination to have more in God and our pain regarding the ways in which we fall short.

In the coming hour untold millions will experience new dimensions of God's heart and power as they come to understand Him as the Bridegroom, King, and Judge. The reward of the Bridegroom fast is the anointing to receive God's love and love Him in return. Fasting before the Bridegroom God brings about renewed tenderness in our hearts, sensitizing us and removing our spiritual dullness.

Our lives are very different when our desires are touched by His grace. David Brainerd, the well-known evangelist to Native Americans, wrote this in his diary on June 14, 1742:

> Feeling somewhat of the sweetness of communion with God and the force of His love and how it captivates my soul and makes all my desires and affections to center in God, I set apart this day for secret fasting and prayer to God, to bless me in view of preaching the Gospel. I had life and power in prayer this afternoon. God enabled me to wrestle ardently in intercession for my friends. The Lord visited me marvelously in prayer. I think my soul was never in such agony before. I felt no restraint, for the treasures of God's grace were opened to me. I wrestled for absent friends and for the ingathering of poor souls. I was in such agony from sun half an hour high till near dark that I was all over wet with sweat. Oh! My dear Savior did sweat blood for these poor souls! I longed for more compassion toward them. I was under a sense of divine love, and went to bed in such a frame of mind, with my heart set on God.[8]

EXAMPLES OF FASTS IN THE BIBLE

Fasts of various lengths:

+ **One-day fast:** The Day of Atonement (Lev. 16:29; 23:27)

+ **Three-day fast:** Paul after his conversion (Acts 9:9)

+ **Seven-day fast:** David before his child died (2 Sam. 12:15–18, 21–23)

+ **Twenty-one-day fast:** Daniel seeking to understand prophetic scriptures (Dan. 10:2, 3)

+ **Forty-day fast:** Moses (Exod. 24:18; 34:28; Deut. 9:9, 18)
Elijah (1 Kings 19:8)
Jesus during His temptation (Matt. 4:2–3)

Corporate Fasting

+ Believers in the early church fasted and prayed for Peter's deliverance from prison (Acts 12:1–19).

+ The church leaders at Antioch fasted to receive prophetic direction (Acts 13:1–3).

+ Paul and his team fasted as they commissioned elders in Lystra, Iconium, and Antioch (Acts 14:23).

+ God's people, the Jews, fasted on Yom Kippur, the Day of Atonement (Lev. 16:29; 23:37; Acts 27:9).

+ The Jews fasted during Purim (Esther 9:30–31).

+ Israel fasted in the fourth, fifth, seventh, and tenth months during the captivity in Babylon (Zech. 7:3–5; 8:19).

+ Israel fasted at Mizpah before the Philistines attacked (1 Sam. 7:3–10).

+ The children of Israel fasted when engaged in civil war with the Benjaminites (Judg. 20:26–28).

+ Jehoshaphat and the people of Judah fasted before going to war with Moab and Ammon (2 Chron. 20:3–4).

+ King Josiah humbled himself with fasting—it is probable that others joined him (2 Kings 22:11–20).

+ The people of Judah fasted in King Jehoiakim's day in obedience to the Lord (Jer. 36:9–10).

+ Joel called the people to national solemn assemblies (Joel 1:13–14; 2:12–15).

+ Esther and the Jews fasted to avert a plot to annihilate all their people (Esther 3:13; 4:3, 7, 16–5:6).

+ Ezra and others fasted to seek God for protection on the way to Jerusalem (Ezra 8:21–23).

+ Nehemiah and the Jews in Jerusalem fasted for spiritual renewal (Neh. 9:1).

+ Nineveh fasted after Jonah's preaching (Jon. 3:3–9).

Individual Fasting

- Believers will fast to experience Jesus as the Bridegroom God (Matt. 9:14–15).

- Jesus fasted for forty days (Matt. 4:1–3; Luke 4:1–2).

- Moses fasted on Mount Sinai for forty days (Exod. 24:18; 34:28; Deut. 9:9, 18).

- Elijah fasted for forty days on the way to Mount Horeb/Sinai (1 Kings 19:8).

- John the Baptist led a fasted lifestyle (Matt. 11:18).

- Paul led a fasted lifestyle (2 Cor. 6:5; 11:27).

- Paul fasted for three days to receive clear direction (Acts 9:9).

- Paul fasted to receive clear direction in ministry situations (Acts 13:1–2; 14:23).

- Daniel fasted to receive end-time revelation (Dan. 9:1–3, 20–23; 10:1–3, 12–14).

- King Darius fasted all night for Daniel's protection in the lions' den (Dan. 6:18–23).

- Anna the prophetess fasted and prayed regularly for more than sixty years (Luke 2:36–37).

- Cornelius prayed and fasted for spiritual breakthrough (Acts 10:1–4, 30–31).

- Esther fasted for the Jews' deliverance (Esther 4:16–5:6).

- King Ahab humbled himself with prayer and fasting (1 Kings 21:25–29).

- Hannah fasted over her barrenness (1 Sam. 1:7–8).

- David fasted often (2 Sam. 12:15–23; Ps. 35:13; 69:10; 109:24).

- Ezra fasted as he mourned over the people of Israel's intermarriage with pagans (Ezra 9:1–6).

- Ezra fasted again as the people joined him in repentance (Ezra 10:1–6).

- Nehemiah fasted in Jerusalem for Israel's spiritual renewal (Neh. 9:1).

- Nehemiah fasted for Israel's restoration (Neh. 1:1–11) and renewal (Neh. 9:32–38).

As we have seen, there are many different reasons to fast and many examples in both the Old and the New Testaments of various types of fasts. But learning about fasting and being convinced that it is something God requires aren't enough. You have to actually *fast* in order to see for yourself the incredible power of this discipline. Add fasting to praying in the Spirit, which you'll learn about in the next chapter, and you'll *really* boost your prayer power!

Chapter 19

PRAYING *in the* SPIRIT

*If the spiritual life be healthy, under the full power of the
Spirit, praying without ceasing will be natural.*[1]
—ANDREW MURRAY

THIRTY-FIVE YEARS AGO I was struck by one verse in the Scripture related to praying in the Spirit, or praying with the gift of tongues. In it the apostle Paul claimed that *he spoke in tongues more than all* the other believers who lived in Corinth.

> I thank my God I speak with tongues more than you all.
> —1 CORINTHIANS 14:18

At that time I had been teaching against speaking in tongues for about five years. I was earnest about it because I thought tongues was a great deception. But this one verse perplexed me. I couldn't explain it away. How was it possible that Paul spoke in tongues more than the rest? Why did he value this gift so much that he engaged in it more than anyone else? I thought surely he was exaggerating.

The verse deeply troubled me. As the apostolic leader of the many new churches in Asia Minor, Paul was incredibly busy, yet he still invested much time in speaking in tongues—so much so that he could boldly claim he used this gift more than everyone in the whole city of Corinth. Why was speaking in tongues so important to Paul?

I wrestled with this verse for more than a year. If Paul valued praying in tongues as much as he seemed to, then I needed to rethink my position. I began to realize that this verse gives us an important glimpse into Paul's personal prayer life and his view on the gift of tongues.

TWO DIFFERENT TYPES OF THE GIFT OF TONGUES

> The manifestation of the Spirit is given to each one *for the profit of all*: for to one is given the word of wisdom…to another different kinds of tongues….Do all speak with tongues?
> —1 CORINTHIANS 12:7–8, 10, 30

> For he who speaks in a tongue does not speak to men but to God....He
> who speaks in a tongue *edifies himself.*...I wish you all spoke with
> tongues.
> —1 Corinthians 14:2, 4–5

In his first letter to the Corinthians Paul described two different types of the
gift of tongues—two different expressions, with two different purposes. I had
missed this key point in my early ministry when I taught that the gift of tongues
was not available to every believer. Once I saw that there were two different types
of tongues in the Bible, I understood that two seemingly contradictory views of
tongues are both biblical: (1) that only *some* believers, not *all*, have the gift of
tongues (1 Cor. 12:30); and (2) that "all" can receive the gift of tongues (1 Cor.
14:5; Mark 16:17). I came to see that there is a significant difference between the
gift of tongues given for the *profit of the corporate body* (1 Cor. 12:7), when the
speaker speaks to men, and tongues given as a devotional prayer language for the
profit of the individual who uses the gift to speak privately to God (1 Cor. 14:2, 4).

Paul distinguished between the public and private use of the gift of tongues:

> I thank my God I speak with tongues more than you all; yet in the
> church I would rather speak five words with my understanding, that I
> may teach others also, than ten thousand words in a tongue.
> —1 Corinthians 14:18–19

He thanked God that he spoke in tongues more than others but said that
when he was in church, he would rather speak five words with his understanding
than ten thousand words in tongues. In other words, his "speaking in tongues
more than anyone" referred to using his personal prayer language, not to giving
utterance in tongues in a public church service. Here he makes a clear distinction between the two types of speaking in tongues.

It is important to understand the difference in the benefits of the two types.
In 1 Corinthians 12, where Paul explained the gifts of the Spirit, he spoke
of tongues that are "*for the profit of all*" and benefit the whole body, while in
1 Corinthians 14, he spoke of tongues that bring *personal edification* to the one
speaking in tongues.

In 1 Corinthians 12 Paul asked a rhetorical question, signifying that not every
believer has the gift of tongues to profit the corporate body: "Do all speak with
tongues?" (v. 30). However, later he indicated that all can have the gift of tongues
for their personal lives. He wrote, "I wish you all spoke with tongues" (1 Cor.
14:5). Later he added, "Do not forbid to speak with tongues" (v. 39). Jesus said
that speaking in tongues was one of the signs that would follow those who believe.

> These signs will follow those who believe...they will speak with new
> tongues.
> —Mark 16:17

Therefore, every believer can receive the gift of tongues for his *personal use* as a devotional prayer language, but not all will receive the gift of tongues for *public use* in a church service. I had been teaching against tongues based on one aspect of Paul's teaching—that all do not have the gift of tongues (1 Cor. 12:30). I had confused the gift of tongues to be used in public with the gift of tongues to be used in private as a devotional tool.

BENEFITS OF SPEAKING IN TONGUES

In 1 Corinthians 14 Paul gave three benefits of speaking in tongues: speaking mysteries (v. 2); edifying oneself (v. 4); and blessing and giving thanks to God (v. 17). Let's examine these three more closely.

Speaking mysteries

> For he who speaks in a tongue does not speak to men but to God, for no one understands him; however, in the spirit he speaks mysteries.
> —1 CORINTHIANS 14:2

In this verse Paul identified the first benefit of speaking in tongues in a devotional or personal way. He wrote that "in the spirit he speaks mysteries." When we speak in tongues, we commune with the Holy Spirit, who often gives us information that helps us to understand God's will and heart for us. Speaking mysteries is not about receiving "special truths" that are available to only a few. In other words, Paul was not imputing an element of secrecy to tongues or saying we gain elite information about spiritual things such as the gnostics claimed to have.

As we speak mysteries in tongues—in our prayer language—our understanding is unfruitful and we do not understand the words we are saying, but as our spirits commune with the Holy Spirit, we may receive faint and subtle impressions from the Lord in the same way that words of knowledge come to us. These impressions may give us insight into how God wants to touch us or someone else through our prayers. They may be insights about our callings, lives, or areas of brokenness and pain where our hearts need healing.

As we pray in tongues, we may receive a mental picture of someone or see his pain or discouragement or a special need he has. We may receive direction about how to pray for or serve God's plans for other people, cities, and nations. Or the Holy Spirit may show us something in our own lives, such as the need to humble ourselves to someone or reach out in a relationship. Often the mysteries that the Holy Spirit highlights are practical issues in which the Lord wants to minister to us or through us to others.

When I am preparing to speak at a church service or conference, I try to spend as much time as possible praying in the Spirit. In this way I position myself to receive impressions, phrases, and direction from the Holy Spirit to guide and help me in preaching or ministering to people. Sometimes as I pray in tongues and speak mysteries, I receive a word of knowledge before a meeting about someone the Lord wants to touch.

When praying in tongues, take time to pray for the interpretation of what you are praying in the Spirit: "Therefore let him who speaks in a tongue pray that he may interpret" (1 Cor. 14:13). As you do, the Holy Spirit may give you insight into what is on His heart for a particular situation.

One of my favorite passages is 1 Corinthians 2:10, in which Paul spoke of the Holy Spirit as searching the depths of God to reveal them to us. The Holy Spirit is our escort into the deep things of God's heart, Word, and will. He feeds us at the banqueting table of the knowledge of God.

> The Spirit searches all things, yes, the deep things of God…we have received…the Spirit who is from God, that we might know the things that have been freely given to us by God.
> —1 Corinthians 2:10, 12

Think of the Holy Spirit's knowledge of the Father and the Son as the ultimate "search engine" of God's heart. He is the only one who knows the deep things of the Father and the Son. He gives us a portion of what He searches out as we engage more with Him by speaking to Him with our minds and by praying with our spirits.

Edifying oneself

> He who speaks in a tongue *edifies himself*, but he who prophesies edifies the church.
> —1 Corinthians 14:4

In verse 4 of 1 Corinthians 14 Paul highlighted a second benefit of speaking in tongues: "He who speaks in a tongue edifies himself." Paul was calling us not to be self-centered but to build up our spiritual lives. He was essentially encouraging us to "charge our spiritual batteries." Edifying oneself simply means being strengthened or built up.

It is important that we value the gift of tongues and use it regularly in our personal prayer times. God gave us this gift as a means of spiritually strengthening ourselves. We may not feel anything when we pray in the Spirit, but we should not judge what is happening by what we feel in that moment.

Jude 20 also speaks of "praying in the Holy Spirit" to build up our personal faith. Doing so causes our hearts to become more tender and sensitive to the things of the Holy Spirit and enables us to receive mysteries and give thanks to God (1 Cor. 14:16). Being edified in our spiritual lives is an essential aspect of walking in the Spirit and ministering in His power. I have never known anyone who operated in the prophetic or the healing ministry who did not speak in tongues regularly in his private prayer time.

How often do you get in the car and turn on music or the news to entertain yourself? If you used some of your time in the car to pray in the Spirit, you may be surprised how much of a difference it would make in edifying your spiritual life. Or how about the hours you spend alone on a bus, walking, or on a plane? I try to pray in the Spirit whenever I am traveling alone. In this way I can redeem the time and edify my spiritual life.

Paul referred several times to the idea of praying night and day, or praying without ceasing (1 Thess. 3:10; 5:17). I'm sure that one way he was able to pray so consistently was by praying in tongues while doing other things, such as making tents (Acts 18:3; 20:34) or walking from one city to the next. When his hands were sewing tents, his heart was engaged in God as he prayed much in the Spirit. As I came to understand that praying in tongues is the key to edifying our spiritual lives and growing in the things of the Spirit, I was provoked to seek to pray without ceasing by praying in tongues at least part of the time.

Blessing and thanking God

> If you bless with the spirit, how will he who occupies the place of the uninformed say "Amen" at your giving of thanks…? For you indeed give thanks well.
>
> —1 CORINTHIANS 14:16–17

In verse 16 of 1 Corinthians 14 Paul stated the third benefit of speaking in tongues: we bless with our spirits and give thanks. Who are we blessing? We are blessing God when we pray or sing in tongues. Paul wrote in verse 2 of this chapter that he who speaks in a tongue speaks to God: "For he who speaks in a tongue does not speak to men but to God." When we pray in the Spirit, we are actually ministering to God by blessing and giving thanks to Him, and He receives our thanks. Thus speaking in tongues is a devotional gift that we use to bless, praise, and worship God in a way that differs from giving thanks only with our minds.

Because we speak to God when we pray in tongues, we should direct our attention to Him and not just speak mindlessly into the air. When I pray in tongues, I often focus my mind on the scene centered on God's throne in heaven (see Revelation 4 in chapter 23 of this book) and talk directly to the Father. At other times I speak to the Holy Spirit, who dwells in my spirit (Rom. 8:9; 2 Cor. 13:14). I encourage people to talk to the indwelling Spirit. Eastern religions look inwardly but to nothingness. This is a great error. We look to a real person, the indwelling Holy Spirit.

Praying and Singing in the Spirit

I will pray with the spirit, and I will also pray with the understanding.
I will sing with the spirit, and I will also sing with the understanding.
—1 Corinthians 14:15

Praying "with the spirit" and praying "in the spirit" are the same as praying in tongues. We can pray with our understanding (our minds) and with our spirits. Both types of praying are important, but praying with our spirits impacts us in a different and deeper way than praying with our minds. Praying in tongues engages our spirits in prayer, and the presence of the Holy Spirit influences and strengthens our inner man, including our thoughts and feelings. Paul prayed for the Ephesians that they would be "strengthened with might through His Spirit in the inner man" (Eph. 3:16), and being strengthened in this way is one of the results of our speaking in tongues. God designed the human psyche so that our spirits could engage with God by speaking or singing in tongues (1 Cor. 14:15; Eph. 5:19; Col. 3:16).

Singing in the Spirit is an important practice. Paul taught that if we sing the Scripture from our hearts, we will experience God's grace and the Spirit's presence:

> Let the word of Christ dwell in you richly in all wisdom, teaching and admonishing one another in psalms and hymns and spiritual songs, singing with grace in your hearts to the Lord.
> —Colossians 3:16

> Be filled with the Spirit, speaking to one another in psalms and hymns and spiritual songs, singing and making melody in your heart to the Lord.
> —Ephesians 5:18–19

Our hearts are warmed and tenderized by spontaneously singing the Word and singing in the Spirit; doing so makes our spirits more sensitive to the Holy Spirit. I have discovered the power of spontaneously singing Bible passages to God and intermittently singing in tongues, which often results in the Holy Spirit's touching the deep chambers of my heart. I encourage you to do this regularly.

Singing the Word impacts our hearts more than just speaking it or hearing others speak it. God designed the human heart to be touched deeply by music and singing. As we sing the Word and sing in the Spirit, we receive mysteries (divine impressions from the Holy Spirit) and gain insight from the Word. The Holy Spirit will give us more and more if we will sing the Word and sing in the Spirit consistently.

Clearly our communion with God is strengthened through praying or singing in tongues because our spirits are engaged with God in a way that extends beyond praying with our minds. Praying or singing in tongues enables us to speak and receive mysteries (1 Cor. 14:2), to edify ourselves (v. 4), to bless God (v. 16), and to pray continually (v. 18) in a way that builds up our faith; thus it tenderizes our hearts and sensitizes us to the things of the Holy Spirit.

The good news is that any believer can pray in the Spirit because it requires no special training or intellectual ability. It is a spiritual gift that can benefit us greatly as we grow in prayer. Employing this gift makes it easier to sustain prayer for long periods because we do not have to keep finding different ways of expressing our ideas. Our spirits commune effortlessly with the Holy Spirit when we pray in tongues.

BEING CONSIDERATE WHEN PRAYING IN TONGUES

> If anyone speaks in a tongue…if there is no interpreter, let him keep
> silent in church, and let him speak to himself and to God.
> —1 CORINTHIANS 14:27–28

Paul spoke of times in church services when it is best not to pray in tongues out loud but rather to pray in tongues to oneself and to God. He spoke of it as a practical expression of edifying others and seeking to excel in love (v. 12). When we speak in tongues to ourselves and to God, we are still praying effectively.

In a public gathering such as a church service or prayer meeting, it is important not to distract others when praying in tongues. A public prayer room is like a public living room. There are many different types of personalities sharing this "living room," and most people are there to connect with God. They may already be struggling to fight other distractions such as wandering thoughts, situations they are anxious about, their cell phones, and other things in the room, including the people around them, the music, the temperature, the lights, and so on. It usually requires effort for people to press through such distractions to connect well with the Lord.

Therefore, in corporate meetings, we must show consideration to others by praying in tongues quietly to avoid adding yet another distraction. If the majority of the people in the prayer meeting are singing in the Spirit or praying aloud in the Spirit together, then by all means join in. But if the vast majority are not singing or praying in the Spirit together, then it is an expression of love to avoid distracting those around you by praying silently in tongues to God (v. 28).

In other words, if you are one of the only people praying in tongues in a meeting, then do it quietly to yourself. Do not pray so loudly that the three rows in front of you and behind you can hear you and are distracted. Remember that some of those near you may be working to keep their minds focused on the Lord. It does not quench the Spirit to pray in tongues quietly; in fact, it honors the Lord when we show love and consideration for His people.

We can pray quietly in tongues under our breath almost anywhere without allowing others to hear us. I do this in my leadership meetings, at family dinners, in the shopping mall, and in restaurants, as well as while driving my car, walking down the hallway to my next meeting, or fellowshipping with a friend.

In his book, *The Walk of the Spirit—The Walk of Power*, Dave Roberson writes:

> People come to me all the time and ask, "How do *you* pray in tongues, Brother Roberson?" I just simply answer, "I pray like this," and then I demonstrate, praying quietly under my breath. "But don't you pray out loud?" "No, not usually," I reply. "God isn't hard of hearing." (Of course, if I do pray louder, He isn't nervous either!) Then someone asked me, "Well, what about warring in tongues?" I asked, "How do you do that?" The person demonstrated, almost screaming in tongues. "Why do you yell like that when you're talking to God?" I asked. "Well, I thought I was talking to the devil." "No, no, First Corinthians 14:2 says you're talking to God. Now, you can pray that loud if you want to."...But the issue isn't whether you shout or whisper when you pray in tongues. You aren't producing any more for the Kingdom of God by yelling in tongues than you are by praying in tongues under your breath, because it's the Holy Spirit who supplies the language. You didn't create it; *He* created it. And if the Holy Spirit is the Originator of the language, it is always full of power. (The same is true with worship: It isn't how loud or how quiet you worship; it's how much of your entire being you pour into every statement of adoration.)[2]

PRAYING IN TONGUES AND THE GREAT COMMISSION

> Go into all the world and preach the gospel to every creature....And these signs will follow those who believe: In My name they will cast out demons; they will speak with new tongues.
> —MARK 16:15, 17

It is significant that Jesus mentioned praying in tongues in the context of the Great Commission. Unfortunately some sincere believers dismiss this part of the Bible, as I did for a few years in my early walk with the Lord. But it is best to honor every passage in the Scriptures. I believe we will disciple the nations more effectively if we include both casting out devils *and* speaking in tongues. They go hand in hand in successfully engaging in the Great Commission.

John G. Lake (1870–1935) was a Canadian-American leader in the Pentecostal movement in the early twentieth century. His ministry was unusually powerful, and God used him in what was possibly the greatest demonstration of the Spirit of any man in the twentieth century. More than five hundred thousand healings were reported in his ministry in a five-year period in South Africa (1908–1913). Lake prayed in tongues for hours a day and said, "Praying in tongues was the making of my ministry." In 1980 I had the privilege of meeting Lake's daughter and son-in-law, Gertrude and Wilford Reidt, who said of Lake, "He was a praying man." Lake's daughter told me personally that praying in tongues for hours a day was one of the keys to his supernatural ministry of healing.

Kenneth Hagin (1917–2003), an American Pentecostal preacher, wrote about his early days of ministry, when he would spend four to five hours a day praying in tongues. The Holy Spirit used him in powerful ways, and many healings and miracles were seen in his ministry.

Smith Wigglesworth (1859–1947), a great British evangelist, uneducated and from a poor family, also had one of the great healing ministries of the twentieth century. His powerful healings are well-known and written about in many books. He spoke of praying in tongues often. For example, he once wrote: "I maintain that, with a constant filling, you will speak in tongues morning, noon and night."[3]

Pastor Yonggi Cho (1936–present) pastored the largest church in history— the famous Full Gospel Church in Seoul, South Korea—with more than five hundred thousand active members. He prayed in tongues four to six hours a day in his early years of ministry. I know several men who know him well. One man told me that after a long morning meeting, several leaders were planning on going to lunch with him. But Cho told them, "I cannot go to lunch because I have to minister at seven o'clock this evening." When they pointed out that it was only two o'clock, he answered, "But I need four hours to pray in tongues before the service to be the most effective in my ministry."

If men with such powerful ministries greatly valued praying in the Spirit, then surely we also will benefit from praying often in tongues. Indeed, the more we pray in tongues, the more the power of God will move in our lives and ministries. We cannot earn the privilege of being used by God by praying more, but by praying more we can position ourselves to receive more from the Holy Spirit.

I encourage believers to start by praying in the Spirit for thirty minutes a day. Often, I find that it takes me about fifteen minutes of praying in the Spirit before my mind quiets down and I get in a flow. Then it is much easier to stay with it and focus on God.

> Therefore, brethren, desire earnestly to prophesy, and do not forbid to speak with tongues.
>
> —1 CORINTHIANS 14:39

Paul told the Corinthians, "Do not forbid to speak with tongues." To forbid ourselves from speaking in tongues is to minimize the blessing of edifying ourselves spiritually and of speaking mysteries, thus diminishing our ability to experience the things of the Spirit. I know of no one who operates in the prophetic ministry or healing who does not speak in tongues.

Praying in tongues is a universal benefit for all believers. It is not a requirement or proof of salvation; rather, it is a benefit available to us through the work of Jesus and the indwelling of the Spirit. It is not reserved for those with a special calling. It does not require any special training, qualification, or preparation. It is a free gift to all because of the blood of Jesus.

RECEIVING THE GIFT OF TONGUES

Every person who has received Jesus and His free gift of salvation has access to the gift of tongues as a personal prayer language. If you have never received your devotional prayer language (the gift of tongues), then you can ask for it now. It is very simple: just ask the Father to release this particular grace of the Spirit to you.

Some say if the Spirit wants them to speak in tongues, then He will make them. However, the Spirit will not "force" anyone to do anything, including speaking in tongues. Some wait for an overwhelming sense of the Spirit, but often the Spirit touches us like a gentle breeze. Therefore, as you pray for the gift of tongues, you may feel the presence of God lightly, or you may feel a gentle urge to speak out. I encourage you to speak out the words the Spirit gives you in your new prayer language and see what happens. It is not always powerful—sometimes it begins very gently and subtly. God is faithful to give good gifts to His children when they ask Him. If you desire to grow in prayer, I encourage you to use this gift regularly.

Chapter 20

RECEIVING *the* SPIRIT *of* PRAYER

Whole days and weeks have I spent in lying pros-
trate on the ground in silent or vocal prayer.[1]
—GEORGE WHITEFIELD

J UST AS JESUS is an intercessor, so the Holy Spirit is also an intercessor. He intercedes for God's will to be done on Earth. He prays both *for* us and *through* us. At times He pours out on intercessors a spirit of supplication that is commonly referred to as "the spirit of prayer." The spirit of prayer is a special grace given by the Spirit that empowers prayer in and through the body of Christ.

When Zechariah prophesied about Israel's end-time national conversion (Zech. 12:10–14), he highlighted that the Holy Spirit would pour out the spirit of grace and the spirit of supplication (which is the same as the spirit of prayer): "I will pour on…the inhabitants of Jerusalem the Spirit of grace and supplication; then they will look on Me [Jesus] whom they pierced" (v. 10). Prayer and supplication can be used interchangeably in this passage. The Spirit of grace and the spirit of prayer are manifest together. This refers to the Holy Spirit's releasing a special work of grace that energizes prayer and results in unbelievers coming to salvation in a powerful way.

The spirit of prayer, or the gift of anointed prayer, is manifest through us in special moments when we are touched with an unusual measure of the Spirit's activity that goes beyond the normal measure of grace we commonly experience in prayer. It is a great blessing when a spirit of prayer rests on us. Our hearts are especially tenderized as the presence of the Spirit rests on us to anoint and ener-gize us in our prayers. These are powerful times of participation with the Holy Spirit in prayer.

I have observed that God's power or grace is usually released in a greater mea-sure when the Spirit releases the spirit of prayer through us in a distinct way. This special grace in prayer has touched me a number of times through the years, and I long to experience it more regularly.

GROANING IN THE SPIRIT

The apostle Paul taught that the Holy Spirit helps us in our prayer lives: "In the same way the Spirit also helps our weakness; for we do not know how to pray as we should, but the Spirit Himself intercedes for us with groanings too deep for words" (Rom. 8:26, NAS). The Spirit helps us to pray beyond the reach of our natural abilities. In our flesh we are all weak in prayer—we do not know how to pray as we should. We need the Holy Spirit to escort us into the deeper things of God related to prayer.

Paul tells us that at times the Spirit prays through us with sighs and groans too deep to articulate with words. He gives impetus to a prayer burden being expressed through us in a form of travail that releases a greater measure of God's power. Through my studies of others and my own personal experience, I have come to understand that the groans that are characteristic of this form of travail have no words and are often accompanied by gentle weeping.

I have been touched by the experience of groaning in the Spirit a number of times through the years. Before I understood it better, I started speaking in tongues when the Holy Spirit began to move on me in this way, but to my surprise the Spirit's burden lifted instead of increasing. At other times I began praying a familiar prayer such as Ephesians 1:17, but again the burden lifted. In other words, I was not responding to the Spirit's work in me in the right way.

Now I stay focused on the indwelling Spirit when He inspires groaning in me. It is not a time to say much. It is not the time to shout in prayer or make prophetic declarations or pray in tongues. There is a time for that, but this is not that time. Some assume that when the Spirit is tenderly or deeply moving on their hearts, they should stir themselves up by saying more. It is better to go in the opposite direction—to quiet our hearts and pay attention to the Holy Spirit's leadership, similar to when we are fellowshipping with the Spirit.

Sighing and groaning is one form of travailing prayer that results when the spirit of prayer is on us, and it will continue to ebb and flow if we stay focused on the Holy Spirit. Some people assume that travail is always related to crying loudly, as a woman often does in giving birth. On the contrary, my experiences have taught me that the burden of the Spirit will be sustained longer and go deeper if we give ourselves to the groaning and tender weeping by "going inward"—focusing on the indwelling Spirit—instead of "going outward" and articulating our prayers in English in a fast and loud way. I have learned through experience that travail is generally more quiet than loud because we are interacting deeply with the indwelling Spirit.

Travailing prayer may be as short as fifteen minutes, or it may last much longer. I have occasionally experienced groaning in the Spirit that lasted for hours. It is not something we can imitate, initiate, or stir up by our own zeal. Travail is a sovereign work of the Holy Spirit, as is every manifestation of the spirit of prayer.

SPIRIT-EMPOWERED PRAYER IS A GIFT

We cannot make the spirit of prayer come on us, nor does it profit anyone to try and contrive this kind of experience by teaching a group of people to sit in a circle and travail in the Spirit. Through the years I have seen various groups decide that they will gather together to "travail in the Spirit" in an attempt to birth a revival. The passage they commonly point to is the one in which the prophet Jeremiah said:

> Call for the mourning women…and send for skillful wailing women….Let them make haste and take up a wailing for us, that our eyes may run with tears, and our eyelids gush with water. For a voice of wailing is heard from Zion: "How we are plundered! We are greatly ashamed…because we have been cast out of our dwellings."
>
> —JEREMIAH 9:17–19

They misinterpret this passage to be an exhortation to gather intercessors to travail and wail as in great anguish. They mimic a woman who is crying out in labor as she births a baby, literally lying on the ground, holding their stomachs, and screaming, "Send revival! Birth it now through us!" They claim that they are travailing for revival and giving birth to it. However, the gift of anointed, Spirit-inspired prayer cannot be manipulated by a group of people going through the motions. It simply does not work that way.

The verses in Jeremiah 9 are not talking about the anointing of intercession but about calling the professional mourners to wail in the city because God's judgment was coming to Jerusalem in the very near future. In Bible times people would hire professional mourners to mourn before and after the funeral of a family member. They were paid to come to the home and scream in mourning for several hours. (See Matthew 9:23.)

Jeremiah was saying that because judgment was sure to come on Israel for its sin, the people should go ahead and arrange for the professional mourners to come so they could start their wailing and the people could begin crying in advance. He was being sarcastic; he was not exhorting them to call the intercessors together to wail and "birth revival."

REVIVAL AND THE SPIRIT OF PRAYER

There is a dynamic connection between the release of the spirit of prayer and revival. By "revival" I do not mean a week of meetings in which an evangelist preaches each night, nightly renewal meetings, or a period of rapid church growth. Nor do I refer to services in which people are getting refreshed, manifesting, falling over, and laughing. I appreciate any genuine touch of the Spirit, but something far greater than the blessing that has occurred in various renewal meetings during the last twenty years in America is on God's heart.

When I use the word *revival*, I am referring to an unplanned, unprecedented historic intervention of the Holy Spirit in power over an extended period of time and a large geographic area. This type of outpouring of the Spirit results in multitudes being saved (hundreds of thousands or millions) and the church's being revived to a state of radical love and obedience to Jesus in the fear of the Lord.

I formed my picture of revival from my studies of the two Great Awakenings in America. The powerful move of God that came to be called the "First Great Awakening" occurred in the mid-1700s, from about 1720 to 1760. During this revival, God's presence and power was manifest throughout most of the East

Coast of America. The intercessors and revivalists associated with it include Jonathan Edwards, David Brainerd, John Wesley (acknowledged as the founder of the Methodist movement), and George Whitefield, who preached to crowds of twenty or thirty thousand with great power. Edwards and Whitefield are generally considered to be the two most influential of these leaders. They both emphasized prayer as essential to the birthing and sustaining of the great revival.

Another move of the Holy Spirit, commonly known as the "Second Great Awakening," took place from about 1790 to 1840. This move also began with a groundswell of prayer, which was the seedbed for the emergence of one of the most significant spiritual seasons in the church in America. The Second Great Awakening is considered to be perhaps the most profound holiness movement in American history.[2]

The manifestation of power during this revival was as dramatic as that in the First Great Awakening and was facilitated by preachers such as Charles Finney, D. L. Moody, Timothy Dwight, Francis Asbury, "Black Harry" Hosier, Peter Cartwright, and others. Of these, Finney and Asbury are considered the most prominent. Finney's preaching was responsible for an estimated five hundred thousand converts, and Asbury (1745–1816) was a famous Methodist circuit rider and the founder of American Methodism.

The leaders in both great revivals had a history of spending long hours in prayer and being energized by the spirit of prayer on many occasions. The result was that the supernatural conviction of the Holy Spirit came upon people throughout entire regions of America, leading many to a long-term lifestyle of wholeheartedness, love, and obedience to God. Jesus promised that when the Holy Spirit came, He would release conviction of sin, righteousness, and judgment (John 16:8). This promise of the Spirit's work of conviction is fulfilled in an unusual measure in genuine revivals.

The verb *convict* speaks of times when the Holy Spirit takes hold of an individual's mind and conscience with the power of the truth. When the spirit of conviction is manifest in an unusual way in an entire geographic location as it was in the First and Second Great Awakenings, then hundreds of thousands—sometimes millions—of people are shaken out of their spiritual lethargy. The Holy Spirit convicts multitudes of those hearing the Word—both unbelievers and believers—of any worldliness in their lives. He presses the truth of God onto their minds and consciences with an intensity that most of us have not ever experienced.

The conviction of God was manifest across large regions in both the First and Second Great Awakenings, and deep repentance occurred in the hearts of many people. Sometimes the majority of the people in a town turned to the Lord, as the public preaching of the Word had a great effect, piercing the hearts of the multitudes like a mighty sword (Heb. 4:12) and shattering the heart of resistance to God like a powerful hammer (Jer. 23:29). Whenever preachers are anointed with an unusual measure of conviction, the church in their regions will be quickly revived, the saints will speak the Word and do the works of the kingdom with great consistency, and a multitude of unbelievers will come to Jesus.

REVIVALISTS ANOINTED WITH CONVICTION

Through my years as a Christian I have been instructed and inspired by studying the lives of some of the revivalists I've mentioned—particularly Jonathan Edwards, David Brainerd, and Charles Finney—who were involved in the First and Second Great Awakenings and who experienced the spirit of prayer in a special anointing on their personal prayer times with a resulting increase of God's power on their preaching. I believe there is a clear relationship between the times when the spirit of prayer rests on us and the times when we see a greater release of God's power in our preaching and in other aspects of our ministries.

What has particularly amazed me is the magnitude of the power of the Holy Spirit's conviction that was released during the ministries of these revivalists. It resulted in large numbers of people being converted and walking with zeal for God for many years afterward. Often people "come to Jesus" with zeal at an altar call, and then after a few years they lose their fire and settle into spiritually passive Christian lives for their remaining years. But the two Great Awakenings are remarkable in that many who were convicted and converted under the anointed preaching remained zealous for God for many years.

History abounds with the testimonies of revivalists—including women such as Maria Woodworth-Etter, Phoebe Palmer, Catherine Booth, Aimee Semple McPherson, and more—who preached with a supernatural unction of the Holy Spirit and saw thousands of unbelievers come under the conviction of the Holy Spirit in their ministries. I will mention just a few examples here.

David Brainerd

I read the biography of David Brainerd (1718–1747) several times when I was a young man. Brainerd served as a missionary to the Native Americans in the New England area during the 1740s. I was greatly inspired by his unusual prayer life and powerful preaching that often resulted in a spirit of conviction falling on those who heard him. His brief ministry ended when he died of tuberculosis at the age of twenty-nine.

During the seven years before his death, Brainerd lived in the wilderness area near the Native Americans in order to preach the gospel to them. He preached through an interpreter to small crowds that were generally made up of fewer than one hundred people. During one season, the only man he could find in the region who knew English well enough to interpret for him was an alcoholic. A few times the interpreter was drunk, but the power of conviction nevertheless greatly impacted the Native Americans who listened to Brainerd preach through this interpreter.

Brainerd prayed for hours at a time, and sometimes the spirit of prayer rested on him with such intensity that his clothing became wet with perspiration. The result was that the power of conviction was manifest in such a great measure during his preaching that many were instantly and radically converted. One well-known story describes a time when a spirit of prayer with deep groanings rested on him for several hours while he was lying in the snow. He wrestled in prayer for new souls with such intensity that the snow around him melted. When he preached the next day, all who heard him were strongly convicted.

As a young man I saw the relationship between the occasions when the spirit of prayer rested on him and the power of conviction was released through his preaching soon afterward.

I highly recommend that you read David Brainerd's diary, which was edited and published by Jonathan Edwards.[3] It is one of the most influential books I have ever read. You can find a free copy of this diary on the Internet.

Jonathan Edwards

I recommend that you also read a biography of Jonathan Edwards (1703–1758).[4] The biography by Iain Murray is a very good one. Edwards was one of the primary leaders of the First Great Awakening and is recognized by many as one of the most influential Christian leaders in American history. He had a remarkable prayer life that was accompanied by powerful preaching. His famous message "Sinners in the Hands of an Angry God," delivered in 1741, resulted in the hearers being powerfully convicted. "Before the sermon was done," wrote eyewitness Rev. Stephen Williams, "there was a great moaning and crying out throughout the whole house, 'What shall I do to be saved?' 'Oh, I am going to Hell!' 'Oh, what shall I do for Christ?' Edwards had to stop and ask for silence, but the wails continued. He never finished the sermon. They closed in prayer, and all the visiting ministers dispersed through the crowd to lead people to Christ."[5]

The power of conviction was released with so much force that people would cry out while he was still preaching and continue for hours afterward. His experience was the same as David Brainerd's—when the spirit of prayer rested on him, the power of conviction would be manifest in great measure during his subsequent preaching, and many were radically converted.

Charles Finney

The autobiography of Charles Finney (1792–1875) greatly inspired me.[6] One of the most influential evangelists in America in the mid-1800s, he was involved in the Second Great Awakening as well as the Prayer Revival of 1857–1858.[7] In 1857 a wave of prayer washed over the church throughout New York and other cities on the East Coast of America, with thousands gathering to pray daily. At a time when the population of America stood at around thirty million, Finney reported that during a few short months in the winter of 1857–1858, five hundred thousand were converted in the northern states. He wrote: "And it will be remembered that it was at this time that a great revival prevailed throughout all the northern states. It swept over the land in such a tremendous manner, that for some weeks it was estimated that not less than fifty thousand conversions occurred per week."[8] Five hundred thousand new converts is a remarkable number to reach in a period when there were no microphones, no large indoor venues, and no public transportation systems to facilitate large gatherings of people.

The northern part of the country was not the only area impacted by the Prayer Revival. Finney reported that "the revival extended all the way from our frontier settlements in the west, to our most eastern boundary on the Atlantic coast." He claimed that "there was such a general confidence in the prevalence of prayer that the people very extensively seemed to prefer meetings for prayer to meetings for preaching. The general impression seemed to be, 'We have had instruction until we are hardened; it is time for us to pray.' The answers to prayer were constant, and so striking as to arrest the attention of the people generally throughout the land. It was evident that in answer to prayer the windows of heaven were opened and the Spirit of God poured out like a flood."[9]

In his autobiography Finney wrote of the outpouring of prayer on ordinary people during the revival:

> I have said, more than once, that the spirit of prayer that prevailed in those revivals was a very marked feature of them. It was common for young converts to be greatly exercised in prayer; and in some instances, so much so, that they were constrained to pray whole nights, and until their bodily strength was quite exhausted, for the conversion of souls around them. There was a great pressure of the Holy Spirit upon the minds of Christians; and they seemed to bear about with them the burden of immortal souls. They manifested the greatest solemnity of mind, and the greatest watchfulness in all their words and actions. It was very common to find Christians, whenever they met in any place, instead of engaging in conversation, to fall on their knees in prayer. Not only were prayer meetings greatly multiplied and fully attended, not only was there great solemnity in those meetings; but there was a mighty spirit of secret prayer. Christians prayed a great deal, many of them spending many hours in private prayer....Answers to prayer were so manifestly multiplied on every side, that no one could escape the conviction that God was daily and hourly answering prayer.[10]

Leonard Ravenhill

Leonard Ravenhill (1907–1994) wrote several books on prayer that are now considered classics. I recommend all seven of his short books on prayer and revival. But I was surprised by what I saw the first time I went to hear him preach in 1978; he was an elderly man of small stature. His appearance did not seem to match the power that attended his ministry.

I went to a morning meeting along with three friends that was held in a Baptist church. The four of us were privileged to sit in the front row, though several hundred other people were also at the service. Ravenhill preached on the need for revival. At the end of his message he invited the people to quietly wait on God. I knelt down, and suddenly I began to sigh and groan in my spirit. Nobody around me could hear me; I was expressing a deep inward groaning for God. Experiencing the spirit of prayer was new to me. I had never experienced anything like it before, especially as the result of hearing someone preach.

More than an hour passed as I continued to kneel and lie before the Lord in the Baptist sanctuary. I heard some people gently weeping behind me, but I assumed that not many of those who had come to the service were still there. Finally, I got up out of consideration for my friends, who I assumed were patiently waiting for me to go to lunch. To my amazement I saw that my friends were on the ground not far away, groaning! I looked around, and more than one hundred people were still kneeling in the pews or lying in the aisles.

Another hour passed, and very few of them had left. There had been no ministry time, no music, no one saying, "Come, Holy Spirit," no one giving direction from the front. There was just one man, Leonard Ravenhill, up on the platform, praying quietly. This was the first time I had witnessed the power of conviction resting on a group of people in response to a sermon.

Some years later I had the privilege of getting to know Leonard personally. I told him that the spirit of conviction had touched me and my friends powerfully during the first message I heard him preach. With humility he shared that a similar type of conviction had accompanied his preaching a number of times over the years. He explained that whenever the spirit of prayer touched him during his private prayer time, power was manifest in his public preaching. I asked how I could experience a similar response in my ministry. He said, "Only one way. Not just long hours of prayer. It will take giving your whole life to God—your time, your words, your eyes—give your all to the Holy Spirit. Do not live differently outside the prayer room. It will cost you everything. Is this what you want?"

"Yes, I really want it," I told him.

My Personal Experiences

Since that conversation the Holy Spirit has gripped me in prayer many times, and God's power is released in a greater measure when the Spirit prays through me in this way. I believe there is a manifestation of power in a person's life or in an event in response to this type of prayer, as the experiences I am about to share will show. However, I am not saying that we should wait until a spirit of prayer is manifest before we can expect demonstrations of power. I have experienced the power of God flowing in my ministry many times without tracing it back to a specific anointed prayer time. I could share several of those testimonies, but instead I am going to recount a few examples of my experiencing the spirit of prayer and then seeing a difference in my preaching or in a person's life the very next day.

My first experience was in 1982. I was in a Saturday-night prayer meeting with five or six young men when the spirit of prayer rested on me. I knelt down and prayed with quiet groaning, sighing, and tender weeping for about an hour, as the Spirit Himself made intercession (Rom. 8:26). I was not loud and did not draw the attention of others to the fact that the Spirit was touching me in prayer. I did not call the other intercessors together and say, "I am groaning; everybody groan and travail with me."

The next morning when I preached at the Sunday service to about five hundred people, I saw the power of God manifest in a way that I had never seen up to that time in my ministry. It was unusual and distinct. As I preached on the call to love God with holiness, I noticed maybe one hundred people gently weeping, repenting, and loving God while I was preaching.

Before that service I had seen people moved to tears either during a message when I was sharing a heartrending emotional story or afterward during a ministry time, but it was unusual for them to weep while the message was being given. Their weeping was the result of the Spirit's touching them as I spoke. In that service more people were saved than was usual for a Sunday service. I understood that the response to my preaching and the increased number of salvations was directly related to the heightened activity of the Holy Spirit praying through me in the prayer meeting the night before.

Two months later something similar happened. The spirit of prayer again rested on me during a small Saturday-night prayer meeting. Again, I knelt down and quietly prayed with tender weeping and groaning for about an hour. I was not drawing the attention of the others to the fact that the Spirit was touching me, nor did I did stop to call them to groan with me. The next morning when I spoke at church, the Spirit moved in our midst in a way that was similar to the way He had moved the previous time.

The spirit of prayer has come on me outside of prayer meetings as well. I remember one time at about three o'clock in the morning I suddenly woke up with a clear picture in my mind of someone in my extended family. I lay in bed and asked the Lord to touch this person. All of a sudden groaning rose up in me, so I quickly went into another room where, being energized by the Holy Spirit, I began to weep and groan. I believe that a crisis was averted in the life of that particular family member. As I prayed, I kept picturing the person barely avoiding a car wreck. I am confident that this short session of prayer resulted in his avoiding a serious injury.

Another time, during one of my regular prayer times, a Bible teacher who had blessed me years earlier came to mind. I prayed for him for one or two minutes, "Lord, just bless him today." Suddenly travailing intercession rose up in me with groans and sighs that lasted for about an hour. I felt strongly that he was on the verge of suicide and that my intercession mattered. I believe it contributed to his averting a crisis in his life.

On a different occasion I was praying for one of our leaders at the International House of Prayer. Suddenly I was in the grip of strong intercession that continued for about three hours with gentle weeping and groaning by the Holy Spirit. I could not let go of it. Later the person told me what happened, explaining that he had shifted from a place of real difficulty in his life to one of breakthrough. The point is that every time we are led into travail, an immediate breakthrough of some type occurs.

My purpose in sharing these personal experiences is to emphasize how glorious and powerful it is when the Holy Spirit releases a spirit of prayer on and through us. It is worth setting everything aside to follow His leadership during these special times of prayer.

THREE MODES OF PRAYER

Unfortunately not all our prayer times are infused with the spirit of prayer. Praying under its influence is only one of three different modes of prayer that I have identified. I use the analogy of an ancient warship, powered by rows of oarsmen and sails, to describe these three modes.

The first mode of prayer is like the warship on a *calm day*, with only a gentle breeze. The gentle breeze helps a little, but in order to make good progress, the oarsmen have to row hard. This mode represents our normal daily prayer times. We put effort into it as the oarsmen do. We advance, and we are grateful for the small breeze, but it takes more effort on our parts to continue in prayer in order to make progress.

The second mode of prayer is like the warship on a windy day. The ship's sails catch a strong wind while the oarsmen are rowing. All of a sudden the ship is carried along at a high speed without much human effort. It may go ten times faster. This mode represents our prayer times under the spirit of prayer. We may start out rowing, but suddenly the wind of the Spirit carries us along so that we make far greater progress that day.

The third mode of prayer is like the warship facing into a heavy wind. The oarsmen are rowing as hard as they can, but the ship is being blown backward instead of forward. This mode represents the prayer times in which we experience heightened demonic resistance. In these times the strong resisting winds of darkness may hit our minds and hearts and make us feel as if we are losing ground, no matter how hard we row. In reality we are not losing ground because it is impossible to pray in God's will and lose ground in prayer.

In times of heightened demonic opposition we must persevere with confidence, knowing that God hears our prayers offered in the name of Jesus and that His authority makes our breakthrough certain. (See 1 John 5:14.) Satan must always flee when we stand with confidence using the name of Jesus against him.

I have found that most of my normal, everyday prayer life takes place in the first prayer mode, comparable to the warship on a calm day, when it is necessary for the oarsmen to exert effort in their rowing to make any headway. However, when I least expect it, the "winds" of the Holy Spirit suddenly help me in my weakness.

I am sure that all who are reading this book long to experience the great blessing that occurs when a spirit of prayer genuinely rests on a believer. It is a glorious thing for the Holy Spirit to tenderize our hearts as He anoints and energizes our prayers, allowing us to participate with Him in fulfilling God's plans and purposes on the earth.

CONTENDING FOR A THIRD GREAT AWAKENING

I believe one plan God has in mind is to send another great awakening to America and the nations of the earth. Based on my study of the lives of revivalists, the activity of the Holy Spirit in previous revivals, and biblical promises related to the end times, I am contending in prayer for just such a great move of God. In both the First and Second Great Awakenings in America in the eighteenth and nineteenth centuries, massive numbers of people came to the Lord as the result of an unusual measure of the power of conviction on the preaching of the Word. We have seen the role the spirit of prayer played in releasing this power.

But during the twentieth century, there was no such awakening in America. Yes, there was the move of the Holy Spirit at Azusa Street that led to the Pentecostal and charismatic movements, but there was no widespread release of the conviction of the Holy Spirit on the preaching of the Word and no large numbers of new converts who walked in purity and the fear of the Lord for years.

I am thankful to God for the Jesus Movement in the 1970s, when many young people were born again. I was saved during that time (June 1971). But again, in this movement we did not see the spirit of conviction with the fear of the Lord being released across entire cities and regions.

It has been almost a hundred and fifty years since our nation has seen a great awakening. However, a great awakening is coming to America again, one that will far surpass the previous two and go beyond all that happened at Azusa Street, in the Jesus Movement, and as a result of the Pentecostal, charismatic, and various regional renewal movements.

I am contending in prayer for many in whole towns and cities to experience the manifest glory of God so that large numbers of people are saved and then walk in the fear of God and obedient love for Jesus. I am believing for the time when the Holy Spirit establishes the first commandment in first place in the whole church. What a day it will be when every believer operates in the gifts of the Holy Spirit on a regular basis, churches live out kingdom community life together, and missionaries are thrust to the nations so that the glory and fame of Jesus's name is known in every tribe and every tongue!

I am desperate for true revival, and I will never be satisfied with anything less than a full measure of what God is willing to give. I know many of you reading this book have the same vision and desire. Continue to petition Him in faith and hope, enter in to the spirit of prayer when it comes upon you, and then give yourself fully to it. It is good to pray for your own local church or college ministry, but I encourage you to focus your prayer on something bigger—that is, revival for your *entire region* or for a third great awakening across our nation. Some of our

Bible-school students gathered together last year to pray and fast for a revival in our Bible school. I encouraged them to get a bigger vision than that and to cry out for an awakening or revival for the *whole church* in our city and region and even more—for a third great awakening in America. I assured them that, in the process of answering their "big" prayer, God would not forget to touch us.

Chapter 21

ENGAGING *in* WORKS *of* JUSTICE

You can do more than pray after you have prayed; but you
cannot do more than pray until you have prayed.[1]
—A. J. GORDON

I HAVE BEEN TALKING a lot in this book about prayer, and there's no question that prayer is essential in helping to bring about God's purposes. However, prayer alone is not enough. Both prayer *and* service are important in God's kingdom; they go hand in hand. *Works* of justice must follow our *prayers* for justice, and prayers must back up our works.

We are witnessing an escalation of injustice in the nations, with human trafficking, poverty, racism, abortion, the mistreatment of orphans, and many other types of oppression on the rise. As the global crisis intensifies, God calls His people to work for justice in a spirit of mercy and humility combined with prayer. The spirit of intercession is expressed in *both* prayer and deeds.

When Jesus was on Earth, He emphasized the importance of prayer and highlighted its relationship to injustice when He said:

> Will not God bring about justice for His elect who *cry to Him day and night*...? I tell you that He will *bring about justice for them quickly.*
> —LUKE 18:7–8, NAS

Jesus is the first social reformer who linked the release of justice to night-and-day prayer, which we will learn more about in Part VI. Why? He understood that continual, persevering prayer confronts the true source of injustice in the spirit realm—demonic powers (Eph. 6:12). When we cry out for justice in intercession, we actually change the spiritual atmosphere in the region in which the injustice is occurring.

There is a spiritual dimension to doing works of justice and compassion in the grace of God. Demons resist justice; they do not easily give up territory they have retained through decades or centuries of oppression.

Jesus knew that our works of justice would be far more effective when combined with night-and-day prayer that addresses the spiritual roots of injustice. But both are necessary. Acts of justice and compassion are a visible expression of our love for God. When we serve the needy, the poor, the fatherless, and the oppressed, we exalt Jesus and demonstrate His love in a practical way. Loving people by "doing justly" is a visible measurement of our invisible love for God.

Our good works declare our love for God. "But whoever has this world's goods, and sees his brother in need, and shuts up his heart from him, how does the love of God abide in him?" (1 John 3:17). Our works of service for others demonstrate that His power has changed us.

Jesus taught us to engage in good works (of justice) "that they may see your good works and glorify the Father" (Matt. 5:16). Believers are to be known by what they *do* instead of by what they do not do. It is not enough to avoid scandalous sin; we are called to be actively engaged in loving people. When we are, unbelievers acknowledge that God is not distant or indifferent but rather committed to the world and active in people's lives.

APPROACHING JUSTICE GOD'S WAY

Just as good works are incomplete without prayer backing them, so prayer is incomplete without good works following it. The clearest instruction concerning the relationship of prayer to justice is found in Isaiah 58:1–12. This passage outlines practical ways of doing works of justice with a spirit of mercy and humility.

At a time when Israel seemed to be seeking God, Isaiah was sent as God's messenger to tell them that seeking Him without helping others was not pleasing to Him. They felt satisfied in themselves because they were seeking God, but they were not also embracing works of justice and mercy. God wanted more than their worship songs and prayer meetings.

The Lord thundered through Isaiah:

> Tell My people their transgression…they seek Me daily, and delight to know My ways…they take delight in approaching God. "Why have we fasted," they say, "and You have not seen? Why have we afflicted our souls, and You take no notice?"
>
> —ISAIAH 58:1–3

The nation of Israel sought God with prayer and fasting. They claimed to delight in knowing His ways through studying the Scriptures and even took pleasure in approaching God's presence. Although these are good and even essential activities, the attitude of the people was wrong because they did not combine their good religious activities with practical works of justice.

When Israel asked the Lord why He had not answered their prayers and responded to their days of fasting, He pointed to their wrong attitude: They had stopped short in their worship; they had been oppressing people and neglecting to do works of justice. The Lord's words through the prophet were, "In the day of your fast you…exploit all your laborers. Indeed you fast for strife and debate, and to strike with the fist of wickedness" (vv. 3–4).

God accused the leaders of Israel of fasting and praying mostly to gain His favor in their businesses and to appear devout while at the same time exploiting those whom God had placed under them. They sought to use God's favor on their lives for their own advancement but without helping the needy. The business leaders of that day were using their influence and resources as a means of increasing their personal comfort with no thought of helping others or sharing their blessings from God.

Our resources and influence may be small, but we can still use them to help others. God is watching to see how we steward a small amount of resource; it is an indication of how we would use a larger amount. To him who is faithful with little, God will give increase and make him ruler over much more (Luke 16:10).

The Lord continued to reveal His heart to Israel by explaining that the approach to fasting and prayer that is pleasing to Him is one that espouses helping the oppressed.

> Is this not the fast that I have chosen: to loose the bonds of wickedness, to undo the heavy burdens, to let the oppressed go free, and that you break every yoke?
>
> —ISAIAH 58:6

Removing bonds of wickedness, heavy burdens, and yokes means relieving people of the bondage that results from oppressive laws and social barriers, many of which have been created over decades and centuries. It speaks of the systemic injustice in society that has institutionalized wickedness. In addition it refers to the cultural mind-sets that prevail as the result of educational disadvantages, lack of preventive or appropriate health care, legal or economic inequalities, and other social factors that negatively affect individuals. The combined impact of these mind-sets and social conditions keeps many individuals in bondage. Whether it is the inner city, the immigrant community, the school system, or any other part of society, God calls us to do our part in helping others.

Social injustice will not be entirely eradicated from the world until Jesus returns. However, we can make a difference today when we combine prayer with works of justice. As we work to change oppressive laws and unjust social barriers, we must meet some of the practical needs of those who are waiting for change by sharing our resources of food, housing, and clothing with them. The fast that God has chosen is to share our bread with the hungry, to bring the poor into our houses, and to provide clothing for them (Isa. 58:7).

As we work to meet the needs of those suffering from injustice, it is essential that we serve in a spirit of humility and treat the oppressed with dignity. We recognize that we do not understand all the complexities that have developed over decades, nor do we fully understand other people's life situations. Therefore, the Lord instructs us to "take away the yoke from your midst, the pointing of the finger, and speaking wickedness" (v. 9). When serving the needs of the afflicted, we must not "point the finger" by judging where they went wrong or how they got into their present situations. In other words, we must not criticize their work ethics, lack of diligence in education, problems with alcohol or drugs, or other issues. Some people may have these deficiencies, but there are many other factors that also contribute to their plights. The greatest minds cannot figure out all the complex factors that lead to their difficult life circumstances.

Our role is to love and serve others with humility rather than trying to ana-lyze their situations or judging and criticizing them. Our true motives are often easily discerned by those we are serving. We are to see the dignity of individuals who are being oppressed—their worth in God's sight—so that we may serve them well and demonstrate that God really loves them.

God will release a supernatural dimension of His powerful light and healing when fasting and prayer are joined to works of justice. The Lord promised to back up our prayers and actions with an increase of His manifest presence when He declared:

> Then your light shall break forth like the morning, your healing shall spring forth speedily, and your righteousness shall go before you; the glory of the LORD shall be your rear guard. Then you shall call, and the LORD will answer.
>
> —ISAIAH 58:8–9

Consistent prayer will result in an increase of the measure of God's power that is released on our works of justice. People do not need only practical help; they need to experience God's power too. Healing a sick person is better than giving him money to go to the doctor, though we often do both. Praying and breaking demonic oppression off people does more than just listening with com-passion to their battles against oppression. We do both, but let's not draw back from the vision to manifest God's justice by demonstrating His power over sick-ness and oppression.

SETTING OUR HEARTS TO DO JUSTLY

We must be zealous to do good works on Jesus's terms and for His reasons. We will never meet the needs of *all* the people in our hurting world, but together we can make an impact on the lives of *some* of them by consistently praying for God's justice and by performing acts of compassion, no matter how small. Together we can make a big difference.

Impacting the lives of a few will impact the lives of many over time. If we ask Him, God will give us creative ideas about how we can help those who are oppressed. He takes delight in us when we dream big and think outside the box.

Don't be limited by what is currently being done in the church or ministry where you serve. God may give you an entirely new idea to reach people in your neighborhood or workplace that is beyond the present spheres of ministry being done by your local church. God is raising up courageous people who will do great exploits without being intimidated by obstacles. Let us join together in giving ourselves to prayer and justice on God's terms, for "we are His workmanship, created in Christ Jesus for good works, which God prepared beforehand that we should walk in them" (Eph. 2:10).

PART V

THE INTEGRATION *of* PRAYER *and* WORSHIP

*It is in the process of being worshipped that God com-
municates His presence to men.*[1]
—C. S. LEWIS

Chapter 22

THE CHURCH'S ETERNAL IDENTITY
as a HOUSE *of* PRAYER

The great people of the earth today are the people who pray. I do not
mean those who talk about prayer; not those who can explain about
prayer; but I mean those people who take time and pray.[1]
—S. D. GORDON

IN ONE SHORT statement Jesus revealed the eternal identity and destiny of His people. He declared, *"You shall be called a house of prayer."* (See Matthew 21:13.) Jesus was quoting Isaiah's prophecy to Israel: *"My house shall be called a house of prayer for all nations"* (Isa. 56:7).

When God calls us by a specific name, it indicates our character and how we are to function in the Holy Spirit. Isaiah's prophecy and Jesus's statement tell us that God's people are to function as a house of prayer both now and in the age to come. Our greatest place of authority, honor, and dignity is found in prayer—that is, in our deep interaction and partnership with Jesus. Being a house of prayer involves much more than having prayer meetings. It involves establishing a prayer culture in the body of Christ and seeing that our spiritual identity is rooted in being a people of prayer forever.

What does it mean to be or to function as a house of prayer? It means that God speaks to us and moves our hearts. Then we speak His words back to Him, and they move His heart. The result is that God's resources are released on the earth—His power, money, wisdom, creative ideas, unity, and favor. This is how the redeemed will operate forever in God's family, being moved by God to ask Him for the things that are on His heart so that He will release them onto the earth.

It is important to understand that the "house of prayer" in a city is the whole body of Christ in that city or region. It is not just the prayer ministries in that city. I tell our Bible-school students that the house of prayer in Kansas City is not made up of only our organization, the International House of Prayer. We are simply a small "gas station"—it is as if we take a "cup of gasoline" and throw it on the prayer fires that burn in the whole house of prayer in Kansas City, which is the entire body of Christ—more than one thousand congregations.

THE CENTRALITY OF WORSHIP AND
INTERCESSION IN GOD'S PLAN

The Holy Spirit wants to establish a culture of prayer integrated with worship in the church. In fact, He is currently raising up the greatest prayer and worship movement in history. Why? Because engaging in worship and intercession is the highest calling of the redeemed in the age to come, and it is the primary means by which He releases His power through them to the earth. Worship and intercession are among the few things that we do both now and forever.

Prayer and worship have always been at the center of God's purpose. Central to God's government and the release of His power is His eternal worship sanctuary as described in Revelation 4–5.

The Scriptures emphasize the centrality and importance of prayer. For example, human history actually began in a "praying meeting" in the Garden of Eden as Adam walked with God each day in the cool of the day (Gen. 3:8). Israel as a nation also began at a fiery "prayer meeting" at Mount Sinai, which was ablaze with God's fire, after the people crossed the Red Sea. At that time God called them to be a kingdom of priests (Exod. 19:6–20). The first mandate He gave Israel as a nation under Moses's leadership was to build a worship sanctuary, a house of prayer, in the wilderness (Exod. 25).

God's purpose for His people to be a "house of prayer" can be seen clearly in the reign of King David. David established worship in the tabernacle, the house of God, led by singers and musicians (1 Chron. 15–16) who "were free from other duties; for they were employed in that work day and night" (1 Chron. 9:33). David financed more than four thousand full-time paid musicians and singers (1 Chron. 23:5; 25:7).

We know from the Bible's descriptions of the reigns of subsequent kings that David commanded the leaders in the generations after him to maintain worship in the house of the Lord in the way that God had revealed to him:

> He [King Hezekiah] stationed the Levites in the house of the LORD with cymbals, with stringed instruments, and with harps, according to the commandment of David, of Gad the king's seer, and of Nathan the prophet; for thus was the commandment of the LORD by His prophets.
> —2 CHRONICLES 29:25

When Zerubbabel returned to Jerusalem after seventy years of Babylonian captivity, he set in place full-time singers and musicians, as commanded by David (Ezra 3:10–11; Neh. 12:47). Each time the Davidic order of worship was reestablished in Israel, a spiritual breakthrough with a military victory soon followed.

Jesus Himself began His public ministry in a prayer meeting in the wilderness (Matt. 4) and ended it in a prayer meeting in the garden of Gethsemane (Matt. 26). The early church began in a prayer meeting in the Upper Room as Jesus's followers waited for "the Promise of the Father" (Acts 1:4): "These [the eleven disciples] all continued with one accord in prayer and supplication, with the women and Mary the mother of Jesus, and with His brothers" (v. 14). The apostles made the ministry of prayer a top priority:

> They continued steadfastly in the apostles' doctrine and fellowship...and in prayers.
>
> —Acts 2:42

> We will give ourselves continually to prayer and to the ministry of the word.
>
> —Acts 6:4

Natural history as we know it will end in the context of a global prayer movement (see Part VI for more about this phenomenon). The conflict at the end of the age will be between two houses of prayer, two global worship movements—one worshipping Jesus and the other worshipping the Antichrist.

Today the Holy Spirit is raising up what will become the most powerful worship movement in history.[2] It will totally defeat the Antichrist's end-time worship movement. In Revelation 13 we read of the worldwide worship of the Antichrist that will come to pass just before Jesus returns:

> So they worshiped the dragon who gave authority to the beast; and they worshiped the beast, saying, "Who is like the beast? Who is able to make war with him?"...And authority was given him over every tribe, tongue, and nation. All who dwell on the earth will worship him, whose names have not been written in the Book of Life of the Lamb slain from the foundation of the world.
>
> —Revelation 13:4, 7–8

We can be confident that Jesus will establish worship and intercession throughout the whole millennial earth in the age to come because His Word declares this truth:

> Yes, all kings shall fall down before Him; all nations shall serve Him.
>
> —Psalm 72:11

> So the nations shall fear the name of the Lord, and all the kings of the earth Your glory.
>
> —Psalm 102:15

> "For from the rising of the sun, even to its going down, My name shall be great among the Gentiles; in every place incense shall be offered to My name, and a pure offering; for My name shall be great among the nations," says the Lord of hosts.
>
> —Malachi 1:11

These verses and others, such as Psalm 138:4 and Psalm 148:11, confirm that the whole earth will worship Jesus. The Scripture makes it clear that worship and intercession are of great value to the Lord in heaven, on earth in this age, and on earth in the age to come.

THE VOW THAT CHANGED HISTORY

Psalm 132 records a vow of King David that is at the heart of the end-time missions and prayer movement. I call it *"the vow that changed history"* because dedicated believers throughout the ages have embraced the spirit of it and set their hearts to live by it. The vow is a commitment to be wholehearted in seeking the fullness of God's purpose.

> He [David] swore to the LORD, and vowed to the Mighty One of Jacob: "Surely I will not go into the chamber of my house, or go up to the comfort of my bed; I will not give sleep to my eyes or slumber to my eyelids, until I find a place for the LORD, a dwelling place for the Mighty One of Jacob." ... Arise, O, LORD, to Your resting place.
> —PSALM 132:2–5, 8

David vowed to live in extravagant commitment to the Lord by seeking to establish a place where God's presence would be honored and fully responded to. David had a higher priority than building his own house—his own comfort, family, ministry, calling, and finances. In this passage David's "house" refers to his domestic life and personal resources. His "bed" refers to his personal comfort and ease. The phrase "not giving sleep to his eyes" refers to his pouring out his strength in contending for God's will to be done.

David's heart was gripped with something bigger than his personal comfort and promotion. As a young man he vowed to dedicate his life to finding a "resting place" (vv. 8, 14) or "dwelling place" (vv. 5, 13) for God. Both phrases speak of the same reality. God seeks a resting place on Earth where His people obey His will and where His presence and purpose are openly manifested.[3]

In principle a "dwelling place" speaks of a place (a city or region) where God's purpose is done to the fullest measure ordained by God in any given generation and where His presence is manifested on Earth in a way that is openly seen and thus discernable even to unbelievers. The Spirit strives with those who resist His leadership to convince them to obey (Gen. 6:3). Thus, a "resting place" in this context is a place where the Spirit "rests" in the midst of His people who live in agreement with His will.

> The LORD said, "My Spirit shall not strive with man forever."
> —GENESIS 6:3

David's main life vision was to find a resting place for God. Walking out this vision implied that he partner with a "radical core" of believers living as a holy, praying community and seeking "revival." David's vow included establishing day-and-night worship by setting singers and musicians in place to join him in contending for the fullness of God's purpose in their generation. The apostle Paul described David as a man who served the fullness of God's purpose, doing all His will in his generation (Acts 13:22, 36).

David's vow included establishing a building in Jerusalem for the ark of the covenant (Ps. 132). The ark was associated with the manifestation of God's power and presence. In the New Testament, God's habitation, or resting place, is in His people (Eph. 2:22).

Notice that in Psalm 132:5 the psalmist gives the ultimate goal of David's mission—to find "a dwelling place" for God in the city in which he lived. Of course, he was speaking of the city of Jerusalem. The fullness of the dwelling place for the Lord in Psalm 132 refers to Jesus's sitting on His throne in Jerusalem after His Second Coming. This will be the ultimate expression of God's dwelling place on Earth in a geographical location (Jer. 3:17).

In a spiritual sense the church on Earth is the dwelling place of God today, and we can contend for a much greater release of God's presence now through the worldwide body of Christ. When people speak of seeking "a dwelling place for God," they are often referring to a place where, in principle, God's manifest presence is released in an unusual way for an extended period of time and where it results in the commitment of many people to love and obey God with all their hearts, live under the leadership of the Holy Spirit, and together experience an unusual measure of His power and manifest presence on a regular basis. Thus a "dwelling place for the Lord" may in principle describe a community of believers who walk in the fear of the Lord with the first commandment in first place in their lives and who obey with gratitude and humility. They will see demonstrations of God's power with signs and wonders so that many come to know the Lord in a deep and glorious way.

Remaining faithful to his vow brought reproach on David. He described the afflictions he endured from his youth related both to his zeal for God's house and the way he lived because of it. The vow was costly and caused him great pressure and persecution.

> For Your sake I have borne reproach; shame has covered my face. I have become a stranger to my brothers, and an alien to my mother's children; because zeal for Your house has eaten me up, and the reproaches of those who reproach You have fallen on me. When I wept and chastened my soul with fasting, that became my reproach....I became a byword to them. Those who sit in the gate speak against me....I am the song of the drunkards.
>
> —PSALM 69:7–12

David was mocked because he boldly stood for what God was zealous for in his generation. He bore reproach for his zeal in fasting that God's house would one day be filled with glory (v. 10). He became a byword to his family and friends (v. 11). In other words, they told jokes about him because of the intensity with which he sought God. The spiritual and political leaders in his community—those who sat at the gate of the city—spoke against him. Even the drunkards mocked him with songs that criticized his zeal for God (v. 12).

Some sincere believers draw back from zealously seeking God due to fear of receiving criticism from others. They cannot bear the reproach that comes as a result of diligently pursuing Him. Some draw back because of the love of comfort—they want things to be easier. Some draw back because they want more money—seeking God takes time away from earning an income.

Does David's vow and vision for a dwelling place stir your heart? As a pastor seeking to establish a foundation of prayer in the local church where I formerly served, I was inspired by David's vow, and as head of the International House of Prayer at Kansas City, I still am. This vow has motivated leaders around the world to build prayer ministries and to seek to establish a culture of prayer in their local churches.

Many dedicated believers throughout church history have embraced the spirit of David's vow. All through the ages the Lord has raised up groups that function as a radical core of holy, praying believers. These groups may be as small as five to ten dedicated, praying believers or as large as several hundred. There are undoubtedly many groups like this in your city in various churches with different denominational affiliations. Surely you want to be a part of one! God will use even a small number who seek to lay hold of His promises. He answers these groups by releasing His power in a way that will inspire others to wholeheartedness.

Find out what God is doing in your generation and then fully throw yourself into it. Determine to be a part of a radical core that will not stop until the fullness of God's purpose is released. Be a revivalist or part of a "revival company" that is fully dedicated to Jesus.

All over the earth in this hour the Lord is raising up groups to live as radical cores that will be catalytic to inspire many others to love, obey, and seek God with all their hearts. Today the Spirit is preparing such groups as "catalytic forerunner communities," with members who will humbly stir others to also seek the Lord in the context of their church families in contending for the fullness of all that God intends to release in their generation.

I offer one important warning. You must never believe that your group is more dedicated than others. That was the error Elijah made. He assumed that he was the only one who was dedicated to the Lord in his generation. The Lord corrected him, informing him that there were seven thousand who had remained faithful to God (1 Kings 19:18).

I am certain there are many more than seven thousand dedicated, radical prayer communities across the earth. The enemy wants those functioning as radical cores to stumble with pride, but don't give him the satisfaction by thinking your group is better than others. It is important to seek the Lord with genuine humility that desires to be a blessing to others and that refuses to harbor even a trace of pride or any sense of spiritual superiority over others in the body of Christ.

Vow, as David did, to live in extravagant devotion, seeking the Lord with all your resources—your time, talents, and treasures—that He may establish places across the earth where He can manifest His presence and kingdom purposes in the way He so desires.

THE GROWING CRISIS IN THE WORLD

Unquestionably the church's identity as a house of prayer is significant, and the Lord desires to use the praying church as His vehicle to release blessing to the nations. We can see Him working now to bring change to the church to prepare it to function in this way now and in the coming hour.

However, the church in the West stands at a critical juncture. The nations are increasing in lawlessness and moral confusion and engaging in escalating conflicts, including those inspired by racism, terrorism, and sexual immorality. In addition we are facing the threat of devastating global economic crisis, the breakdown of marriage and the family, the rapid, wholesale acceptance of the gay agenda, and many other pressures. The prevailing sentiment worldwide is one of growing fear, unbelief, and mistrust, as the earth shudders under the weight of man's escalating sin. Psalm 2 and Isaiah 24 describe our current state:

> Why do the nations rage, and the people plot a vain thing? The kings of the earth set themselves, and the rulers take counsel together, against the LORD and against His Anointed, saying, "Let us break Their bonds in pieces and cast away Their cords from us."
>
> —PSALM 2:1–3

> The earth is also defiled under its inhabitants, because they have transgressed the laws, changed the ordinance, broken the everlasting covenant.
>
> —ISAIAH 24:5

The most significant crisis in the world today is in the church itself, particularly in the West. More and more church leaders are promoting a distorted grace message, making light of heterosexual fornication, celebrating the ordination of homosexuals, endorsing abortion, denying the authority of Scripture, rejecting Jesus as the only way of salvation, discarding the doctrine of hell, and even renouncing the divinity of Christ. Yet some of these congregations continue to grow.

Many leaders have substituted methodology and church-growth mechanics for God's calling on the church to function as a "house of prayer for all nations" (Isa. 56:7). They have hidden their barrenness behind the fig leaves of superficial cultural relevance instead of pressing in to walk out the two great commandments—to love God and people (Matt. 22:37–40)—and to deeply engage in the Great Commission (Matt. 28:19).

There will be two clear trends in the church as we draw nearer to the coming of the Lord: many will fall away from the faith,[4] and at the same time many will rise up in wholehearted love for Jesus to participate in the most glorious and powerful time in the church's history.

The evils and pressures we see in our world today provide an impetus and opportunity for the church to bring change. During dark times such as those in which we are living, God's people are to rise up in faith, wholly resolve to take hold of what God is saying, and then do it with all their hearts. We can take direction from the Book of Joel, which gives us insight into God's solution for the growing crisis and tells us how to respond in these dark times.

GOD'S SOLUTION FOR THE CRISIS

Let's first take a look at what Israel was dealing with in Joel's day. Joel gave a graphic picture of the situation (Joel 1). Israel had just endured a national economic crisis caused by a locust plague that was quickly followed by a drought that destroyed their crops (vv. 4, 16–20). The result was that both the food and the finances of the nation were in ruin. No class of society was exempt from the effects of the crisis; it affected everyone, from the elders or political leaders (v. 2) to the priests or spiritual leaders (v. 13; Joel 2:17) to the drunkards (Joel 1:5), the young couples (v. 8), the farmers (v. 11), and even the children. And this crisis was only the beginning of troubles for Israel in that generation. Joel prophesied that a greater crisis was soon to come in the form of a military invasion by the mighty Babylonian army (Joel 2:1–9).

The Scripture is clear that a national crisis is not God's ultimate aim. His desire is that His people walk in relationship with Him and that the oppressed are delivered. However, God does allow certain crises to awaken the attention of whole nations so that they pay attention to His will and ways and His calling for them.

The message God gave to Israel through Joel in the midst of their crisis was good news—that the people could minimize the devastation and see total restoration by responding to the Lord in the way He desired. Joel told the leaders to call a sacred assembly, to gather the old and the young to turn to God with all their hearts with prayer and fasting, to repent of their sins, to blow the trumpet in Zion, and to cry out to experience more of God's mercy and power.

> "Turn to Me with all your heart, with fasting, with weeping, and with mourning." So rend your heart, and not your garments; return to the LORD your God, for He is gracious and merciful, slow to anger, and of great kindness; and He relents from doing harm....Blow the trumpet in Zion, consecrate a fast, call a sacred assembly....Let the priests, who

minister to the LORD, weep between the porch and the altar; let them say, "Spare Your people, O LORD."
—JOEL 2:12–13, 15, 17

The encouraging news of Joel's message applies to God's people today. Thus, it is wise to pay close attention to his model of responding to the Lord in times of national crisis and pressure. Joel's book is a must-read for all who are committed to growing in prayer and who want to see the church fully functioning in its role as a house of prayer called to fulfill God's purposes on the earth.

Turn to God with all your heart

The primary response God is looking for in a national crisis is that His people turn to Him with all their hearts and repent for the compromise in their lives. Sadly it is common for leaders in the body of Christ today to refuse to address the need for believers in compromise to repent because the leaders don't want to preach negative messages. Some go to the extreme of saying that because Jesus died on the cross, born-again believers no longer need to repent when they stumble into sin and compromise in their lives. This is a very serious false teaching.

The call to repentance was foundational to the kingdom message of Jesus, John the Baptist, and the apostles.[5] Repentance is the way *into* the kingdom—we repent and receive the free gift of God's righteousness by faith. It is also the way *of* the kingdom—we repent regularly for our weakness as we seek to walk under the leadership of the Holy Spirit. We are to walk with Jesus in the same way that we received Him—by faith and repentance:

As you therefore have received Christ Jesus the Lord, so walk in Him.
—COLOSSIANS 2:6

Turning to the Lord with all our hearts involves fasting and repenting with mourning, or godly sorrow, for our sins. The apostle Paul wrote, "For godly sorrow produces repentance leading to salvation, not to be regretted; but the sorrow of the world produces death" (2 Cor. 7:10). Jesus taught, "Blessed are those who mourn, for they shall be comforted" (Matt. 5:4). The type of mourning Jesus referred to is an expression of the grace of God working in our hearts. It is the result of the conviction of the Holy Spirit, which leads us to repent. It is not the same thing as Satan's condemnation after we repent.

In Joel 2:13 Joel called the people to show their repentance with profound sincerity by rending their hearts. The people were familiar with rending, or tearing, their garments to show their grief and desperation. However, Joel urged them to tear their hearts and separate themselves from all their compromises.

Tearing one's heart is intensely personal and painful. Speaking symbolically of this spiritual tearing, or radical obedience, Jesus said, "If your right eye causes you to sin, pluck it out" (Matt. 5:29). In other words, remove everything in your life that quenches the Spirit! Jesus was encouraging us to deal radically with the issues in our hearts that hinder our relationships with God. It is costly to "tear" our hearts, but it is powerful in terms of positioning ourselves to receive the Lord's blessings and intervention in a crisis.

By turning to the Lord with all our hearts, we bring God—His power, wisdom, and blessing—into the crisis. This element is missing in the approach that many take to national crises. Joel's approach may seem overly simplistic, but when the Lord's blessing is restored, many social, agricultural, financial, political, and spiritual dynamics change for the good.

The Lord spoke to Solomon in a dream and showed him the same way to deal with a national crisis that He showed Joel.

> The LORD appeared to Solomon by night, and said to him: "I have heard your prayer...when I shut up heaven and there is no rain, or command the locusts to devour the land, or send pestilence among My people, if My people who are called by My name will humble themselves, and pray and seek My face, and turn from their wicked ways, then I will hear from heaven, and will forgive their sin and heal their land."
> —2 CHRONICLES 7:12–14

Repent with confidence in God's mercy

Joel summoned the people to return to the Lord, knowing that He would respond in a way that was gracious, merciful, and filled with great kindness.

> Return to the LORD your God, for He is gracious and merciful, slow to anger, and of great kindness; and He relents from doing harm. Who knows if He will turn and relent, and leave a blessing behind Him.
> —JOEL 2:13–14

We have confidence to rend our hearts when we know that the Lord will respond to us with kindness and that He delights in restoring our lives and our fellowship with Him.

During King David's time, David assured the people that if they repented, the Lord would not discipline them in the way their sins deserved. "He has not dealt with us according to our sins, nor punished us according to our iniquities" (Ps. 103:10). The prophet Micah confirmed that the Lord actually delights in showing us mercy:

> Who is a God like You, pardoning iniquity...because He delights in mercy.
> —MICAH 7:18

God is slow to anger and not easily provoked by our sin and weakness. He desires to forgive all who sincerely repent. Our repentance will never be met with rejection. According to Zephaniah, God is even willing to stop judgment that is about to be decreed in His heavenly court.

> Before the decree is issued...before the day of the LORD's anger comes upon you! Seek the LORD, all you meek of the earth...it may be that you will be hidden in the day of the LORD's anger.
> —ZEPHANIAH 2:2–3

Joel assured the people of the Lord's desire to "relent" and leave a blessing behind (Joel 2:14). God is willing to transform a disaster zone into a revival center of His blessing, to make a way of deliverance and bring total restoration, if only we will repent and cry out to Him in a loyal relationship of love.

Blow the trumpet

According to God's instructions through Joel, we are to "blow the trumpet" (Joel 2:15) in a time of crisis; that is, to boldly proclaim the necessity for a sacred assembly by speaking of the coming restoration that is available and the coming judgment that is inevitable if God's people do not turn to the Lord. We all know the familiar Scripture passage that says, "If *My* people who are called by My name will...pray and...turn from their wicked ways, then...I will...heal their land" (2 Chron. 7:14). It is the people of God who are called to return to wholehearted obedience to the Lord.

A "sacred assembly" is a time set aside for the people of God to gather in corporate prayer with fasting and turn to the Lord in repentance for all the compromise in their lives. Fasting and prayer are expressions of our wholeheartedness. Fasting positions us to receive more from God; it enhances our ability to give ourselves to God and deepens our heart-connect with God's heart.

Perhaps no one in your area is blowing a trumpet. Or perhaps only a few are responding to the call. I urge you not to delay. Gather a few and cry out to God today. Even a small number of devoted believers crying out to God can make a way for His judgments to be withheld and His blessings to be restored in answer to their prayers.

How many people does it take to respond to God before He will relent and withhold His judgment? We do not know the exact number, but we can be encouraged by the Lord's promise to Abraham that He would spare the city of Sodom if only ten people responded to Him in righteousness (Gen. 18:20–33).

Cry out in earnest prayer

Through Joel, God called the spiritual leaders in Israel to weep and cry out for mercy so that they would be spared even greater trouble. Often in times of national disobedience one crisis escalates to a greater crisis. So the leaders were called to pray and cry out for mercy. "Let the priests, who minister to the LORD, weep between the porch and the altar [a place in the courtyard of Solomon's temple where the people gathered]; let them say, 'Spare Your people'" (Joel 2:17).

In times such as those in which we are living, we must insist on prayer as the priority in our prayer meetings. This admonition may sound redundant, but I have been to many "prayer meetings" in which there was much preaching, testimony, and giving of praise reports, but not much prayer.

GOD WILL RESPOND

The call of Joel comes as an urgent plea to rightly interpret the seriousness of the ungodly trends and events happening today and then respond in the way that God requires, knowing that a national crisis will eventually escalate unless God's people cry out for mercy. A culture of prayer and fasting in the church is not optional. Prayerlessness leads to a lack of spiritual discernment, individually and corporately, which in turn leaves many without the motivation to respond rightly to a crisis.

God's answer for a national crisis is the same in every generation. We have a clear road map set forth in the Book of Joel for the specific response God wants from His people in times of crisis. The Lord does not leave us guessing about what He desires from us. We can act with confidence. It will take faith to carry out the Lord's plan, but following it is something anyone can do, regardless of education, ministry experience, gifts, economics, or ministry influence. As we turn to God with all our hearts, He will release a historic visitation of His Spirit to revive the church and restore many things in our nation and the rest of the world.

Chapter 23

PRAYER BEFORE GOD'S THRONE

A glimpse of Jesus will save you. To gaze at Him will sanctify you.[1]
—MANLEY BEASLEY

LTHOUGH WE MAY not often think of it in this way, when we pray we actually come before God's throne—a real throne, with a real person sitting on it. "Let us then approach God's throne of grace with confidence, so that we may receive mercy and find grace to help us in our time of need" (Heb. 4:16, NIV). What an amazing privilege, that mere mortals can approach the throne of the eternal One, who rules the universe and waits for us to ask for help!

We are strengthened in our prayer lives by learning about the One to whom we pray, and that includes the place where He dwells and the majestic scene that surrounds Him. When we understand the kind of God He is, our relationship with Him deepens, our minds are renewed by the truth, and the way that we pray changes: prayer becomes more significant, more vital, more enjoyable, intensely practical, and increasingly fruitful.

Rather than speaking my words into the air or praying in a mental vacuum, I focus my mind on the biblical description of God's throne as set forth by the apostle John in Revelation 4. The majestic beauty of the Father's throne, revealed to John in exile on the island of Patmos, is the clearest and most detailed depiction of God's throne in the Bible.

In this chapter we will reflect on the scene around the Father's throne, the place where He receives our prayers. Of course, I will describe it imperfectly, but my goal is to give you a starting point on which to focus your mind when you are worshipping and praying. The throne scenes in the Scriptures are a great gift to the body of Christ; they show us what God wanted us to understand about His throne. I encourage you to give much time to studying what the Word tells us about God's throne and to meditate on it. All who desire to grow in prayer will reap benefits from such study and meditation; my own prayer life continues to bear out this truth.

THE BEAUTY REALM OF GOD

I sometimes refer to the scene around God's throne as the beauty realm of God because it is the place where the beauty of God is most manifest. God chose to surround Himself with specific things to express His beauty to creation. His royal court is the ultimate place of honor, majesty, strength, and beauty:

Honor and majesty are before Him; strength and beauty are in His
sanctuary.

—PSALM 96:6

I organize Revelation 4 according to four main categories, each having three
themes; thus, I think of twelve specific themes in this throne scene. The implications are vast. Each of these themes could fill a book itself, and they warrant a
lifetime of diligent study.

Ask the Holy Spirit to escort you into a greater understanding of the truth
about the Father. It is the Spirit's delight to escort us on a great treasure hunt
into the beauty of God—a lifelong treasure hunt. The Spirit has so much more
to show those who are hungry. A billion years from now we will still be discovering new things related to these twelve themes of the beauty of God.

FOUR CATEGORIES OF GOD'S BEAUTY

As you read the following account of a vision, witnessed and recorded by John,
take your time, and pay special attention to all the details that God wants us to
understand.

> Behold, a throne set in heaven, and One sat on the throne. And He
> who sat there was like a jasper and a sardius stone in appearance; and
> there was a rainbow around the throne…like an emerald. Around the
> throne were twenty-four thrones, and on the thrones I saw twenty-four
> elders sitting, clothed in white robes; and they had crowns of gold on
> their heads. And from the throne proceeded lightnings, thunderings,
> and voices. Seven lamps of fire were burning before the throne, which
> are the seven Spirits of God. Before the throne there was a sea of glass,
> like crystal. And…around the throne, were four living creatures…they
> do not rest day or night, saying: "Holy, holy, holy, Lord God Almighty,
> who was and is and is to come!"
>
> —REVELATION 4:2–6, 8

The four categories into which I organize the description in this passage, each
with its three themes, are listed below, followed by a few brief thoughts on each
category:

+ The beauty of God's person: how God looks, feels, and acts (v. 3)

+ The beauty of God's people: the church enthroned, robed, and
  crowned (v. 4)

+ The beauty of God's power: manifestations of power in lightning,
  thunder, and voices (v. 5)

◆ The beauty of God's presence: His fire on lamps, seraphim, and the sea (vv. 5–7, 15:2)

The beauty of God's person

He who sat there was like a jasper and a sardius stone in appearance; and there was a rainbow around the throne, in appearance like an emerald.

—REVELATION 4:3

The first category I find is the beauty of God—how God looks. John saw the Father sitting on His throne with the most glorious and beautiful jasper, sardius, and emerald light radiating from His throne. John did not see God's face directly; what he saw was the light emanating from God and His throne. As Moses said, "No man can see God's face." (See Exodus 33:20.) Only those with resurrected bodies can see the face of God directly. As a man, still living on the earth, John saw the glorious light of many colors radiating from God's presence, including the brightness of diamonds (precise identification of the term *jasper* from the ancient world is difficult, but several scholars equate jasper to a diamond), fiery red glory (sardius), and the hues of the emerald rainbow.

The jasper brilliance speaks of His splendor; the sardius, His fiery desires; and the emerald rainbow, His mercy. Modern-day jasper is different from the diamondlike jasper stone of the ancient world. In Revelation 21:11 John speaks of jasper as "a most precious stone…clear as crystal." The jasper-diamondlike radiance that is around the Father is beautiful, fascinating, and terrifying in its glory.

The magnificent light that shines forth from the Father is also like a sardius stone. Some translations put the word *ruby* because sardius is a deep red gem. There is deep red, rubylike brightness coming from the throne of God. I believe this speaks of His fiery desire for His people that is like a consuming fire.

Additionally John saw a rainbow around the throne. The rainbow that we know has many colors, but the dominant color of this rainbow is emerald. In my mind's eye I picture this rainbow arching over the throne. The Old Testament prophet Ezekiel also saw a vision of the throne scene, and he describes the same rainbow:

Like the appearance of a rainbow in a cloud on a rainy day, so was the appearance of the brightness all around it [the throne]. This was the appearance of the likeness of the glory of the LORD.

—EZEKIEL 1:28

The rainbow refers to God's tender mercies. God set a rainbow in the clouds after Noah's flood as a promise of His mercy (Gen. 9:13). This emerald rainbow of mercy encompasses all the plans and actions that issue forth from God's throne. The redeemed will forever sing of the Lord's mercy: "The Lord is good, for His mercy endures forever" (Jer. 33:11; see also Ps. 136).

At the right hand of the Father sits another; Paul tells us that the Father seated Jesus "at His right hand in the heavenly places" (Eph. 1:20). In the Book of Hebrews we read that our High Priest is "seated at the right hand of the throne of the Majesty in the heavens" (Heb. 8:1).

Ezekiel saw the glory radiating from Jesus's throne as sapphire blue.

> ...the likeness of a throne, in appearance like a sapphire stone; on the likeness of the throne was a likeness with the appearance of a man [Jesus] high above it.
>
> —EZEKIEL 1:26

John the Apostle described Jesus, the Son of Man, thus:

> His eyes like a flame of fire...and His countenance was like the sun shining in its strength.
>
> —REVELATION 1:14, 16

Can you imagine Jesus, with eyes of fire and His face shining like the sun, sitting on a sapphire throne beside the Father?

The beauty of God's people

> Around the throne were twenty-four thrones...I saw twenty-four elders sitting, clothed in white robes; and they had crowns of gold on their heads.
>
> —REVELATION 4:4

Next we consider the beauty of the people whom God establishes in partnership with His eternal reign. I imagine the twenty-four elders in front of the throne, sitting in a semicircle facing the Father. They sit on thrones, clothed in white robes, with golden crowns on their heads—they are enthroned, robed, and crowned. They are a foreshadowing of the redeemed in the age to come, who will also be enthroned, robed, and crowned. All the details are significant, but we do not have space here to elaborate on them. What dignity, honor, and beauty the redeemed receive by sitting in God's presence and ruling with Christ forever![2] Jesus gives us, His people, His own beauty in place of our ashes (Isa. 61:3). Imagine: the very beauty that God possesses is the beauty He imparts to His people (Ps. 90:17).

The beauty of God's power

> From the throne proceeded lightnings, thunderings, and voices.
>
> —REVELATION 4:5

Out of God's throne come beautiful, glorious, and even terrifying manifestations of His power. He makes known what He is thinking and feeling through these different manifestations. Flashes of lightning go forth continually from His throne. I think they speak of the impartation of the Spirit's power to His people. When the Holy Spirit falls on people, I think of it as the lightning of God striking them in a glorious way, as when "the Holy Spirit fell upon all those who heard the word" in Cornelius's household (Acts 10:44). In other words, these flashes of lightning proceeding from God's throne may speak of power encounters with the Spirit. I pray, "Lord, let the lightning of Your Spirit touch me." I want my heart alive with the power of God.

Thunder also proceeds from God's throne. Thunder from God is often related to specific messages. (See John 12:28–29; Revelation 10:4; 19:6.) When I worship, I think of receiving insight into specific messages from God's Word and say, "I want my being to resonate with Your Word. I want it to reverberate throughout my entire being like thunder. I want Your heart and message to thunder in me."

God's royal courtroom is also filled with awesome, beautiful voices, along with heavenly noises (music) that surround His throne (Rev. 5:9; 8:5; 11:19; 16:18).

The beauty of God's presence

> Seven lamps of fire were burning before the throne, which are the seven Spirits of God. Before the throne there was a sea of glass, like crystal...around the throne, were four living creatures.
>
> —Revelation 4:5–6

The beauty of God's manifest presence is seen in the divine fire associated with it on the sea of glass, the lamps of fire, and the living creatures.

Before the throne is a vast sea of glass, like crystal. It is glistening in the diamondlike splendor and glory of God that reflects off it as light reflects off glass. The saints stand on this sea of glass that is mingled with the fire of God.

> I saw something like a sea of glass mingled with fire, and those who have the victory over the beast...standing on the sea of glass, having harps of God.
>
> —Revelation 15:2

The prophet Daniel saw God's throne as blazing with fire, with a river of fire flowing from it. "His throne was ablaze with flames...a river of fire was flowing and coming out from before Him" (Dan. 7:9–10, nas).

I assume that the fire that rests on the sea of glass comes from the river of fire that flows from the throne. I see this fiery, glassy sea as the great heavenly "conference center" before the throne. I do not know how many believers there will eventually be in God's family. Perhaps several billion believers will one day worship before the throne on this vast crystal sea. Can you imagine how much space is needed for several billion people to stand together? This is a vast sea, not merely a pond or a lake.

The beauty of God's presence is further represented by seven lamps of fire burning before the throne of God, which refer to seven manifestations of the Spirit. Isaiah spoke of these in greater detail, and each one teaches us more about God and expands our view of Him:

> The Spirit of the LORD shall rest upon Him, the Spirit of wisdom and understanding, the Spirit of counsel and might, the Spirit of knowledge and of the fear of the LORD.
>
> —ISAIAH 11:2–3

When I think of these seven lamps, I do not envision them as five feet tall. They are probably massive torches and may be moving in power across the sea of glass, just like the pillar of fire moved with the Israelites in the wilderness in the days of Moses. The pillar of fire probably reached from the ground to the sky. I think of it as a token of the heavenly lamps before the throne. I picture these seven torches moving in the midst of the people of God as they stand on the glassy sea (Rev. 15:2). I imagine the lamps to be in front of the throne. Or maybe these are massively large torches of fire that move, hovering over the vast congregation on the glassy sea as the Spirit once hovered over the face of the earth (Gen. 1:2).

My final theme in the beauty realm of God is the four living creatures. I imagine them flying all around the throne, even in the area above God's face, saying, "Holy, holy, holy."

> And they do not rest day or night, saying: "Holy, holy, holy, Lord God Almighty, who was and is and is to come!"
>
> —REVELATION 4:8

When Isaiah saw these living creatures, he called them "seraphim" (Isa. 6:2). Because the suffix "-im" expresses the plural in Hebrew, today we would call them "seraphs."

> Above it stood seraphim; each one had six wings: with two he covered his face, with two he covered his feet, and with two he flew. And one cried to another and said: "Holy, holy, holy is the LORD of hosts…"
>
> —ISAIAH 6:2–3

The word *seraphim* means "the burning ones." They are the ones closest to the manifest glory and beauty of God, a special category of angelic beings that are deeply associated with God's fire.

The Scripture tells us about the four seraphim—the four living creatures— around the Father on His throne. The seraphim seem to be the highest-ranking angels in the Bible. They are higher than the archangels. Under the seraphim in rank are the cherubim. The two are not the same. The seraphim seem to have the greater spiritual capacity because they are in the immediate presence of God.

When the seraphim look at God, they cover their eyes with one set of wings to keep from being overwhelmed by fresh insights into His transcendent glory. It is as if the power of what they see races through their beings, overwhelming them so that they must cover their eyes. After a while they "come up for air," but as they catch another glimpse of His glory, they are overwhelmed again, causing them to cover their eyes. Before long, they look up, only to be overwhelmed once more. For eternity they never exhaust the splendor and the glory of the One whom we call "our Father who art in heaven." Yes, this is our Father. This is the One who desires us—desires *you*—the One who sent Jesus for us.

There are myriads of angels surrounding God's throne and the royal court as His angelic attendants.

> I looked, and I heard the voice of many angels around the throne, the living creatures, and the elders; and the number of them was ten thousand times ten thousand, and thousands of thousands.
>
> —Revelation 5:11

> A thousand thousands ministered to Him; ten thousand times ten thousand stood before Him.
>
> —Daniel 7:10

When I pray, I often begin by saying, "Father, I come before You in the presence of Your holy angels." I imagine billions of angels surrounding the throne.

Conclusion

My own prayer time has been helped greatly as I picture myself seated in heavenly places (Eph. 2:6) and, thus, standing before the throne of God when I pray. This is what is implied in coming to the throne of grace when we pray (Heb. 4:16).

Let me describe the scene as I picture it in my mind after considering the details given in the Scripture. I am sure that what I picture is not very accurate when compared to what the throne scene actually looks like. But when I pray, I picture the following scene:

I see the Father on His throne with a diamondlike radiance and fiery red brightness emanating from Him. I picture Jesus sitting at the Father's right hand on a sapphire throne, with His face as bright as the sun and His eyes like fire, with an emerald rainbow arching above them and with the four living creatures flying around the top area of the throne, crying, "Holy, holy, holy" as myriads of angels surround the throne.

I imagine twenty-four elders in white robes, with golden crowns, sitting in a semicircle facing God's throne. I think of a river of fire coming out of the Father's throne and flowing into the sea of glass. I imagine twelve elders on each side of the river of fire. I picture flashes of lightning and peals of thunder continually going forth from His throne, along with the most glorious music and beautiful fragrances. And I imagine standing with multitudes of believers on the sea of glass in the midst of fire, with lamps or torches hovering over it.

When we pray, we are actually talking to someone, not just verbalizing our ideas to the air. The Father and the Son are listening to us, and they gave us this picture to use, so as we intercede, let us set our minds on God's throne—the place of ultimate beauty, as well as the governmental center of the universe.

As I mentioned in a previous chapter, David, the man after God's own heart, made it his life's purpose to gaze on the beauty of God.

> One thing I have desired of the LORD, that will I seek: that I may dwell in the house of the LORD all the days of my life, to behold the beauty of the LORD, and to inquire in His temple.
> —PSALM 27:4

Like David, we can posture our minds to gaze into this glorious throne scene and be fascinated with God's beauty all the days of our lives. As we do, we too can become people after God's heart—as well as intercessors who have a strong foundation for understanding what worship in heaven looks like.

Chapter 24

PRAYER *and* WORSHIP *on* EARTH
as IT IS *in* HEAVEN

Surely that which occupies the total time and energies of heaven [worship and prayer] must be a fitting pattern for earth.[1]
—PAUL E. BILLHEIMER

IN GIVING US what we call "the Lord's Prayer," Jesus exhorted us to pray for the kingdom to be manifested on Earth as it is in heaven (Matt. 6:10). Praying as He directed logically includes asking God to establish worship on Earth just as it is in heaven. In the previous chapter we discussed the Father's throne and the surrounding scene. In this chapter we will consider the activity of worship around the throne.

The Book of Revelation gives us a glimpse into the worship order around God's throne (Rev. 4–5). Of the many aspects that may be identified, I will mention five: worship in heaven is God-centered (Rev. 4:8; 5:11–14), relational (Rev. 5:9–10), continual (Rev. 4:8), musical (Rev. 5:9), and antiphonal-interactive (vv. 8–14). Each of these characteristics was expressed in the worship order that King David established in Israel. I believe that each will also be reflected in the end-time worship movement, as we will see in the next chapter.

1. Worship in heaven is God-centered.

> The four living creatures and the twenty-four elders fell down before the Lamb.... And they sang a new song, saying: "You are worthy..." Then I looked, and I heard the voice of many angels around the throne...saying with a loud voice: "Worthy is the Lamb."
> —REVELATION 5:8–9, 11–12

The worship order of heaven is decidedly God-centered. Those nearest God's throne continually proclaim the truth about who God is and what He does. The truth about the supremacy of God invokes a response; therefore, those nearest His throne cannot be silent. He is worthy, and His great worth demands expression. Treasuring God and adoring Him as the worthy One is the first priority in the worship order of heaven. It is a necessary and fitting response to His matchless beauty and immeasurable worth.

2. Worship in heaven is relational.

> You are worthy...for You were slain, and have redeemed us to God by
> Your blood...and have made us kings and priests to our God; and we
> shall reign on the earth.
>
> —REVELATION 5:9–10

Around the throne, the four living creatures and twenty-four elders sing about the facts that Jesus was slain and that He has made His people kings and priests in partnership with Him. One aspect of magnifying Jesus is to praise Him because of His desire for deep relationship and partnership in ministry with us. The way He loves us reveals much about who He really is. Why was He slain? The answer is found in the quality of love He possesses for His Father and His people.

Our lives have great value because of the way God loves and values us. God is love; therefore, He greatly values His people. We see the truth of this statement more vividly when we consider the opposite: our lives are not valuable to Satan because he is a murderer (John 8:44). We are immensely valuable because the most worthy One attributes great worth to us and because He wants relationship with us.

In heaven multitudes worship and give glory to Jesus. Love, infinite power, great wisdom, and majestic splendor all define who Jesus is. But His greatness is seen most clearly in the quality of His love. He uses His power and wisdom to establish His plan to forever fill heaven and Earth with love (Rev. 21–22).

We worship Jesus as the altogether worthy One, who being high, went low to bring us near to Himself because we are dear to Him. Jesus was high in heaven. He transcends humanity in every way, being infinitely superior to all of creation. And yet He made Himself low for our sakes, taking on human form. All His actions throughout time have one purpose—to bring us near to Him. He wants us with Him as "kings and priests" (Rev. 1:6; 5:10) who will reign with Him for eternity. And the reason? Because we are dear to His heart, the objects of His unfailing love. So it is that the worship songs around the throne magnify God's great love—a love that expresses itself in His desire for relationship with us and that results in His making us kings who share His authority and priests who draw near to His heart.

Because God is relational, to magnify Him and extol His worth is to make much of who He is and what He cares about. He is love, and He cares deeply about expressing His love toward us. Forever we will sing of His great love, which led to His washing us in His blood and making us kings and priests (Rev. 1:6; 5:10), and of His worthiness because He was slain (Rev. 5:9).

> ...Jesus Christ...the ruler over the kings of the earth. To Him who loved us and washed us from our sins in His own blood, and has made us kings and priests to His God.
>
> —Revelation 1:5–6

At the end of the age He will "show the exceeding riches of His grace in His kindness toward us" (Eph. 2:7). Therefore, an important aspect of understanding Jesus's glory is seeing our worth to Him in His grace.

3. Worship in heaven is continual.

The worship order of heaven is continual. The four living creatures, those nearest to God's throne, offer unceasing worship.

> The four living creatures...do not rest day or night, saying: "Holy, holy, holy."
>
> —Revelation 4:8

The value of 24/7 worship was established in heaven around the throne. Why do they offer unceasing worship? Because God's majesty and supremacy demand to be continually extolled by those who see Him most clearly.

Isaiah prophesied of a time when worship and intercession will be offered in a way that will never stop (Isa. 62:6–7). Jesus referred to Isaiah's prophecy when He spoke of those who would pray continually (Luke 18:7–8).

4. Worship in heaven is musical.

> The four living creatures and the twenty-four elders...each having a harp...sang a new song, saying: "You are worthy."
>
> —Revelation 5:8–9

> I heard the sound of harpists playing their harps. They sang as it were a new song before the throne.
>
> —Revelation 14:2–3

The worship order of heaven is musical. God's beauty is seen in the glorious music, songs, choirs, voices, and noises that surround His throne (Rev. 4:5; 8:5; 11:19; 16:18). There beautiful songs are sung before Him, proclaiming the glory that is due His name (Rev. 5:9–14; 14:2–3; 15:2–4).

The Lord Himself sings over His people (Zeph. 3:17), and Jesus sings praise to the Father (Heb. 2:12). The apostle John highlighted harps and trumpets in the heavenly symphony around God's throne (Rev. 5:8; 8:2, 6, 13; 14:2; 15:2).

5. Worship in heaven is antiphonal.

Around God's throne antiphonal singing is the model of God's choice (Rev. 5:8–14). "Antiphonal singing" means "responsive singing." It is the norm in the Book of Revelation. In this model musicians and singers flow interactively together to worship God with prayers and prophetic proclamations. For example, in the worship setting described below, we can identify five responsive movements of different groups ministering to God:

> The four living creatures and the twenty-four elders...sang a new song, saying: "You are worthy..." I heard the voice of many angels...saying with a loud voice: "Worthy is the Lamb..." Every creature which is in heaven and on the earth...I heard saying: "Blessing and honor and glory and power be to Him..." Then the four living creatures said, "Amen!" And the twenty-four elders fell down and worshiped Him.
>
> —REVELATION 5:8–9, 11–14

First, the four living creatures and twenty-four elders sing (vv. 8–9). Second, the myriads of angels respond to them (vv. 11–12). Third, every creature contributes to what the first two groups proclaimed (v. 13). Fourth, the four living creatures answer with a chorus, crying, "Amen!" (v. 14). Fifth, the twenty-four elders respond with worship (v. 14).

THE WORSHIP ORDER ESTABLISHED BY KING DAVID

King David received understanding from the Holy Spirit related to how the temple was to be designed and how the priests and Levites (singers and musicians) were supposed to function (1 Chron. 28:11–19).

> David gave his son Solomon the plans...for all that he had by the Spirit...for the division of the priests and the Levites...."All this," said David, "the LORD made me understand in writing, by His hand upon me, all the works of these plans."
>
> —1 CHRONICLES 28:11–13, 19

The Lord used David to establish a new worship order in Israel. In this order he was expressing on Earth some of the worship principles that exist in heaven around God's throne. The worship order established by David—in other words, "Davidic worship"—had many elements, but again, I will mention only five: It is God-centered, relational, continual, musical, and antiphonal, or interactive, just like the worship in heaven described above.

1. Davidic worship was God-centered.

> One thing I have desired of the LORD, that will I seek: that I may dwell in the house of the LORD all the days of my life, to behold the beauty of the LORD.
>
> —PSALM 27:4

The premier distinction of David's life was his preoccupation with God, particularly His majestic beauty. Many of the songs used in David's tabernacle were God-centered in magnifying God's beauty and honor and declaring the truth about who God is and what He does. Some of David's many songs were included in the Book of Psalms. They reflect his heart's desire to make God supreme in his life. David treasured and adored God and sang about His beauty and immeasurable worth.

2. Davidic worship was relational.

A number of the songs in the Book of Psalms were sung by the Levites in the temple and in David's tabernacle before the temple was built. Many of them emphasize God's love for His people and His desire for relationship and partnership with them.

> Because Your lovingkindness is better than life, my lips shall praise You.
> —PSALM 63:3

> I have called upon You....Show Your marvelous lovingkindness by Your right hand....Keep me as the apple of Your eye.
> —PSALM 17:6–8

David wrote songs about how God loved him and treated him, about his future destiny along with his love for God, and about crying out for mercy and help in times when his love was weak. Such themes were often expressed in the worship songs that David and the Levites wrote. They sang about how God wanted to relate to them and use them in this age and in the age to come. David also magnified the Lord for loving His people as He does and for desiring to involve them in His kingdom purposes.

> LORD, our Lord, how excellent is Your name in all the earth....What is man that You are mindful of him, and the son of man that You visit him?...You have crowned him with glory and honor. You have made him to have dominion over the works of Your hands; You have put all things under his feet.
> —PSALM 8:1, 4–6

He was overwhelmed at seeing the dignity of the redeemed in God's sight and God's commitment to rule the earth in partnership with them (Ps. 8). He asked why the Lord is mindful of humans (v. 4). He wanted to know what it is about humans that deeply moves the Lord. The answer is found not in any inherent goodness in us but in the greatness of God's love for us.

David praised the Lord because He was kind and loving, because He took pleasure in weak people and imparted His own beauty to them (Ps. 149).

Let them praise His name...for the LORD takes pleasure in His people;
He will beautify the humble with salvation.

—PSALM 149:3–4

And let the beauty of the LORD our God be upon us.

—PSALM 90:17

David sang praise to God for exalting him as a king who would partner with
God in bringing God's glory to Israel and the nations, for making him blessed
forever (Ps. 21), and for giving him many benefits in this age and in the age to
come because God loved him and longed for a blessed and deep relationship with
him (Ps. 103).

The king shall have joy in Your strength, O LORD....For You meet him
with the blessings of goodness....His glory is great in Your salvation;
honor and majesty You have placed upon him. For You have made him
most blessed forever.

—PSALM 21:1, 3, 5–6

Bless the LORD...and forget not all His benefits: who forgives all your
iniquities, who heals all your diseases, who redeems your life from
destruction, who crowns you with lovingkindness and tender mercies.

—PSALM 103:2–4

3. Davidic worship continued day and night.

As I mentioned in chapter 22, David established singers and musicians to sustain day-and-night worship before the Lord.

These are the singers...who lodged in the chambers, and were free from
other duties; for they were employed in that work day and night.

—1 CHRONICLES 9:33

David provided financial support for these musicians and singers to worship God as their full-time occupation. He set in place four thousand musicians
(1 Chron. 23:5) and two hundred eighty-eight singers (1 Chron. 25:7). Organizing
these groups and supporting them required a massive amount of work and was
very expensive. Nevertheless, David insisted on making this costly investment
of time and money, knowing that the Lord commanded it and that the God of
Israel is worthy of praise.

Behold, bless the LORD, all you servants of the LORD, who by night
stand in the house of the LORD! Lift up your hands in the sanctuary,
and bless the LORD. The LORD who made heaven and earth bless you
from Zion!

—PSALM 134:1–3

The Scripture makes it clear that the Levites ministered to God "night and day" and that there was a special blessing for those who praised the Lord in the night. Many people believe that Davidic worship was 24/7; however, there is no clear statement in the Scripture that proves beyond doubt that David's order of worship was continual in the sense of ongoing worship twenty-four hours a day. We know for sure that it was continual in the sense of going night and day.

4. Davidic worship was musical.

After David became king, he established a tabernacle of worship in Jerusalem. From our reading of 1 Chronicles 15–16, and other chapters, we understand that David set Levites as singers and musicians before the ark—which represented God's throne—to worship God night and day using their musical instruments.

> They brought the ark of God and set it in the midst of the tabernacle that David had erected for it....He appointed some of the Levites to minister before the ark of the LORD, to commemorate, to thank, and to praise the LORD God of Israel.
>
> —1 CHRONICLES 16:1, 4

First Chronicles 16 names the leading Levites who ministered in music before the Lord in the new order of worship in the tabernacle of David—including Asaph the chief musician—and lists their instruments, which consisted of stringed instruments, harps, cymbals, and trumpets (1 Chron. 16:5–6). The second Book of Chronicles speaks again of the musicians and singers David established:

> And the Levites who were the singers...having cymbals, stringed instruments and harps...
>
> —2 CHRONICLES 5:12

David made instruments and mobilized thousands of Levites to praise the Lord and prophesy on their instruments:

> And four thousand praised the LORD with musical instruments, "which I made," said David, "for giving praise."
>
> —1 CHRONICLES 23:5

> David...separated for the service some of the sons of Asaph, of Heman, and of Jeduthun, who should prophesy with harps, stringed instruments, and cymbals....All these were under the direction of their father for the music in the house of the LORD, with cymbals, stringed instruments, and harps, for the service of the house of God.
>
> —1 CHRONICLES 25:1, 6

In a list of the Levites' responsibilities in Jerusalem we learn that praise was offered to the Lord in song day and night (1 Chron. 9:33).

5. Davidic worship was antiphonal.

The worship order that David established in Israel included antiphonal, interactive singing (Neh. 12:24), just as the worship order around God's heavenly throne does (Rev. 5:8–14). Why did David command it? Possibly because he understood that God had organized the choirs of heaven to respond to one another antiphonally.

David organized antiphonal choirs to respond to each other (Neh. 12:8–9, 24, 31, 38, 40). The choirs stood across from each other and alternated as they sang responsively:

> Mattaniah who led the thanksgiving psalms, he and his brethren. Also Bakbukiah and Unni, their brethren, stood across from them in their duties....And the heads of the Levites were Hashabiah, Sherebiah, and Jeshua the son of Kadmiel, with their brothers across from them, to praise and give thanks, group *alternating with group*, according to the command of David the man of God.
> —NEHEMIAH 12:8–9, 24

> And they sang *responsively*, praising and giving thanks to the LORD: "For He is good, for His mercy endures forever toward Israel."
> —EZRA 3:11

MAINTAINING THE DAVIDIC ORDER OF WORSHIP

After David established the heavenly order of worship that he had received by revelation, he commanded God's people to honor it because it had come to him as a direct commandment from the Lord (2 Chron. 29:25; 35:4, 15; Ezra 3:10; Neh. 12:45). Whenever Israel went astray, God raised up spiritual reformers with a vision to restore worship as David had commanded. All seven "revivals" in the Old Testament included the restoration of Davidic worship. Notice how many times the Scripture refers to the leaders of Israel setting the singers and musicians in place because it was "according to the command of David."

> He [Hezekiah] stationed the Levites in the house of the LORD with cymbals, with stringed instruments, and with harps, according to the commandment of David...for thus was the commandment of the LORD.
> —2 CHRONICLES 29:25

Around 970 BC Solomon established the singers according to the command that God had given his father David.

> According to the order of David his father, he [Solomon] appointed the divisions of the priests for their service, the Levites for their duties (to praise and serve before the priests) as the duty of each day required…for so David the man of God had commanded.
> —2 Chronicles 8:14

Around 870 BC Jehoshaphat's reform included establishing singers and musicians in their place to sing to the Lord.

> The Levites…stood up to praise the Lord…he [Jehoshaphat] appointed those who should sing to the Lord….So they came to Jerusalem, with stringed instruments and harps and trumpets, to the house of the Lord.
> —2 Chronicles 20:19, 21, 28

In about 835 BC Jehoiada the high priest restored temple worship in the order of King David with singers and musicians. The high priest was functioning as the main leader in Israel at that time because the young future king, Jehoash (Joash), was only seven years old.

> Jehoiada appointed the oversight of the house of the Lord to…the Levites…with singing, as it was established by David.
> —2 Chronicles 23:18

Around 625 BC Josiah's revival restored full-time singers and musicians to their places just as David had commanded the kings of Israel.

> He said to the Levites…"Prepare yourselves…following the written instruction of David…" The singers…were in their places, according to the command of David.
> —2 Chronicles 35:3–4, 15

In 536 BC Zerubbabel established full-time singers and musicians to worship God as their full-time occupation because King David had commanded that this be done in Israel.

> The Levites [stood]…with cymbals, to praise the Lord, according to the ordinance of David.
> —Ezra 3:10

Ezra and Nehemiah in 445 BC also established full-time singers and musicians because King David had commanded it.

> The Levites were…to give thanks…according to the command of
> David….Both the singers and the gatekeepers kept the charge of their
> God…according to the command of David.
>
> —NEHEMIAH 12:24, 45

We learn from Nehemiah that the practice of apportioning provision for the singers was reinstituted in the days of Zerubbabel, the governor of Judah (Neh. 11:23; 12:44–47; 13:5–12), in accordance with the way that David had financially supported the singers who were worshipping as their full-time occupation (2 Chron. 8:14; 31:5–16).

> In the days of Zerubbabel and in the days of Nehemiah all Israel gave
> the portions for the singers…a portion for each day.
>
> —NEHEMIAH 12:47

I believe that the order of worship God commanded David to embrace—establishing the full-time occupation of singers and musicians in God's house along with worship that is God-centered, relational, continual, musical, and antiphonal—was not only for David's time but also for ours. It is ageless because God's desire to be worshipped on Earth as He is in heaven remains the same. Though it has not always been a focus, the Holy Spirit is now calling many ministries to embrace Davidic worship. The application will be different in each city, but I believe over time the Lord will raise up 24/7 worship in each city or region of the earth as local churches partner together to establish it. I do not believe that 24/7 worship is supposed to flow from each church building but rather from as many as one hundred churches coming together to see 24/7 worship offered to God from their geographic area.

The prophet Amos, in about 750 BC, prophesied that David's tabernacle would be restored. "On that day I will raise up the tabernacle of David, which has fallen down, and repair its damages; I will raise up its ruins, and rebuild it as in the days of old" (Amos 9:11). Restoration will include Davidic worship in the spirit of the tabernacle of David. The fullness of the tabernacle of David refers to Jesus's government based on 24/7 Davidic worship in the millennial kingdom, as we will see in chapter 25.

PART VI

THE END-TIME GLOBAL PRAYER MOVEMENT

When God gets ready to do something new with His people, He always sets them a-praying.[1]

—J. EDWIN ORR

Chapter 25

SEVEN CHARACTERISTICS *of the* END-TIME PRAYER MOVEMENT

Prayer is both starting point and goal to every movement in which are the elements of permanent progress. Wherever the church is aroused...somebody, somewhere has been praying.[1]
—A. T. PIERSON

JESUS IS NOT coming back to a prayerless church but to one that is operating in close partnership with Him in intercession for the end-time harvest (Rev. 22:17). The Holy Spirit is on the move, raising up a worldwide prayer and worship movement throughout the whole body of Christ. It will surpass any other such movement in history in terms of depth of insight, release of power, and the number of people involved. The outcome will include the gospel's being preached to all nations in the power of the Holy Spirit (Matt. 24:14; Rev. 7:9, 14).

The end-time prayer and worship movement is rapidly growing in the nations (see chapter 28) as the Holy Spirit works to establish a prayer culture in the body of Christ worldwide before Jesus returns. Throughout the world He is raising up people with what I refer to as the "Anna calling." Anna was a prophetess at the time of Jesus's birth who served God with much prayer and fasting in the temple most of her life (Luke 2:37). The end-time Annas are radical believers who function as what I call "intercessory missionaries," engaging in the work of intercession with worship as their full-time occupations. (See chapter 30 for more about the Anna calling and what I mean by the term "intercessory missionary.")

The prophet Isaiah and King David in the Psalms gave us the most information about the end-time prayer and worship movement in terms of its earthly dimension, whereas the apostle John described it from a heavenly perspective in the Book of Revelation. In this chapter we will look closely at what they said.

The Book of Isaiah and the Psalms, along with other scriptures, describe many characteristics of this glorious movement. I will identify just seven of them, though there are many more. The end-time prayer and worship movement will be God-centered, relational, continual, musical, global, missional, and intergenerational. You will notice that I am including four of the five aspects mentioned in the last chapter pertaining to the worship order in heaven and in David's time. I believe that the end-time prayer movement will express worship "on earth as it is in heaven" (Matt. 6:10) in a greater way than the worship-intercession model David established with the Levites in his generation did.

1. The end-time prayer movement will be God-centered.

The premier distinction of the end-time prayer and worship movement will be the understanding of the supremacy of Jesus, particularly His majestic beauty as Bridegroom, King, and Judge. End-time worship songs will emphasize the majesty of the Lord. Prophesying about the end-time prayer and worship movement, Isaiah said:

> They shall sing; *for the majesty of the Lord* they shall cry aloud....From the ends of the earth we have heard songs: "Glory to the righteous!"
> —ISAIAH 24:14–16

The songs will focus on the Lord's majesty and bring "glory to the Lord, as the Righteous One." Some translations clarify Isaiah 24:16 by translating the phrase "the righteous" as "the Righteous One" (see the NIV and the NAS). Through these songs worshippers will magnify the majesty of God.

Worship is a response to the revelation of God. It is a response to something that we see and to someone we love. Around the globe people of all ages are catching a glimpse of the beauty, worth, and supremacy of Jesus and are responding in genuine love as they treasure and adore Him, giving a witness on the earth to His indescribable value.

The truth of Jesus's worth and greatness *must* be declared in song and in prophetic proclamation because it is the ultimate truth on which the whole created universe exists. Jesus told the Pharisees when they were insisting that He rebuke His disciples for worshipping Him that if the people kept silent in His presence, the very stones would immediately cry out in their place (Luke 19:37–40). The end-time prayer movement on Earth will join the worship symphony in heaven, crying out, "Worthy is the Lamb" (Rev. 5:12).

2. The end-time prayer movement will be relational.

The end-time prayer and worship movement will have a relational focus, which will be reflected in our singing of the wonders of God's love for us and our response of love for Him. God is love, and He wants relationship with us—not because He is needy but because He wants to share His love and to rule the earth in a deep partnership with His people. Love finds pleasure in relating to others and working closely with others.

Jesus desires to make us feel loved; He celebrates our dignity and value and wants us to do so too. He delights in us, in sharing His heart with us, and in relating to us. He wants to partner with us in the work that His Father has entrusted to Him. He is pleased when we love, honor, and magnify Him.

As King David did, we will sing songs about God's love for us. We will also sing new songs about our destiny as kings and priests ruling the earth with Jesus forever. We will sing of our love for Jesus, thanking Him for mercy and asking Him for help in times when our love is weak. We will sing of His kindness and of the marvel that He takes pleasure in weak people and imparts His very own beauty to us (Isa. 61:3; Ps. 90:17; 149:4).

> To proclaim the acceptable year of the LORD...to give them beauty for ashes...
>
> —ISAIAH 61:2–3

> And let the beauty of the LORD our God be upon us.
>
> —PSALM 90:17

In tandem with the revelation of the Father-heart of God is the understanding of Jesus as our Bridegroom King and of the body of Christ as His cherished bride (Eph. 5:29–32). Thus we will sing of the Father's relating to us with tender mercy and of Jesus's expressing His desire for His people as their Bridegroom God (Isa. 54:5; 62:5; Rev. 22:17). Before the Lord returns, the church will see themselves as a bride crying out to her Bridegroom King to come to her (Rev. 22:17, 20). Even now the Holy Spirit is emphasizing the church's identity as His cherished bride.

In Revelation 22:20 John prophesied that the Spirit and the bride would say, "Come, Lord Jesus!" This is one of the most informative and significant prophecies describing the end-time church. In the end times, for the first time in history, the Spirit will universally emphasize the church's identity as Jesus's bride.

As sons of God we are positioned to experience His throne—His power operating through us. As the bride of Christ we are positioned to experience God's heart—His desire for us. The Bridegroom message is focused on Jesus's emotions for us, His beauty, and His commitment to share His heart, home, throne, secrets, and beauty with us. Many verses in the Scripture refer to God as the bridegroom of His people.[2]

We are "heirs of God and joint heirs with Christ" and thus have access to both His power and His heart (Rom. 8:17). The end-time worship movement will sing of many aspects of this glorious relationship as we grow in our understanding and experiences of His affections for us.

A word of caution: it is wrong and wholly inappropriate to mix the truth of Jesus as our Bridegroom God with the concept of a sensual lover or "boyfriend God." We must absolutely avoid any sensual overtones in the bride-of-Christ message. I have known some women who applied the glorious truth of Jesus as our Bridegroom God in a wrong way by viewing Jesus as their lover or boyfriend in the natural sense. This is a grave error.

Isaiah emphasized the relational aspect of the end-time prayer movement when he described the Messiah as our Bridegroom God.

> For your Maker is your husband, the LORD of hosts is His name.
>
> —ISAIAH 54:5

> As the bridegroom rejoices over the bride, so shall your God rejoice over
> you.
> —ISAIAH 62:5

Isaiah declared to Israel that their maker was their husband. The idea of a God with deep emotions of love was a difficult concept for the people in his day to grasp because they saw God only as their transcendent Creator. Jewish tradition emphasized His holiness and majesty, so it was shocking for the people to learn that God had desire for them and not just power over them.

Isaiah connected the revelation of Jesus as the Bridegroom with the end-time prayer movement that will continue night and day until the Lord returns to make Jerusalem a praise in the earth:

> You shall be called Hephzibah . . . for the LORD delights in you. . . . For . . . as
> the bridegroom rejoices over the bride, so shall your God rejoice over
> you. I have set watchmen [intercessors] on your walls, O Jerusalem; they
> shall never hold their peace day or night . . . till He makes Jerusalem a
> praise in the earth.
> —ISAIAH 62:4–7

He prophesied that in the end times God's people would be called "Hephzibah," which in Hebrew carries the meaning of the Lord's delighting in His people.

The God who delights in us is the very One who will set intercessors in place to worship and pray 24/7 until Jesus returns (vv. 6–7). His Holy Spirit is moving right now to raise up a multitude of men and women—singers, preachers, evangelists, writers, marketplace leaders, and intercessors—all over the world who will proclaim that God delights in His people.

I have found that people are best motivated to sustain night-and-day intercession when they understand that God delights in them as a bridegroom delights in his bride (vv. 4–5). In fact, one reason people burn out in intercession and ministry to others is that they lack the intimacy with God that comes from encountering Jesus as their Bridegroom God who delights in His relationship with them. In other words, the revelation of the church as Jesus's cherished bride is essential to keeping our hearts alive through the years as we diligently do the work of the kingdom.

3. The end-time prayer movement (worship element) will be continual (Isa. 62:6–7; Luke 18:7–8).

As the worship order around God's throne in heaven is continual, so worship on Earth will be continual in many nations before Jesus returns. Isaiah prophesied of a time just before Jesus returns when the Lord would set intercessors in place who would never be silent day or night. He referred to these intercessors as watchmen "who remind the Lord."

> On your walls, O Jerusalem, I have appointed watchmen [intercessors];
> all day and all night they will never keep silent. You who remind the
> LORD, take no rest for yourselves; and give Him no rest until He estab-
> lishes and makes Jerusalem a praise in the earth.
>
> —ISAIAH 62:6–7, NAS

Isaiah described prayer ministries that would continue 24/7 until the time
when Jerusalem becomes a praise in the earth—that is, when Jesus returns to
reign from Jerusalem. Jeremiah prophesied the Lord's reign in Jerusalem when
he decreed, "At that time Jerusalem shall be called The Throne of the LORD" (Jer.
3:17). And Jesus spoke of Jerusalem as "the city of the great King" (Matt. 5:35),
anticipating the day when He would dwell there among His people, ruling the
nations in partnership with them after He returns to the earth.

Only one generation will see the fulfillment of God's promise to appoint
watchmen-intercessors to pray "all day and all night" on Jerusalem's walls. Do
you understand the significance of this promise? God will sovereignly appoint
and place intercessors in prayer ministries *who will not stop praying for Jerusalem
until Jesus returns.* In ministries in Jerusalem and around the world believers are
taking hold of this prophetic promise and standing on the "wall of intercession"
to cry out for the salvation of Jerusalem and the nations. Perhaps you will be one
of them.

Jesus made reference to the prophecy given by Isaiah when He spoke of those
who would pray day and night and whose prayers would result in the release of
justice (Luke 18:1–8). Jesus connected the call to continual prayer to the timing
of His Second Coming (vv. 7–8). Also notice that in Luke 18:1 Jesus started His
parable with "then," tying it back to what He had just taught about the end times
in Luke 17:22–36.

> Then He spoke a parable to them, that men always ought to pray and
> not lose heart.... "Shall God not avenge His own elect who cry out
> day and night to Him...? I tell you that He will avenge them speedily.
> Nevertheless, when the Son of Man comes [the Second Coming], will
> He really find faith on the earth?"
>
> —LUKE 18:1, 7–8

In place of the word *avenge* in verses 7 and 8, many Bible translations use
the phrase "bring about justice." Jesus connected night-and-day prayer to God's
releasing justice on the earth, especially in the generation in which the Son of
Man comes back.

In verse 8 Jesus posed an important question about finding faith on the earth.
He was not asking if there would be believers on Earth who had faith to become
born again. He was asking if there would be people who would have the faith *to
agree with Him in bringing about justice through night-and-day prayer.*

The Spirit is raising up many leaders in the body of Christ who have faith (agreement with God) to work for justice in a way that flows from praying night and day for it. Most often, 24/7 prayer will arise from many local churches working together across a city or region. I don't believe the Lord is calling most individual local churches to start 24/7 prayer ministries on their own; rather, He is calling them to build a culture of prayer in their churches and to work with other ministries to see 24/7 prayer and worship set up in their cities. In other words, unless the Lord specifically calls you to start 24/7 prayer in your congregation, it is best to participate in the collective effort of many local churches, including hundreds of people leading prayer meetings in homes, churches, universities, and the marketplace across your city.

4. The end-time prayer movement will be musical (Isa. 42:10–13).

Another aspect of the end-time prayer movement is that it will involve music. Isaiah emphasized the place of singing and music in the end-time prayer movement.[3] Music is one expression of the kingdom of God "on Earth as it is in heaven."

Music is an essential part of our human makeup. The human spirit is musical because we were created in the image of God, who is musical (Zeph. 3:17; Heb. 2:12). The Bible tells us the Lord sings over His people:

> The LORD your God…will rejoice over you with singing.
> —ZEPHANIAH 3:17

The writer of Hebrews describes Jesus's singing praise to the Father (Heb. 2:12). Jesus is surely the greatest singer, musician, and songwriter in human history.

Music touches the deepest part of the human spirit. Anointed worship music helps God's people express their hearts to God in adoration and love. It also draws them together in unity by giving them the opportunity to sing the same thing to the same Man at the same time. In addition it helps people learn and remember the truth of God's Word. Most important, the anointing of the Spirit on worship music tenderizes our hearts, increasing our ability to receive love from God and return it back to Him.

In his book *The Evidential Power of Beauty* Thomas Dubay quotes Michael Platt: "Music reaches the passions without passing through the mind…[even] those who have devoted no study whatever to listening to music are moved by it."[4] Dubay believed that "music…sparks a thirst for the divine."[5] Both the orchestra conductor and the blue-collar factory worker can be equally moved in their hearts by the music to which they listen.

Think how many special events in our lives are accompanied by music— ceremonies, weddings, birthdays, football games, funerals, graduations, romantic outings, church services. Many of us listen to music throughout the day, whether we are attending a special event or not. Music is not only enjoyable, it is also essential in the economy of God. The Holy Spirit has a musical dimension to His being. God the Father and God the Son sing, create music, and enjoy music.

For years before we started the International House of Prayer at Kansas City (IHOPKC), music was not central to our daily prayer meetings at the church I pastored. Eventually we added music to our times of prayer and worship, and the meetings became not just bearable but enjoyable!

Isaiah called end-time Israel to sing while the people were still spiritually barren, before the fulfillment of God's promise of mercy and restoration: "Sing, O barren, you who have not borne! Break forth into singing, and cry aloud, you who have not labored with child!...For you shall expand to the right and to the left, and your descendants will inherit the nations" (Isa. 54:1, 3).

In a similar way Isaiah is calling those who are a part of the end-time worship movement to sing even before we see revival. God will raise up a prayer movement that will break forth in intercessory singing until the fullness of God's salvation is manifest.

The Holy Spirit is committed to filling the earth with songs that extol Jesus (Ps. 96–98).

> Sing to the LORD a new song! Sing to the LORD, all the earth....Worship the LORD....Tremble before Him, all the earth...for He is coming to judge the earth.
> —PSALM 96:1, 9, 13

> Sing to the LORD a new song...all the ends of the earth have seen the salvation of our God. Shout joyfully to the LORD, all the earth; break forth in song, rejoice, and sing praises....For He is coming to judge the earth. With righteousness He shall judge the world.
> —PSALM 98:1, 3–4, 9

Though it is characterized by music, the end-time worship movement is not a Christian music festival. It is an environment in which music flows from those who grow deep in the knowledge of God. Young adults especially are responding with great zeal. Around the globe they are catching a glimpse of the beauty and worth of Jesus and of how He is worshipped in heaven.

As we saw in the previous chapter, the worship order that David established included antiphonal, interactive singing (Ezra 3:11; Neh. 12:8–9, 24) just as the worship order around God's heavenly throne does (Rev. 5:8–14). Here in Kansas City, at the International House of Prayer, the "harp and bowl" model of intercessory worship includes antiphonal singing in an interactive relationship between the worship team and the intercessors. Antiphonal singing provides an opportunity for them to operate in team ministry in worship and prayer. It also provides diversity in night-and-day prayer, making the prayer time more interesting and sustainable.

We have established three ways to antiphonally sing the Word in our prayer meetings.

1. Echo the phrase. The singer sings the exact words of the person who prayed or sang before him. Repeating the same phrase increases the impact.

2. Paraphrase the phrase. The singer summarizes the theme in similar words.

3. Expand the phrase. The singer uses totally different words to enhance the idea.

You can actually watch our worship teams through our live Web stream. We broadcast our prayer room live 24/7. To view it, go to www.ihopkc.org/prayerroom.

5. The end-time prayer movement will be global (Isa. 24:14–16; 42:10–12; Mal. 1:11).

The Scripture is clear that the end-time worship and prayer movement will extend all across the earth, even to the most remote and difficult-to-reach places. It contains numerous prophecies of a global worship movement that will involve singing to the Lord from the ends of the earth (Ps. 96:1; Isa. 24:14–16; 42:10–12).

> Sing to the LORD a new song…all the earth.
>
> —PSALM 96:1

> From the ends of the earth we have heard songs: "Glory to the righteous!"…
>
> —ISAIAH 24:16

> Sing to the LORD a new song, and His praise from the ends of the earth.
>
> —ISAIAH 42:10

King David and others prophesied that the worldwide worship movement would involve all the kings of the earth.[6]

> Yes, all kings shall fall down before Him; all nations shall serve Him.
>
> —PSALM 72:11

> All the kings of the earth shall praise You, O LORD, when they hear the words of Your mouth. Yes, they shall sing of the ways of the LORD, for great is the glory of the LORD.
>
> —PSALM 138:4–5

Isaiah prophesied that a global intercessory worship movement would usher in Jesus's return:

> Sing to the LORD a new song, and His praise from the ends of the earth, you who go down to the sea, and all that is in it, you coastlands....Let the wilderness and its cities lift up their voice, the villages that Kedar inhabits. Let the inhabitants of Sela sing, let them shout from the top of the mountains....The LORD shall go forth [Jesus's Second Coming] like a mighty man; He shall stir up His zeal like a man of war. He shall cry out, yes, shout aloud; He shall prevail against His enemies.
>
> —ISAIAH 42:10–13

In his prophecy Isaiah is saying that the redeemed will worship from one end of the earth to the other until Jesus returns. Simply put, the end-time worship and prayer movement will be in every place—even the hardest and darkest places—offering up worship to Jesus (Mal. 1:11). Isaiah highlighted that God's people will sing to the Lord in the islands, which are often remote and hard to get to (Isa. 42:10). He spoke of worship going forth in the wilderness, or desert places, even in Islamic villages such as Kedar in Saudi Arabia and Sela in Jordan (v. 11). The prophecy reveals the zeal with which the Holy Spirit is raising up a worldwide worship movement. Jesus is not coming in a vacuum but in answer to a global worship movement.

6. The end-time prayer movement will be missional (Rev. 7:9, 14).

The end-time worship and prayer movement will be instrumental in ushering in the greatest harvest of souls in history and the fullness of God's justice on the earth (Matt. 24:14; Luke 18:7–8; Rev. 7:9, 14). Jesus said that we must ask the Lord to release laborers into the harvest (Luke 10:2). We can identify a pattern by studying the account of the early church, in which communities such as the one in Jerusalem mentioned in Acts 2 and the one in Antioch mentioned in Acts 13 gathered together in worship and prayer. The result was that missionaries were sent out, evangelism movements were unleashed, and a significant harvest of souls was reaped. Jesus connected night-and-day prayer to the release of justice on the earth (Luke 18:7–8), in the context of the end times (Luke 17:24–37), with specific reference to His Second Coming (Luke 18:8).

7. The end-time prayer movement will be intergenerational (Mal. 4:5–6).

The end-time prayer movement will be intergenerational, joining physical and spiritual fathers and mothers with their children. Malachi prophesied that the Holy Spirit would turn the hearts of the fathers to the youth in the generation in which the Lord returns:

> Behold, I will send you Elijah the prophet before the coming of the great
> and dreadful day of the LORD. And he will turn the hearts of the fathers
> to the children, and the hearts of the children to their fathers.
>
> —MALACHI 4:5–6

The Holy Spirit desires for spiritual fathers and mothers to focus on God's
purpose for young people, causing the young people to respond with honor and
love so that there is great unity and power in God's house.

Statistically most people who turn to Jesus do so before they are twenty-five
years old. The majority of the current population of the earth is under this age.
I believe the Holy Spirit is emphasizing prophetic worship and the revelation of
Jesus's beauty in this hour to draw a massive number of youth to Jesus once again,
as He has drawn them in many of the great revivals of history.

Just before He died, Jesus prayed and prophesied in what I call His "high
priestly prayer" that He would pour out His glory, enabling His people to walk
in a level of unity that would greatly enhance the effectiveness of the gospel
(John 17:21–23). The end-time worship and prayer movement will function in
gracious cooperation because God has entrusted different aspects of His purposes and plans to different parts of His body. Out of necessity the prayer movement will be profoundly unified as we experience the fullness of God's purpose
by honoring and serving one another in relationship. Unity will be achieved
because God's supernatural grace will be poured out upon the church, enabling
His people to walk in love and in a spirit of unity, for unity is the place where
God commands His blessing in the greatest measure:

> Behold, how good and how pleasant it is for brethren to dwell together in
> unity…for there the LORD commanded the blessing—life forevermore.
>
> —PSALM 133:1–3

As we can see, the Holy Spirit is calling the church to rise up in unity and participate in an end-time global prayer movement, offering fervent, continual intercession and worship that flows from prophetic music and intimacy with God.
From our position of strength as intercessors we will work together to fulfill the
Great Commission and bring in the greatest harvest of souls in history.[7] Jesus
will respond to the voice of His bride calling out as one with the Spirit for Him
to "come in power" to vanquish His enemies and fill the earth with the knowledge of the Lord.

As I have mentioned, the great conflict at the end of the age will be between
two "houses of prayer"—two global worship movements. The Holy Spirit
is raising up the most powerful prayer and worship movement in history. To
combat this worship movement of the Spirit, the Antichrist will establish a
state-financed, worldwide, false worship movement (Rev. 13:4, 8, 12, 15). But
Jesus has a plan in His heart, and His plan will not fail. Jesus's worship movement will be stronger, more creative, and more anointed than anything Satan

can produce. The end-time prayer movement will be God-centered, relational, continual, musical, global, missional, and intergenerational and will come closer than any other movement in history to offering worship "on earth as it is in heaven" (Matt. 6:10).

At this point, you may be asking yourself, "What does the end-time prayer movement have to do with *me*? I'm not living on the IHOPKC missions base, and I'm not called to be an Anna, spending all my days in unceasing prayer and worship before God's throne." Clearly not everyone is meant to be an intercessory missionary. However, each of us is called to play a role in the prayer movement and accompanying harvest in our generation. We are not exempt from helping to bring about His purposes simply because prayer is not our full-time occupation.

You may not be called to be an Anna, but perhaps God is asking you to attend a prayer meeting once a week at your local church to intercede. Perhaps He wants you to lead worship for a prayer group meeting in someone's home. Perhaps He desires for you to sing on a worship team made up of members from the body of Christ in your area or to engage in street evangelism. As Mary, Jesus's mother, told the servants at the wedding in Cana, "Whatever He [Jesus] says to you, do it" (John 2:5). And don't delay.

Chapter 26

PRAYER *in the* SPIRIT *of the* TABERNACLE *of* DAVID

The man who mobilizes the Christian church to pray
will make the greatest contribution.[1]
—ANDREW MURRAY

THROUGH THE PROPHET Amos, God gave an indication that the end-time global prayer movement will operate "in the spirit of the tabernacle of David." He declared: "On that day I will raise up the tabernacle of David, which has fallen down" (Amos 9:11). Previously we considered the worship dimension of David's tabernacle described in 1 Chronicles 16 and learned that David built a tent, or tabernacle, to house the ark of the covenant and then organized four thousand musicians and two hundred eighty-eight singers to stand before it to minister to God in shifts that continued day and night.[2]

When I refer to prayer "in the spirit of the tabernacle of David," I mean prayer combined with worship that has similarities to the worship order that David instituted in the tabernacle. It includes prayer that contends for the fullness of all God has promised regarding the throne of David. As we have already seen, foundational to the tabernacle of David was this specific "order of worship" that was established by David.[3] David received the worship order by revelation from the Lord (1 Chron. 28:19).

> They were ministering with music before the dwelling place of the tabernacle…and they served in their office *according to their order.*
> —1 CHRONICLES 6:32

> *According to the order of David his father,* he appointed…the Levites for their duties (to praise and serve before the priests).
> —2 CHRONICLES 8:14

Again I repeat that the Lord told David to command the kings of Israel after him to uphold this worship order:

> And he stationed the Levites in the house of the LORD with cymbals, with stringed instruments, and with harps, according to the commandment of David…for thus was the commandment of the LORD by his prophets.
> —2 CHRONICLES 29:25

The tabernacle of David included King David's government in Jerusalem, functioning in righteousness and founded on worship that was offered to God day and night. In other words, it consisted of a worship order *and* a governmental authority, plus more. David was the first king in history to base his kingship and national government on worship and prayer that continued day and night (1 Chron. 9:33).

In the generations after David's death, the tabernacle fell into ruin, but through the prophets God later promised to restore David's tabernacle:

> In mercy the throne will be established; and One will sit on it in truth, in the tabernacle of David, judging and *seeking justice* and *hastening righteousness*.
>
> —Isaiah 16:5

> "On that day I will raise up the tabernacle of David, which has fallen down, and repair its damages; I will raise up its ruins, and rebuild it as in the days of old; *that they may possess the remnant of Edom* [an Islamic nation], and *all the Gentiles* [nations] who are called by My name," says the Lord who does this thing....I will bring back the captives of My people Israel [1948]; they shall build the waste cities and inhabit them; they shall plant vineyards and drink wine from them...I will plant them in their land, and no longer shall they be pulled up from the land I have given them," says the Lord your God.
>
> —Amos 9:11–15

The fullness of God's promise to restore the tabernacle of David refers to Jesus's righteous government over all the nations in the context of 24/7 worship with prayer.

The restoration of the tabernacle of David is being fulfilled in part in this age and will be established in fullness after Jesus returns to the earth. In other words, this promise will be completely fulfilled only in the millennial kingdom, when Jesus rules all nations, both Jew and Gentile, from the throne of David in Jerusalem in the context of worship and intercession. However, the Holy Spirit is restoring a measure of the spirit of the tabernacle of David today, and the restoration includes much more than prayer meetings led by prophetic worship. It speaks of God's government on the earth flowing from prayer with worship (Rev. 4:8). We must embrace and contend for all the glorious aspects of the tabernacle of David that are set forth in the Scripture.

The Tabernacle of David: Seven Expressions

The restoration of the tabernacle of David has at least seven expressions that are deeply connected:

1. A spiritual expression—emphasizing prophetic worship with prayer based on intimacy with God (1 Chron. 16, 25)

2. A political expression—contending for justice and righteousness in government (Isa. 16:5)

3. A messianic expression—establishing a believing remnant in the state of Israel (Amos 9:14–15)

4. A missional expression—impacting all nations with the gospel of the kingdom (Amos 9:12)

5. A supernatural expression—releasing God's power, glory, and miracles (Ps. 145:11–12)

6. A transformational expression—restoring cities, agriculture, economics, and so on (Amos 9:13–14)

7. An eschatological expression—receiving Jesus as King over all nations, reigning from Jerusalem (Matt. 25:31–32; Jer. 3:17).

The spiritual expression of the tabernacle: worship with prayer based on intimacy with God

> They brought the ark of God, and set it in the midst of the tabernacle that David had erected for it.... And he [David] appointed some of the Levites [as singers] to minister before the ark of the LORD, to commemorate, to thank, and to praise the LORD.
>
> —1 CHRONICLES 16:1, 4

The spirit of the tabernacle of David has a spiritual expression—doing the work of the kingdom from a foundation of prayer led by prophetic worship that flows from intimacy with God (1 Chron. 25). The first reference to the tabernacle of David in the Scripture is related to David's establishing singers and musicians before the ark to praise God (1 Chron. 16:1–4).

David put singers before the ark because the Lord commanded him to do so (2 Chron. 29:25). Then he commanded the kings of Israel after him to uphold the worship order that God had revealed to him, including musicians and singers being supported in their full-time occupations.[4]

First Chronicles gives us valuable insight into the singers and musicians and their ministry in the tabernacle of David (1 Chron. 13–16; 23–25). In his tabernacle David valued singers and musicians who operated in the prophetic spirit, the spirit of inspiration:

> David...separated for the service some of the sons of Asaph...who should prophesy with harps, stringed instruments, and cymbals.
>
> —1 CHRONICLES 25:1

As we have seen, David's order of worship included responsive singing and antiphonal choirs that answered one another in song (Ezra 3:11; Neh. 11:23–24). In this hour many prayer ministries are learning how musicians and singers can flow more freely in a "prophetic spirit" and how their songs can interact with the prayers being offered by the intercessors.

Central to the worship order that David established was prayer energized by intimacy with God, as a result of beholding God's beauty and seeking His direction.

> …to behold the beauty of the LORD, and to inquire in His temple.
> —PSALM 27:4

We have found that one of the keys to enjoyable prayer is to combine prayer with prophetic worship that has a focus on the beauty of God. In Psalm 27 David gives us another key that he employed in his tabernacle—inquiring of the Lord. David engaged in strategic prayer, asking to know God's will and the specific plans and strategies to accomplish His will. All over the earth, the Lord is raising up prayer ministries that include gazing on God's beauty and encountering His love alongside inquiring about His strategies for the nations—all in a setting of prophetic worship.

The political expression of the tabernacle: justice and righteous government

> In mercy the throne will be established; and One [Jesus] will sit on it in truth, in the tabernacle of David, judging and seeking justice and hastening righteousness.
> —ISAIAH 16:5

The spirit of the tabernacle of David has a political expression. In prayer we are to contend for justice and righteousness to be released in a spirit of mercy, and we are to pray for the leaders in government that they will establish God's will in their sphere of authority (Isa. 16:5; 1 Tim. 2:1). The Lord promised to raise up David's throne, and the fulfillment of the promise includes the Holy Spirit's raising up godly leaders in government who will work to achieve justice. Thus, prayer in the spirit of the tabernacle of David includes praying for the release of God's justice with mercy according to what Jesus taught in Luke 18:7–8.

The messianic expression of the tabernacle: a believing remnant in the land of Israel

> I will bring back the captives of My people Israel….I will plant them in their land, and no longer shall they be pulled up from the land.
> —AMOS 9:14–15

The spirit of the tabernacle of David has a messianic expression. The prophets spoke of a believing remnant of Jewish people in the land of Israel, professing faith in Jesus as their promised Messiah. Amos prophesied that God would plant Israel in their own land in such a way that they would never again be uprooted. This speaks of the restoration of the state of Israel. The land had been given to them (first to Abraham) by God as an everlasting possession.[5] But in AD 70 the Jews were scattered to the nations as a result of the Roman siege and conquest of Jerusalem. For almost two thousand years the Jewish people did not have their own land, but God is faithful to all His promises, and on May 14, 1948, Israel became a nation once more. This is one of the most striking events in biblical prophecy.

The Lord has planted Israel in their land three times—in Joshua's generation (around 1400 BC), in Zerubbabel's generation (536 BC), and in May 1948. The state of Israel, established in 1948, *will not be cast out of the land.* How do we know? The Scripture prophesies that Israel will remain in the land in the end times—"in that day"—even though surrounded by hostile nations and that a remnant will be supernaturally preserved in the land (Joel 2:32; Zech. 12:1–10; 14:1–5).

Amos's prophecy linked the timing of the rebuilding of David's tabernacle to one specific generation—when Israel would be restored to her land in such a way that she would *never be pulled up from it* (Amos 9:15). This prophecy could be fulfilled only after 1948 because Israel was pulled up from the land in the previous two gatherings to the land (under Joshua and Zerubbabel). Israel's restoration to the land in 1948 signaled the beginning of the time when the spirit of the tabernacle of David would be released, which is connected to the harvest of the remnant of Edom.

The ancient land of Edom is in modern-day Jordan. The prophecy refers to both the geography and the people identified with ancient Edom. Thus, "Edom" encompasses the Arab nations and the Islamic peoples, though these are not exactly the same in that some Arabs are not Muslims and some Muslims are not Arabs. Nevertheless, there is major overlap between the two.

Messianic congregations in Israel—congregations of Jews who believe that Jesus is the Messiah—are growing at a rapid rate and seeing more Jewish people come to Jesus than at any time since the first century. More than fifteen thousand believers make up over one hundred fifty messianic congregations in Israel today. The number of believing Jews in Israel may seem small compared to the overall population of around eight million (75 percent Jewish, 20 percent Arab, 5 percent internationals), but it represents an increase of more than 500 percent in the last ten years.

Prayer for the release of God's purposes in Israel includes praying for the believing remnant of Jewish believers in the restored land and state of Israel. This is a vital aspect of the spirit of the tabernacle of David.

The Lord promised to bless all who pray for the peace of Jerusalem. "May they prosper who love you" (Ps. 122:6). Peace in Jerusalem, as anywhere, comes from Jesus and on His terms. In Ezekiel's day, God blessed those who prayed for Jerusalem by supernaturally protecting them in a time when God's judgment fell on the city (Ezek. 9:4–6).

We are exhorted to pray for and declare God's purpose for Jerusalem to the nations:

> For thus says the Lord: "Sing with gladness for Jacob, and shout among the chief of the nations; proclaim, give praise, and say, 'O Lord, save Your people, the remnant of Israel!' Behold, I will bring them from the north country, and gather them from the ends of the earth…a great throng shall return there.…Hear the word of the Lord, O nations, and declare it in the isles afar off, and say, 'He who scattered Israel will gather him, and keep him as a shepherd does his flock.'"
>
> —Jeremiah 31:7–10

The missional expression of the tabernacle: impacting all nations with the gospel

> I will raise up the tabernacle of David…that they may possess the remnant of Edom [Islam], and all the Gentiles [nations]…called by My name.
>
> —Amos 9:11–12

The spirit of the tabernacle of David has a missional expression: Our prayers and worship will impact all nations with the gospel of the kingdom (Amos 9:12; Matt. 24:14). Amos referred to winning the nations to Jesus when he prophesied of Israel's possessing the remnant of Edom (Arab nations and Islamic peoples).

God has an appointment with the Muslim world, but the battle for their salvation must first be won in the spirit realm. We cannot counteract Islam with a political spirit. In other words, the body of Christ will never win Muslims to Jesus through political agendas and appeals alone. It will take the power of God with signs and wonders, which will be released in fullness only as the result of continual prayer in the spirit of the tabernacle of David.

The first application in the Scriptures of the restoration of David's tabernacle relates to Gentiles being saved (Acts 15:17). In about AD 50 James quoted Amos's prophecy about David's tabernacle being restored to emphasize the point that God is committed to bringing the Gentiles to Jesus.

> I will…rebuild the tabernacle of David…so that the rest of mankind may seek the Lord, even all the Gentiles [nations] who are called by My name…
>
> —Acts 15:16–17

The word *Gentiles* in this context is interchangeable with the phrase "the nations," which refers to every nation other than Israel. Here, application of the promise of the restoration of the tabernacle of David in the New Testament is related to the Gentile nations receiving salvation through Jesus. The greatest harvest of souls in all history will occur in the generation in which the Lord returns (Matt. 24:14; Rev. 7:9, 14). Thus, prayer in the spirit of the tabernacle of David includes prayer for the harvest.

The supernatural expression of the tabernacle: the release of God's power and glory

Prayer in the spirit of the tabernacle of David has a supernatural expression: It is prayer that results in the manifestation of God's power, direction, and protection. David spoke often of and prayed much for the release of God's power, glory, and miracles.

> They shall speak of the glory of Your kingdom, and talk of Your power, to make known to the sons of men His mighty acts, and the glorious majesty of His kingdom.
>
> —PSALM 145:11–12

David inquired of the Lord for His prophetic direction and strategies (Ps. 27:4) and for divine protection (vv. 1–14).

> One thing I have desired of the LORD…to behold the beauty of the LORD, and to inquire in His temple. For in the time of trouble He shall hide me in His pavilion.
>
> —PSALM 27:4–5

When Solomon's temple was dedicated, God's glory fell on the singers and musicians, including one hundred twenty trumpeters (2 Chron. 5:13–14; 7:1–3). The event was a foreshadowing of the supernatural event that occurred on the Day of Pentecost, when one hundred twenty intercessors were gathered in prayer and God's manifest presence was released on and through them.

> And suddenly there came a sound from heaven, as of a rushing mighty wind.…Then there appeared to them divided tongues, as of fire, and one sat upon each of them. And they were all filled with the Holy Spirit.
>
> —ACTS 2:2–4

Prayer in the spirit of the tabernacle of David is prayer that zealously contends for the fullness of the release of God's power and presence as seen in the famous vow of David in Psalm 132:1–5 (see chapter 22). In other words, foundational to understanding David's tabernacle is seeing that David was zealous to contend for the "fullness" of God's purposes. The Scripture is clear that the church will be filled with God's glory and that God's glory will fill the earth (Eph. 5:27; Hab. 2:14).

We must contend for a "historical revival" in our day. The commitment to seek for the fullness of all God will give in our generation is in sharp contrast to the popular trend of being content with the status quo in the church.

The transformational expression of the tabernacle: restoration of cities

> "Behold, the days are coming," says the LORD, "when the plowman shall overtake the reaper . . . they shall build the waste cities and inhabit them."
> —AMOS 9:13–14

The spirit of the tabernacle of David has a transformational expression: it is connected to the restoration of cities, which includes blessed agriculture, economics, and so on. When Amos prophesied about the plowman overtaking the reaper, he was referring to an unusually abundant agricultural blessing that would come as a result of God's glory being manifest. George Otis Jr., maker of the award-winning *Transformations* and *Transformations II* documentaries, highlighted God's supernatural blessing on agriculture in places where God's people repented and cried out to God in prayer. He documented the healing of the land, which included cases of extremely large fruits and vegetables in those places. For example, he reported that the land in Almolonga, Guatemala, was healed to such a degree that it produced giant vegetables along with a thousand percent increase in agricultural productivity. Once unproductive fields began to yield crops of "biblical proportions" in shortened growing cycles.[6] Another example is Fiji, where the coral reefs that were once dying are now coming back to life to the amazement of the scientific world.[7]

Transformation of society can occur in part in this age but in fullness only in the Millennium after Jesus returns to Earth. However, even partial transformation in this age is significant as it results in changed lives and glory given to Jesus.

The eschatological expression of the tabernacle: Jesus received as King over all nations

> At that time Jerusalem shall be called The Throne of the LORD, and all the nations shall be gathered to it, to the name of the LORD, to Jerusalem.
> —JEREMIAH 3:17

The spirit of the tabernacle of David has an eschatological, or end-time, expression, which emphasizes Jesus's role as the son of David, reigning from Jerusalem over all the nations. Thus, we pray for the full release of God's purpose for Israel, which includes Jesus's reigning in Jerusalem on the throne of David.[8]

> When the Son of Man comes in His glory, and all the holy angels with Him, then He will sit on the throne of His glory. All the nations will be gathered before Him.
> —MATTHEW 25:31–32

And the Lord God will give Him [Jesus] the throne of His father David. And He will reign over the house of Jacob forever, and of His kingdom there will be no end.

—LUKE 1:32–33

The Lord is releasing understanding about the tabernacle of David to the church across the earth so that we pray not only for our own ministries, nations, and cities but also for the throne of David to be established in Jerusalem and for the earth to be filled with God's glory (Hab. 2:14).

THE RELEASE OF THE SPIRIT OF THE TABERNACLE OF DAVID

In the past God anointed a solitary man named David, but now He is anointing a generation to be like David. The Lord is restoring His house of prayer not as a casual endeavor but as a means of bringing all nations to Him.

The spirit of the tabernacle of David includes prayer meetings led by prophetic worship, but it involves much more than that. Amos emphasized that the restoration of David's tabernacle would be "as in the days of old." That means it will include both the physical and the political aspects of David's tabernacle as seen in David's generation (Amos 9:11).

Because David was the first person to establish day-and-night prayer with prophetic worship in Jerusalem; because he was the king (with governmental authority over Israel's society); and because he proclaimed God's kingdom to both the Jews and the Gentiles (Ps. 67–68), the tabernacle of David links the restoration of prayer, worship, and the spirit of prophecy in the church with the missions movement and the messianic remnant in the restored land of Israel. It connects three dimensions—the praying church, the messianic movement, and the state of Israel—with a righteous government under Jesus's authority as the Son of David.

The spirit of the tabernacle of David will be expressed through the church in every Gentile nation of the earth and through the messianic remnant in the restored land and state of Israel. It will be manifested in part in this age (it is continually increasing) and in fullness in the Millennium. The fullness of the restoration of the tabernacle of David will occur only after Jesus returns to rule all nations from the throne of David in Jerusalem in the context of worship with intercession. Let us be zealous to embrace, pray for, and declare all that is implied in the Scripture by the spirit of the tabernacle of David.

Chapter 27

NIGHT-*and*-DAY PRAYER THROUGHOUT HISTORY

Every great movement of God can be traced to a kneeling figure.[1]
—D. L. Moody

WHEN WE CONSIDER the end-time global prayer movement, it is good to remind ourselves that the idea of unceasing worship and prayer is not a new idea. From before the creation of the earth, seraphim have surrounded God's heavenly throne, continuously crying out, "Holy, holy, holy is the Lord of hosts" (Isa. 6:3; see also Rev. 4:8). Throughout the centuries, the Lord has raised up different ministries that mobilized night-and-day prayer and worship to give a small reflection on the earth of the worship that occurs in heaven (Matt. 6:10).

THE KINGS OF JUDAH

Around 1000 BC, as we learned in chapter 24, King David established two hundred eighty-eight singers and four thousand musicians to minister before the Lord day and night (1 Chron. 9:33; 16; 23; 27). In the generations after him David's daily worship order was upheld by at least seven kings or governors of Judah: Solomon (2 Chron. 8), Jehoshaphat (2 Chron. 20), Joash with Jehoiada the priest (2 Chron. 23–24), Hezekiah (2 Chron. 29–30), Josiah (2 Chron. 35), and Ezra and Nehemiah (Ezra 3:10; Neh. 12:28–47).

MARTIN OF TOURS

Around AD 371 Martin was appointed Bishop of Tours (France), though he had no desire to fill this post. He wanted to devote himself to prayer. He built himself a small retreat hut seven kilometers from Tours, but soon eighty men joined him in prayer as his disciples. Two hundred years before the word *monastery* was used, Martin began what came to be known as the monastery of Marmoutier. Martin mandated that the majority of the monks engage full time in prayer and worship.[2]

ALEXANDER AKIMETES

Around AD 400 Alexander established a monastery in Constantinople that maintained 24/7 worship and prayer. He organized his three hundred to four hundred monks into six choirs that rotated in shifts to create a flow of uninterrupted prayer and worship twenty-four hours a day. He first organized this *laus perennis*, or perpetual prayer, near the Euphrates River, where it lasted for twenty years. Then he and seventy monks moved to Constantinople, where another three hundred monks joined them in 24/7 prayer with worship. Because their prayer with worship never stopped, the group was referred to as "the order of the *Acoemetae*" (literally, "Sleepless Ones"). Eventually they were driven from Constantinople, and Alexander founded a monastery in another location that functioned similarly.[3]

After Alexander's death in AD 430, this monastery grew in numbers until, by the end of the fifth century, it housed more than one thousand monks committed to day-and-night prayer. They sang hymns and doxologies non-stop. Similar ministries of 24/7 prayer and choral psalm-singing were established in other monasteries at that time along the Euphrates and in Persia.[4]

KING SIGISMUND

In AD 515 King Sigismund of Burgundy (France) founded the monastery of Saint Maurice at Agaunum in Switzerland. Following Alexander's practice of *laus perennis*, he instituted the recitation of the divine office—consisting of the Psalms, hymns, and other prayers—around the clock by seven shifts or choirs called *turmae*. The monks in the *turmae* were referred to as the *Akoimetoi* ("Sleepless Ones") because they prayed "a monastic round of twenty-four offices to fill every hour."[5]

COMGALL

In AD 433 Patrick, a native of Roman Britain, returned to Ireland—where he had previously been kept as a slave for several years—to preach the gospel. In the twelfth century the monk Jocelin reported that when Patrick came to a valley on the shores of the Belfast Lough near Bangor, Ireland, he and his comrades beheld a vision of heaven. Jocelin wrote, "They beheld the valley filled with heavenly light, and with a multitude of the host of heaven, they heard, as chanted forth from the voice of angels, the psalmody of the celestial choir."[6] From then on the valley was known as "The Valley of Angels."

Patrick didn't institute 24/7 prayer, but a little more than one hundred years later, the monk Comgall established a monastery in the very same valley where Patrick had seen the vision of angels. More than three thousand monks joined him full time, and together they maintained a 24/7 house of prayer with worship that continued its ministry for more than three hundred years. The monks practiced continuous worship that was antiphonal in nature and based on Patrick's vision.[7]

The monastery at Bangor became famous for its choral psalmody. In the twelfth century Bernard of Clairvaux spoke of Comgall and Bangor, stating that "the solemnization of divine offices was kept up by companies, who relieved each other in succession, so that not for one moment, day or night, was there an intermission of their praises."[8]

The monks experienced intimate relationship with Jesus through their continual worship and, as a result, were stirred to evangelize the lost. Many were sent out from Bangor as missionaries to Europe and had widespread influence. Wherever they settled, they first established continual praise and adoration to God, so their missions work flowed from a foundation of prayer.

These missionaries preached the gospel throughout Europe, leading multitudes to Jesus. One example is Columbanus. In AD 590 he set out from Bangor with twelve brothers to plant monasteries throughout Switzerland that combined prayer and missions work.

Deicola, also trained at Bangor under Comgall, traveled with Columbanus through Gaul. Upon reaching the Church of St. Martin in Tournans, France, he left the company of Columbanus to establish a Bangor-type monastery there.[9]

Monks from Bangor also established three monasteries in Wales: Bangor Iltyd, Bangor Elwy, and Bangor Wydrin. At Bangor Iltyd, more than one hundred men were engaged every hour in chanting, so that without intermission, psalms were rendered night and day. At Elwy, Wales, nearly four hundred men were devoted, day and night, to the singing of psalms so that the praise of God never ceased there.[10] In each of these Bangor monasteries day-and-night praise and prayer was offered without intermission in one-hour shifts.[11]

Cluny Abbey

Around AD 1000 William I, Duke of Aquitaine, founded a monastery at Cluny, in central France, that departed from the Benedictine rule by removing manual labor from the monks' days and replacing it with more prayer. "Great importance was given to praying the Liturgy because the monks of Cluny were convinced that it was participation in the liturgy of Heaven as seen in Revelation 4."[12] Hundreds of monastic communities throughout Europe followed the example of Cluny by embracing night-and-day prayer with worship.

Bernard of Clairvaux

Just after AD 1100 Bernard, together with seven hundred other monks in Clairvaux, France, organized day-and-night prayer that continued for many years and resulted in a dynamic release of evangelism through signs and wonders across Europe. We know Bernard promoted continual prayer because reports from visitors to the monastery at Clairvaux describe the monks as singing their prayers through the night and working in silence while communing with God during the day.[13]

COUNT ZINZENDORF AND THE MORAVIANS

In AD 1727 Count Zinzendorf, a young, wealthy German nobleman, committed his estate in Germany to a twenty-four-hour-a-day prayer ministry. He renamed the estate "Herrnhut," which means "the watch of the Lord."

The origins of the Herrnhut prayer and missionary community go back to 1722, when Zinzendorf met a Moravian preacher, Christian David, who told him of the persecuted Protestants in Moravia. The Moravian believers were the remnants of John Huss's followers in Bohemia who had suffered at the hands of Catholic monarchs.

Zinzendorf offered the Moravians asylum on his land. In response about three hundred persecuted believers moved from Bohemia to his estate, forming the Herrnhut community. At that time, Zinzendorf gave up his court position to lead the group.[14]

The radical believers at Herrnhut covenanted to pray in hourly shifts around the clock, all day and all night, every day, taking inspiration from Leviticus 6:13: "A fire shall always be burning on the altar; it shall never go out." Their "prayer meeting" continued nonstop for the next one hundred years.[15]

From the prayer room at Herrnhut came an unsurpassed missionary zeal. By 1776 more than two hundred missionaries had been sent out from the small community.[16]

Zinzendorf became the leader of the first Protestant missionary movement in history. His policy was to send out missionaries, two by two, to the unreached people groups of the earth. As they went out, the prayer furnace back home in Herrnhut covered them in prayer. In other words, the first Protestant missionary movement married the prayer aspect of the Great Commission with the proclamation, or evangelism, aspect. Count Zinzendorf saw prayer and missions as inseparable.[17]

I do not have space to describe the many other tremendous movements of prayer that have arisen throughout church history. But it is important to mention the strong relationship that exists between continual prayer and revival. The First Great Awakening (1720–1760), the Haystack Prayer Meeting leading to the first missionaries being sent out from the US in 1806, the Second Great Awakening in the early nineteenth century (1790–1840), the Welsh revival (1904–1905), the Azusa Street revival (1906–1915), the Pyongyang revival in Korea (1907–1910), and the revivals in China (1927–1937) and Indonesia (1964) all bear witness to this truth. Each of these revivals followed a similar pattern: a radical group of believers committed themselves to continual intercession and then revival broke out, which in turn led to significant missionary activity.

An irrefutable law in God's kingdom holds that in God's timing revival in the church, with evangelistic zeal and effectiveness, will always follow wherever night-and-day prayer is established. Now you can see why it is so important!

Chapter 28

THE GLOBAL PRAYER MOVEMENT TODAY

There has never been a spiritual awakening in any country
or locality that did not begin in united prayer.[1]
—A. T. Pierson

THOUGH THE DIFFERENT worship and prayer movements throughout history inspire us, I believe that the greatest prayer movement is still ahead of us. J. Edwin Orr, a well-known historian on revival and missions, often said, "When God gets ready to do something new with His people, He always sets them a-praying."[2] The Holy Spirit will establish a prayer culture in the whole body of Christ before Jesus returns. Currently He is raising up a worldwide, worship-based prayer movement that has many diverse styles and emphases. It is a sovereign work of God that has grown rapidly in many cities during the last ten years. This movement is only the firstfruits of what the Spirit will do before the Lord returns.

One of the most significant events in the prayer movement in this generation was the first International Prayer Assembly in Seoul in 1984, which was cosponsored by the Lausanne Committee for World Evangelization and the Korean church. More than three hundred thousand Korean believers participated, along with three thousand international leaders. Much of what has happened in the global prayer movement since then can be traced to that catalytic gathering thirty years ago. Many prayer strategies and initiatives have been birthed from it, including the International Prayer Council, which has been influential in establishing numerous houses of prayer.

In 1984 the number of 24/7 houses of prayer in the world was fewer than twenty-five. Today there are more than ten thousand, and most of the growth has occurred in the last ten years. Prayer initiatives are springing up all over the globe at a staggering rate. Such momentum in prayer must be attributed not to human ingenuity but to the sovereign work of the Holy Spirit.

PRAYER MINISTRIES AROUND THE WORLD

The significant increase of 24/7 prayer ministries and large prayer events, including those in stadiums, is a prophetic sign of the times that the Lord is doing something important. In cities all over the globe new 24/7 prayer ministries are being established. From Kiev, Bogota, and Jerusalem to New Zealand, Cairo, Cape Town, and Hong Kong, men and women are responding to the Spirit's leadership. Despite the pressures and inherent dangers, 24/7 prayer centers are even being set up in primarily Muslim nations such as Egypt, Turkey, Syria, Indonesia, and Lebanon.

Due to space restraints I will mention just a few examples of the growth of prayer ministries in the nations. But these examples will be sufficient to give you a picture of what God is doing around the world.

Asia

The prayer movement in Korea, China, and Indonesia is charging forward with great momentum. More than one hundred million Chinese and Koreans are praying, and their intercession has led to an unprecedented increase of new prayer ministries.

South Korea. Korea has clearly been leading the global prayer movement during the last fifty years. In 1973 David Yonggi Cho, founder of the Yoido Full Gospel Church, established Osanri Prayer Mountain just outside Seoul. This prayer mountain has hosted non-stop night-and-day prayer for forty years. Its prayer ministry is second to none in all history.

Osanri Prayer Mountain has attracted more than a million visitors per year and has inspired hundreds of other prayer mountains throughout Korea and the world. The ten thousand-seat sanctuary has generally been full every day throughout the last twenty years. More than two hundred prayer mountains exist in Korea.

The result of the prayer ministry at Osanri during the last forty years has been remarkable: multitudes have come to the Lord, and spiritual breakthrough has occurred in Korea and other nations. As the youth of South Korea pick up the mantle of leadership from their fathers and mothers and add worship and intimacy with God to the chorus of intercession, we expect the spiritual impact of this nation in the next fifty years to surpass its influence during the previous decades. I believe that the prayer ministry in Korea has taken the lead in the Spirit in inspiring the prayer movement we are witnessing in the nations in this hour.

Indonesia. About five hundred city prayer networks have been established in Indonesia as well as 24/7 prayer towers in numerous cities. More than five million intercessors from all over the country are involved in the national prayer network. Indonesians hosted the World Prayer Assembly in the national stadium in May 2012. More than three hundred fifty cities in Indonesia held citywide prayer rallies simultaneously in local indoor stadiums and public halls. The rallies involved more than five million believers, who joined with the one hundred thousand intercessors in the national stadium to pray for the nation.

China. There are literally thousands of "24/7 prayer chains" established throughout the People's Republic of China. Every Home for Christ, based in Colorado Springs, Colorado, and run by Dick Eastman, has started what they refer to as "walls of prayer" that host 24/7 prayer chains. They report that more than five thousand are going strong today in China. I believe that China will have the mightiest spiritual prayer force in all history before Jesus returns, due to its size and the decades of difficulty and persecution believers have endured since the Communist revolution in 1949.

Taiwan, Hong Kong, and Singapore. Numerous houses of prayer are springing up in these Chinese-speaking nations. The Tabernacle of David house of prayer in Taipei was launched by Miriam Chang in April 2000. They continue for more than twelve hours a day in prayer meetings that combine worship with intercession.

India. Houses of prayer are also springing up all over India. For example, Patrick Joshua has mobilized nearly five hundred thousand intercessors and six million children through his National Prayer Network for India. The Royal Kids Prayer Ministries combines prayer with care for destitute orphans. Its impact is remarkable.

Thailand. The Thailand House of Prayer network trains and mobilizes intercessors across the nation. The Bangkok House of Prayer mobilizes various congregations, each covering a full day of prayer with worship. The Southeast Asia House of Prayer mobilizes daily prayer fourteen hours a day. OneThing Thailand is a network of houses of prayer and churches that sponsor a day of twenty-four-hour worship with intercession every other month.

New prayer ministries are starting and growing all over Asia in countries such as Japan, Malaysia, Singapore, the Philippines, Vietnam, Myanmar, Bangladesh, Pakistan, and more.

The Middle East

Israel. Tom Hess founded Jerusalem House of Prayer for All Nations in 1987; it is the most notable prayer ministry in Jerusalem. Today there are eight prayer rooms in Jerusalem that seek to organize 24/7 prayer, including Succat Hallel, the Prayer Pavilion, and the Korean House of Prayer. In Tel Aviv the VIP Prayer Tower hosts twenty-five hours of prayer each week. Nazareth has a well-established prayer room. More prayer rooms are being developed in Yad HaShmona, Beersheva, and Eilat. Throughout Israel monasteries conduct prayer meetings many hours a week, some hosting 24/7 prayer.

Egypt. Kasr El Dobara Church in Cairo—the largest evangelical church in the Middle East—has done much to organize and inspire prayer throughout this region. Pastor Sameh Maurice leads a well-known Monday-night prayer meeting for which two thousand people gather; multitudes throughout the Middle East join by live television and the Internet. The Cairo House of Prayer began in 2002 and is led by Lillian Sobhy. It operates 24/7 except when government curfews prohibit it, and the leaders host annual three-day prayer conferences attended by nearly ten thousand young adults. The Alexandria House of Prayer is well-established and working toward 24/7 worship and prayer.

Day-and-night prayer watches are held in various places in Kuwait, Algeria, Sudan, and Turkey, with numerous new 24/7 watches being raised up, including the Istanbul House of Prayer in Turkey and other houses of prayer in Iraq, Dubai, and Syria.

Europe

UK. Under Pete Greig's leadership, the 24/7 movement spread across Europe to twenty-eight nations. They have established more than one hundred prayer communities, some called "boiler rooms," in urban hubs throughout England and in twenty-eight nations across Europe. Ken Gott in Sunderland is inspiring many young people to embrace the call to raise up 24/7 prayer with worship in the UK.

Germany. The Augsburg House of Prayer led by Johannes Hartl started in 2007. By 2011 it was functioning 24/7, with worship teams leading each prayer meeting. The ministry has one hundred staff members and several thousand visitors per year. Their annual prayer conferences regularly draw four thousand people. There are more than ten houses of prayer in Germany, including those in Berlin and Freiburg, each of which has at least a few full-time intercessory missionaries. The Watchman's Call Initiative organizes twenty-four-hour prayer chains involving more than three hundred cities in Germany.

Poland. There are many praying communities across this nation. Twelve cities hold twelve-hour, citywide solemn assemblies once a month. Under the leadership of Maciej Wolski and Marcin Widera, houses of prayer have been established in Warsaw and Wrocław that mobilize prayer with worship four to six hours each day.

Italy. Numerous prayer gatherings occur throughout Italy: daily prayer with worship hosted by the Sardinia Prayer Mountain, "One Day" in Rome, "The Tabernacle" in Turin, prayer watches in Naples, the Milan House of Prayer, 24/7 Italia in Montecalvo, the "Italy in Prayer" conferences, and many more. House of Prayer (HOP) Italia in Caserta has a full-time music school and a school of prayer. Kim Kollins leads the Burning Bush national prayer initiative. In Sicily Corrado Salmè organizes prayer events at which thousands of young people gather.

The Netherlands. Amsterdam's Tabernacle of the Nations, led by Robin van Ommen, who was formerly a part of the IHOPKC leadership team, prays night and day in the city's red-light district.

When I stop to consider what has happened in Europe in the last decade, I am filled with awe and gratitude to the Lord. Some people have given up on seeing a great revival in Europe, but the fact that there are so many new houses of prayer with worship teams and full-time intercessory missionaries gives us some insight into the Holy Spirit's zeal for this continent. There are houses of prayer with prayer meetings led by worship teams in the UK, Scotland, Ireland, Germany, Austria, Switzerland, Poland, France, Italy, the Netherlands, Spain, Sweden, Norway, Finland, Romania, Greece, Iceland, the Czech Republic, Croatia, Belgium, Cyprus, Malta, Macedonia, Turkey, Spain, and other places as well. The European House of Prayer Leader's Summit, led by Johannes Hartl, hosts leaders from fifty different houses of prayer in Europe.

Russia and Ukraine

The ministry giving the most visible leadership to the prayer movement in Russian-speaking countries is the God Seekers Movement led by Sergey Shidlovskiy from Kiev, Ukraine. This ministry hosts daily prayer meetings plus international prayer events that are broadcast live on television and that have gathered fifty thousand people during the last three years. The Kiev House of Prayer has full-time paid intercessory missionaries. Regular prayer events, as well as prayer events in the local stadium, are led by Boris Grisenko, who leads the Jewish Messianic Congregation in Kiev. Houses of prayer are growing in many cities in Russia, including Moscow, Murmansk, Yekaterinburg, Khabarovsk, and Nizhny Novgorod, as well as in other Russian-speaking countries such as Moldova, Armenia, Kazakhstan, Latvia, and Belarus.

Africa

Nigeria. The most well-known prayer ministries in Africa are the monthly all-night prayer meetings in southern Nigeria, which sometimes have a million in attendance, and the Global Day of Prayer launched from South Africa. Each year, through the Global Day of Prayer, more than one hundred million believers gather on Pentecost Sunday in more than two hundred nations to pray for a global outpouring of the Holy Spirit.

South Africa. Thousands of 24/7 prayer rooms have been established in townships and cities by many different prayer ministries that are working together.

Rwanda. Many 24/7 prayer watches have been established. In the city of Kigali, Paul Gitwaza, pastor of Zion Temple, leads both a twenty thousand-member church and the most well-known house of prayer in Rwanda. Launched in 2000 it has continued 24/7 with musicians and/or singers for more than fourteen years.

Uganda. Since 1995 World Trumpet Mission and Watchman Intercessors Network based in Kampala has helped to establish twenty-four-hour prayer watches in forty-three districts in Uganda. Many strong prayer ministries also exist in Zimbabwe, Congo, Tanzania, Kenya, and Ethiopia.

North America

US. There are more than four hundred houses of prayer in the US, in addition to prayer rooms on one thousand university campuses, plus a multitude of national prayer ministries that are too numerous to mention in this book.

Mexico. In 2003 Benjamin Nuñez started a house of prayer on his university campus that hosted prayer meetings for six hours a day. Within ten years his team helped to start seventy-two more houses of prayer in Mexico. In addition, other ministries have established more than one hundred houses of prayer. Lalo Garcia mobilizes citywide prayer ministries in Juarez, one of the most dangerous cities on Earth. We respect Garcia and the other intercessors for their courage and sacrifice as they faithfully stand for Jesus and diligently persevere in prayer in Juarez.

Canada. In Ottawa the National House of Prayer (NHOP) has led regular prayer meetings for the Canadian government since 2004. There are nearly fifty houses of prayer in Canadian cities, some going 24/7. There are an additional twenty-five prayer furnaces or houses of prayer on university campuses. Stacey Campbell's role in the prayer movement throughout Canada has been invaluable. Other prayer ministries in Canada include The Cry, which rallies people to solemn assemblies consisting of twelve hours of prayer with fasting. Prayer Canada is establishing a weekly prayer meeting in every city hall across Canada.

South America

Brazil. In the last ten years more than thirty-five houses of prayer have been started in Brazil. Notable prayer ministries include Gideões de Oração in Lagoinha, which has had a 24/7 "prayer tower" going since 2003. They have launched twelve more prayer towers throughout Brazil. Brasil de Joelhos is a national network of prayer leaders.

The Lord has blessed Brazil with a unique measure of grace for worship. Some worship events gather one million people. Dwayne and Jennifer Roberts, who were on the original team that started IHOPKC in May 1999, moved to Florianopolis, Brazil, in the summer of 2013 to start a 24/7 house of prayer as well as to serve God's purpose in strengthening houses of prayer throughout the land in partnership with other ministries.

Colombia. Cesar Fajardo leads the Bogotá house of prayer. Others in Colombia, Bolivia, and Venezuela are building houses of prayer.

Australia, New Zealand, and the Pacific Islands

Australia. There are a number of houses of prayer in Australia, such as Canberra House of Prayer situated near the Australian Parliament, the Australian House of Prayer in Adelaide, and Fremantle (New Life Church prayer room).

New Zealand. Aaron Walsh launched the Tauranga House of Prayer in February 2006. At this time he has one hundred staff, students, and interns who lead prayer meetings that continue for fifty hours a week. They have raised up a training center for the wider South Pacific region.

Solomon Islands. In July 2013 Prime Minister Gordon Darcy Lilo helped to launch a house of prayer in the capital city Honiara. A house of prayer began in 2009 in the jungle village of Fa'arau on the island of Malaita, where there is no electricity or running water. The intercessors there use a diesel generator to operate their sound system and musical instruments.

Papua New Guinea. Prime Minister Peter O'Neill helped start the Goroka House of Prayer in August 2013.

OTHER PRAYER MINISTRIES TODAY

Campus Crusade for Christ, founded by Bill Bright (1921–2003), is one of the largest missions organizations in history. In the fifteen years before his death Bill zealously called the body of Christ and the missions movement across the earth to prayer and fasting, inspiring many to combine prayer and world evangelization. He insisted that the Great Commission could be fulfilled only in the context of much prayer and fasting.

Lou Engle founded **TheCall** prayer events, which began in September 2000 when more than four hundred thousand people, mostly young adults, gathered at the National Mall in Washington DC to fast and pray for revival in America. Since then Lou has hosted more than a dozen TheCall events, including one in New York City in 2001 with more than one hundred thousand people in attendance and one in Nashville in 2007 with more than seventy thousand people. Lou is passionate about launching houses of prayer. From 1996 to 1999 he led a 24/7 house of prayer in Mott Auditorium in Pasadena, California. Then in 2004 he launched the Justice House of Prayer (JHOP) in Washington DC to pray for the ending of abortion and for revival in America. Similar JHOPs have been planted in New York, Boston, San Francisco, San Diego, and Montgomery, Alabama. For five years, from 2007 to 2012, Lou served on the senior leadership team of IHOPKC before returning to his home in Pasadena to start the **Ekballo House of Prayer**, which he founded to pray for unreached people groups in partnership with the US Center for World Mission.

Dick Eastman's **Every Home for Christ** has started more than ten thousand 24/7 prayer chains in Asia. The three books in Eastman's Intercessory Worship Series are standard textbooks for many prayer ministries. I know of no one who is bolder or more consistent than Dick Eastman in calling for prayer watches in the spirit of the tabernacle of David connected to the Great Commission. His headquarters in the Jericho Center in Colorado Springs, Colorado, hosts eight hours of daily prayer meetings led by worship teams.

Brian Kim, who served on the International House of Prayer leadership team for many years, helped to establish **Luke18 Project**, which has set up prayer furnaces on more than one thousand college campuses in America. Through the **Antioch Center for Training and Sending** (ACTS), he also serves at Every Home for Christ in planting prayer furnaces focused on breakthrough in difficult and challenging places around the world.

Loren and Darlene Cunningham founded **Youth With A Mission** (YWAM) more than fifty years ago. It is one of the largest missions organizations in the world. For many years the Cunninghams, together with Joy Dawson, have trained young believers around the world to hear the voice of God and then to pray back to Him what they hear in strategic prayer. The result is more effective work in missions. Today YWAM has more than fourteen hundred ministry locations in nearly two hundred nations. The YWAM base in Kona, Hawaii, hosts a house of prayer led by worship teams that operates many hours each day. Loren has been a strong voice in this generation in encouraging young people to combine missions with hearing God's voice and then responding in prayer.

Andy Byrd, a key young leader in the YWAM movement, has emerged as an important voice in calling young people to plant houses of prayer around the world through his **Fire and Fragrance** discipleship training school and the **Circuit Rider** initiative. He has been integral in helping to establish a prayer center at the YWAM base in Hawaii that is rooted in worship-fueled intercession.

Larry Lea's book *Could You Not Tarry One Hour?* has been distributed to more than twenty million people worldwide since 1987. Lea has spoken to numerous gatherings of ten thousand people across the nations, calling them to prayer, and has preached on prayer in more than sixty nations. Some claim that he has spoken to more people on prayer than any other person alive today.

Books on prayer by Leonard Ravenhill (1907–1994) have inspired multitudes to pray during the last fifty years. His most notable book, *Why Revival Tarries*, has sold well over a million copies worldwide. His teaching continues to inspire the next generation to pray consistently for revival and a great harvest.

John Robb leads the **International Prayer Council**, the largest global network of prayer ministries. He has mobilized more than one hundred thousand intercessors across the nations and worked closely with Patrick Joshua, who has mobilized in excess of four hundred thousand intercessors and six million children in a prayer network.

Jane Hansen leads **Aglow International**, a movement of praying women, with approximately four thousand local groups in one hundred seventy nations. Each month they mobilize two hundred thousand women in prayer and Bible study to become more effective in the harvest.

C. Peter Wagner was at the forefront of the prayer movement in the nations throughout the 1990s, leading the **Spiritual Warfare Network**. Along with Cindy Jacobs, Dutch Sheets, Chuck Pierce, and others, he has mobilized hundreds of thousands to fast and pray for a greater kingdom breakthrough.

George Otis Jr.'s award-winning **Transformations** documentaries have been seen by tens of millions worldwide. They have been greatly used by the Lord to inspire multitudes to gather together for consistent prayer and repentance.

Graham Power, a South African businessman, started the **Global Day of Prayer** in 2000. Through his efforts and those of the other people associated with the ministry, more than one hundred million believers in two hundred twenty nations gather each year on Pentecost Sunday for the Global Day of Prayer.

Terry Tykel has for decades effectively equipped and inspired multitudes of **prayer ministries** in Methodist congregations as well as in many other denominational churches.

The **National Day of Prayer** established in 1952 by President Harry S. Truman has effectively mobilized millions of people to gather in their cities for corporate prayer and repentance.

The **National Prayer Committee** was established in 1979 and has given birth to many prayer initiatives in the United States and other nations. It has been led by people of prayer such as David Butts, Vonette Bright, Dick Eastman, and David Bryant.

Intercessors for America started in 1973 with a commitment to pray and fast for America. Gary Bergel has given leadership to Intercessors for America for more than twenty years.

Sean Feucht, the leader of the **Burn 24/7** ministry, has been a consistent voice in calling young people to a Davidic lifestyle of worship and prayer as he has helped multiply young adult prayer furnaces on college campuses in many different nations.

There are many others who have contributed to the growth of prayer in the nations—way too many to mention. But this list is enough to let us know that God is using numerous people and ministries to fuel the worldwide, worship-based prayer movement He is raising up across the earth today. We live in a glorious hour of history!

Chapter 29

THE CONVERGENCE *of the* MISSIONS
and PRAYER MOVEMENTS

*All great revivals have been preceded and carried out by per-
severing, prevailing knee-work in the closet.*[1]
—SAMUEL BRENGLE

IT IS EXCITING to note that the missions movement, along with many church-
planting movements, is growing just as the prayer movement is. And because
these movements are interdependent, we can expect to see them coming
together more and more to fulfill God's purposes on the earth before Jesus
returns.

I want to highlight two significant biblical signs of the approach of the return
of the Lord. The first is the gospel's being preached to all nations:

> This gospel of the kingdom will be preached in all the world as a witness
> to all the nations [*ethnos*], and then the end will come.
> —MATTHEW 24:14

Jesus linked the evangelizing of every nation to His return. The top leaders
of the largest missions organizations today are saying that all twelve thousand
ethnic groups on Earth will have heard the gospel preached to them by 2025.
The degree to which the task of reaching "every nation" has been accomplished
may be determined by comparing the ratio of non-Christians to believers in the
world. There are an estimated one billion Christians today.

According to the US Center for World Missions, in AD 100 the ratio was
three hundred sixty unbelievers to one believer (*a fraction of 1 percent* of the
world believed in Jesus); nine hundred years later, in AD 1000, the ratio was two
hundred twenty to one (still *a fraction of 1 percent*); in AD 1500 the ratio was
sixty-nine to one (*just over 1 percent*); by 1900 it was twenty-seven to one (*about
4 percent*); and by 2000 the ratio was an astounding six to one (*about 20 percent
of the population of the earth currently believes in Jesus*).

The second sign is unity in the church, which is closely connected to the evangelization of the nations. Jesus is bringing a new level of unity to His body as three
generations combine their gifts to work together in the prayer, justice, missions,
and church-planting movements to fulfill the Great Commission. The world will
believe that Jesus is from the Father when the church operates together in unity.

That they all may be one ... that the world may believe that You sent Me.
—JOHN 17:21

Before Jesus returns, the church will see the greatest harvest of souls in history. Leading to this success in the missions movement and many church-planting movements is the growth of the greatest prayer movement in history—the one you have been reading about in this book that the Holy Spirit is raising up today.

Jesus's command to pray for laborers to be sent out by the Lord to bring in the harvest of souls carries with it the promise of His enabling us to overcome obstacles so that the laborers succeed. Thus, in the Scripture, there is a strong relationship between missions and intercession. When Jesus pointed out that "the harvest truly is plentiful, but the laborers are few," He was clear about the solution: "Therefore pray the Lord of the harvest to send out laborers into His harvest" (Matt. 9:37–38).

Jesus,[2] Paul,[3] John,[4] David,[5] Solomon,[6] Isaiah,[7] Joel,[8] Zephaniah,[9] and Zechariah[10] all connected the prayer movement to the missions and justice movement in God's global plan to win the nations. The work of missions and justice is most effective when combined with prayer, sharing the gospel, and good works. It is essential that we do not separate these activities that God has joined together. Prayer addresses the root causes of injustice in the spirit. That is one reason Jesus exhorted us to pray night and day for justice (Luke 18:7). Prayer changes the spiritual atmosphere of the region in focus so that the work of the gospel goes forth more effectively. (See Daniel 10:13, 20.)

MISSIONS AND PRAYER MINISTRIES WORKING TOGETHER

As many ministries work together, we will see the gospel preached to every tribe and tongue on Earth as well as 24/7 worship and prayer offered to God. Yes, the prayer and missions movements are both accelerating. The Holy Spirit is bringing a convergence of these two movements. Convergence means that we can do something together that we cannot do separately.

Several times in the last century, the Holy Spirit has stirred the call to missions and prayer on a global level. In 1910 the Edinburgh World Missionary Conference, led by senior leaders of the Student Volunteer Movement (SVM), was held. In 1974 Billy Graham gave leadership to a worldwide convocation on missions in Lausanne, Switzerland. The convocation led to the formation of the Lausanne Committee for World Evangelization, which has held regional and global strategy meetings and prayer gatherings for nearly forty years. This remarkable collaboration among Christian leaders is truly a work of the Holy Spirit.

The AD2000 & Beyond Movement was a collaborative effort through the 1990s that was focused on completing the task of world evangelization by the year 2000. This ministry sponsored the May 17–25, 1995, Global Consultation on World Evangelization (GCOWE '95). Nearly four thousand Christian leaders representing one hundred eighty-six countries gathered to formulate evangelism plans focusing on the year 2000. People attended GCOWE '95 from more countries than any other Christian gathering in the history of the world.

In 1990 Luis Bush coined the term "the 10/40 window" to refer to the area located between 10 and 40 degrees north of the equator, which contains the largest and most dense populations of unreached peoples. Since that time the church has targeted the 10/40 window and emphasized the transformation of communities.

Bill Bright zealously called leaders in the missions movement to pray and fast in an effort to combine the work of prayer with the work of world evangelization. He insisted that the Great Commission could be fulfilled only in the context of much prayer and fasting. He wrote, "I believe the power of fasting as it relates to prayer is the spiritual atomic bomb that our Lord has given us to destroy the strongholds of evil and usher in a great revival and spiritual harvest around the world."[11]

In January 2008 Mark Anderson led a historic gathering in Orlando, Florida, named "Call2All Orlando." It was the first of many Call2All congresses, and it drew more than six hundred leaders, most from top international missions organizations and prayer ministries. They came together to strategize about completing the task of giving a witness of the gospel to every people group of the earth before the Lord returns. The purpose of the Call2All congresses is to reach "all"—the least, the last, and the lost.

At the Call2All Orlando congress the Holy Spirit began to call the missions movement back to its roots in prayer. At this congress both the missions leaders and the prayer leaders recognized the Lord's hand in establishing them together in new, strategic alliances for completing the task of bringing the gospel to every nation by 2025. God is arranging a glorious convergence throughout the nations of the prayer movement and the missions movement together with local church leaders.

Some speak of "the prayer movement" and "the missions movement" as though they are distinct or even in conflict. Each of these movements has attracted some criticism—missions groups for not praying enough and prayer groups for not evangelizing enough. In God's heart the two movements are one. Only in man's eyes are they two separate movements. They constitute one reality in His heart because *evangelism* is not the ultimate goal, *worship* is. As John Piper writes, "Missions exists because worship doesn't."[12] Worship is ultimate because Jesus is ultimate. Worship is both the fuel and the goal of missions. Worship is a response to the worth of Jesus—it is the reward of His suffering.

On December 25, 2006, Mark Anderson, the leader of Call2All, had a prophetic dream in which the Lord showed him that the missions movement and the prayer movement are the *same movement* in God's heart. At Call2All Orlando the leaders of international prayer movements agreed to partner with leaders of international missions organizations as they reach out together to all nations. They determined to see each missions organization and missionary covered in prayer. They have asked each prayer ministry and each intercessor across the earth to specifically adopt one mission organization, three individual missionaries, and one city or nation to cover in prayer on a regular basis. In January 2004 IHOPKC adopted YWAM as our primary missions organization, and in December 2007 we adopted Egypt as our primary area to cover in prayer.

Leaders of the missions movement (church-planting movements with marketplace ministries) and the prayer movement are working together with intensity on a global level for the first time in history to see the kingdom of God impact every sphere of society. In twenty-two Call2All congresses (2008–2012), thirty-five thousand leaders made commitments to start *seven million new church plants* and *seven hundred thousand new prayer watches or houses of prayer* by 2020.

The prayer leaders at Call2All Orlando made a definitive commitment to the missions leaders: "Mission leaders, as you go to the four thousand zones, we are going with you, intentionally and strategically. We will pray before you go, we will cover you while you are there, and we will continue to pray as you increase your ministry in those parts of the earth." The missions leaders answered back with an affectionate response born of revelation: "We need you because we cannot do our job without partnership with you."

Jesus is bringing a new level of unity among His people so that all the gifts in His body—in all nations, from three generations—work together. We can do so much more when we embrace each other's different callings with love.

He is also bringing about a fruitful cross-pollination of the missions and the prayer movements. For example, YWAM's University of the Nations in Hawaii and Every Home for Christ World Headquarters in Colorado—both primarily missions organizations—are pioneering night-and-day prayer rooms. Intercessors are giving themselves to the missionary effort, and missionaries are giving themselves to focused prayer and worship. Something big is going on!

THE ROLE OF YOUNG PEOPLE

One of the most exciting aspects of the growth of the missions and prayer movements is the huge number of young people who are embracing it with zeal. Hunger for real encounter with God is increasing in the youth of America and other nations. We are witnessing a spiritual resurgence among young people in both the missions and the prayer movements. Young men and women may be dissatisfied with religious programs, but they sincerely desire to embrace a vibrant faith rooted in intimacy with God through prayer and His Word.

In recent years tens of thousands of young adults have gathered in stadiums and arenas for massive solemn assemblies organized by Lou Engle and TheCall. They did not come to hear a well-known preacher or Christian worship band. In fact, the names of speakers and worship bands were not announced in advance of these large, solemn assemblies. Young people simply responded to the call to worship, fasting, and prayer for revival in America.

Other nations, including Korea, Egypt, Taiwan, the Philippines, Thailand, and Brazil, have held similar large, young-adult prayer conferences or solemn assemblies.

More than one hundred years ago, God raised up the Student Volunteer Movement (SVM) in North America. In this movement more than twenty thousand college students and young professionals abandoned their pursuit of the "American dream" and, ignited by the Holy Spirit, went to foreign lands to proclaim the gospel. Trading in the potential for lucrative careers, powerful influence, and comfortable lifestyles for lives of prayer and evangelism, these young men and women were motivated not by earthly pleasures and human accolades but by the desire to wholeheartedly commit themselves to the fame of Jesus.

Writing about the SVM, John L. Cumming described their commitment to prayer:

> The early Student Volunteer Movement believed firmly in the power of prayer. They did not pray just because it was the right thing to do. They prayed because they believed God would answer. They made prayer a first priority both in their individual lives and in the Volunteer Bands (also called Prayer Bands).[13]

One of the movement's own leaders, John R. Mott, confirmed Cumming's observation when he said, "The vital things pertaining to the Movement…hinge on prayer."[14]

Today the Lord is once again raising up what I call "intercessory missionaries"—missionaries who preach the gospel out of a lifestyle rooted in prayer (see chapter 30). Brian Kim, a senior leader at the International House of Prayer of Kansas City, launched the Luke18 Project, which works together with many ministries in an effort called "2020 Vision." This project is focused on planting "prayer furnaces" on all twenty-six hundred college campuses in our nation by 2020 and making the universities the recruiting ground for a new student volunteer movement of missions and prayer. The vision includes recruiting and training ten thousand of "the best and the brightest" young people in our nation as intercessory missionaries and then releasing them into the hardest and darkest places of the earth. By the grace of God and together with other ministries, we have trained and resourced campus ministries and students to plant prayer furnaces on more than one thousand college campuses to date. History will continue to be made on our college campuses as students respond wholeheartedly to the call of God.

The rapid growth of the prayer movement worldwide is only the beginning of what Jesus Himself is orchestrating in His beloved church in this generation. As I have said before, I believe that what we are witnessing is nothing less than a Holy Spirit–inspired movement of worship and prayer that will result in a great global harvest prior to the return of Jesus.

HOW THE PRAYER MOVEMENT CAN SUPPORT MISSIONS

In order to facilitate the convergence of the missions and prayer movements and support the efforts of Call2All, we are asking that every house of prayer ministry and every individual intercessor do three things:

1. Adopt one missions organization to support with your regular prayer and finances.

2. Commit to pray regularly for three specific individual missionaries who are serving in foreign lands.

3. Commit to pray regularly for one city or nation (besides your own).

In addition to these three things we are calling born-again believers to pray for God's purposes to be released in Israel. Praying for this nation must be a global effort. We are believing God for one hundred million intercessors to cry out for the breakthrough of the power of God in Jerusalem, "the city of the great King" (Ps. 48:2; Matt. 5:35). If we all work together—some in prayer and some in evangelism—we will certainly see the fulfillment of God's plans for the harvest and for the restoration of justice throughout the earth.

Chapter 30

THE CALL *to* BE *a* FULL-TIME INTERCESSORY MISSIONARY

What the church needs today is not more machinery or better, not new organizations or more and novel methods, but men whom the Holy Spirit can use—men of prayer, men mighty in prayer.[1]
—E. M. BOUNDS

ONE SIGNIFICANT ASPECT of the global prayer movement—and essential to it—is the large numbers of believers the Lord is calling to engage in prayer ministry as a full-time occupation. I refer to those who are called to this level of commitment as "intercessory missionaries." An intercessory missionary is one who does the work of the kingdom (as his full-time occupation) from the place of prayer and worship while embracing a missionary lifestyle and focus.

People sometimes ask me what an intercessory missionary is and where this ministry title is mentioned in the Bible. In principle the calling and occupation of intercessory missionary appears throughout the Scripture, though it is not referred to by the name I have coined for it. However, I will show in this chapter that its function can be found in both the Old and the New Testaments, particularly in passages that focus on end-time prophecy, as well as throughout church history and in contemporary ministries.

The New Testament gives only a few specific ministry titles and job descriptions, but it does encourage us to participate in kingdom-related activities such as winning the lost, caring for people, helping the poor, and praying. "Apostle" is the title with the clearest job description. But we don't find the titles of "senior pastor," "marriage counselor," "youth pastor," "children's pastor," "outreach pastor," and many other titles used in the church today. In fact, most of the titles we currently use are not specifically mentioned in the New Testament.

It's understandable that the Bible does not provide a comprehensive list of ministries the Holy Spirit has used to meet the needs of every culture in every generation throughout the history of the church. As long as biblical values are upheld, the church has the liberty to name specific ministry focuses in a way that applies to a particular generation and culture so that God's purposes are fulfilled.

INTERCESSORY MISSIONARIES IN THE OLD TESTAMENT

As we have seen, the Old Testament contains important information about the full-time occupation of singers who ministered to God night and day. After King

David established a new order of worship that he had received from God, he commanded all the kings after him to uphold it because it was God's command (2 Chron. 29:25; 35:4, 15; Ezra 3:10; Neh. 12:45).

David was the first leader in the Bible to establish worship and intercession as a full-time occupation.[2] He set into place eight thousand intercessory missionaries—four thousand singers and musicians and four thousand gatekeepers—all of whom were Levites (1 Chron. 23:3–5). (Today I would add sound technicians to this list, because, in my opinion, the soundboard is the most important "instrument" on a worship team.) The gatekeepers took care of the buildings and finances and carried out many other activities to support the ministry to God in the temple. In our context "gatekeepers" are those who help in financial or event management, janitorial or organizational service, running seminars, and so on.

The singers were employed in the work day and night and thus were freed from other duties (1 Chron. 9:33). In other words, they did not have other jobs outside their temple responsibilities. What they did—singing and playing their instruments—was hard work. I imagine they had many "worship team practices" and had to grow in musical skill, knowledge of the Scripture, and other related activities.

Establishing the ministry of night-and-day prayer and worship required a significant amount of effort, and it was very expensive. But David insisted on making the costly investment of time and money because the Lord had commanded it and because he knew that the God of Israel is worthy of extravagant praise.

In the generations that followed David, when Israel went astray, God raised up spiritual reformers with a vision to restore worship as David had commanded it. Seven generations in the Old Testament experienced "revival." Each honored the command that God had given David and restored Davidic worship, complete with full-time intercessory missionaries. (See chapter 24 for a list of these spiritual reformers and the actions each took to reestablish night-and-day Davidic worship in Israel.)

INTERCESSORY MISSIONARIES IN END-TIME PROPHECY

The Scripture gives many indications of the significance of prayer in the end times.[3] In fact, prayer is one of the major themes of end-time prophecy. As I have mentioned previously, *the conflict at the end of the age will be between two global worship movements.* The Antichrist will empower a worldwide, state-financed, false worship movement (Rev. 13:4, 8, 12, 15), but the global prayer movement led by Jesus will be far more powerful.

Isaiah prophesied about prayer ministries that would continue 24/7 until Jesus returns and restores Jerusalem as a praise in the earth. Isaiah was referring to the watchmen-intercessors the Lord Himself would appoint and set in place who would not keep silent day or night.

On your walls, O Jerusalem, I have appointed watchmen [intercessors]; all day and all night they will never keep silent. You who remind the LORD, take no rest for yourselves; and give Him no rest until He establishes and makes Jerusalem a praise in the earth.

—ISAIAH 62:6–7, NAS

Isaiah's prophecy clearly states that God will raise up 24/7 prayer ministries in the end times that will never be silent until Jesus returns. The 24/7 aspect of this promise implies that some intercessors and ministries will be called to engage in prayer as a full-time occupation. It also implies that God will make a way for them to walk in this calling, including providing for them financially.

In his prophecy Isaiah is referring to New Testament believers who will be on the earth when Jesus returns. Some will be full-time occupational intercessors. Their hard work in prayer is meant to serve and strengthen the prayer ministries in local churches in their regions and to be catalytic in inspiring others in prayer.

Only one generation will see the complete fulfillment of God's promise to appoint, or set, watchmen (intercessors) in place to cry out all day and all night until Jerusalem becomes a praise in the earth. The prophecy speaks specifically about prayer ministries being established by the Lord that will continue until He returns. At that time all nations will see Jerusalem as Jesus's own city, the city of the great King (Ps. 48:2; Matt. 5:35).

Isaiah's prophecy speaks of a "spiritual wall" of intercession from which the end-time watchmen-intercessors will cry out 24/7 for the release of God's promises. Ezekiel also spoke of "spiritual walls" of prayer (Ezek. 13:3–5; 22:30). God will establish end-time watchmen-intercessors in their places to function as a "wall of prayer." These watchmen are to "make the wall" by standing in the gap in prayer before God and the people so that the land will be blessed rather than destroyed.

Through Isaiah, God promised sovereignly to appoint intercessors and establish them in the work of intercession, which will never stop until Jesus returns. Those called will include full-time occupational intercessors—intercessory missionaries—who will stand on the wall of intercession to cry out for God's purposes for Jerusalem.

INTERCESSORY MISSIONARIES IN THE NEW TESTAMENT

Some people ask me where intercessory missionaries are found in the New Testament. My response: Where in the New Testament do we find leaders who do *not* prioritize prayer? Beginning with Jesus and the apostles, the New Testament highlights many leaders who gave themselves to prayer in an extravagant way.

Jesus personally spent long hours in prayer,[4] and He placed great value on Mary of Bethany's choice to sit before Him rather than busying herself with other things. In fact, He called it the "one thing…needed" (Luke 10:38–42).

He also emphasized prayer, or "watching," more than any other specific activity when speaking about the generation in which He would return.[5]

The apostle Paul embraced night-and-day prayer in various seasons and called widows to this ministry (1 Thess. 3:10; 1 Tim. 5:5; 2 Tim. 1:3). John the Baptist spent much time communing with the Lord in the wilderness of Judea (Matt. 3), and the apostles were committed to their prayer lives (Acts 6:4). An angel declared to Cornelius, a man who "prayed to God always," that his continual prayers were a memorial before God (Acts 10:2–4).

Prayer was a high priority for all the leaders mentioned in the New Testament.[6] As proof, consider just a few of the many verses that reflect the value they placed on prayer:

> They continued steadfastly in the apostles' doctrine and fellowship…and in prayers.
>
> —Acts 2:42

> We will give ourselves continually to prayer and to the ministry of the word.
>
> —Acts 6:4

It is easy to find leaders in the New Testament who were consistently engaging in prayer and the Word. God's kingdom work is accomplished both in the place of prayer and outside it. The three dimensions of missions work—continual prayer, mercy deeds, and sharing the gospel—must go together. Prayer causes the work of outreach to the lost and needy to be much more effective. Oswald Chambers said, "Prayer does not *fit* us for the greater work; prayer *is* the greater work."[7]

Some people are concerned that intercessory missionaries may develop lazy, isolated lives in prayer, detached from the real needs of people. Anyone who has prayed four hours in one day, with fasting, and then gone out to preach the gospel will know that the call to be an intercessory missionary is not for lazy people.

Others ask if too much prayer leads intercessors to neglect walking in love for others. I have observed just the opposite. Night-and-day prayer is a practical expression of the commandment to love one another because it fosters an environment in which multitudes are blessed and delivered. When a person is being tormented by a demon, he needs someone to cast the demon out. Jesus linked greater effectiveness in casting out demons to prayer and fasting (Matt. 17:21). The rigorous lifestyle of an intercessory missionary prepares him to engage in this type of ministry. By praying for and serving people, the missionary seeks to walk out the first and second commandments to love God and others with all his heart.

The Anna calling

One of the most powerful examples in the New Testament of an intercessory missionary is Anna, an elderly Jewish widow who prayed in the temple night and day prior to Jesus's birth. She was empowered by the grace of God to spend long hours in His presence for many years.

> Now there was one, Anna, a prophetess...She was of a great age, and had lived with a husband seven years from her virginity; and this woman was a widow of about eighty-four years, who did not depart from the temple, but served God with fastings and prayers night and day....She gave thanks to the Lord, and spoke of Him [Jesus] to all those who looked for redemption in Jerusalem.
>
> —LUKE 2:36–38

Anna was a "watchman" set on the wall in Jerusalem. We see in her an expression of Isaiah's prophecy: "All day and all night" she "never kept silent" (Isa. 62:6, NAS). Through Isaiah, the Lord promised to set intercessors in place for His end-time purposes, and Anna was a token of what will happen across the nations during the generation in which the Lord returns.

Notice that the passage in Luke describes Anna as a prophetess (Luke 2:36), an intercessor (v. 37), *and* an evangelist (v. 38). In this one woman the grace for all three ministries—prophecy, intercession, and evangelism—came together.

Anna was widowed after living with her husband for seven years (v. 36), probably when she was in her midtwenties, and that is when she began giving herself to prayer night and day. At eighty-four years old—approximately sixty years later—she was still ministering to the Lord in much prayer with fasting. Anna remained faithful in her calling to long hours of prayer. What a remarkable woman!

Anna is representative of intercessors with grace to sustain long hours of prayer for many years. Her calling—what I refer to as "the Anna calling"—transcends gender and age. *It is for male and female, young and old.* When I refer to an intercessory missionary as having a specific "Anna calling," I mean he or she has grace for much prayer and fasting.

In this very hour the Lord is wooing those with a heart and a calling like Anna's to the full-time occupation of worship and prayer. He is personally appointing them and setting them in their places. The Lord is calling forth modern-day "Annas" in churches and prayer rooms around the world, and we must celebrate them as a great gift to the body of Christ and the prayer movement, recognizing and releasing them to obey their God-given mandates.

INTERCESSORY MISSIONARIES THROUGHOUT HISTORY

The Lord has led many throughout the two thousand years of church history to establish night-and-day prayer ministries. Looking back, I see a golden thread of the Spirit testifying that 24/7 prayer is on God's heart. Although it is clear that the Holy Spirit has not called the entire body of Christ to this ministry during any generation, He has clearly called some. Thus, we see a witness of night-and-day prayer through the centuries, a testimony that God desires this kind of extravagant ministry from His people.

The order of worship that God commanded David to establish—full-time singers and musicians in God's house—is timeless and valid today, but the application of this command differs according to each generation and culture. Through the years intercessory missionaries have been known by different titles, but the biblical values behind their occupation were evident: they did the work of missions from a lifestyle of being deeply engaged in prayer, worship, and the Word.

One of the most dramatic expressions of 24/7 intercessory prayer began with Comgall, a monk in Bangor, Ireland, who founded a monastery in AD 558. After his death in AD 602 the annals reported that three thousand monks had joined his monastery, which maintained a 24/7 prayer ministry for more than three hundred years. It became an influential missions-sending community, famous for its choral psalmody and unceasing prayer.[8]

In those days most of the people who sustained 24/7 prayer ministries did so as their full-time occupation; therefore, I refer to them as intercessory missionaries, although they themselves did not use that term. Most of the people who embraced this calling in medieval times were monks, priests, or nuns who lived in monastic communities. Most monastic communities that sustained 24/7 prayer were also involved in various outreaches to the cities nearby.

Ministries from all streams of the body of Christ—including those of Celtic, Orthodox, Catholic, and Protestant traditions—have mobilized 24/7 prayer ministries through the years. For more information about some of them, including Comgall's Bangor monastery, see chapter 27.

INTERCESSORY MISSIONARIES TODAY

As we read in chapter 28, the Holy Spirit has raised up thousands of new prayer ministries in the last ten to twenty years. The number of 24/7 houses of prayer in the world has increased from fewer than twenty-five in 1984 to more than ten thousand, and most of the ministries have been founded in the last ten years.

Clearly God's desire to be worshipped on Earth as He is in heaven has not changed. I believe that many of the principles expressed in the order of worship God commanded David to embrace, including establishing the full-time occupation of singers and musicians in God's house, are timeless. We seek to apply these principles at the International House of Prayer in Kansas City (IHOPKC) where, as a rule, we ask those who enter the full-time occupation of intercessory missionary to commit to fifty hours per week, which includes at least four hours per day, six days a week, in the prayer room. If this seems like a lot, remember Anna: she probably spent more hours in prayer in the temple each day than we ask the intercessory missionaries at IHOPKC to do! (For more about IHOPKC, see Appendix A.)

You may be wondering: Exactly what do intercessory missionaries *do* in the prayer room? We engage in several important activities:

- **Worship.** We minister to God by declaring His worth unceasingly, reflecting the way He receives worship continually in heaven (Matt. 6:10). We magnify the supremacy of Jesus, declaring His worth, beauty, and riches. Millions of people across the nations join the choirs of heaven by ministering to God in this way.

- **Intercession for revival.** We labor in intercession for the release of God's power to spread the fame of Jesus and to win the lost, revive the church, and impact society. We also engage in works of justice and compassion outside the prayer room.

- **Intimacy with God.** We seek to grow in intimacy with God by personally encountering Him through His indwelling Spirit, receiving greater grace (James 4:6) to love, obey, and partner with Him as we are fascinated by who He is.

- **Feeding on the Word.** We seek to grow in understanding of God's Word, gaining insight into His will, ways, and salvation, and seeking to learn about the unique dynamics of His end-time plan. We serve others in an important way by taking the time and effort to grow in our understanding of the Word so that we may help them understand God's heart and will for this hour of history.

Lest, after reading this chapter, some believers mistakenly feel that they are "second class" or somehow inferior if they do not have a call to night-and-day prayer, let me be absolutely clear. As I have stated before, *not everyone is called to be an intercessory missionary.* Certainly not everyone is called to be an Anna. We are *all* called to pray but not necessarily as our primary occupation.

The greatest ministry is to do the will of God, whatever that may be for each one of us. In other words, the greatest ministry you can have is the one to which God calls *you.* The pressure of trying to operate in another's calling leads to all types of problems, including burnout, disappointment, and discouragement. So I urge you: do not despise your calling, and do not try to imitate the ministry of another. Embrace your own individual calling, whether it is serving God full time in the marketplace; in your home, school or neighborhood; or in the prayer movement, because it is the highest calling for you.

God is calling both Annas (full-time intercessors) and faithful believers in the marketplace and the home to participate in the end-time prayer movement. If

God asks you to participate in one corporate prayer meeting a week, be faithful to attend it and do your part. That is His will for you. Think about it: if you go to one weekly two-hour prayer meeting, in one year you will have prayed for your city, your nation, or the lost for more than one hundred hours. That is no small accomplishment! Now consider the possibility of *thousands* of people praying together for one hundred hours a year—their intercession will have a serious impact!

The Holy Spirit has not emphasized the calling to night-and-day worship and prayer *worldwide* throughout all two thousand years of church history, but as we have seen, He is now calling many ministries around the globe to work together to establish it in each city and region of the earth. The practical application of 24/7 prayer will differ from city to city and from nation to nation according to the local cultures, the personalities involved, and the resources available.

Join us and many others as we ask the Lord to establish 24/7 prayer with worship in every tribe and tongue before the Lord returns by uniting multiple ministries together in each region to engage in this type of prayer. Just imagine a missions movement that reaches every nation, with the gospel being preached in every language, and that is deeply connected to 24/7 prayer with worship in every tribe and tongue!

Will you also join me in asking the Lord to establish one million full-time intercessory missionaries—singers, musicians, sound technicians, intercessors, and gatekeepers maintaining the systems that support these prayer ministries—before the Lord returns? For some of you, full-time intercession is not your calling, but the Lord may lead you to support someone emotionally and/or financially who is called to this occupation. For others, this *is* your calling—your personal story is deeply linked to God's plan related to the end-time prayer movement. If you sense that this is the case, what should you do?

Certainly the Holy Spirit will direct the steps of each believer who is called by God to be an intercessory missionary, and He will undoubtedly have different steps for different people. He may inspire one person to join a ministry and live on a prayer-focused missions base like that at IHOPKC or one of many other similar places. He may tell another to help develop a culture of prayer in his local church and region. (Pastors who are called to do this, please see Appendix E.) He may direct yet another to begin a prayer meeting or series of prayer meetings, and so on. (For information about starting and participating in a prayer meeting, see Appendix F.) The important thing is to take the first step God gives you as you begin to fulfill this glorious calling, and watch what He does to further His end-time plan through you.

Appendix A

WHAT IS *the* INTERNATIONAL HOUSE *of* PRAYER *of* KANSAS CITY?

THE INTERNATIONAL HOUSE of Prayer of Kansas City is an evangelical missions organization that engages in outreach from the place of 24/7 worship with prayer. We have continued in 24/7 worship with prayer since September 19, 1999.

Our staff of approximately one thousand raise their financial support to serve as "intercessory missionaries"—believers who engage in outreach from the place of prayer. The majority serve full time, investing a minimum of fifty hours per week in the prayer room, in service, in outreach, in building relationships, and so on. (Some of our staff serve part time, investing twenty-five hours a week.) Most of our full-time staff members invest about twenty-four hours each week in our worship-based prayer room and another twenty-four hours a week in service, ministry outreach, building relationships, and becoming further equipped in the Word.

Two hours per week are designated for raising financial support. We are inspired by the successful financial model of support-raising that Campus Crusade for Christ and Youth With A Mission missionaries have used for more than fifty years. Today each of these missionary ministries has more than twenty thousand full-time missionary staff members who raise their own financial support. These two ministries have proven that raising support as a full-time missionary works when approached in a biblical way while embracing a few practical steps.

We have four different worship-led prayer rooms on our missions base—the Global Prayer Room, the All Nations Prayer Room, the Hope City Prayer Room (in Kansas City's inner city), and the Justice Prayer Room. Our largest prayer room, the Global Prayer Room, is 24/7; its name reflects the facts that many join us from around the globe and that we pray for many different nations, issues, and ministries around the world. It seats seven hundred people.

The 24/7 schedule in the Global Prayer Room consists of eighty-four prayer meetings each week, each lasting two hours and being led by worship teams of about ten to twelve staff members. Most of our worship teams lead six two-hour prayer meetings per week as part of their full-time jobs.

Our worship teams and intercessors flow together in what we call "the harp and bowl model" of prayer. Revelation 5:8 describes the twenty-four elders and the four living creatures around God's throne, "each having a harp, and golden bowls of prayer." The *harp speaks of music and worship* and the *bowl speaks of intercessory prayer*. Thus, we combine worship and intercession in our prayer meetings in each of our four prayer rooms.

We train our singers, musicians, and intercessors to flow in the harp-and-bowl model, an interactive relationship of worship and prayer. For example, an intercessor will pray for a few moments and then pause so that the singers can respond with a short song that usually lasts less than ten seconds. The intercessor prays again and then pauses, allowing the singers to again echo the prayer back in a responsive way. This pattern continues twenty-four hours a day, seven days a week. You can watch our worship teams through our live Web stream. We broadcast our prayer room live 24/7. To view it, go to www.ihopkc.org/prayerroom.

We utilize this model with our worship teams of ten to twelve singers and musicians. The New Testament prayers of Jesus and the apostles, the hymns found in the Book of Revelation, and the Psalms are the foundation for our prayer model. In our intercessory worship sets we pray for the harvest, revival in the church, justice in society, and righteousness in the government—for different cities and nations across the earth.

In conjunction with highlighting the importance of intercession for revival, justice, transformation, and evangelism, we emphasize intimacy with God, knowing that God desires for His people to encounter His heart and love in a deep and personal way. We worship the Father with confidence that He relates to us with tender mercy. We come before Jesus in worship and intercession, knowing that He is our Bridegroom King and that He greatly enjoys and delights in His people as His bride.

With our worship grounded in intimacy with God, we bring our petitions to Him in an expression of intercession. Our 24/7 sanctuary of worship with prayer is both a place of personal encounter and a gathering of corporate intercession, where we boldly approach the throne, lifting our voices as one. We ask the Lord to pour out His Spirit across Kansas City and our nation and in various cities throughout the earth. Jesus loves the whole church in all the different denominations and ministry streams. Therefore, we have joy in praying for many different parts of the body of Christ. We petition Him for a greater release of His power on our outreach and the ministry of the church so that His people will be more effective in the work of ministry. We are committed to prayer for the harvest, with music, from the place of intimacy with God.

We train young people at our full-time Bible school, the International House of Prayer University (IHOPU), which is built around the centrality of the Scriptures. Each year about a thousand students and interns join us to be equipped in the Word so that they may be faithful disciples of Jesus with godly character and may have a fruitful ministry in their local church as well as in the marketplace; in a house of prayer; or in a missions organization.

Rather than building an organizational network of related houses of prayer, we encourage many of our staff, students, and interns to return home to serve the Lord in the marketplace as well as in their local churches or to help build a prayer ministry in whatever city the Lord sends them to.

Our vision is to train people to serve alongside others and to develop a culture of prayer in the church family wherever God places them. We encourage churches to work together to establish 24/7 prayer with worship in their regions. In fact, we discourage pastors from seeking to establish 24/7 prayer with worship in their local churches alone without working with others.

A BRIEF HISTORY OF OUR BEGINNINGS

The *primary calling* of every Christian ministry is to work together with other churches and ministries to build the church and engage in the Great Commission. This mandate includes spreading the fame of Jesus by declaring His worth to everyone and calling people to love and obey Him with all their hearts. Our primary calling also includes loving people by winning the lost, making disciples, building godly families, healing the sick, doing works of justice, and impacting society. Alongside this primary calling, the Lord often gives *specific assignments* to ministries. The International House of Prayer's specific assignment includes maintaining a 24/7 sanctuary of worship with prayer as a foundation from which we engage in outreach ministry.

In May 1983 our church engaged in twenty-one days of prayer and fasting for revival. We interceded for God to release a greater measure of power to revive the church and win the lost. During this time, the Lord spoke to us in a dramatic way, telling us that one day He would *"establish twenty-four-hour-a-day prayer in the spirit of the tabernacle of David"* in our midst. Back in 1983 we did not have any idea what this would look like, how we would do it, or when we would do it.

We sought to be faithful in small beginnings, preparing to see this promise fulfilled. The Lord graciously helped us to establish intercessory prayer meetings in 1983 that continued daily for sixteen years while we waited for Him to give us understanding about when and how we were to begin a 24/7 schedule of prayer with worship. Then suddenly in January 1999 God confirmed that it was time, and the International House of Prayer began on May 7, 1999, in a small, three hundred-seat building. We started with thirteen hours of intercession a day, led by worship teams, and continued for four months. Then on September 19, by the grace of God, we launched our 24/7 schedule.

The journey that began that day has included many miracles of provision and sustenance. What an adventure it has been these last fifteen years! God has sent us full-time intercessors and musicians from many nations, believers who are fully committed to serving God as Anna did—with prayer and fasting by night and day (Luke 2:36–38).

In our first year about ten to fifteen people, in addition to the worship team, gathered for most of the prayer meetings. But it was not uncommon, especially during the night, for a worship team to have only two or three musicians and singers. The Lord often encouraged us not to despise the day of small beginnings

(Zech. 4:10). Today we continue to seek to understand what it means to function *"in the spirit of the tabernacle of David."*

SHARING OUR BLESSINGS WITH OTHERS

In 2003 we began to Web stream our 24/7 prayer room. Then in 2007 GOD TV began to broadcast it live around the globe. Throughout the year multitudes from about two hundred nations pray with us via the Web stream. In 2012 alone we had more than one million different people watching the live Web stream from one hundred ninety-six nations.

Now more than fifty thousand visitors each year come from different nations to visit us in Kansas City, primarily to spend time in the prayer room and receive training at conferences or seminars, and so on. They often come in groups and usually stay several days or weeks. Many visitors, international and local, leave encouraged to return home to establish daily worship and prayer meetings in their local churches.

Our All Nations Prayer Room (ANPR), located on our IHOPU campus, is another sanctuary of corporate worship and intercession, staffed by internationals whom the Lord has added to our community. Prayer meetings run fourteen hours a day, led by full worship teams singing in one of *nine languages*—Chinese, Korean, Spanish, Portuguese, Russian, Arabic, Farsi, German, and French. These worship-led prayer meetings are broadcast live on the Internet each day. We provide regular short-term training programs in most of those languages on our missions base—Chinese, Korean, Spanish, Portuguese, Russian, Arabic and Farsi—and we began one-year programs in Chinese and Korean at IHOPU in 2013.

My purpose in sharing some of our story is to give others confidence that they too can establish a prayer ministry in their region as many churches work together. If weak and broken people like us in Kansas City can do it by the grace of God, then surely weak and broken people in other cities can do it too, if churches will work together. It will have a different expression in different cities, ministries, and churches, but the principles are the same.

Appendix B

PRAYERS *for the* RELEASE *of the* SPIRIT

THE FOUNDATIONAL PREMISE of our prayers is to ask for a greater release of the power and presence of the Holy Spirit—in other words, for a greater manifestation of the gifts, fruit, and wisdom of the Holy Spirit (Luke 11:13; 18).

How much more will your heavenly Father give the Holy Spirit to those who ask Him!

—LUKE 11:13

THE FRUIT OF THE SPIRIT: GODLY CHARACTER IN OUR LIVES

1. Pray for the release of conviction of the Holy Spirit that results in godly character in those who hear the preaching of the Word (John 16:8). In other words, pray for the release of the power of God on His Word for those who hear it. Pray that God's power would cause His Word to be like:

   • A sword that pierces the hearts of hearers (Heb. 4:12).

   • A fire that consumes the hearts of hearers (Isa. 33:13–14; Jer. 23:29).

   • A hammer that shatters the hearts of hearers (Jer. 23:29).

   • An arrow that pierces the hearts of the hearers (Ps. 45:5; Acts 2:37–41).

2. Pray for the spirit of revelation of Jesus's beauty to be given to believers, that their hearts would be filled with love for God (Eph. 1:17).

3. Pray for the release of the fear of God in the church (Ps. 86:11).

4. Pray for the release of righteousness, peace, and joy on the church (Rom. 14:17; 15:13).

THE WISDOM OF GOD: GOD'S WAYS AND PLANS IN OUR LIVES

1. Pray for the wisdom of the Spirit to be released in the church and on its members so they will walk in the will of God (Col. 1:9–11).

2. Ask the Lord for direction for the church and its ministries (Col. 1:9–10; 4:12).

3. Pray for personal direction for individuals (James 1:5; Ps. 25:5; 43:3–4).

THE GIFTS OF THE SPIRIT: GOD'S POWER IN OUR LIVES

1. Ask the Holy Spirit to release His power and gifts to deliver people so they can fully love God (1 Cor. 12:31; 14:1).

2. Ask for the release of the prayers of Jesus through the empowering of the Spirit working in us (Heb. 7:25).

3. Ask for the manifestation of God's power through the ministry of the gifts of the Holy Spirit (1 Cor. 12:7–9).

OTHER PRAYER THEMES FROM THE NEW TESTAMENT

1. For individuals and traveling ministries:

   + Protection (Rom. 15:31; 2 Thess. 3:2; Philem. 22; Acts 12:5, 12).

   + Open doors of opportunity for ministry and favor (Col. 4:3).

   + Deliverance from temptations and evil (Matt. 6:13; Luke 22:31–32; 2 Cor. 13:7).

   + Personal needs met (Phil. 4:7, 19).

   + Release of the spirit of boldness (Eph. 6:19).

   + Mercy on their homes (2 Tim. 1:16–18).

2. For those in secular authority (1 Tim. 2:1–3).

3. To release the power of God to magnify Jesus's name in a specific city or region (Phil. 2:9–11; Isa. 45:22–25; 52:13–15; Ezek. 36:22–32, 37).

Appendix C

A NEW TESTAMENT APOSTOLIC PRAYER LIST

CATEGORIES OF PRAYER IN THE NEW TESTAMENT

1. Prayers for wisdom to be given to believers (Eph. 1:17; Col. 1:9; 4:12; James 1:5).

2. Prayers for a greater measure of strength in the heart (Eph. 3:16–19; Col. 1:11; Heb. 13:20–21).

3. Prayers for a greater release of God's power and comfort (2 Thess. 2:17; 3:5; Heb. 13:21).

4. Prayers to grow in receiving and expressing love (Eph. 3:18–19; Phil. 1:9; 1 Thess. 3:12; 2 Thess. 3:5).

5. Prayers that the church grow in purity (John 17:11–17; 2 Cor. 13:7–9; 1 Thess. 3:12–13).

6. Prayers for unity in the church (John 17:21–23; Rom. 15:5–6).

7. Prayers to release peace, joy, and hope (Rom. 15:13; 2 Thess. 2:16–17).

8. Prayers to overcome evil and to be delivered from evil men (John 17:11–15; 2 Thess. 3:3; Rom. 16:20).

9. Prayers to release boldness in the saints (Acts 4:29–31; Eph. 6:19).

10. Prayers to release anointed laborers (Matt. 9:37–38; Luke 10:2).

11. Prayers that the influence of the Word will spread by God's power and examples of this (Acts 12:24; 13:48; 19:20; 2 Thess. 3:1–2).

12. Prayers for the opening of a door for the gospel with miracles (Acts 14:27; Col. 4:3–4).

13. Prayers for grace to be found worthy to fulfill one's calling (2 Thess. 1:11–12).

14. Prayers to grow in patience, endurance, and steadfastness (Col. 1:11; 2 Thess. 3:5).

15. Prayers and promises for Israel, for restoration and blessing (Ezra 9:5–15; Neh. 1:4–11; Ps. 44; 45:3–5; 65; 67; 80; 83; 85;

86; 90:13–17; 102:12–22; 110:1–5; 132:1–17; Isa. 63:15; 64:12; Dan. 9; Hab. 3:2).

The Prayers of Jesus, the Chief Apostle (Heb. 3:1)

1. The Lord's Prayer (Matt. 6:9–13).

2. Prayers for anointed laborers in the harvest (Matt. 9:37–38; Luke 10:2).

3. Jesus exhorted us to pray for the release of the Spirit's ministry (Luke 11:13), for justice to prevail (Luke 18:1–8), and for strength for the saints (Luke 22:31–32).

4. Jesus prayed for strength in the garden (Matt. 26:40–41; Luke 22:39–46), before choosing the apostles (Luke 6:12–13), during the Transfiguration (Luke 9:28–29), and for Peter's faith (Luke 22:31–32). Jesus prayed long hours alone (Matt. 14:23; Mark 1:35; 6:46–47; Luke 5:16; 6:12).

5. Jesus prayed in John 17 to keep the saints in the Father's name (v. 11), to keep the saints from the evil one (v. 15), to sanctify the saints by truth (v. 17), and for the saints to experience God's glory and love (vv. 21–26).

Jesus's Answers to and Exhortations on Prayer

1. Jesus answered the prayer of the leper (Matt. 8:1–4), the centurion (vv. 5–13), the disciples in the storm (vv. 23–27), Jairus (Matt. 9:18–19, 23–25), the sick woman (vv. 20–22), the two blind men (vv. 27–31), Peter (Matt. 14:28–31), and the Syro-Phoenician woman (Matt. 15:21–28).

2. Jesus spoke about prayer with fasting (Matt. 17:21; Mark 2:18–20; 9:29), unified prayer (Matt. 18:19–20), the prayer of faith (Matt. 21:18–22), and prayer to overcome temptation (Matt. 26:40–41).

3. Jesus's teaching on prayer in the Gospel of John (John 14:13–15; 15:7, 16; 16:23–26).

Paul's Prayers in Romans

1. Prayer to visit that he may impart spiritual gifts to establish them (Rom. 1:8–11).

2. Prayer for Israel and for the lost to be converted (Rom. 10:1).

3. Prayer for unity in the church across a city (Rom. 15:5–7).

4. Prayer for believers to be filled with all joy, peace, and hope (Rom. 15:13).

5. Prayer for unity, to be delivered from persecution, to be effective in ministry, and to be able to visit in joy to be refreshed (Rom. 15:30–33).

6. An intercessory prophetic proclamation of victory over Satan (Rom. 16:20).

7. An intercessory benediction to receive insight into the mystery (Rom. 16:25–27).

PAUL'S PRAYERS IN 1 AND 2 CORINTHIANS

1. Prayer that the church would not come up short in spiritual gifts (1 Cor. 1:4–8).

2. Prayer for the release of grace for the church (1 Cor. 16:23–24).

3. Prayer for the release of God's comfort in pressure and persecution (2 Cor. 1:2–5).

4. Prayer for grace to avoid evil, to walk in godliness and honor (2 Cor. 13:7–9).

5. Prayer to experience abundant grace that leads to intimacy with God (2 Cor. 13:14).

PAUL'S PRAYERS IN EPHESIANS, PHILIPPIANS, AND COLOSSIANS

1. Prayer for the release of a spirit of revelation on the church (Eph. 1:15–23).

2. Prayer for strength in the inner man by experiencing God's love (Eph. 3:14–21).

3. Prayer for the release of the anointing of boldness in ministry (Eph. 6:18–20). Paul testified of the anointing of boldness (2 Tim. 4:17). The early church was strengthened with boldness (Acts 4:29–31).

4. Prayer for supernatural peace and love, faith, and grace (Eph. 6: 23–24).

5. Prayer for love and to walk in excellence and fruitfulness (Phil. 1:9–11).

6. Prayer for grace to be manifest upon the church and its members (Phil. 4:23).

7. Prayer for wisdom, intimacy with God, and spiritual strength (Col. 1:9–12).

8. Prayer that God would open a door of evangelism (Col. 4:2–4). A door of opportunity for the gospel opened for Paul (Acts 14:27; 1 Cor. 16:9; 2 Cor. 2:12).

9. Prayer for maturity and wisdom for the church (Col. 4:12).

Paul's Prayers in 1 and 2 Thessalonians

1. Prayer to release anointed ministry to the church that helps them abound in love and holiness (1 Thess. 3:9–13).

2. Prayer for passion for Jesus with purity through the Spirit (1 Thess. 5:23–25).

3. Prayer for grace to be manifest on the church (1 Thess. 5:28).

4. Prayer to be equipped to fulfill God's highest purposes for our lives (2 Thess. 1:11–12).

5. Prayer for the church to be comforted in God's love and established as effective and fruitful in ministry (2 Thess. 2:16–17).

6. Prayer to be delivered from persecution and for the influence of the Word to increase, resulting in new souls being saved and the saints growing in love and perseverance (2 Thess. 3:1–5). The increase of the influence of the Word results in many being born again (Acts 6:7; 12:24; 13:12, 48; 19:20).

7. Prayer for peace in circumstances and intimacy with God (2 Thess. 3:16).

Paul's Prayers in 1 and 2 Timothy

1. Worshipful benedictions to magnify God (1 Tim. 1:17; 6:15–16).

2. Prayer for governmental authorities and civic leaders (1 Tim. 2:1–4).

3. Prayer to receive more spiritual understanding (2 Tim. 2:7).

4. Prayer for God to open hearts with understanding and to grant repentance to those in deception (2 Tim. 2:24–26). The Lord opens hearts (Luke 24:45; Acts 16:14).

5. Prayer for a persecutor, Alexander the coppersmith, who harmed Paul (2 Tim. 4:14–15).

6. Prayer that disloyal believers would receive mercy and not be held accountable for not standing with Paul (2 Tim. 4:16).

7. Prayer for deliverance from every evil work and for protection (2 Tim. 4:18).

APOSTOLIC PRAYERS FROM PHILEMON TO JUDE

1. Prayer for effectiveness in one's faith (Philem. 1:4–6).

2. Worshipful benediction esteeming God's power in creation (Heb. 1:10–12).

3. Prayer to be made complete as a mature believer (Heb. 13:20–21).

4. James's exhortation to pray for wisdom (James 1:5–6).

5. Peter's doxology of thankfulness for salvation (1 Pet. 1:3–5).

6. Prayer to be established in maturity in the face of persecution (1 Pet. 5:10–11).

7. Prayer to grow in grace and the knowledge of God (2 Pet. 1:2–3).

8. Prayer for prosperity (3 John 1:2) in all things, including physical health and one's soul.

9. Jude's doxology and prayer for holiness (Jude 24–25).

APOSTOLIC PRAYERS AND EXHORTATIONS TO PRAY IN ACTS

1. Prayer of the apostles for boldness and for signs and wonders (Acts 4:24–31).

2. Stephen's martyrdom prayer (Acts 7:55–60).

3. There is much teaching and emphasis on prayer in the Book of Acts (Acts 1:13–14; 2:42–47; 3:1–4; 4:23–31; 6:4–7; 7:55–60; 8:9–25; 9:5–6, 11; 9:36–43; 10:2–4, 9, 31; 12:5, 12–17; 16:13, 16, 18, 25; 20:36; 27:29, 35; 28:8, 15).

4. Singing both the Word and our prayers has a significant place in a Spirit-filled lifestyle (1 Cor. 14:14–18; Eph. 5:18–19; Col. 3:16; James 5:13).

PRAYERS AND HYMNS IN REVELATION

1. John's doxology of thanksgiving for salvation (Rev. 1:5–6).

2. The song of the living creatures before the Father's throne (Rev. 4:8–9).

3. The song of the twenty-four elders before the Father's throne (Rev. 4:10–11).

4. The living creatures and elders declare Jesus's worth (Rev. 5:8–10).

5. Song of the angelic host declaring the worthiness of Jesus (Rev. 5:11–12).

6. Song of all creation glorifying the Father and the Son (Rev. 5:13–14).

7. The prayer of the martyrs for righteous vengeance and vindication (Rev. 6:10).

8. Worship from believers in all the nations magnifying God (Rev. 7:9–10).

9. The angelic host responding to all the nations worshipping God (Rev. 7:11–12).

10. Worship before the throne in anticipation of Jesus's return (Rev. 11:15–19).

11. Worship inspired by God's salvation and Satan's being cast to the earth (Rev. 12:10–12).

12. The tribulation saints worship God because of His righteous judgments (Rev. 15:2–4).

13. Worship in light of God's end-time righteous judgments (Rev. 16:4–7).

14. Worship as God's salvation is fully manifest on the earth (Rev. 19:1–4).

15. Worship at the wedding supper of the Lamb (Rev. 19:5–9).

16. Prayer for the presence of Jesus to come to His people (Rev. 22:17, 20).

OTHER NEW TESTAMENT PRAYERS

1. The prayer of Zacharias (Luke 1:8, 13, 67–80).

2. The prayer of Mary (Luke 1:46–55).

OLD TESTAMENT PRAYERS OF DEVOTION TO GOD

1. Prayers of personal devotion (Ps. 25–27; 40–43; 45; 63; 65; 69; 84; 86; 88; 119:12–21, 57–68, 145–160, 169–176; 130).

Appendix D

PRAYERS *for* VICTORY OVER CULTURAL STRONGHOLDS

IN ADDITION TO encouraging believers to pray for the Lord to release a greater measure of the Spirit with His gifts, fruit, and wisdom on the church, I also encourage people to pray apostolic prayers and/or to remind God of biblical promises when interceding for a kingdom victory over cultural strongholds in society that are caused by persistent sin and demonic spirits.

1. *Justice issues.* Pray for a greater release of God's power, love, and provision in relation to abortion, human trafficking, genocide, economic slavery, injustice, and so on.

2. *Crisis events.* Pray for a greater release of God's power, love, and provision in relation to catastrophic events in nature (weather, earthquakes, famines, wars, plagues, and so on).

3. *Political issues.* Pray for the government, especially political and civic issues (1 Tim. 2:1). Ask the Lord to put the person of His choice into office. Ask Him to inspire leaders to make choices for righteousness and to stop unjust policies, appointments, laws, and so on.

4. *Economic issues.* Pray for a greater release of God's power, blessing, creative wisdom, and provision with regard to market-place assignments and for an end to economic crisis.

5. *Family issues.* Pray for a greater release of God's love, wisdom, and power with regard to the fatherless, youth issues, marriages, divorce, domestic violence, widows, the elderly, the disabled, and so on.

6. *Media issues.* Pray for the Lord to raise up media messengers with prophetic ideas and creative wisdom about how to do the work of the kingdom through media. Ask Him to silence the violence, sexual perversion, and occult themes that are flooding the media channels today.

7. *Educational issues.* Pray that God's favor and blessing, with righteousness and excellence, be released in our educational institutions, on teachers, and in classrooms.

Appendix E

HOW DO WE DEVELOP *a* CULTURE *of* PRAYER?

We start with the senior leader.

When the senior leader of a local church or ministry embraces a *lifestyle* of prayer, then that local church or ministry will develop a *culture* of prayer. It has often been said, "The character of the kingdom is set by the character of its king." This is particularly true of prayer. Prayer cannot be delegated. We may think we are too busy to lead another ministry initiative; however, prayer is one initiative we *cannot* be too busy to lead. Once we realize that developing a lifestyle of prayer means cultivating intimacy with God—not just leading prayer meetings—we know we can't afford to do ministry any other way.

We make prayer the top priority for the ministry staff.

As pastors we may need to rethink the way we spend our time in the office. What if we dedicated the first hour or two to worship and prayer with some of the people on our staffs? Why not gather several mornings a week for an hour to seek the Lord together?

We teach on prayer and subjects that encourage prayer.

The culture of our churches is largely based on what we emphasize in our preaching. Intimacy with God, the majesty of God, the Sermon on the Mount, revival, holiness, and key themes related to the end times are all subjects that motivate people to pray.

Appendix F

STARTING *and* PARTICIPATING
in a PRAYER MEETING

IF YOU BELIEVE God is calling you to begin a prayer meeting or a series of meetings in your local area, don't let lack of experience hold you back. Here are some steps to get you started.

1. **Invite other believers to pray together with you on a regular basis.** If it is difficult for you to find someone who is willing to do this, don't be discouraged. Ask the Lord to lead you to people who want to pray. The Holy Spirit knows how to bring you together.

2. **Start small.** It doesn't take many people to start a weekly prayer meeting.

3. **Be consistent.** If you commit to pray every Thursday, then be consistent, regardless of who is out of town. Do not easily cancel the prayer meeting, even if the numbers are small. Consistency is important—and it shows others that you are committed to your prayer meeting.

4. **Commit.** It is common for people to start prayer meetings with zeal but for their zeal to quickly fade. Encourage the team to commit for a specific time period, perhaps three or six months. Then, at the end of that time, they can recommit to another set period of months.

5. **Involve young people.** Involve as many young people as possible by encouraging them to join your leadership team and to pray out loud in the prayer meetings. Consider asking them to give a three-minute devotional teaching or to present a prayer focus at the start of the prayer meeting.

6. **Incorporate music.** Try to involve worship music, even if you use an instrumental worship CD as background music. Many groups use the IHOPKC live prayer room Web stream as their worship team until they gather their own team.

7. **Decide on a purpose.** Determine what the purpose of the prayer meeting is. For example, decide that you will focus on

praying for revival, for justice, or for another kingdom issue God has put on your heart.

8. **Pray for one another.** Consider asking each intercessor to pray for at least one personal prayer request for someone in the group during the coming week. Maybe ask group members to report on answered prayer in their lives.

9. **Keep the meetings short.** Most believers are not accustomed to prayer meetings that last longer than two hours. I recommend limiting the prayer meeting to two hours at a time or less.

10. **Limit the number of meetings at first.** Do not start with too many prayer meetings a week. Some people are in a hurry to cover a large number of hours. Start with one or two prayer meetings and grow to more only when you have about ten to twenty intercessors at your meetings.

11. **Advertise.** Use Facebook and other means to advertise your times of prayer. Usually other people just like you want to pray with a group but don't know how to start. Putting up signs on school or church bulletin boards, sending out an e-mail, or posting on your Facebook account the times that you are praying and what you are praying for may encourage others to participate in your prayer meeting(s).

12. **Write out the "ground rules."** Write out the main principles for what will happen or what you do not want to happen in your prayer meetings so that people will know what is expected and accepted in your prayer meetings. For example, we ask people who are praying on the mic to use prayers from the Bible; not to pray longer than five to ten minutes; and not to relate dreams, give exhortations, or share testimonies at that time.

TIPS FOR PRAYING IN A PUBLIC PRAYER MEETING

Some believers are eager to set up prayer meetings but aren't certain what to do after the other intercessors show up. Below are some tips for how to pray.

1. **Use biblical prayers.** There are many different ideas about how to pray, so we encourage all intercessors to simply use the prayers in the Scripture (Eph. 1:17–19; 3:16–19; Phil. 1:9–11, and so on) as discussed in this book (see chapters 9 and 10 as well as Appendix C).

2. **Pray over biblical promises.** Remind God of His promises (Isa. 62:6–7; 43:26).

3. **Speak to God.** Encourage the people to *pray to God* instead of *preaching to people* when they pray in public prayer meetings. Focus on *asking* God to intervene in power rather than explaining or preaching to people about the value and details of obedience. Be more conscious that God is listening to you than that others are listening. Ask the people to avoid "preaching prayers."

4. **Pray for holiness in the church.** Instead of mentioning the specific sins of the people, pray for the release of the Holy Spirit's conviction of sin, righteousness, and judgment (John 16:8). The release of conviction on the church will cause many areas of sin to be dealt with and will release grace for repentance in the lives of those we are praying for. Ask for the release of the spirit of the fear of God and righteousness (Rom. 14:17; 15:13; Acts 8:6–8; 9:31).

5. **Avoid too many specifics.** Avoid informing God or people of the details of specific circumstances. Avoid praying for things that involve too many details, personal concerns, and issues that the majority of the group does not really care about.

6. **Do not dominate the meeting.** As a rule limit your prayer to five minutes or less unless there is an extra-special anointing on it. Don't pray out loud *while* another is leading in prayer.

7. **Avoid distraction.** Don't do anything that causes the majority in the group to be distracted or that draws undue attention to you or disturbs other intercessors.

8. **Value short prayers.** Encourage people to pray short prayers. Let them know that short prayers are valid, even if they consist of just one sentence. Don't be concerned about silence in the prayer meeting either.

WHAT TO DO IN A PRAYER MEETING WHEN ANOTHER IS PRAYING

In a corporate prayer meeting, it is good to engage with God by actively agreeing with the person praying on the microphone. How do we do this? By quietly *repeating some of the phrases* that others publicly pray aloud. I'm not saying *every* phrase, but I try to repeat every third or fourth phrase nearly word for word to the Lord. For example, if the intercessor prays a prayer with several phrases, such as, "Lord, pour out Your Spirit on the upcoming high school conference; release a spirit of conviction, and release Your power in great measure," I may repeat just one of those phrases word for word to the Lord, and then repeat another phrase when the intercessor prays the next sentence.

This is a very simple principle, but it keeps my heart engaged with the Lord during the prayer meeting. I have found that it is surprisingly easy to sit in a prayer room and not actually pray. It is also common for our minds to wander in a prayer meeting, but if we softly verbalize even just a part of the prayer that is being offered by another, then our minds will stay focused. Often I just softly whisper what the person leading in prayer is praying.

It is not enough to just be in the prayer room; we want to actually talk to God. I compare not talking to Him to being in a restaurant and reading the menu without actually eating. You can be a menu connoisseur and yet still die of starvation!

In addition to praying, I encourage people to follow a simple Bible-reading plan while sitting in a prayer meeting. If you read five chapters of the New Testament six days a week, you will read through the entire New Testament every two months. (If you want to read through the New Testament each month, you will need to read approximately ten chapters per day.)

NOTES

PART I—THE FOUNDATION FOR PRAYER

1. As quoted in Elizabeth George, *A Woman Who Reflects the Heart of Jesus* (Eugene, OR: Harvest House Publishers, 2010), 176.

CHAPTER 1—CALLED TO PRAY

1. As quoted in Gary L. Thomas, *Simply Sacred* (Grand Rapids: Zondervan, 2011).
2. See also Romans 9:23; Ephesians 3:16; Philippians 4:19; Colossians 1:27.

CHAPTER 2—THE FELLOWSHIP OF THE BURNING HEART

1. Tentmaker.org, "Prayer and Intercession Quotes," http://www.tentmaker.org/Quotes/prayerquotes2.htm (accessed June 20, 2014).
2. Bernard of Clairvaux, *The Four Loves*, from public domain material at Christian Classics Ethereal Library at Calvin College (www.ccel.org), modernized and abridged by Stephen Tompkins, edited and prepared for the Web by Dan Graves. In this treatise Clairvaux relates that the fourth degree of love is to love oneself for God's sake.
3. Thomas Dubay, *The Evidential Power of Beauty: Science and Theology Meet* (San Francisco: Ignatius Press, 1999).
4. As quoted in Thomas Dubay, *Faith and Certitude* (San Francisco: Ignatius Press, 1985). Dubay is quoting a statement made by a character in Fyodor Dostoyevsky's novel *The Brothers Karamazov*.
5. As quoted in Dubay, *The Evidential Power of Beauty*, 14. Dubay is quoting from Book I of St. Augustine's *Confessions*.

CHAPTER 3—CHARACTERISTICS OF EFFECTIVE PRAYER

1. Arthur T. Pierson, *George Muller of Bristol* (London: James Nisbet & Co., Limited., 1899), 456.

CHAPTER 4—ABIDING IN CHRIST

1. As quoted in Mary Ann Bridgwater, *Prayers for the Faithful* (Nashville, TN: B&H Publishing Group, 2008).
2. See Romans 6:22; 7:4–5; Galatians 5:22; Ephesians 5:9; Hebrews 12:11; James 3:18.
3. See John 4:36; Romans 1:13; 15:28; Philippians 1:22; Colossians 1:5–6.

CHAPTER 5—A PRACTICAL PLAN TO GROW IN PRAYER

1. As quoted in Alice Smith, *Spiritual Advocates* (Lake Mary, FL: Charisma House, 2008), 21.
2. See Zechariah 1:14–17; 2:10–12; 8:2–3; 12:1–10.
3. Mike Bickle, *Passion for Jesus* (Lake Mary, FL: Charisma House, 1996, 2007).
4. The following scriptures will elaborate on these themes: Isaiah 54:4–12; 62:2–5; Jeremiah 3:14; 31:32; Hosea 2:14–23; Matthew 9:15; 22:2; 25:1–13; John 3:29; 2 Corinthians 11:2; Ephesians 5:25–32; Revelation 19:7–9; 22:17.
5. See Mark 1:35; 6:46; Luke 5:15–16; 6:12; 9:18, 28; 21:37.
6. See Mark 1:35; 6:46; Luke 5:15–16; 6:12; 9:18, 28; 21:37.
7. Henry David Thoreau, *Walden* (Radford, VA: Wilder Books, 2008), 9.
8. Dubay, *The Evidential Power of Beauty*.

CHAPTER 6—ORGANIZING YOUR PRAYER TIME

1. As quoted in James Ford Jr., *When a Man Loves a Woman* (Chicago: Moody Publishers, 2011).

CHAPTER 7—A BIBLICAL PARADIGM FOR PRAYER

1. R. A. Torrey, *How to Pray and Study the Bible* (Peabody, MA: Hendrickson Publishers, 2004).
2. Basil Miller, *George Muller: Man of Faith and Miracles* (Minneapolis, MN: Bethany House Publishers, 1941), 146.

PART II—INTERCESSORY PRAYER

1. Tracey M. Sumner, ed., *The Essential Works of Andrew Murray* (Uhrichsville, OH: Barbour Publishing Inc., 2008).

CHAPTER 8—RELEASING GOD'S POWER THROUGH INTERCESSION

1. Goodreads.com, "Andrew Murray Quotes," https://www.goodreads.com/author/quotes/13326.Andrew_Murray (accessed June 20, 2014).
2. The Millennium is a literal thousand-year period in which Jesus will rule the whole world from Jerusalem in righteousness, peace, and prosperity (Rev. 20:1–6). This period of worldwide blessing will be initiated by Jesus's Second Coming. See Psalms 2; 110; Isaiah 2:1–4; 9:6–7; 11:1–16; 35:1–8; 51:3; 65:17–25; Ezekiel 34:29; 36:35; 47:6–12; Matthew 6:10; 17:11; 19:28; 28:19–20; Acts 1:6; 3:21; Revelation 20:4–6.

CHAPTER 9—THE VALUE OF USING BIBLICAL PRAYERS

1. Goodreads.com, "John Calvin Quotes," https://www.goodreads.com/author/quotes/30510.John_Calvin (accessed June 20, 2014).
2. Adapted from Mike Bickle, *After God's Own Heart* (Lake Mary, FL: Charisma House, 2004, 2009), 143.

CHAPTER 10—THE MOST FAMOUS APOSTOLIC PRAYER

1. S. D. Gordon, *Quiet Talks on Prayer* (New York: Fleming H. Revell Company, 1904).
2. A. W. Tozer, *The Knowledge of the Holy* (San Francisco: HarperOne, 2009).
3. **The kingdom is here in part now:** Matthew 3:12; 4:17, 23; 6:10, 33; 10:7; 12:28; 13:11; 16:18–19; 19:12; Mark 4:11, 26; 9:1; Luke 16:16; 17:20–21; 18:16, 29–30; Acts 14:22; 19:8; 20:25; 28:23, 30–31; Romans 14:17; 1 Corinthians 4:20.

    The kingdom is also future: Matthew 8:11–12; 25:34; Luke 13:28–29; 14:15; 19:11–19; 22:16–18, 29–30; Acts 1:3–6; 1 Corinthians 15:24–28, 50; 2 Timothy 4:1, 18; Hebrews 6:5; 12:28; Revelation 11:15–18; 12:10; 20:1–6.

CHAPTER 11—PRAYER AND PROPHETIC PROMISES

1. Greg Laurie, *New Believer's Guide to Prayer* (Wheaton, IL: Tyndale House Publishers, Inc., 2003).
2. **The kingdom is here in part now:** Matthew 3:12; 4:17, 23; 6:10, 33; 10:7; 12:28; 13:11; 16:18–19; 19:12; Mark 4:11, 26; 9:1; Luke 16:16; 17:20–21; 18:16, 29–30; Acts 14:22; 19:8; 20:25; 28:23, 30–31; Romans 14:17; 1 Corinthians 4:20.

    The kingdom is also future: Matthew 8:11–12; 25:34; Luke 13:28–29; 14:15; 19:11–19; 22:16–18, 29–30; Acts 1:3–6; 1 Corinthians 15:24–28, 50; 2 Timothy 4:1, 18; Hebrews 6:5; 12:28; Revelation 11:15–18; 12:10; 20:1–6.

Chapter 12—The New Testament Model for Spiritual Warfare

1. "What Various Hindrances We Meet" by William Cowper. Public domain.
2. See 2 Chronicles 5:13; 7:3, 6; 20:21; Ezra 3:11; Psalms 52:1; 100:5; 106:1; 107:1; 117:2; 118:1–4, 29; 136; Jeremiah 33:11.

Chapter 13—Lifestyle of an Effective Intercessor

1. William Law, *A Practical Treatise Upon Christian Perfection* (London: William and John Innys, 1726).

Part III—Devotional Prayer

1. Goodreads.com, "Brother Lawrence Quotes," https://www.goodreads.com/ quotes/141767-there-is-not-in-the-world-a-kind-of-life (accessed June 20, 2014).

Chapter 14—Prayers to Strengthen Our Inner Man

1. Gordon, *Quiet Talks on Prayer*.

Chapter 15—Fellowshipping With the Holy Spirit

1. D. L. Moody, *Notes From My Bible* (New York: Fleming H. Revell Company, 1895).

Chapter 16—How to Pray-Read the Word

1. Edward M. Bounds and Harold J. Chadwick, *The Classic Collection on Prayer* (Gainesville, FL: Bridge-Logos, 2001), 79.

Chapter 17—Appropriating God's Names

1. Andrew Murray and Al Bryant, *Daily Secrets of Christian Living* (Grand Rapids, MI: Kregel Publications, 1978).
2. Larry Lea, *Could You Not Tarry One Hour?* (Lake Mary, FL: Charisma House, 1987), 55–65.

Part IV—Going Deeper in Prayer

1. As quoted in Dick Eastman, *No Easy Road* (Grand Rapids, MI: Chosen Books, 2003).

Chapter 18—Adding Fasting to Prayer

1. As quoted in Charles Stanley, *Charles Stanley's Handbook for Christian Living* (Nashville, TN: Thomas Nelson Inc., 2001), 517.
2. Richard J. Foster, *The Celebration of Discipline* (San Francisco: Harper and Row, 1978), 44–45.
3. Andrew Murray, *With Christ in the School of Prayer* (Old Tappan, NJ: Spire Books, 1979), 74.
4. A. M. Hills, *The Life of Charles G. Finney* (Cincinnati, Ohio: Office of God's Revivalist, 1902). The information about Finney in my book was taken from pages 63 of an online version, http://www.libraryoftheology.com/writings/biographies/Life_of_Charles_ Finney.pdf (accessed June 18, 2014).
5. Gordon Lindsay, *John G. Lake: Apostle to Africa* (Dallas, TX: Christ for the Nations, 1987), 53.
6. *Evangelical Magazine*, "National Prayer: Spurgeon's Sermon to the Nation," February 4, 2011, http://magazine.emw.org.uk/2011/02/national-prayer/ (accessed June 18, 2014).
7. For information about the congressional resolutions calling for national days of prayer and fasting, see the *Journals of the American Congress from 1774-1788 in Four Volumes* (Washington DC: Way and Gideon, 1823). For information about Lincoln's

proclamation appointing a day of national humiliation, fasting, and prayer, go to www
.presidency.ucsb.edu/ws/index.php?pid=69891 (accessed June 20, 2014).

8. Jonathan Edwards, ed., *The Life of David Brainerd* (Grand Rapids, MI: Baker Book
House, 1988), 40.

CHAPTER 19—PRAYING IN THE SPIRIT

1. Andrew Murray, *The Ministry of Intercession* (London: James Nisbet & Co., Limited.,
1899), 202.

2. Dave Roberson, *The Walk of the Spirit—The Walk of Power: The Vital Role of Praying
in Tongues* (Tulsa, OK: Dave Roberson Ministries, 1999).

3. Smith Wigglesworth, *Ever Increasing Faith* (N.p.: Zao Ministries International, n.d.),
81. This work is in the public domain and has been released in different versions by
various publishers.

CHAPTER 20—RECEIVING THE SPIRIT OF PRAYER

1. John Gillies and George Whitefield, *Memoirs of Rev. George Whitefield* (Middletown,
CT: Hunt & Noyes, 1838) 17.

2. Dr. Gardiner Spring, pastor of the Brick Presbyterian Church in New York, said in
1856 that the period between 1792 and 1842 was "a memorable period in the history
of the American Church." He declared that "scarcely any portion of it…but were graciously visited by copious effusions of the Holy Spirit. From north to south, and from
east to west, our…academies, our colleges and our churches drank largely of this foun-
tain of living waters." Gardiner Spring, *The Brick Church: The Old and the New* (New
York: M. W. Dodd, 1858), 16. Viewed online at Google Books.

3. Jonathan Edwards, ed., *The Life and Diary of David Brainerd.*

4. Many people have written about the life of Jonathan Edwards. I recommend the fol-
lowing biographies: George Marsden, *A Short Life of Jonathan Edwards* (Grand Rapids,
MI: Wm. B. Eerdmans Publishing Co., 2008); Iain H. Murray, *Jonathan Edwards: A
New Biography* (N.p.: Banner of Truth, 1987).

5. George M. Marsden, *Jonathan Edwards: A Life* (Harrisonburg, VA: Donnelly & Sons,
2003), 220.

6. Charles Finney, *The Original Memoirs of Charles Finney* (Grand Rapids: Zondervan,
2002).

7. The Prayer Revival of 1857–1858 goes by many names: The Businessman's Revival; The
Layman's Prayer Revival; The Noon Prayer Revival; The Great Revival of 1857–58;
and simply The Revival of 1857–58. It was birthed when people from various denominations began to gather to cry out to God to pour out His Spirit on the land. A great
impetus to the revival were the noon prayer meetings held at the North Dutch Church
on Fulton Street in New York City by Jeremiah Lanphier. A forty-eight-year-old businessman who had taken on the role of lay city missionary, Lanphier believed God
was leading him to begin a weekly prayer service at noon for men in the business district to pray for a spiritual awakening. Only six men came the first week, twenty the
second week, and thirty to forty the third week. Before long, however, three thousand
men were coming daily to the prayer meetings, and within six months, ten thousand
men (out of a city of eight hundred thousand people) gathered daily to pray at noon
in twenty locations across the city. The noon prayer meetings had a great effect on the
church in the New York City as well as across the country, inspiring numerous prayer
meetings and services throughout America.

8. Finney, *The Original Memoirs of Charles Finney*, 112.

9. Charles Finney, *The Memoirs of Charles G. Finney* (New York: Fleming H. Revell Company, 1903), 444.

10. Ibid., 141.

CHAPTER 21—ENGAGING IN WORKS OF JUSTICE

1. E. M Bounds, *Purpose in Prayer* (New York: Fleming H. Revell Company, 1920), 20.

PART V—THE INTEGRATION OF PRAYER AND WORSHIP

1. C. S. Lewis, *Reflections on the Psalms* (New York: Houghton Mifflin Harcourt, 1964).

CHAPTER 22—THE CHURCH'S ETERNAL IDENTITY AS A HOUSE OF PRAYER

1. Goodreads.com, "S. D. Gordon Quotes," https://www.goodreads.com/quotes/124496 -the-greatest-thing-anyone-can-do-for-god-and-man (accessed June 20, 2014).

2. See Isaiah 62:6–7; 24:14–16; 25:9; 26:8–9; 30:18–19; 42:10–13; Luke 18:7–8; Revelation 22:17; 5:8; 8:4.

3. See Psalm 132:5, 8, 14; Isaiah 11:10; 18:4–7; 63:14; Zechariah 6:8.

4. See Matthew 24:9–13; 2 Thessalonians 2:3; 1 Timothy 4:1–2; 2 Timothy 3:1–7; 4:3–5; 2 Peter 2:1–3.

5. Verses that call God's people to repentance: Matthew 3:2, 8, 11; 4:17; 9:13; 11:20–21; 12:41; Mark 1:4, 15; 2:17; 6:12; Luke 3:3, 5, 8; 5:32; 10:13; 11:32; 15:7, 10; 16:30; 17:3–4; 24:47; Acts 5:31; 8:22; 11:18; 13:24; 17:30; 19:4; 20:21; 26:20; Romans 2:4; 2 Corinthians 7:9–10; 12:21; 2 Timothy 2:25; Hebrews 6:1, 6; 2 Peter 3:9; Revelation 2:5, 16, 21–22; 3:3, 19; 9:20–21; 16:9, 11.

CHAPTER 23—PRAYER BEFORE GOD'S THRONE

1. As quoted in Lindsay Terry, *I Could Sing of Your Love Forever* (Nashville, TN: Thomas Nelson Inc., 2008), 105.

2. See Revelation 2:26–27; 3:21; 5:10; 20:4–6; 22:5.

CHAPTER 24—PRAYER AND WORSHIP ON EARTH AS IT IS IN HEAVEN

1. As quoted in Terry, *I Could Sing of Your Love Forever*, 205.

PART VI—THE END-TIME GLOBAL PRAYER MOVEMENT

1. C. Peter Wagner, *The Rising Revival* (Ventura, CA: Renew Books/Gospel Light, 1998), 7.

CHAPTER 25—SEVEN CHARACTERISTICS OF THE END-TIME PRAYER MOVEMENT

1. Arthur T. Pierson, ed., *The Missionary Review of the World* (New York: Funk and Wagnalls Company, 1898), 1.

2. See Isaiah 54:4–12; 62:2–5; Jeremiah 3:14; 31:32; Hosea 2:14–23; Matthew 9:15; 22:2; 25:1–13; John 3:29; 2 Corinthians 11:2; Ephesians 5:25–32; Revelation 19:7–9; 22:17.

3. See Isaiah 24:14–16; 26:1; 27:2; 30:29, 32; 35:2, 10; 42:10–13; 54:1.

4. Dubay, *The Evidential Power of Beauty*, 58.

5. Ibid., 56. See Psalms 102:15; 148:11; Isaiah 62:2; Revelation 21:24.

6. See Isaiah 24:14–16; 25:9; 26:8–9; 27:2–5, 13; 30:18–19; 42:10–13; 43:26; 51:11; 52:8; 62:6–7; Jeremiah 31:7; Luke 18:7–8; Revelation 5:8; 8:4; 22:17.

CHAPTER 26—PRAYER IN THE SPIRIT OF THE TABERNACLE OF DAVID

1. As quoted in Scott Dawson, ed., *The Complete Evangelism Guidebook* (Grand Rapids, MI: Baker Books, 2008), 55.
2. See 1 Chronicles 6:31–33; 9:33; 15:16–22; 23:4–6.
3. See 1 Chronicles 6:32; 25:2; 29:35; 2 Chronicles 8:14.
4. See 1 Chronicles 9:33; 16:37; 23:5; 25:7; 2 Chronicles 8:12–14; 31:4–6, 16; 29:25; 34:9, 12; 35:4; Ezra 3:10–11; Nehemiah 10:37–39; 11:22–23; 12:24; 44–47; 13:11–12.
5. See Genesis 12:7; 15:17–18; 17:8; 48:4; Exodus 32:13; Deuteronomy 31:7; Joshua 1:6; 2 Chronicles 20:7; Jeremiah 7:7; 11:5, and others.
6. *Transformations: A Documentary* (Monument, CO: Exploration Films, 1999), DVD.
7. *Let the Sea Resound* directed by George Otis Jr. (N.p.: TransformNations Media, 2004), DVD.
8. See Isaiah 2:3; 4:4–6; 24:23; 62:1, 7; 65:18; 66:20; Jeremiah 3:17; Joel 3:17; Micah 4:2; Zechariah 6:12–13; 8:2–3; Luke 1:32–33.

CHAPTER 27—NIGHT-AND-DAY PRAYER THROUGHOUT HISTORY

1. Goodreads.com, "D. L. Moody Quotes," https://www.goodreads.com/quotes/ 288517-every-great-movement-of-god-can-be-traced-to-a (accessed June 20, 2014).
2. Régine Pernoud, *Martin of Tours: Soldier, Bishop, Saint* trans. Michael J. Miller (San Francisco: Ignatius Press, 2006), 92–93.
3. Daniel Caner, *Wandering, Begging Monks* (Berkeley, CA: University of California Press, 2002), 131–132. See also Alban Butler, *Butler's Lives of the Saints, vol. 1*, ed. Paul Burns (Collegeville, MN: Liturgical Press, 1995), 105.
4. Caner, *Wandering, Begging Monks.*
5. Barbara H. Rosenwein, "Perennial Prayer at Agaune," in Sharon Farmer and Barbara Rosenwein, eds., *Monks & Nuns, Saints & Outcasts: Religion in Medieval Society* (Ithaca, NY: Cornell University Press, 2000), 37–42.
6. Jocelin, *The Life and Acts of Saint Patrick: the Archbishop, Primate and Apostle of Ireland* (Dublin: Hibernia Press Company, 1809), 116.
7. Ian Adamson, *Bangor Light of the World* (Minneapolis, MN: Fairview Press, 1979). See also Parish of Bangor Abbey, "A Short History of Bangor Abbey," http://www .bangorabbey.org/history.htm (accessed June 19, 2014).
8. F. E. Warren, ed., *Antiphonary of Bangor* (London: Harrison and Sons, 1892), xi. See also Parish of Bangor Abbey, "A Short History of Bangor Abbey."
9. Margaret Stokes, *Three Months in the Forests of France* (London: George Bell and Sons, 1895).
10. Rowland E. Prothero, *The Psalms in Human Life* (London: Forgotten Books, 2013), 54–55.
11. Margaret Evans and Isabel Southall, *Songs of Siluria* (London: Elliott Stock, 1890), 15.
12. Libreria Editrice Vaticana, "Benedict XVI General Audience," November 11, 2009, http://www.vatican.va/holy_father/benedict_xvi/audiences/2009/documents/hf_ben -xvi_aud_20091111_en.html (accessed June 19, 2014).
13. James Cotter Morison, *The Life and Times of St. Bernard, Abbot of Clairvaux* (London: MacMillan & Co, 1894).
14. August Gottlieb Spangenberg, *The Life of Nicholas Lewis Count Zinzendorf*, trans. Samuel Jackson (London: Samuel Holdsworth, Amen-Corner, 1838), 39, 85, 88.
15. D. A. Carson, ed., *Teach Us to Pray* (WEF Theological Commission, 1999).
16. J. E. Hutton, *A History of Moravian Missions* (London: Moravian Publication Office, 1922), 521.

17. Ruth A. Tucker, *From Jerusalem to Irian Jaya* (Grand Rapids, MI: Zondervan, 1983), 69–72.

CHAPTER 28—THE GLOBAL PRAYER MOVEMENT TODAY

1. Barbara Wentroble, *Praying With Authority* (Ventura, CA: Gospel Light, 2003), 146.
2. Wagner, *The Rising Revival*, 7.

CHAPTER 29—THE CONVERGENCE OF THE MISSIONS AND PRAYER MOVEMENTS

1. Samuel Logan Brengle, *Take Time to Be Holy* (Carol Stream, IL: Tyndale House Publishers Inc., 2013), 186.
2. See Matthew 6:10; 9:38; Luke 10:2; 18:7–8; John 17:20–26.
3. See Romans 10:1; Philippians 1:9–11; Colossians 4:2–4; 2 Thessalonians 3:1–2.
4. See Acts 4:29–31; Revelation 6:9–11; 8:3–5; 22:17.
5. See Psalms 2:8; 102:12–22.
6. See 2 Chronicles 7:14.
7. See Isaiah 30:18–19; 42:10–13; 54:1–3; 62:6–7; 64:1–6.
8. See Joel 2:12–17.
9. See Zephaniah 2:1–3.
10. See Zechariah 8:20–23; 12:10.
11. Bill Bright, *7 Basic Steps to Successful Fasting and Prayer* (Orlando, FL: Campus Crusade for Christ, 1995).
12. John Piper, *Let the Nations Be Glad* (Grand Rapids: Baker Academic, 2010), 35.
13. Joseph L. Cumming, "The SVMFM: Its Seeds and Precedents, Its Origins and Early History, Its Growth and Decline," bachelor's thesis, Princeton University, 1982.
14. John R. Mott, "The Place of Prayer in the Volunteer Movement," *The Student Volunteer* 3, no. 1 (N.p.: Student Volunteer Movement for Foreign Missions, 1894), 2.

CHAPTER 30—THE CALL TO BE A FULL-TIME INTERCESSORY MISSIONARY

1. Edward M. Bounds, *Power Through Prayer* (Chicago: Moody Publishers, 2009), 18.
2. See Isaiah 24:14–16; 25:9; 26:8–9; 27:2–5, 13; 30:18–19; 42:10–13; 43:26; 51:11; 52:8; 62:6–7; Jeremiah 31:7; Luke 18:7–8; Revelation 5:8; 8:4; 22:17.
3. See 1 Chronicles 9:33; 16:37; 23:5; 25:7; 2 Chronicles 8:12–14; 31:4–6, 16; 34:9, 12; Nehemiah 10:37–39; 11:22–23; 12:44–47; 13:5–12.
4. See Mark 1:35; 6:46; Luke 5:16; 6:12; 9:18, 28.
5. See Matthew 24:42–43; 25:13; Mark 13:9, 33–38; Luke 21:36; Revelation 3:3; 16:15.
6. See Acts 1:14, 24; 2:42; 3:1; 4:31; 6:4; 9:11; 10:2, 9, 30–31; 11:5; 12:5, 12; 13:3; 14:23; 16:16, 25; Romans 8:26; 10:1; 12:12; 1 Corinthians 7:5; 2 Corinthians 1:11; 9:14; 13:7–9; Ephesians 1:17–19; 3:14–20; 6:18; Philippians 1:4, 9–11; 4:6; Colossians 1:3, 9–11; 4:2–3; 1 Thessalonians 3:10; 5:17, 25; 2 Thessalonians 1:11; 3:1; 1 Timothy 2:8; 4:5; Hebrews 13:18; James 5:13–18; Jude 20.
7. Oswald Chambers, *My Utmost for His Highest* (Grand Rapids, MI: Discovery House, 1935), October 17 entry, emphasis added.
8. Parish of Bangor Abbey, "A Short History of Bangor Abbey."

INTERNATIONAL HOUSE *of* PRAYER

· ·

24/7 LIVE WORSHIP AND PRAYER
ihopkc.org/prayerroom

· ·

Since September 19, 1999, we have continued in night-and-day prayer with worship as the foundation of our ministry to win the lost, heal the sick, and make disciples, as we labor alongside the larger Body of Christ to see the Great Commission fulfilled, and to function as forerunners who prepare the way for the return of Jesus.

By the grace of God, we are committed to combining 24/7 prayers for justice with 24/7 works of justice until the Lord returns. We do this best as our lives are rooted in prayer that focuses on intimacy with God and intercession for breakthrough of the fullness of God's power and purpose for this generation.

For more information on our internships, conferences, Bible school, and more, please visit our website at ihopkc.org.

The Best *of the* Prayer Room Live
SIX LIVE WORSHIP ALBUMS PER YEAR

· ·

Every other month we release a new volume of worship
and prayer recordings from our Global Prayer Room.

Subscribe today at ihopkc.org/bestof

International House of Prayer Missions Base, 3535 E. Red Bridge Road, Kansas City, MO 64137
(816) 763-0200 | info@ihopkc.org | ihopkc.org

INTERNATIONAL
HOUSE *of* PRAYER
UNIVERSITY

MINISTRY • MUSIC • MEDIA • MISSIONS

••

ENCOUNTER GOD. DO HIS WORKS. CHANGE THE WORLD.
ihopkc.org/ihopu

••

International House of Prayer University (IHOPU) is a full-time Bible school which exists to equip this generation in the Word and in the power of the Holy Spirit for the bold proclamation of the Lord Jesus and His return.

As part of the International House of Prayer, our Bible school is built around the centrality of the Word and 24/7 prayer with worship, equipping students in the Word and the power of the Spirit for the bold proclamation of the Lord Jesus and His kingdom. Training at IHOPU forms not only minds but also lifestyle and character, to sustain students for a life of obedience, humility, and anointed service in the kingdom. Our curriculum combines in-depth biblical training with discipleship, practical service, outreach, and works of compassion.

IHOPU is for students who long to encounter Jesus. With schools of ministry, music, media, and missions, our one- to four-year programs prepare students to serve the Great Commission and obey Jesus' commandments to love God and people.

International House of Prayer Missions Base, 3535 E. Red Bridge Road, Kansas City, MO 64137
(816) 763-0200 | info@ihopkc.org | ihopkc.org

International House *of* Prayer
INTERNSHIPS

ENCOUNTER GOD. DO HIS WORKS. CHANGE THE WORLD.
ihopkc.org/internships

Each of our five internships are committed to praying for the release of the fullness of God's power and purpose, as interns actively win the lost, heal the sick, feed the poor, and minister in the power of the Holy Spirit. Our vision is to work in relationship with the larger Body of Christ to serve the Great Commission, as we seek to walk out the two great commandments to love God and people. Our desire is to see each intern build strong relationships and lifelong friendships.

INTRO TO IHOPKC
Two three-month tracks designed to impart the vision and values of the International House of Prayer, along with the practical skills necessary to succeed long-term as an intercessory missionary. For singles, couples, and families. Classes for children available.

FIRE IN THE NIGHT
Come and behold the beauty of Jesus in the night hours. Grow in love for God and take your stand in intercession as a watchman of the night. Fire in the Night is for young adults, ages 18–30.

ONE THING INTERNSHIP
A six-month residential program for single young adults, ages 18 to 25.

SIMEON COMPANY
Two three-month tracks for over-50s, married or single.

HOPE CITY INTERNSHIP
A three-month internship program equipping intercessory missionaries to minister in the inner city, serve in the soup kitchen, lead in our inner-city prayer room, and minister to gang members, drug addicts, and the homeless.

International House of Prayer Missions Base, 3535 E. Red Bridge Road, Kansas City, MO 64137
(816) 763-0200 | info@ihopkc.org | ihopkc.org

MIKE BICKLE
TEACHING LIBRARY
—— *Free Teaching & Resource Library* ——

This International House of Prayer resource library, encompassing more than 25 years of Mike's teaching ministry, provides access to hundreds of resources in various formats, including streaming video, downloadable video, and audio, accompanied by study notes and transcriptions, absolutely free of charge.

You will find some of Mike's most requested titles, including *The Life of David*, *The First Commandment*, *Jesus, Our Magnificent Obsession*, *The Book of Romans*, *The Book of Revelation*, and much more.

We encourage you to freely copy any of these teachings to share with others or use in any way: "our copyright is the right to copy." Older messages are continually being prepared and uploaded from Mike's archives, and all new teachings will be added immediately.

Visit mikebickle.org

International House of Prayer Missions Base, 3535 E. Red Bridge Road, Kansas City, MO 64137
(816) 763-0200 | info@ihopkc.org | ihopkc.org

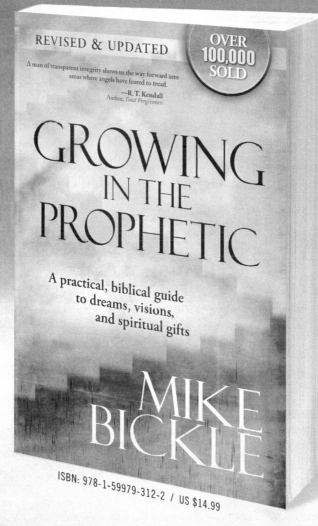